PROLOGUE:

 MW01245671

It was odd how much the _ _ _ _ .... uuilding always left Jonah uneasy. The whole structure should be at least thirty meters high, leading to an endless bottom os scariness, but he knew that fear was an illusion in that situation and his mind was the only thing hindering him from concentrating on what should be his final quest. Something longed for his presence down there, something he had no idea of what it was, but he was sure it was paramount he'd find out.

No matter how hard he tried, he couldn't see what was waiting for him, his vision was blurred by oddly shaped and eerie silhouettes that indicated the presence of random people all over the place. A few voices hailed his name and pleaded him not to abandon them, and whenever he tried to jump, his mind would bring him back to the beginning of that unwanted never-ending mirage.

Every time he would attempt a jump, he could feel his legs giving away his weight, surrendering his whole body to the sole force of gravity. He felt like a superhuman, like someone who could do whatever he wanted without having to deal with any of the consequences of his actions.

That feeling could sometimes seem even stronger, something unexplainable. It was imaginable, although not tangible, as he had never really experienced it before. Every time he jumped he felt like he was experiencing what he thought people felt just before dying. An adrenaline so intense that his body would started squirming, waiting for an unavoidable end to come. He would squeeze his own hands until his nails would pierce his callous skin. He would stretch his arms and legs, leaving no room for it to go any further, and just before his legs would hit the ground and his whole body would be shattered by impact, his mind would bring him straight back to the starting point, leaving no remnant, no recollection what so ever that he had ever left the top of building. Then, he would jump again and, even that his mind was already used to the adrenaline that would take control of his every motions, he would fell the whole thing over again, as if he had never felt it before, allowing him to fell some of the most amazing feelings a human being could ever feel.

The wind would pass through his hair, and the euphoria caused by the freedom of a non-stop free fall would give him goosebumps all over his body. Nothing could stop him from going down, there wasn't a sole obstacle in the world that could prevent him from enjoying the strong cold breeze that was giving him such a high. It was a strange dichotomy caused by two opposite effects of an experience that he had never had, even if that didn't make any sense. His mind was spinning whilst his eyes were trying to fix a point to which he could find the answers he didn't know the the questions to, because the crucial point of the whole so-called adventure would never come. He was never able to touch the ground and follow the next steps of what he was apparently supposed to do. Sometimes he'd even try to climb down the building, little by little, leaning on beams and low walls that gave perfect support to his hands and feet, but seeking different results to an unsolvable puzzle was the one and only goal of that almost-poetic loop that would come into his mind without invitation.

It was oddly satisfying for him to think that something was waiting at the end. He wasn't even sure that anyone could see him up there as the reciprocal was not possible, but the anxiety and the momentum that made him try it over and over again told him that he had to keep trying, as giving up was not a feasible option. He craved for answers, longed for solutions, and begged for and end, no matter what that would be. He only wanted for the exhilarating anxiety to be over, even if that meant he had to die. He couldn't take it anymore.

Jonah would wake up to cold sweats and fail to fall back asleep. That was a dream he had had since he was a small child, as little as he could remember. He would even try sleeping at his grand-parents' bed as he was scared to find himself in the same dream when he'd finally manage to close his eyelids and set his mind at ease, but nothing he would do mattered. He always had the same faulty plan to an endless and unescapable task. It was something he had never been able to decipher and would never be able to understand.

The weirdest thing he felt that morning is that Jonah hadn't had that dream in years, he couldn't even remember

2

the last time that happened. Actually, to his mind, he had finally been able to control his nightmares, to a point he no longer needed any therapy, even though none of the professionals he had hired throughout his life had been able to help him understand whatever it would mean.

Well, the soothing felling of control had come to an end. It had been like that until that chilly Friday morning, the one he had been longing for quite some time, as he couldn't wait to spend his weekend doing something different for a change. The cold sweats came back with the eerie dream after years of it being cloistered in the depths of his subconscious, and he would have to face it all the way until he'd be able to control it again.

CHAPTER 1:

After spending the whole day thinking about the return of his haunting dream, he left his shower soaking wet to what was one of the most beautiful nights of the year. The stars illuminated a partially clear sky and the mid-seasoned temperature made the windy climate incredibly pleasant. 'From a perfect night to a perfect weekend.', he thought as he got dressed and looked at himself in the mirror. Jonah Albuquerque was a man who liked to admire himself, he was arrogant that way. He had thin, dark hair and a stubble shave gave him a cool look to someone of his age. Not too short, but not to tall, he'd consider himself a perfect-height lad with white enough teeth that could attract any girl if he'd put his mind into it. His good genetics gave him a fair look for a man in his mid-twenties.

Lately his life had been settling into a routine, he had been working in the same job for over two years, the same amount of time he had moved to that quiet little town. 'This situation is temporary ...', he thought as he was getting off the bus and realised where he was. He was used to a busy life as he had lived in several cities across the globe and his utmost dream had always been to go out and see the world free of obligations or setting roots anywhere that had a chance of feeling like home. He was there to save money as the job paid well and there weren't many places where he could spend his hard earned money.

Two years after that fateful moment, he was still looking through the same small window, in a central apartment, which faced the same noisy traffic and the same lifeless people who repeatedly did the same aimlessly boring things in a daily basis, but Jonah was not the kind of man to whine and think his life was sad, that was his life for now, but he was sure he could change it anytime he wanted. Since he had arrived, he'd managed to make a few friends at work, with whom he would go out to the only bar in town, the Black Hole, but that wouldn't change the fact that as soon as he got home from work, or even a night out, boredom and solitude would strike his confidante self-steam as he was always alone and his mind would end up drifting to the same old point, with the same old thought: the routine had taken over his dreams, and his life choices provided him with a loneliness that was not always welcome.

That Friday, he had been preparing to attend another event. Patrick Skies could be considered his best-friend in that town, even though Jonah didn't like that term very much. He thought it was quite cheeky for a man his age to have a so-called 'best-friend', and he would never tell anyone in the world he felt that way about him.

'There's this super cool party at a hotel this weekend, shall we?' said Patrick when showing the invitation on his mobile last Monday.

His eyes gave up the answer right away, he really enjoyed a good party, and spending a night in a hotel would be something very welcomed to his routine.

'Are you ready?' he heard Patrick ask when answering the phone.

'Almost, give me ten more minutes and stop by.' said Jonah, who needed a lift every time they went somewhere that wasn't within walking distance.

He did not know where the so called hotel was, in fact, he was terrible in any situation that depended on a location skill set, in addition to not knowing the town very well outside the city center, where he lived and worked. Either way, his mind was set on having a good time that weekend, maybe meeting someone new or having a conversation that wasn't based on the same monotonous usual crap he had to endure every day at work. Feeble minded people and boring conversations had turned him into an auto-pilot person, as he would refrain from starting arguments that would only lead to a disappointing outcome.

He heard the horn of Patrick's car and quickly went down the stairs - he lived on the first floor and was terribly afraid of elevators, despite using them whenever he needed to.

'How's it going?' he asked as he got into the car and shook hands with his friend. 'Where is this hotel then?'

'Will it make any difference if I try to explain it to you?' asked Patrick rhetorically without even looking at him.

'I was just making conversation...' said Jonah as he laughed at the situation, he was already used to that kind of joke, it was what made their friendship something he liked to cultivate.

'So, tell me, what's the deal with this party?' Jonah started talking again as they started to move away from the city center.

'I actually think it's a super cool idea. Each person must rent a room for the night, and the rest, such as food and drinks, will be all inclusive.' replied Patrick, looking excited about the night ahead.

'Interesting, but I hope the rates for the night won't be too high.' Jonah always looked for something that would take away any expectations he could have about what was coming. He liked to be surprised.

The path was longer than Jonah expected. They were already leaving town and entering unknown lands. Even Patrick seemed a little confused by the GPS's directions, but he followed its instructions very carefully. The path forked along an unpaved road, and Patrick's car, which wasn't something to really brag about, started to be flooded with dust, which made Jonah close the window to keep his clothes and hair from getting messy.

'Thank you.' said Patrick when noticing the kind gesture.

'How much time till we get there?' asked Jonah as he was getting more and more excited, seeming like an uneasy child.

'Well, it should be right here...'

Patrick started hitting the breaks when the two saw the magnitude of the building that gave form to the hotel. 'Welcome to the Dartagnan Brothers Hotel', displayed the sign hovering over a grand arch of stones through which the car passed until it could reach the door that led to the main hall. The place was huge, Jonah couldn't understand how he had never heard of it before, much less what would lead someone to set up such a structure in a small town like that.

The building's facade was composed of two huge pillars that were connected by thick vines, which gave it an incredible charm, mixed with the brick coloured walls from the rest of the building. Its height did not impress as much as its beauty, and, despite not having more than two floors, Jonah was unable to see the end of the structure in its

6

extension. Patrick seemed ashamed to be arriving with that old car in a place of such magnitude, but his expression also showed euphoria and anxiety for the party that awaited for them. Jonah could no longer contain his desire to go inside, he was certainly hoping to find very interesting people there, since he was tired of always going back to the Black Hole, seeing the same faces and having the same boring conversations.

'Good evening sir, you can leave the key in the ignition, I will park the car for you.' said the sole valet who were standing by the main entrance.

Patrick just nodded and showed a feeble smirk, whilst Jonah took the lead so the two could make their way towards the reception. The hotel lobby was even more stunning, the building's right foot was at least five meters high - Jonah wondered what awaited him in the rooms on the second floor - and the ground floor was all covered in marble. The walls were white, full of mirrors, and the ceiling held a dazzling chandelier that illuminated the room only by the gleaming of its crystals. With each step he took, Jonah increased his speed, the reception desk was guarded by a lone woman, and, oddly enough, there was no queue for registration at the Dartagnan Brothers Hotel.

'Are you sure we've arrived on time?' asked Jonah, finding it strange that no one else was around.

'Yes, it says 8 p.m right here. We're actually fifteen minutes late.' Patrick replied as he glanced at the digital invitation he had received on his mobile.

'A little late, we should be among the first to arrive,' thought Jonah as he calmly approached the reception. The woman behind the counter was exuberantly beautiful. Loose and messy blond hair and shiny little earrings that broke the hair barrier and matched the incredible blue of her eyes. Jonah had never seen teeth so white except in toothpaste commercials. She was wearing a short dress that covered her entire torso, and just above her right breast a name tag indicated her calling: 'Lara Farlet, Receptionist'.

'Good evening gentlemen, how may I help you today?' the woman's voice left Jonah gasping and speechless.

'I've got an invitation to the party today, we would like two rooms.' Patrick went ahead, showing the digital invitation so that the discomfort from the silence could be broken.

'Let me check it...' said Lara whilst Jonah couldn't make enough effort to take his eyes off her face.

'Can you be a little more discreet?' whispered Patrick as he nudged him with his elbow.

Jonah realised he was static and went off to admire the beauty of that place, disguising his awe inferred by Lara's presence. 'What a woman.', he thought whilst realising how superficial his desire for beautiful women was.

'Your invitation only entitles you to one ticket, Mr. Skies.' said Lara, turning her eyes towards Jonah, who was now looking silly again without understanding anything that was happening.

'I understand, but when they sent me the invitation they told me that I was entitled to a plus one.' replied Patrick with confidence.

'Exactly, a plus one. But as far as I can tell, your friend should not be a plus one.' she said, emphasising the words as she opened an uncomfortable smile, realising Jonah still stared at her.

'Oh well, do you have any problems with my sexual orientation?' said Patrick with a politically correct tone. His wits amazed Jonah, who had not agreed to that approach.

'No problem at all, I believe you will be needing only one room then...' she reciprocated trying to end that little game she knew was a way to circumvent the rules, after all, by the way Jonah looked at her, it was very unlikely that those two were a couple.

'I thought it was two rooms, despite the love, we'd like to have some privacy.' replied Patrick whilst trying to get out of that mess.

'I think I can make an exception.' she said as she went back to type on the computer.

Within a few minutes the two were each holding different room keys.

'I made sure of putting you in interconnected rooms, so you won't be far from each other after enjoying the party. I apologize, but Mr. Dartagnan did not warn me about the sexual orientation of each individual guest.' Lara tried to correct the mistake, whilst Jonah kept looking directly into

8

her eyes. 'The price is one hundred and fifty for each room, which includes the ticket to the party.' she finished whilst Patrick handed her a credit card.

'Thanks for the comprehension. Jonah?' Patrick kept his seriousness as he nudged Jonah once again, bringing him back to reality.

'Yes thank you very much!' he said whilst trying to look a tad more serious and also handing over a credit card. He was finding the situation quite amusing, not to mention uncomfortable.

'Your room is on the second floor, I see that you didn't bring any luggage for the weekend... Will you be needing anything? I might be able to arrange something....' said Lara whilst Jonah acted surprised once again. Each time one of them opened their mouth, he learned more unknown information about the so called weekend.

'Good! If we need it, we will let you know.' said Patrick, trying not to look directly at Jonah.

'You can call me Lara, sir.' she said as she pointed, with the most delicate hand Jonah had ever seen, to the badge holding her name. French-style painted nails with a white gold ring loaded with a small diamond.

'And you can call me Patrick.' he said, trying to be courteous. 'This is my partner Jonah.'

'Sure...' grunted Jonah with sadness as he realised the most beautiful woman he had ever laid eyes in thought he was on a date with another man.

The two finally took off to the building's elevators holding nothing but the small magnetic card that served as a key to the bedroom doors.

'What fucking idea was that?' whispered Jonah as they walked quickly to the elevators.

'Shush. I'll explain later!' replied Patrick as he tried to take Jonah's hand, before having it slapped away.

Jonah reached the front of the elevator and started looking for any set of stairs that would relieve him from an upcoming headache. At the other end of the lobby, he could see two huge marble stairs that intertwined at the end, he even felt how good it would be going up each step so he didn't have to go into that deadly cubicle.

'Maybe we could take...'

'Don't even think about mumbling off about the stairs Jonah, do not embarrass me!' Patrick interrupted before Jonah could suggest anything.

'Embarrass him?' thought Jonah with sheer indignation. They hadn't been there for ten minutes and Patrick had already make that whole scene at the reception and forgot to comment that the party would last for the whole weekend. 'I'm going to have to stay in the same underwear for three days.', he stomped as he realised his upcoming shame whilst his friend pressed one of the buttons on the elevator so the doors would close.

As the elevator went up, Jonah clung to the small banister that ran at the back of the motorised box. His elevator phobia came from his childhood, when both of his parents died in a tragic accident, in an old building, on a visit to a foreign country, when he was still too young to remember anything. Since then, after being raised by his grandparents, Jonah had never had any idea of what was to have a father or a mother.

As it was mentioned by the beautiful receptionist, the two rooms were separated by a sole door. They went straight into Patrick's room, and to Jonah's surprise, who expected a stunning room, it contained nothing more than a small bathroom and a single bed. There was no television, telephone, air conditioning, not even a ceiling fan. 'One hundred and fifty for this?', he thought as he opened the door to his own room and lost any hope that his bedroom were to be any different. The bed looked good. On top of it were some white towels that smelled of fabric softener and just two pillows, which led Jonah to think that he would have to go back to the reception to ask for another one, he had this weird habit of always having three pillows and would not be able to sleep without satisfying it.

'Please, don't get into it. This party will be so good that you won't even feel like sleeping!' said Patrick whilst realising that Jonah had an expression of disappointment towards his own bed.

'It's two nights, Patrick! Two!' he repeated with a strong tone. 'You could have mentioned it, couldn't you?'

'I had no idea that the party would go on for the whole weekend, but you heard the girl at the reception, anything you need, just ask!' said Patrick as he threw himself on Jonah's bed whilst looking at him with confusion in his eyes.

'Her name is Lara, and speaking of her, what chances do I have now?' he asked rhetorically as he reminded his friend of the scene at the reception.

'Just stop with the nonsense, what chances did you even have before? There will be so many women at this party that you'll soon forget about this so called Lara.' he made a mocking tone when saying the woman's name.

'Oh, I'm sure it will, I've already lost any hope, did you not see the empty reception when we arrived?' asked Jonah as he opened each drawer on the nightstand to see if there was any clue as to how they were supposed to get to the so called party.

'Relax! Soon someone will come to pick us up for the party, so just stop whining for a bit.' he finally explained what Jonah really wanted to know 'I'm off to a quick shower to wash off the dust from the road, you should do the same.'

'And how am I supposed to fix my hair if you didn't tell me that we would be here for all this time?' he asked angrily. If there was anything Jonah was vain about, it was his hair.

Patrick didn't even give him the courtesy of an answer, as Jonah realised that all that nuisance was already starting to tire the atmosphere on that room. As soon as he was alone, he laid down on the bed to fiddle with his mobile. 'No bars...', he thought as he decided to go back to the front desk to ask for the internet password, but this time he would appreciate the beauty of the artist who designed that magnificent staircase. The hotel corridors were tiny, two people walking side by side would be crammed by it, and if one of them was too fat, they would have to walk in a line. He could not understand how all that magnitude could turn into petty and badly decorated rooms, maybe it was Lara trying to get them back for all that ragged lying of being a couple. There was no reason why Jonah should be angry, after all, if Patrick hadn't lied, they would already be on their way back home, and the only destination would be another tedious night at the Black Hole.

'You again...' said Lara, noticing his presence as she moved around behind the front desk.

'Yes.' he started by expressing an embarrassed laugh. 'There's no cellphone reception here? Could you give me the internet password, please?' he asked, trying to remember the good manners he had learned from his grandparents.

'No reception, no internet.' she replied dryly without even looking at him.

'Really? What if I need to speak to someone?' he asked, looking deeply at her as he sought attention.

'We have a phone at the reception, you can use it anytime you want.' she replied pointing to the old device the laid in front of her, one of those table phones that you'd still have to rotate a wheel to dial the numbers, Jonah had not seen something like that since he had left his grandparents' house over ten years ago. 'If you don't want to use it, just wait in your room and soon someone will be there to pick you up for the party. And may I suggest you take a shower?'

He soon turned his head and made his way back to his bedroom. That shower nonsense was starting to irritate him. 'What about my fucking hair?', he thought as he got even more angry with Patrick for not giving him all the information he needed about the weekend. He was one of those people that appreciated leaving his house prepared for whatever may come. He climbed back up the stairs - as he would avoid getting into that elevator as much as he could - and knocked on Patrick's bedroom door. Nobody answered. He decided to enter through his own door this time as he took the magnetic card out of his pocket and waited for the small green light to allow him access.

He crossed the door that connected the rooms in search of Patrick. No sign of him. The bathroom door was wide open and the bed was already all messed up. 'Typical... and he still left me here alone.', he thought as he returned to his room in the hope that his friend would soon return to pick him up. Three ringings echoed inside the room as someone knocked on the door. 'Patrick must have forgotten his key.', he thought as he got out of bed and ran to open the door.

'I see you ignored my advice about taking a shower...' said Lara whilst Jonah tried to hide the surprised expression on his face as he found himself admiring her radiant beauty once again.

'Hmm, what are you doing here?' he said, ignoring the unnecessary commentary.

'I told you that soon someone would come to pick you up for the party. Nice to meet you, I'm someone.' she replied sarcastically.

'I did not have a shower because nobody told me to bring a suitcase, and I wouldn't have the means to fix my hair.' he tried to explain himself when he realised how ridiculous it sounded as the words left his mouth.

'I told you to ask me for anything you might need, I would have brought you some ointment for your hair, but you just want to know about cellphones and the internet. Now there is no more time, the Dartagnan brothers must wait for the arrival of every single guest before they can start the party.' she finished with a slightly more friendly tone, maybe she realised that Jonah was a bit out of his comfort zone.

Jonah started walking next to Lara as soon as he closed the room's door behind him. He hadn't noticed, whilst he was at the reception, but besides being beautiful, she smelled very nice and had a body that was sculptural. 'I need to pay more attention to things,' he thought as he found himself daydreaming.

'Is this your first time here?' she asked, trying to lighten up the tension.

'Yes, I didn't even know about this place, I'm not from around here.' replied Jonah, seeking a normal conversation.

Silence reigned as they passed the reception again after what seemed like an eternity inside the elevator. Jonah was embarrassed to show such a tiny fear to such an interesting woman, with each step they took, she became more mysterious and attractive.

They passed through a huge glass door behind the desk where Lara was then working, which, by the way, was now empty. 'The organisation of this hotel does not live up to its facade.', he thought as he realised that anyone who was late would have no chance of being found. Despite the beauty of all the decor, after crossing the glass door, Jonah realised that all that extension was just more and more of an extensive and narrow corridor with doors that, according to his imagination, could not lead anywhere other than to more rooms .

'Are we there already?' he asked, looking like an impatient child who couldn't wait for things to come.

'No sir, we'll be in the ballroom soon. Then, later on, I can show you your room.' she replied keeping her tone.

'My room?' asked Jonah implying his surprise about what Lara had just said. 'What about the room I was in?'

'Do you really think that Mr. Dartagnan would leave his guests in a room like the one you are in? As I told you, it was just so you could take a quick shower.' she looked at him and winked as if she knew how that conversation was irritating him.

'Well, I've already told you! I didn't...'

'Yeah, yeah, I understand.' she interrupted the conversation before he could start whining again.

To Jonah's surprise, Lara stopped in front of a small wooden door painted white as she stood in front of him to interrupt his walk. She ran a delicate hand through his hair as if she was fixing a strand that was out of place. 'I hate it when people touch my hair.', thought Jonah as he felt strangely comfortable with the soft touch that Lara infringed on him.

'Now.' started she. 'I need you to sit in the place that I will indicate to you, the Dartagnan Brothers will only start the party after everyone arrives. I think you're the last one, so you won't have to wait much longer.'

'Aren't you going to join the party as well?' he asked gallantly as he leaned against the door that would soon be opened.

'Yes I will.' she said smiling. 'But first I'm going for a quick shower...'

Jonah felt the tone of the joke and decided to join the laughter, after all, the woman was now giving a little opening to whatever his strategy might have been. The door opened and the astonishment began. That place was indescribably incredible. The chandelier that had impressed Jonah in the lobby had become a small lamp in front of the many huge chandeliers that shone over the huge ballroom. The light was off, instead, little sparks distinguished the nuances of the room as they shone from the dangling lights that hovered over every corner. Not much could be seen through the darkness, but Jonah could see that the immensity of the main room forked in several corridors and open rooms. He could see a bar and several waiters walking around with trays covered with champagne flutes, the smell of some delicious food fed the hunger of those who hadn't eaten in hours, and several very well-dressed people, all sitting around gigantic tables covered with towels and white huge plates made of heavy marble. 'These people have some weird fetish with these stones,' thought Jonah who was of humble origin and had never seen so much extravagance concentrated in only one place.

'Now you stay here.' whispered Lara in his ear as he, once again, smelled something he could not distinguish from a very good perfume to just the natural sent that such a perfect genetic creation had given that woman.

She left him in front of one of those giant tables where Jonah was surrounded by strangers. They were exquisitely well-dressed and pompously standing people. He tried to find Patrick's ugly face somewhere, but no luck. Beside him, a man with gray hair and a practically full white beard, on the other side, an extremely elegant, tall, and extravagant middle-aged woman. Everyone seemed to be dressed for the occasion, suits and tuxedos prevailed the people's choice, but did not seem to be mandatory, all-though recommended. He, on the other hand, was wearing some old shoes with skinny jeans and a shirt he hadn't washed in months. The pitch black, slightly lightened by the shine of the chandeliers, did not allow him to see much further than that. Patrick could be far away or even at his table, he could not be sure as its far end was nowhere near visible. He had no idea of how many people were there, but he could see a simple and classic sign that hovered above one of the doors saying: 'Sleeping area', which sounded oddly suspicious, as if sleeping wasn't something extremely important to human life.

Jonah realised that he would not sleep in the small room without air conditioning after all, which gave him a slight feel of happiness, although he was still annoyed with Patrick for not having told him that the party would be off such elegance. He imagined Lara dressed in a shiny long dress as he tried to untangle the tight pants he was wearing.

Much less than suddenly, the lights began to flash rapidly, the chandeliers no longer sparkled the crystals and the music began to play. It seemed like an incredible introduction, something worthy of kings and queens, but before Jonah could be even more impressed, as he looked for Patrick between a wink and another, a man holding a red staff, with slightly predominant belly, walked down an even bigger and more beautiful staircase than the one he had seen at the reception. 'He must be one of those Dartagnan brothers.' thought Jonah as he felt intimidated by the presence propagated by the mysterious man as he descended each step.

'Ladies and gentlemen!' announced a low-pitched voice over the speakers. 'Please, a round of applause for Mr. Giovanni Dartagnan!' the echo of the clapping hands took over any other noise that could be heard, as people stood up as if they knew the routine to be followed. Jonah just went with the flow, imitating the gesture by the masses.

CHAPTER 2:

As soon as Jonah got up - following the myriad of people around him - he realised he was sitting at the main table of the event. The huge straight marble staircase led directly to two free seats in front of it. 'The less important Dartagnan should come later on.', he thought as he realised that the so called Giovanni was coming down the stairs by himself. The crowd continued to applaud to every step the man took, in the two years he had been living in that quiet little town, he had never set eyes on such a man. By his pompous appearance and eccentric dress code, he must have been in his sixty's; Jonah could feel the envy hovering over the looks of the numerous men who longed to be able to grow a beard like that.

He went back searching around the room - now slightly more visible due the presence of light - to see if he could find his friend Patrick. He could see several different people, women and men of all ages of which most seemed to know each other, something that made Patrick's absence even more uncomfortable. Giovanni Dartagnan bore a simple pace as he calmly observed everyone around him whilst holding up his chin and showing no sign of pretentiousness at the same time, quite the opposite, he felt so at ease that he smiled proudly through his yellow teeth and greeted every person whose eyesight crossed his.

'His an admirable man, isn't him?' asked the elegant stranger who sat beside him with an arrogant tone.

Jonah just nodded as he couldn't care less for the feeble attempt of small talk. The euphoria depicted by all of those people was captivating, and he felt a lot of awe for all that reverence that could be cast upon only one person.

After that brief interruption, he went back to his search for Patrick, but, to his surprise, his eyes fixed on the angelical walk that followed Lara's footsteps from across the room. She was the only person, besides Giovanni, who was standing. In fact, she was in tune with the host in every aspect. Jonah continued to watch Lara walking, it was now clear that she was coming towards him. 'She must be sitting at my table.', he thought, realising he would have someone to talk to, but as she walked, steered away from him and went towards Giovanni. She took a circular walk around the table whilst he waited standing behind a chair that was supposedly hers. Jonah had lost sight of the old man until he saw that he had suddenly materialised to the seat right in front of him. Lara began to walk slower until she stopped beside Mr. Dartagnan, who had now turned around to face the beauty who had just arrived.

To Jonah's surprise, as soon as Lara stopped, Giovanni leaned forward until his lips met hers. For a few seconds, what seemed like an eternity, they kissed slowly as they held hands and made a sign of reverence to the entire audience in front of them. Jonah followed the crowd as they leaned over to pay homage to the woman he had spoken to a few minutes earlier.

'Please take your seats.' said Giovanni. He had a hoarse intoned voice that became clean after a subtle cough.

Lara sat beside the host whilst Jonah felt into the illusion of her beauty once again. She now wore a black dress with a low back cut, her hair was tied up in a bun that let two small blond streaks slide down the side of her face. She wore what seemed to be an incredibly expensive diamond necklace, and the then small earrings were then replaced by long, flashy pieces.

'Jonah, how are you?' she asked shortly after sitting down.

'All is fine, I see you've managed to enjoy that infamous shower after all.' he joked as he realised that Giovanni had his attention caught by another guest and was not looking at them. 'I didn't know you had a date!' he exclaimed in a low tone.

She laughed without bothering to give him an answer and went back to pick up a champagne flute that was posed in front of her. Her elegance affected every women around her, and there wasn't a single man in that immensity of a room who wouldn't turn his neck at one point or another to observe how beautiful that young woman was.

Dinner was served with astonishing class, and anything Jonah could possibly desire to drink would instantly materialise in front of his eyes. He talked to everyone around him whilst he was still trying to catch any sing of Patrick's presence, but his friend should be at some distant table, as he could not lay his eyes on him. The dinner ceremony lasted for about two hours and in the end Jonah was already feeling the drunkenness taking over the actions of his mind. He exchanged a few more words with Lara, without worrying about what Giovanni would think, since he was sure the old man had no idea of who he was. He was there as a mere companion for Patrick, which further increased the mystery of why he was sat at the main table whilst his friend was nowhere to be found.

As soon as people started to get up, he realised that he no longer needed any parsimony to get out of his chair and look for a bathroom, which would give him the chance to get to know the place a bit better.

'Do you mind telling me where the toilets are?' he asked the same lady who was still sitting next to him.

'Everyone has their own bathroom, you should find yours in your chambers...' she replied with a slightly aggressive tone whilst looking at Jonah's outfit. He was really starting to feel uncomfortable about being the only one who was poorly dressed.

'Haven't you been shown to your room yet?' interjected Lara.

'Of course not, you were the one who brought me here.' he replied even more aggressively. The drinking always gave him a little more confidence.

'I'll come with you then, show you the rest of the place whilst we're at it.' as soon as Lara finished speaking, she stood up and went for Giovanni, said a few words to his ear, and left without waiting for an answer. Jonah could see, for the first time during the evening, the old man's gaze crossing his as he raised his glass as if he was making a toast whilst winking at him.

The two walked out and Lara soon hooked her arm around his, saving him the embarrassment of a possible rejection. Everyone there seemed very refined and knew every rule of etiquette by decorum, which was not something Jonah had in common with those people.

'Why am I sitting at the main table?' was the first question that came to his mind.

'Giovanni wants to meet you, I'm not sure why, but he will talk to you sometime during the evening.' she replied without giving the subject more importance than it should have.

Jonah was apprehensive about that answer, but decided not to insist in the matter any further.

'Can you tell me where Patrick is?' he continued with the interrogation.

'Sure, he's right over there.' she replied pointing to a place right in front of them, where Jonah could see his friend who was now elegantly bearing a suit and tie that was making him fit right in.

'Fucking what now?', he thought when he remembered that Patrick was dressed just like him when they arrived at the hotel. 'Where did he get those clothes from?' he continued to think as he strode towards him.

'Patrick' he said calmly as he nudged him.

'Jonah!' he exclaimed in a drunken tone.

'Where the hell have you been?' he asked as he shrugged.

'Right fucking here! With all these incredible people, let me introduce you.' he went through every different person in his conversation circle, introducing Jonah. He already knew everyone's names and was even intimate with few of the women.

Patrick explained that, as soon as he got out of the shower, he came face to face with that suit lying on his bed - he had no explanation for how that happened - and that shortly after being dressed, a distinguished woman had come to pick him up in his room .

'Well I did tell her we should wait for you, but she said you'd be in good hands.' he completed whilst quickly grabbing a glass of champagne from one of the waiters who was passing by.

'Still need the toilet?' interrupted Lara.

'Yes, would you mind showing me the way?' he tried to remain polite.

'Haven't you seen your room yet?' asked Patrick in awe. 'Wait until you see the facilities they have here...'

Jonah moved away again, hitched to Lara's arm once again, and followed her towards one of the bifurcations in the main hall, the same one that contained the sign indicating where the rooms were to be placed.

'Do you still have that card?' asked Lara as she stopped in front of the door.

'Yes I do.' he replied, taking out the only thing he had in his pocket besides his useless phone.

'Just go in and look for your name.' she said whilst standing still after the door made an opening noise. 'It would be unusual if I were to go to your room, but I'll be right here when you get back and we can go for a quick tour around the place.'

Jonah finally understood that the woman was indeed committed to the old Dartagnan man. He could not hide the brief sadness that struck upon him as he realised he would not have the chance to talk in a more intimate way with Lara. He would say that such a situation was normal for him, being the new guy in a place and fixating his attention to a sole person.

'You should take the advantage of changing those clothes, even if showering is not your forte, you could still be a bit more presentable.' said Lara as the door closed behind him.

The only way out was to laugh. He was indeed barely presentable and he knew that people were staring at him with a repressive look. He was not used to all that exacerbation of elegance, in fact, he could not remember the last time he wore a suit. The corridors were now a little wider than those in the other part of the hotel. The rooms were closed by frosted glass doors, and each one them had a name above the door, indicating that, indeed, it had all been very well planned by the hosts. He walked for a few meters until he found a sign with his name on it. 'Jonah Albuquerque'. Upon entering the room that had been assigned to him, Jonah was surprised at how little his expectations had been to the facilities in that place. The excess of exuberance in that huge lobby was extended to the rest of the hotel. He wondered what the regular guests, who were not invited to those parties, would think if they knew about those rooms.

The one assigned to him was at least five times bigger than the one he was last in. It was air conditioned and decorated by a bookcase surrounded by refined sofas - no television - and a bathroom, which was open, containing a nice hot tub, in addition to a large shower that seemed to be the wish of his life. Below the mirror he could notice a shelf full of hygiene products, including some hair wax, making him realise he would be able to take a quick shower after all. Upon the huge bed that struck his sight, Jonah could see a luxurious suit laid whilst a selection of shirts and ties filled an open wardrobe right next to it. On the other side of the room, he noticed a huge table full of drinks and snacks, which he couldn't bear to see after having eaten so much during dinner. However, he poured himself a glass of neat whiskey and set it down beside the nightstand whilst glancing with awe at that suit. 'I'm going to need someone to tie one of these ties.', he thought as he remembered he had no idea of how to do it.

He realised that, like the other room, that one was also connected to Patrick's by a door, but time was way too short for him to continue admiring the beauty and nuances of that newly found place. He quickly put on the suit, grabbed a white shirt and stuffed a black tie into his pocket. 'Maybe Patrick knows how to tie this fucking thing.', he thought before closing the bedroom door as he started making his way back to the main ballroom, it was time to visit the rest of the facilities and enjoy the party for a change.

Lara, as promised, was awaiting for him right where he last saw her, but as soon as he opened the door, he saw her talking to someone before she could give him her undivided attention one more time.

'Where's the tie?' she asked.

'I don't know how to tie the knot.' he whispered with shame so that no one else would hear him.

'In here.' she pulled him back into the door, which was still half-open, holding it with one foot that wore a beautiful high-heeled black shoe that highlighted her curves.

Quickly, Lara knotted Jonah's tie with perfection and, after wrapping it around his neck, pushed the door open again before it could close. The two headed towards the party as his gaze returned to contemplate the stunning beauty of that woman.

'Would you like to see the rest of the facilities?' she asked whilst looking at him. 'I believe we have a few minutes before the party starts, the staff still have to collect the tables.'

Jonah wondered how many people it would take to lift a table of that size and weight, but he was also excited by the idea of visiting the other rooms that connected to the main one. Lara re-engaged his arm and the two of them left in the opposite direction of the door they had just left behind.

'Your perfume is different.' he said as he tilted his face to her side.

'Yes, I changed it after taking a shower.' she answered. 'By the way, wasn't the shower to your liking in the new room?'

'How long will you keep this going?' replied Jonah with a friendly tone. He knew that that kind of conversation was the best way to break the ice with someone he had just met.

Lara laughed, but did not answer. Apparently that cheeky joke would be one of those ice breaking lines one uses until intimacy has reached a certain point, in that case, until the weekend came to an end. They continued walking as Lara introduced him to each room they passed through. None of them had a door like the one that led to the bedrooms. The first contained a wide passage that held several leather sofas and velvet couches where some people were already snuggling. Fruit platters were displayed in every corner and a bar full of waiters was ready to serve each and everyone of the guests.

'So this is where the rest of the people who work at the hotel hide. Is that why you were alone at the reception?' he asked as he stopped to observe the beauty of the decoration that dressed up the place.

'Yes, normally people arrive early for these events, in fact, you and your friend were the only ones left...'

'Were you waiting for me? You did mention at the reception yourself that Patrick was supposed to have brought a plus one...'

'I was just checking something. Giovanni was sure that your friend would bring you, which is why he invited him.' she spoke without looking him in the eyes, as if she didn't want to continue that conversation.

'How do you mean?' Jonah ignored the deviation in the subject as he was very intrigued by that thought.

'I told you, Mr. Dartagnan wants to meet you, I can't say anything else for now, but he'll come for you at the right time.'

'May I ask you something private?' he turned around until he came face to face with her.

'You want to know what am I doing with a man that is so much older than me?' Lara, to Jonah's surprise, had guessed every word of the question he was about to ask.

'No' he denied as he started to blush. 'You realised that I was stroked by your beauty, didn't you?' that was the best lame excuse he could come up in such a short notice.

'I did, but this is not really an appropriate conversation subject for today. I told you, Giovanni is going to talk to you, just have a little patience.' she finished, indicating that she wanted to re-engage his arm. 'Shall we see the rest of the place?'

The word patience was not really a part of Jonah's vocabulary, his anxiety often prevented him from making the best of hasty situations, something he had already become accustomed to. The two went on to the next room, when, to Jonah's surprise, dark lights illuminated black walls filled with amateurish designs whilst people sat on small cushions scattered on the floor. The music there was completely different from the rest of the party; as soon as he went through the huge opening, he became aware of electronic music beats in an environment completely conducive to trying different things. He found it a tad inelegant to ask if that was some kind of safe-haven for using drugs, but the very image depicted by the room made it clear that no one there was eating the fruits from the other room. Once again, he was able to notice a bar, again full of waiters working around the clock. 'At least there's no lack of alcohol.', he thought as he was pulled by Lara until they returned to the main hall.

'I reckon we should go back to our table. Soon the party will begin and you will be able to see the rest of the facilities for yourself. It's one surprise after the other.' she said as they headed back to her chairs.

He even thought about going out looking for Patrick again, but the lights were already dimming down and, as far as he could tell, the introduction to such a party would be extremely interesting. That distinguished Mr. Dartagnan had a pose of confidence and sobriety that was to be envied. 'With all of that money, even I would be confident.', he thought as he imagined what kind of fortune one must have to hold a place like that open.

As he was tidy and properly sat, Jonah took a slight tug from the elegant lady who was standing about two meters from the table. For a brief moment, Jonah realised that no one would move those huge tables from their place, in fact the floor opened and, slowly, the tables and chairs began to be swallowed by it. It was unimaginable. Mr. Dartagnan appeared again at the bottom of the staircase, illuminated by a strong spotlight now holding a microphone in his hand.

'Most of you already know how our parties work. All I ask from you is: go ahead and have fun. As for the first timers, watch, learn, and enjoy the night!' he finished as pitch-black took over the main hall and people started applauding him once more.

Jonah went back looking for one of the waiters who would walk back and forth with champagne flutes on a silver platter, not needing to go too far so he could grab a glass and drink it all in one huge sip.

The party started super excited. People danced and exchanged glances, some even made the effort to stop and talk. He passed by Patrick a few times, he was talking and dancing with everyone who he could stumble upon, he was so drunk that some people even avoided approaching him. Not that anyone in there was sober, but his friend had taken a night off to nurse all the bottles he could find.

Jonah summoned up the courage to visit another room. This was the most distant from where the party was happening, the music could barely be heard from there. Before he even noticed what the room had to offer, he looked for a place to sit, when suddenly, one of the waiters came towards him offering something to drink.

'Can I get you anything, sir?' he asked politely.

'How about some whiskey?' asked Jonah naively as the waiter fired a list of bottles that were available that night. 'Whatever you think is best.' he interrupted the waiter so he wouldn't have to say he didn't understand a thing he was talking about.

At the other corner of the room, he saw Mr. Dartagnan. The old man was surrounded by men and women who were drowning him with questions and smiles of admiration. As incredible as it seemed, this was a break room, and the music was practically inaudible, which gave Jonah a moment of silence so he could listen to his own thoughts.

In a few minutes the waiter was back, he had a glass of whiskey with some ice cubes on the tray and a friendly smile on his face that made Jonah make the effort to open his mouth and say thank you.

'I'll take it from here.' he heard Giovanni's hoarse voice approaching the waiter who just held out the tray as he took the glass.

Giovanni sat on the cushion next to Jonah's and handed him the glass, indicating a gesture of goodwill. Jonah tried not to look surprised, but people, who had previously spoken to Mr. Dartagnan, were looking at him with suspicion, as if he held some kind of importance among so many beautiful and interesting people.

'Pleasure, my name is Giovanni Dartagnan.' he said as he held his hand a few inches away from Jonah.

'Jonah Albuquerque.' he replied as if he was not giving so much importance to the situation.

'I'm glad you and your friend took the time to attended my humble party, I hope you're enjoying yourself.' said Giovanni, taking a small metal box from his coat pocket that contained cigarettes inside. 'Will you take one?'

'Why not.' replied Jonah without knowing why he had accepted a cigarette from that man since he had never had a smoke in his life. 'The party is great, I had no idea of the existence of this place. I'm quite happy, and grateful, that you decided to invite us here.' he stammered as the old man lit the cigarette in his mouth.

'Few people know about this place! Very rarely I invite strangers to come here. Always with a purpose, of course.' he said whilst having another drag.

'I feel very flattered, but what would that purpose be?' he asked, showing interest and no patience for small talk.

'For now, nothing that should keep you from enjoying yourself. The mere presence of fascinating people gives me an enormous joy to keep parties like this going on.' replied Giovanni whilst keeping the mystery.

'This place is incredible.' he repeated, feeling flattered and not knowing how to continue that conversation. 'Does the party continue tomorrow?'

'The party doesn't stop until Sunday, young man. Stay free, of course, to rest in your chambers and return whenever you want, the food and drink never stop either.' he said as he held out his glass of champagne to propose a toast to Jonah.

'Admirable.', he thought as he reciprocated, realising that someone much older than him would have the energy to endure such long hours without having to sleep.

'Smart choice, this whiskey is excellent.' Giovanni kept on trying to engage in small talk.

'I did have the help of that great waiter over there, it's been such a long time since I had something as good as this.' he lied without even knowing what he was drinking.

'Well, all of them were very well trained.' said Mr. Dartagnan as he sighed and laid back down on the cushion whilst holding his cigarette in the corner of his mouth.

'Would this be some kind of a break room?' asked Jonah as he realised he was boring the old man.

'For now yes! But soon the party will start here too and, if I may be so bold, the best part of it...'

Once again, Jonah was amazed at the contagious energy of that place. He seemed to be the youngest there and, at the same time, the most exhausted. Giovanni stubbed out his cigarette in his own cup and, with a gentle movement, got up and dropped it on the tray of a waiter passing by. His gestures were smooth and majestic, like those of someone who really had enormous self-confidence.

'I see you had a chance to talk.' Lara's voice came from behind the pillows when Jonah stood up abruptly.

'A little, my dear. I think we will soon have the chance to get to know each other a bit better.' he replied, giving her a smooch on the lips.

Jonah caught himself, once again, admiring Lara's beauty as Mr. Dartagnan was looking at him with a grin on his face. Silence reigned for a few seconds, until he decided to put an end to it.

'Youth does not cease to amaze me. People like you encourage me to live, it's amazing how beauty has taken over this generation.'

The three were now standing on their feet whilst making small talk when, little by little, more people began to infiltrate the host's conversation circle. Jonah was able to meet some interesting people, speeding up time so quickly that soon the lights in the room dimmed down and soft music started to play. As he was looking at the other corner of the room, he noticed his friend's Patrick stranded presence, who seemed to be a bit lost and way over drunk to be amongst all of those people.

'If you'll excuse me.' he began, looking directly at Mr. Dartagnan. 'I just noticed my friend's in the room , and he seems to be a bit lost.'

'Please go! Get him and join us.' replied Giovanni whilst steering away from the people he was having a warm conversation.

'It felt more like an order than an invitation,' thought Jonah as he left for Patrick. His friend had half-closed eyes and an expression of someone who couldn't handle another ounce of alcohol.

'Are you alright?' asked Jonah as he approached.

'Never been better!' he said, trying to show excitement.

'I think I'm going to excuse myself and get some rest, Mr. Dartagnan told me that the party never stops, I don't know if I can take much more for now.' he said as he laughed.

'Will you just stop with the fucking whining for a while... I heard that the best part is yet to come. The party is just beginning.' replied Patrick who, little by little, returned to his sober self.

'I can literally see you getting unconscious...'

'I know that. That's why I took one of those pills that they are distributing. It will soon kick in.'

'What fucking pill? Why am I always the last to hear about these things?' he asked as he was tired of always being left out.

'Here, take one...'

Using drugs was not in Jonah's habit list, but it was also not an odd thing to him. He did enjoy losing control of his actions from time to time, as long as he was sure he would find his way back to sobriety eventually. He swallowed the pill without even asking what it was, it didn't matter that much at that time of night. The two exchanged words for a brief moment, until Jonah realised that Lara was looking at him and gesturing an invitation for them to join the host's group. They slowly walked towards the crowd and sought to infiltrate unnoticed. Jonah strategically positioned himself next to Lara, who was now talking directly to Giovanni Dartagnan.

'The Dream Room is yet to be open, but I think we'll soon have the opportunity to introduce our new friends to the most brilliant idea I have ever had.' said Giovanni as he realised that Jonah and Patrick were now amongst them.

'Don't spoil the surprise.' said Lara when noticing the curious look on Jonah's face. 'Everything in its due time'

'I won't deny my desperate curiosity, but I believe that everything has its moment.' he lied, trying to hide his anxiety.

'Have you manage to get your hands in one of these pills they are giving out' whispered Mr. Dartagnan in his ear as he took Lara's place.

'Indeed I have...' he replied hesitating. 'Is it now normal for everyone to be popping pills?' he thought, noticing that the old man was more anxious than him.

'Great! You will soon realise what you took...'

Mr. Dartagnan left before he could even think about replying to another stupid question. He went out to the bar and, from there, pointed to Jonah's direction at the same time he said something to the waiter. Within a few minutes,

29

he was walking towards him with another glass of whiskey. Apparently, Giovanni had shown an interest in Jonah's good taste for the beverage and selected something even better for him to try.

'I don't know what you did to deserve this, but enjoy. This whiskey was aged for a hundred years before being bottled.' said the waiter, handing him the glass.

Jonah accepted the drink as he raised his glass to toast Giovanni, who, on the other side of the room, raised a glass in the exact same way, apparently holding the same rare and expensive liquid. The time was short for Jonah to finish what, in his humble opinion, was the best thing his lips had the pleasure of touching.

The lights dimmed down again. The small room was practically empty, and as far as he could see, many had been left out of the event that would follow. The big cushions had been collected, without Jonah being aware of it, and Mr. Dartagnan was isolated and ready to speak into a microphone. Jonah was startled again when chairs rose from the floor. Each of them being part of some elaborated structure with cables and a small monitor, what made him start to move away from the audience until he could feel a tug on his arm.

'You needn't be scared. The pill will soon kick in and you will understand what is going on.' Lara got so close to his mouth that he was able smell the magical sent from her breath. He didn't need anything else to convince him. He wasn't scared anymore.

CHAPTER 3:

Jonah couldn't believe his eyes when he saw that even Mr. Dartagnan was removing his coat and shirt to lie on one of those chairs. No explanation was given. Nothing. The only thing Giovanni had said on the microphone was: 'The Dream Room is open.', which was followed by a loud round of applause and excitement by everyone around, even Patrick, who was did not understand a thing, was thrilled by the contagious euphoria exhaled by the guests.

'What is he going to do?' he asked Lara in a very low tone.

'When the time comes, you'll see...' as soon as she finished speaking, she hasted to sit on the chair next to Giovanni's and as soon as she too removed the top of her dress, they helped each other to secure a few cables on each other's body.

The feeling of euphoria only increased as each guest followed the same steps as Giovanni and Lara.

'Shall we?' asked Patrick, who had returned to approach Jonah.

'Are you out of your fucking mind? Do you have any idea what any of these chairs do?'

'Hasn't the pill kick in yet?'

'No, it hasn't.'

'That must be why you're not felling it then, come sit next to me, as soon as it kick in you'll understand.' he said, giving Jonah a huge nudge of confidence.

Jonah had never had any reason to doubt Patrick. Since his arrival in that peaceful little town, he had shown himself to be a person he could always trust. Everything he needed - and Patrick could provide - was within reach. They met in the Black Hole in his first week living in the city.

'"That brunette is looking at you.' Patrick's voice, still unknown, sounded close to him.

'I can see that...' lied Jonah with a credulous tone.

'I know her, let me introduce you.'

After that night, they started to go out together almost every weekend, not to mention the occasional day during the week where they would just get together to have a conversation. Patrick had grown up in that city and still had both his parents living within close range, what made lunch invitations always a possibility."

'Are you coming or not?' he returned to his senses, noticing that Patrick was looming with impatience.

'What is this pill making you fell? And why don't I feel anything?' he asked as they walked towards the two closest chairs.

'I don't know how to explain what I feel, but sitting in that chair makes all the sense in the world to me right now. I feel like sleeping, weird, ain't it?'

Now, nothing else was making any sense to Jonah. 'Sleeping pills in the dream room, what kind of fucking party is this?', he thought and laughed as they continued to walk towards the infamous chairs. Patrick soon removed his shirt - he hadn't been wearing his jacket for some time now - and sat down the chair unceremoniously. 'I hope this pill just kicks in before I'm trapped to that fucking chair.', he thought as he started to get jealous of others. Except for him, everyone seemed very excited about the idea of lying in one of those devices, Patrick was already trying to wire the cables to himself without Jonah even having the opportunity to try and help him.

'Let me help you.' he said, starting to attach the wires to his friend's body.

'Yes, I should do the same for you.'

'Fuck no! Not until I start felling the same as you.' he replied by slapping away Patrick's hand holding one of those wires.

'Hi!' whispered Lara from a chair nearby. 'The drug is only for the possible side effects... You can start the program without it.'

'But how is Patrick feeling like sitting in the chair?' he asked as he air-quoted his friend's own saying, thinking that the drug would bring him some magical insight about how things should work.

'He's just drunk, it has nothing to do with the pill.' she replied trying to be as clear as possible.

Things started to make more sense. Jonah had let go of his anxiety and tried to focus on what he was doing. He let Patrick help him with the strands, one on the left side of his forehead, another two on his bare chest, and another two on each wrist. On the monitor next to him, a green light began to flash, followed by numbers - which he assumed were his heartbeats and vital signs - despite the fact he couldn't see any doctors nearby. Patrick was practically asleep, he didn't know if the machine helped him or if he passed out from the excessive drinking. Besides him, other people already had their eyes closed, that scene was getting more and more likely to be something seen in a horror movie , the eccentricity of those rich people was over the limits. He still had no idea of what was going to happen, or how that pill was supposed to work, or even how he was going to fall asleep like those around him.

'Hi!' he whispered to Lara. 'What should I do?'

'Just lie down!' she exclaimed as she pointed to the back of the chair.

Jonah observed a magnetic plate embedded in the backrest where he would lay his head down in a few seconds, he was still afraid of anything that could happen, but the fact that the pill was only for possible side effects made him a tad more relaxed. He felt a weird little shock and left out a high-pitched noise out of his mouth as he ran his finger over the plate, making Lara come to the rescue as she noticed his hesitation, telling him to take his feet off the floor and lie them on the chair.

The lights were getting dimmer and dimmer. Jonah decided to finally lay his head back as he realised that even Lara had already had her eyes closed. Before he could be induced by the chair into a deep sleep, he was able to see that the waiters were being replaced by men and women who wore white coats and carried strange equipment. He tried, but he couldn't open his mouth to say anything else. His mind was gone.

"The image that appeared before his eyes was one the most realistic things he had ever seen. Jonah was fully aware of the situation, despite having a strong headache. He was fast asleep, or rather, he was dreaming - and he knew it - and could feel everything with the most perfect intensity. His mind was still drunk and he was still lying in the same chair when he found himself in control of his own brain. Patrick was by his side, and he had the same expression of surprise on his face. The rest of the people started to get up slowly as if they were waking up from a deep sleep, Giovanni and Lara were already walking amongst the other guests and welcoming those who had already managed to get up.

'Welcome to the Dream Room. The best lucid dreaming experience that money can buy.' said Mr. Dartagnan as he intertwined his steps between chairs and rubbed the forehead of every person who was trying to face that new reality.

Jonah had read something - in some sensationalist article - about those things they called lucid dreams, but something like that was so far out of his reach that he had never delved into the subject. In recent years, science had been trying to achieve the reality of making that possible, but the price to be paid for such a chair did not suit Jonah's financial reality.

His subconscious started to shape his reality, and despite knowing that he was dreaming, Jonah felt, in his own body, that that experience was not real.

'Each of you is now free to imagine the impossible.' began Giovanni, with a sensationalist tone, as he realised everyone was already supported by their own feet. 'As most of you know, everyone has the freedom to navigate the depths of their own subconscious. Let me, please, give voice to the one who will have the honor of taking us on this exciting journey.

'I hope you appreciate the beauty of the incredible feeling that will be presented to you tonight.' said Lara, extending her arms and starting what seemed like a baptism ceremony.

Despite feeling that his mind was under control and that everything seemed safe, Jonah had a multitude of questions that needed answers, but the speed of which everything was happening would not allow that anytime soon.

Little by little, people began to dissipate out of thin air.

Jonah stood still. Waiting for some scenario to magically appear in front of his eyes, but nothing changed as he was still standing in that room, in fact everything looked normal. Patrick seemed to suffer from the same affliction as he, whilst Lara and Giovanni watched their surroundings

34

and appreciated the beauty of people taking their separate paths.

'Don't just stand there!' said Lara when she noticed they were static. 'Everything is possible in the Dream Room, just imagine it.'

'But what scenario is this?' asked Patrick when looking for something different that could catch his attention.

'The scenario is just an emotional concept. I control the main feeling of the lucid dream. The rest is up to you...'

'Beg you a pardon?' Jonah interjected as nothing made sense anymore.

'First-time dreamers don't get any explanations, my dear. Your job here is just to enjoy and let your imagination take you to the deepest limit of your subconscious.' said Giovanni before Lara could spoil any more future surprises.

'But I don't understand anything...'

'You will understand. The idea is to imagine! Now go!' Giovanni interrupted Jonah before he could ask anything else.

'Do you have any idea of what to do?' he asked Patrick, who had closed his eyes.

His friend was then gone. As simple as that. In the blink of an eye he had disappeared from his sight before he could hear Jonah's question. His expression, despite showing great ecstasy, was incredulous. He could feel that any of that would make him very scared in a normal situation, but Lara controlled the main feeling, whatever that meant, and he felt that he could trust her. Jonah deduced that the only plausible explanation would be happiness, or perhaps the pill they gave him was a very strong drug. 'The idea is to imagine', Mr. Dartagnan had exclaimed a few seconds ago.

Jonah closed his eyes, imitating what Patrick had just done, and thought of the house he had spent his early childhood in, one of the few memories he still had left of his dead parents. In the blink of an eye he was there, standing in the front-yard of where he used to play football with his father. In less than a second his mind was filled with nostalgia, but as much as it brought him sadness and longing, he could not assimilate the image with any negative feelings. His father's face was vivid, just as he remembered. 'Am I the small me or the big me?', he thought as he got more confused by every single thought that would go through his mind. He looked down and saw that he was still wearing his clothes from the party. 'Just use your imagination.', was when, suddenly, he found himself dressed in shorts and had his bare feet touching the lawn, showing him that he was definitely his big self. Happiness returned to take over the neural synapses that worked his brain whilst he tried to focus on the ball he would kick to his deceased father.

'Is that really you, father?' he said aloud as the old man continued to kick the ball in the same direction.

Nothing. Not even a word. His father continued to look in the same direction in which he was kicking the ball, whilst Jonah was already at his side, trying to touch him and get his attention. That was when he turned back to the position he had came from and realised that he could see his young self in the other end, kicking the ball back. 'But how? I felt that ball hitting my foot.', he thought as he vividly remembered the hard leather of the ball touching his bare foot.

'Lunch is ready!' shouted a female voice from the inside of the house.

Jonah knew it was his mother. Before he could run into the house, he saw his body materialised sitting at the dining table in the room where he had grown up. Once again, he tried to observe his arms, which were big, hairy, and strong, far from being those of a child. He was his old self, the same as before, but this time he would not make the mistake of moving. 'I will do exactly as my memory tells.', he thought before he went back to observing his own young self devouring the food in front of him.

Skepticism still dominated most of the events that followed. He was absolutely sure of that memory. In fact, he hadn't thought about that situation for many years, but his subconscious did him the favour of bringing him one of the happiest moments of his youth. He could see what Lara meant by the 'scenery I designed for you.', It had nothing to do with the appearance of anything, but with the feeling that took over his whole body. His arms and legs shivered every few seconds, it was some kind of euphoria he had never experienced before. Happiness didn't come with that intensity and frequency, it wasn't normal, and every aspect of the dream could be controlled - he realised that now. If he wanted to observe or experience the moment, he could, and all he had to do was to imagine it.

His subconscious continued to surprise him, as he was still very young at the time of that memory and couldn't remember every detail with precision, but with each word said and each look exchanged between him and his parents, he realised that everything was there, lodged in some forgotten corner of his mind.

'How was school?' asked his mother as she served him a spoonful of rice and sliced up pieces of meat so he would be able to chew with his yet feeble teeth.

The response was automatic, just as his subconscious commanded. He felt like crying, but his brain continued to block the presence of any possible negative feelings.

His memory took another leap, and before he knew it, he was lying on a small bed in his old childhood room. He looked at his feet and realised he had more than half his legs out of the bed. Next to him, his father covered him with a thin blanket and started to open a small illustrated book that he recognised very well. It was his favorite book as a child, giving off an image that the world could be a box of surprises and that life was simple enough to be lived without worries. Whenever he had time, his father would read him a story or two before he would fall asleep. But sleep had already come that night - it was getting hard do keep track of it - and suddenly the remembrance stopped. The image was static as he was up and out of bed, seeing his young self with his eyes closed and his father holding the book whilst staring at his sleeping son.

Before he could imagine what would come next, his body materialised back into the Dream Room. He was alone, all by himself. The feeling of nostalgia started to take over his mind, and a tear fell from his left eye before he could realise that sadness had taken over his feelings. 'Is it over already?', he thought as he was hoping someone else would just materialise in the room.

Jonah forced his brain to imagine anything else he had experienced before that could bring back a some sort of happiness, but his effort was in vain. All he could think about was the image of his father's fixed eye reading a book whilst he fell asleep. 'The scenario is one of happiness.', he thought as he was now understanding how things were supposed to work. He forced his brain again and again so that his subconscious would take him to another moment of happiness, it didn't matter which one, he just wanted the sadness to leave his mind. 'This main room shouldn't be part of the scene.', he thought as he tried to calm the anxiety of not being able to control his own feelings. That same thought started to repeat itself in his mind in an endless loop. With every turn that loop took in his mind, the anxiety increased even more, and he had no idea of how to make it stop.

He found himself crouched on the floor with his arms crossed over his legs. Now tears streamed from his eyes in an incessant cry, whilst that unwanted thought created even more roots inside his head. 'This main room shouldn't be part of the scene.', he continued as he sought a logical explanation for what was happening as nothing else made anymore sense.

He then rose quickly from the floor and did the only thing he thought was congruent. He lied his back on the chair and put his head on the metal backrest, but the magnetic plate was now gone. He didn't wake up. He opened his eyes and the atmosphere was the same. The same room: empty and lifeless. The loop became more and more intense and the tearful expression had been replaced by an intense feeling of agony. The walls started to close towards him, and the only thing Jonah managed to do was to force his eyelids close and wait for the end to come once and for all."

'Jonah! Jonah!' he heard a familiar voice after feeling that someone was fierily slapping his face.

As he woke up he was facing Patrick looking at him whilst some of the others were already standing up and a few were still waking up from what seemed to be a deep sleep in their chairs.

'What happened? Are you alright?' asked Patrick as he saw that he had opened his eyes and was conscious.

'I... I don't know...' he replied with a weak and discouraged voice.

'Get up and stay calm, nothing you have experienced is real, it is just a dream. Incredible, isn't it?' said Patrick as he noticed Jonah was, little by little, coming back to his senses.

'Yes, really incredible.' he said as he wiped his shirt sleeve over his forehead to dry the cold sweat that was dripping down.

There was no need to lie, that experience had really been something incredible. A roller coaster of emotions had taken over his mind, but now that he was awake, he felt a complete emptiness in his heart.

'What was your experience?' asked Jonah as he got up.

'I've never felt so happy! I don't know how to explain it, but I saw memories and new things too. All at once.' replied Patrick who seemed ready to lie down in that chair and do it all over again.

'Same for me...' he said once more without having to lie. Despite the confusion and fear he had felt at the end of his sleep, happiness was still the predominant feeling throughout the whole experience.

'This main room shouldn't be part of the scene.', he would repeat the loop again and again before anything could bring him what seemed to be an imminent felling of sadness. Little by little, he was becoming more self-aware of the situation and being able to organise his thoughts, remembering exactly what had happened to him whilst he was immersed in that deep sleep.

'How long has it been since we started?' he asked Patrick directly, still trying to assimilate it all.

'You can see it there.' he said, pointing to a stopwatch on the wall.

The numbers on a digital clock marked exactly thirty minutes. He couldn't say whether his perception of time was greater or lesser than that as it had been unthinkable during his lucid dream, but thirty minutes sounded normal. 'It might be right.', he thought.

'I reckon I'm going to spend a few minutes in my room. This thing got me terribly sleepy.' said Jonah as

Patrick ordered another drink from the waiter who was passing by once again.

'Sleepy? I feel like I've slept for fucking hours.' said Patrick looking at Jonah with awe.

He was worried again about what was happening to him. Clearly he had not had the same experience as Patrick on that machine. He was tired and the feeling of happiness, despite reigning, was not the only sensation he had had whilst immersed into lucid dreaming. He needed some explanation about what had just happened to him, he looked around to see if he could find Lara as she would be the one holding all the answers to his questions.

'So what do you think?' asked Lara, realising that Jonah was approaching her.

'Weird, to say the least. But tell me one thing, is it normal for me to be tired?' he asked as he saw that everyone else had already a glass in their hands and were returning to partake in the party as if they were not even a little bit tired. 'I even have a little bit of a headache.'

'Hmm.' she mumbled with worry. 'Did you take the pill before lying down the chair?'

'Yes, I did. Patrick gave me one.' he replied as the anxiety was starting to make another unannounced appearance.

'So it wouldn't be normal. That drug is designed exactly to maintain the balance on the disposition of hormones during the lucid dream, in addition to providing intense rest for the brain in a matter of only a few minutes. You should feel rested, at least mentally.' concern had now taken over Lara's expression.

'How was it?' Giovanni's voice intruded the conversation as Jonah started to panic.

'Maybe the pill didn't work on me?' asked Jonah, ignoring the host's question.

Lara and Giovanni looked at each other whilst Jonah became more and more concerned about his well-being. The chairs had already returned to their places below the floor and the cushions were re-set to their designated area. Jonah sat in disbelief. The expression on his face defined exactly what he was feeling, there was no need to ask if he was okay to know that something was wrong.

'Tell me exactly what happened.' said Giovanni with a demanding tone as he showed off concern.

Jonah told him everything he had been through, from the moment he took the pill given by Patrick until the moment he woke up in a cold and fearful sweat. Lara Farlet and Giovanni Dartagnan were sitting next to him and listened very carefully to every word he had to say. They then exchanged looks of concern as Jonah became increasingly anxious about the whole situation.

'I'll be honest with you.' began Giovanni as Jonah felt that it was going to be a bad conversation. 'This have never happened before, but don't worry, these machines are completely safe and have never been a problem for anyone who has used them.' he finished, showing comfort as he looked deeply into Jonah's eyes.

'It is true! Nothing to worry about.' said Lara. 'Here, just take a sip of my drink then go back to the party, Im'm sure this tiredness will soon be gone.' she finished by offering him the glass of champagne she had in her hands.

'Actually, I don't really feel like drinking. I've got a bit of a headache.' he replied as he politely rejected the alcohol.

'Weird...' began Giovanni before he could be interrupted.

'Did I hear someone say something about a headache?' Patrick appeared out of nowhere and threw himself on a cushion next to Jonah.

'Yes, I think I've drank way too much.' he lied not to worry his friend.

'I've got a pill here. Take this, and soon it will be gone.' Patrick, who was already drinking again, took the pill out of his pocket and handed it to Jonah.

Jonah saw an expression of dismay on Mr. Dartagnan's face, who immediately threw himself in front of him and took the pill before Jonah could reach out for it.

'Where did you get this?' he asked in amazement.

'I brought it from home, I always get headaches after a party.' replied Patrick innocently.

'Impossible! This is the pill we all took before being immersed into lucid dreaming. Only I know how to get one of these.'

As soon as Giovanni finished speaking, Lara, Jonah and himself made the same astonished expression on their faces. What had happened was clear, but Patrick still had a look of confusion in his eyes.

'What the fuck just happened?' he asked as he was felling sort of left out of the conversation.

'You gave me the wrong fucking pill!' said Jonah, panicking.

CHAPTER 4:

Whilst heavily breathing, Jonah stood motionless with his eyes fixed on the horizon. Patrick was beginning to understand what he had done as Lara and Giovanni whispered inaudible words in each other's ears. The rest of the people did not seem to know anything about what was happening, everyone continued to enjoy the party and to compare experiences of what they had just went through.

Several things were passing through Jonah's mind. He had always been apprehensive about taking drugs because he was afraid he would never return to reality, but that night was so good that he didn't even think twice about taking that pill from Patrick's hand.

'I reckon we'd better take you to see one of the doctors we keep here on retainer.' said Giovanni Dartagnan, finally, after crouching in front of Jonah and placing his hand on his shoulder.

He did not reply. He was astonished and was not sure of what he was experiencing at that point, other than the clear feeling of fear that ran amok through his mind. Lara offered him an empathetic look, but the gesture brought Jonah no comfort. He just got up and followed Giovanni through the path that led to the room where the doctor was supposed to be.

'So... this has never happened before?' he asked with a tone of concern.

'No, but just try to stay calm, I strongly believe it's nothing serious.' said Giovanni in a comforting tone.

The journey to the doctor's office was longer than he expected. They passed through all the rooms - Jonah had a sudden urge to go into his and try to sleep until it all went away - until they reached the very end of the building. A small door, without any sings, was opened by Giovanni so that they could enter a tiny room that held two men sitting and talking in an uneasy way.

'Mr. Dartagnan.' said one of them as they stood up to greet him.

Jonah could hear the old man telling them every detail of what had just happened in the Dream Room. The expression on each of their faces was of surprise, that particular situation really seemed to have never happened before, but as good professionals, they tried to keep a good posture and calmed Jonah in a comforting way.

'Let's examine you, rest assured that nothing worse will happen.' said one of them.

'Thank you very much doctor.' he said. 'Your name is?'

'Douglas, and this is my colleague William.' replied him whilst indicating a small bed for Jonah to lie down.

The first doctor, who seemed to be in charge there, started examining Jonah. His nervousness had not yet passed, in fact, his breathing became increasingly stiffed with every foreign object that the doctor laid on his body.

'Try to stay calm.' said Douglas whilst Giovanni and William maintained a conversation on the other side of the small room.

'There really isn't any protocol for this type of situation. I suggest that he should return to the party and try to enjoy himself. First thing Monday morning, go to the hospital so we can run a few more tests.' William's tone of voice, who had approached his colleague to make himself aware of the situation, did not seem to be worried.

'You can rest assure, Jonah. I will do everything in my power to get this all sorted off.' said Giovani as he realised that Jonah was looking incredulously in his direction.

'You won't have to do much.' began Douglas. 'From what I can see here, he just had a bad experience, which would not happen if he had taken the right pill.'

'What should I do then?' asked Jonah.

'Nothing. Just go back to the party. I think it's best that you don't take anything for the headache.' replied the doctor. 'Being alone in your room now can bring you even more anxiety. It is best to be busy with friends and try to have some fun, as difficult as it may be.'

Giovanni thanked the doctors for their attention and indicated the way back so Jonah could follow him. The old man had a comforting smile on his face, the expression of concern had passed and the mood was already shifting from a terrifying fear to a sense of wellness.

'You see? No need to worry anymore.' he started. 'What are you feeling right now?'

'Still a bit tired, but after hearing the doctors I feel kinda better.' he said, realising he was already felling much more comfortable.

'No need to worry about the expenses as well, I'll take care of it all on Monday, I believe this mistake was my fault. I should have given you the pill myself.' he spoke with sincerity.

'Thank you.' Jonah didn't even try to refuse the offer. He had no health insurance and he knew that those tests could be quite expensive.

Patrick and Lara had already left the Dream Room and were talking closely by the table where Jonah had dined. The main hall was restless. People danced and talked at the same time as they refilled their glasses with more alcohol. Everyone seemed well rested. 'How jealous...', thought Jonah, already feeling calm about everything, but the recovering headache was still giving him a tired look. Lara stopped beside him and laid a comforting hand on his arm. The sensitive touch of her hand washed away every single feeling of distress from Jonah's mind.

'Feeling better?' she asked as she looked him in the eye.

'Indeed I am. Everything will be fine, just tired.' replied Jonah. 'I even think I'm going to have something else to drink, we still have a lot of party ahead of us, don't we?'

'Good to see you're getting back on your feet.'

Jonah held a smile to his face as he couldn't see any reason to be worried. He felt great comfort after having spoken to the doctors.

'What were you two laughing about before I got here?' asked Jonah as he approached Patrick and Lara.

'We were just remembering the situation at the reception. Lara told me that she knew you would come as my date.' replied Patrick.

'I forgot to mention. Everything has been clarified.' he said as he winked at Lara.

Jonah remembered that he had lost the chance to talk to Mr. Dartagnan whilst they were alone. He still couldn't understand why he was invited to that party; he didn't want to disturb the host with a boring conversation, but he would love to know why he was chosen to be there. Giovanni was already surrounded, once again, by the most diverse people at the party; everyone seemed to want some time by his side, and he left no one waiting unattended. Even though he acted as a simple man, he seemed to have a clear opinion about everything. 'Maybe some other time I'll get the chance to speak to him.', thought Jonah as he realised Lara was all by herself and Patrick had disappeared from his field of vision.

'Why don't you tell me a little bit more about the Dream Room.' said Jonah as he approached the gorgeous woman.

'What would you like to know?' she asked, slightly smiling after taking another sip of what appeared to be an endless champagne flute.

'That scenario you designed... Why happiness?'

'That had nothing to do with happiness. There is no way to project such deep feelings.' she replied.

'Well, that was all I could feel, happiness. What did you design then?' Jonah seemed to be confused again.

'You felt happiness because of the memories that were brought back to the scene, which was family.' she replied honestly.

Jonah consented with a brief smile. He could now understand why he didn't felt like crying by the remembrance of his late parents, the few memories he had of them were all about happiness, even though the brief scene of his late father brought him a weird sense of nostalgia.

'At first, you told us we could imagine anything, but the only thing I could think of then was my family.'

'Well, yes, that's why the scenario! All of those chairs were connected to mine. Your memories would only take you to what I programmed. It's automatic.'

'I was happy, I could only think of very old memories. Things I didn't even remember that were in my subconscious.' he said looking happy to have been able to relive that experience.

'Didn't you have more recent memories?' she asked curiously.

'My parents passed when I was a very young boy.' replied Jonah.

'I'm sorry.' she started. 'I have no way of knowing what each person will dream, but you could have thought of other people in your family.' she replied, bringing Jonah another unanswered question as why he had not thought about the people who had raised him.

'No need to apologize, on the contrary, I found the experience to be an incredible thing.' he said as he did not want to talk about that subject any longer.

The silence covered the sound of unsaid words. Jonah didn't know what else to say and Lara started looking around with some discomfort. The riddle in her expressions left him unsure of what was going on in her mind. Perhaps Lara's discomfort came from his uncontrollable and constant insistence on looking straight into her eyes; he found it hard to realise what he was doing.

'I'm sorry.' he finally mentioned.

'Why is that?' she asked confused.

'For staring at you. I think you must have realised that I've been doing this since we've met at the reception.' he said, running his hand through his hair and laughing uncomfortably.

'I did realise it, but it doesn't bother me. I feel flattered.' she replied with a sincere smile.

'Why the discomfort then?' he asked, quite curiously.

'I like looking at you too... But I shouldn't.' she replied whilst being keen to put an end to that subject.

Silence reigned with discomfort again. Jonah knew he shouldn't have said anything, let alone flirt with the woman who was accompanied by host and owner of the place he stood; he was very lucky to be there among that select group of people. When he started opening his mouth to try and fix the conversation, Lara was already turning around and heading towards Giovanni. Jonah stood motionless and embarrassed, there was no one else at his side to whom he could talk, the level of intimacy that the conversation had taken seemed to have driven away anyone who was around. He could not contain the euphoria that went through his entire body when he heard those words coming out of Lara's mouth; even if that didn't mean much, he felt something was going on between them.

As he had not rested like the others, Jonah was already starting to feel slightly drunk. The headache and the fear were completely gone so he decided to explore a little more of that magnificent place, since, despite being the last room he had been in, the Dream Room was not the last he could lay his eyes on. He took another champagne flute from a waiter who was just passing by and continued to stroll around the room. People kept talking and dancing, and another good part of them were lining up outside the Dream Room, probably another wave of people that would be submerged into the wonders of lucid dreaming.

He continued walking towards another variant of the main hall that he had not yet visited. Before he got there, he managed to finish with two more glasses of champagne.

The next room he stumbled upon looked even stranger than the others. Wooden swings and thrones raised in not very strategic places gave the small room a medieval feel. There, for the first time, he couldn't see any waiters or even a bar. 'That must be why this room is empty.', he thought wryly. Dark lights and dark-red walls completed the eerie aspect of that place, but the strangest thing was the swords and other sorts of medieval devices hanging off the walls. 'If anyone who's drunk gets one of those things...', he thought again when he heard a female voice coming from the back of the room.

'What's that curiosity all about?' she asked him.

'Nothing in particular. I was just walking around to get to know the place a bit better.' he replied as he saw that the woman came from a dark corner of the room.

'My name is Catarina.' she said as she held out her hand for Jonah to kiss.

He awkwardly returned the gesture courteously as he was not used to that kind of thing; it was not ordinary for one to do something like that in those modern days. Catarina was at most at her fifties. She had black hair in a bun - like most women at that party - and a very thin face that emphasised the size of her nose. She wore a long black dress and had an old-fashioned charm to her walk.

'Would you like to know what this room is?' she asked as she saw the curiosity on Jonah's face.

'If you wouldn't mind, ma'am' he replied as polite as he could be.

'Catarina is fine.' she corrected him. 'Are you one of the new guests? I've never seen you around here.'

'Yes, it is indeed my first time here, I just left the Dream Room...'

'This place is really amazing and it surprises me every time I come here.' she spoke as she held a smile to her face.

'So are you going to tell me what this room is for?'

'Let's just say this is a museum for Mr. Dartagnan's relics.' she deviated from the subject. 'But I'll let him tell you at the right time about what is it that his guests do here.'

'What an odd woman.' he thought as he watched his surroundings for a few seconds. As soon as he turned his attention back to Catarina, he realised that she had simply disappeared. Jonah quickly turned around and went out through the dark opening that led to the main hall. 'Isn't this a room I won't be coming back to...', he thought as he walked quickly to where people could be witnesses in case something happened.

There must have been one or two other rooms that he hadn't been able to visit yet, but he was tired of walking around and had a recent urge to talk to some of the guests. He looked around for Patrick in the midst of the uproar that concentrated the vast majority of the guests. He could see Lara exchanging ideas with some other women her age, but he couldn't see any trace of his friend.

'Will you join me for another cigarette?' asked Giovanni as he approached Jonah.

'Hey there!' he exclaimed as he tried to disguise his startle. 'Of course, are we allowed to smoke in here?' he asked without knowing why he had accepted another one of those things, even though it would allow him a few minutes alone with the man he had been seeking to speak.

'We can do whatever the fuck we want.' he whispered in a confident tone. 'But let's go outside, that door leads to an incredible garden!'

Jonah hadn't even noticed the presence of that glass door that was literally a few meters away from where he was sitting during dinner time. Perhaps it was the darkness of the ambiance or the excitement of being in that place, but that door should not have gone unnoticed.

'Beautiful isn't it?' said Mr. Dartagnan as he held out a lit cigarette so Jonah could grab it.

Jonah nodded his head as he dazedly admired the beauty of the garden slightly lit by a few lights and a strong moonlight that further increased the magnitude of the entire state. Several species of trees surrounded a huge maze decorated with flowers of different colours; at the very end, a fountain lit elegantly by a light so feeble that it would mix in a gradient shade with the moonlight.

'Are you feeling better already?' Mr. Dartagnan broke the silence.

'I actually am, I'd even forgotten about what happened.' he said trying to leave behind the bad experience he had just had. The idea of lucid dreaming seemed like a good escape from his boring everyday life, and it would be really exciting to be able to enjoy that place more often.

'Great. Maybe we can go to the Dream Room again later on, as long as you take the right pill at this time.'

'Can I ask you a question?' said Jonah, ignoring the old man's invitation.

'You can, of course.'

'Why did you insist on me and Patrick coming here?' he said whilst building up the courage to ask the question he had been longing to, even though Giovanni didn't seem to be the type who liked explaining himself.

'I've already told you, young man.' he started looking a little impatient. 'There is no special reason... I saw you in the Black Hole one of these days and I thought it would be interesting to welcome you and your friend here.'

'But we are so... How can I put it...'

'Socially different?' Giovanni jumped in to complete his sentence as he noticed the hesitation in Jonah' voice.

'I was going to say poor, but sure, let's go with your term.' he said, laughing so that the atmosphere would not get so tense.

'I do not consider myself a person who relies on social classes to choose who I relate with. I come from a humble background myself and I believe that, given a chance, everyone has the potential for achieving success.'

'That sounds so...'

'Cliche?' he interrupted again as that started to irritate Jonah.

'Noble...' he corrected the old man with a sarcastic tone.

'Wouldn't say that, Jonah... Not at all.' he said as he puffed his cigarette once again. 'Shall we get back to the party?' he asked as he flicked half his cigarette away.

Upon hearing his voice tone, Jonah realised that Giovanni did not like to be upset or even questioned about his choices and decisions and, despite the smile on his face, he realised that the man had taken him out of his comfort zone for a brief moment.

'I didn't mean to offend you.' said Jonah as he awkwardly copied the movement with the unfinished cigarette in his hand.

'You couldn't if you tried, but there's no need for distrust either. Enjoy the party!' he said and turned his back before Jonah could say anything else.

Finally, Jonah had realised that the reason for being there meant nothing extraordinary. One of the many great traits he could see in the old man, besides noticing a remarkable characteristic of his personality: he did not like to be questioned.

As he was left alone in that huge balcony, he admired the garden for one last time before returning to the party. Patrick were to be found talking amidst a huge group of people. Jonah tried to place himself beside him and interact with the conversation; everyone was intoxicated, which was no surprise since the party had started for a second run a couple of hours ago, and those who were in the first wave of the Dream Room had all their energies renewed. People seemed to be loyal to those who were part of the same group they had experienced lucid dreaming with, but he still did not know the name of anyone other than Patrick's.

'This kind of experience should be instituted for the whole society.' said a man who was facing Jonah.

'I most certainly agree! If I hadn't been invited to come here, I would never have dreamt about such a thing.' replied Patrick with an intended pun as those surrounding him seemed fascinated by his simplicity.

He saw his friend as a strange being, among so many refined people. In a way, it disgusted him, but Jonah knew that, like him, other people were curious to know what the grass felt like on the other side, however, that type of conversation was not for him, or at least not for that particular moment. After hours without realising it, he went back to looking at his mobile to check if he could get any reception somewhere in that place, but his phone was still silent and unreachable. 'There must be some kind of firewall in here.', he thought as he walked aimlessly through the main ballroom.

The lights oscillated between bright and dim, the beautiful chandeliers attached to the ceiling sparkled in sync with the music, it was really something else. For a brief moment, Jonah realised that he was walking amidst different people, bumping into one or another whilst receiving warnings from some inpatient drunks all around. The blinking of the lights led him to lose some of his motor control as his headache started to make a new appearance inside his mind. He could see the people who, around him, continued to dance and talk whilst they drank more and more of anything that could be offered to them.

'You should not insist on it!' he heard Douglas' distinct voice when suddenly finding himself lying on a weird bed.

'What the fuck is this now? Where am I?', his voice echoed inside his own head in vain as he tried to understand where he had magically been materialised.

He inter-called between opening and shutting his eyes tightly to try and make sense of where he was, as he appeared in the main hall once again to watch everyone around him dancing and celebrating. His head was now pounding with an intensity, until then unknown, as someone gave him a nudge and he fell sitting on on his own ass.

'Hey!' he shouted at the person who pushed him, he could clearly see the face of that old lady who had sat beside him during dinner time.

'Stay calm, Jonah. All of this will soon be over.' he found himself lying on that odd little bed again whilst Giovanni spoke from behind his back to try and comfort him for some incomprehensible reason.

A strong light overshadowed his vision as he desperately tried to move within the bed. He looked at his own hands and noticed the shackles that prevented him from freeing himself, turning him into a prisoner of his own body.

'Where the fuck am I?' he tried to scream with all the air he was able to hold inside his lungs, even though the words didn't seem to come out of his mouth

'Soon everything will be fine.' repeated Mr. Dartagnan as he was unable to imagine the despair Jonah was experiencing.

The sound of his words kept echoing inside his own head and, although he felt his own mouth moving, he could not hear the words that were deferred to those surrounding him. Even though the strong light obscured his view, he could clearly distinguish Douglas and Giovanni in front of the bed to which he was tied. The two talked indistinctly as Jonah could only hear the sound of some comforting words when they approached him, but as soon as they spoke to each other, the sound became mute and his perception became blurred again. He felt a strong scratch on his left arm, but as he tried to look he couldn't focus on what caused the pain. Jonah continued to try to detach himself from the shackles with all the strength he could find inside him, but paralysis had taken over every single muscle of his body.

'What is happening to me?', he thought as he began to feel a mild despair.

Even if he wanted to show he was scared and scream from the top of his voice, his head would not allow him to think of anything but the pain he was feeling. He could perceive that his mind oscillated between two different realities, but he couldn't say which was a dream and which was real, or even understand whether any of them made any sense.

He found himself sitting on the floor of the main ballroom once again as he could now see his slowly bleeding arm through the white of his shirt; he must have fallen onto his cup or some other shard of sharp glass that was laying on the floor. A few people looked at him with an expression of astonishment, making him realise he was starting to become the centre of attention. He got up quickly before he could draw more attention to himself 'I must be hallucinating.', he thought optimistically and sensibly as he sought any feasible meaning that would explain what was happening to his state of mind. He staggered for a few meters until he found a wall, where he leaned to take a deep breath and try to calm down. He closed his eyes tightly once again so that reality could reign in his thoughts, but as he opened them he realised things wouldn't be that easy.

'Do you think we've managed to remove all of his memories?' asked the known voice of Giovanni coming from behind his head.

'What? Let me out of here!' he shouted into his own mind as he pointlessly tried kick-boxing the air around him.

'I can't say for sure if that wouldn't kill him.' replied Douglas, looking at a small monitor that controlled his vital signs.

He tried to close his eyes tightly, repeating that gesture as if it was some kind of magic trick that would set him free, trying to get back to what seemed to be the reality he yearned for, but that was now out of question as he felt a slight twinge of small pieces of iron that kept his eyes forcibly open. Giovanni approached him with some kind of dropper that he dripped into his eyes, he could feel a liquid seeping down from each side of his face.

The image that spread before his eyes looked like something straight out of a horror show. He had no control over his own body and his mind was working like some kind of derailed train. Whatever he might think ended up leading him to believe that he was going to die there, in that unknown bed, yet he didn't understand how he got there. 'This has to be a dream.', he thought constantly as he watched Douglas and Giovanni, again, talking without being able to hear them.

'Jonah! Wake up!' he heard Patrick's comforting voice screaming into his ear whilst a few more people from his Dream Room group materialised in front of him.

'What?' he asked without being able to understand what had just happened.

'What? What are you on about? Why are you sleeping on the floor, Jonah?' asked Patrick as he tugged on his arm to get him back on his feet.

'I don't remember anything...' he said as he ran his hand through his hair and wiped the drool that ran down the corner of his mouth.

His head was hurting and his clothes were in a deplorable state. He had no ideia of what had happened or even how he got to that corner where he was leaned against.

'You need to accept this condition.' a small flash of memory came to torment his thoughts, overshadowing the reality as he blinked his eyes whilst rubbing them to clear his vision.

'What?' he asked when he saw Patrick reappear.

'What? I said nothing. Why don't you go to sleep in your room?' he said as he let Jonah rest his arm on his shoulders.

'I don't feel sleepy at all.' he said confused. 'I actually feel completely renewed.' he continued without having to lie, it felt like he had slept for hours. 'How long was I out?'

'It was less than ten minutes, I would say.' replied Patrick as he stared briefly at his wristwatch.

'I think it was just a dream, I just can't properly remember what it was about...' he lied as to not let anything out before he could grasp his mind around what was happening.

CHAPTER 5:

'I'm going outside... need to get some air...' he told Patrick as he walked out towards the balcony he had just left whilst gasping for air.

With long strides, Jonah paced on without looking around. He was extremely anxious about what had just happened. 'How can I have dreamed all of this in such a short time?', he thought as he tried to unscramble the visions he had just had and understand them in line with the alternating reality that was presenting itself to him.

He didn't have to lie to Patrick as he really felt much better and the hallucinations seemed to have given his head a break, no longer aching as badly, but what really interested him at that particular moment was to seek an answer to the anxiety he was feeling. He opened the balcony doors and leaned over the porch to vomit.

He forced it, but nothing came out.

He felt suffocated by his own thoughts as he tried to organise the order of the events.

He searched the deepest of his memories to assemble the direct order of the facts, trying to understand how he could have been in two places at the same time. How could Mr. Dartagnan - who had just been in that same balcony smoking cigarettes with him a few minutes ago - be with him in that small room. Every few minutes he felt the urgency to look around, trying to find the presence of a figure that seemed to run through his peripheral vision, but every time he twisted his neck, hoping for an answer, he'd realise that his mind continued to play poorly elaborated tricks on him. The party atmosphere was still going strong inside. 'Funny how these people have a habit of changing the course of the party.', he thought, realising that the mingle inside would take alternate directions every little bit.

Jonah had no desire to return to that crowd. He observed the immensity of the garden that spread in front of his eyes whilst trying to take a deep breath and calm down. He decided he did not need to comment on what he had just experienced with Mr. Dartagnan, as he did not want to cause any more problems to the celebrations he was kindly invited to.

The size of that maze left Jonah even more curious and intrigued by how large the state of the Dartagnan Brothers Hotel was.

The shape that gave form to the maze seemed simple to unravel from there. Nothing out of the ordinary, it was similar to every other one he had seen in movies or even in parks as he was just a child playing around. As he glanced at the very last corner, he could see the fountain that spurted water whilst glowing white lights. 'A bit tacky.', he thought as he re-thought how it would look like at close range, even though he couldn't see the monument in its entirety.

The balcony extended on both sides with a huge staircase covered by a white granite floor with small black stripes that gave it an incredible contrast. The floor was moist and the handrail was cold, he went down slowly so that he wouldn't fall on the slippery, damp floor that gave way to the grass. At that moment, he could see that the cold was coming as he remembered that humidity used to make an appearance in that region during the winter, but the mid-season still made it possible to enjoy the fresh air with enough comfort.

As he reached the lawn that faced the main entrance to the maze, Jonah noticed that a gloomy air hovered right above where the vines came to an end, it was not so cold, but his left arm felt a little shiver as a slight breeze passed by and moved the direction that his hair was combed. He felt a slight burning sensation on that arm, something he had noticed before, when Patrick had pulled him off, but now it seemed to be bothering him a bit more as the friction of his shirt scratched what appeared to be a small cut. He took off his coat as he laid it on the floor and was able to notice a small blood stain between his shirt and the inside of his forearm, something he had seen before, but thought it was just part of the hallucination. Although he felt a small pain whilst living that weird dream, he couldn't remember getting hurt at any time, but it wasn't unusual for him to wake up with one or two injuries after a night of drinking.

He unbuttoned his shirt and rolled up his sleeve until his forearm was in contact with the air left by the fresh breeze that was passing by. The situation was critical. Jonah could constantly cross the line in a slight charming way that women would find attractive, but he, in any possible way imaginable, could understand how what had just sprung before his eyes could have happened. Beneath a small layer of dried blood, he could see a tiny little drawing. It was a small black cross drawn upside-down as from the point of view he was looking. It didn't make any sense that that thing was there, on his arm, even though in his dream he had been experiencing headaches, he couldn't remember any noise or pain that resembled that of getting tattooed. With great difficulty, as the wound still seemed recent, he removed the small skin of blood that was still forming to look at that thing more closely.

Despite being able to see the little cross more clearly now, Jonah couldn't notice anything different that would make any sense, in fact, nothing else made sense that night. Drugs, lucid dreams, a palace hidden by a hotel and a bunch of weirdly refined people were some of the many things that became part of his life. He stopped to observe his surroundings and realised that he had been looking at his new tattoo for quite some time now. He went back to fetch his mobile so he could at least have some clarity about what time it was, he got so lost that night that he had no idea of how much time had passed since he got there - not much time had passed anyway. The moon light was even brighter now as the sky was clear and lit by sparkling bright little stars, highlighting a strong crescent moon that stamped the sky as if it was a masterpiece.

He decided to forget about the tattoo for a moment so he could go back to observing his surroundings. The grass stretched till the entrance of the maze as a small passage indicated by a sign said 'Welcome'. His affection and desire for mystery was pulling him towards that entrance, which made Jonah decide to take a few steps into the maze, as he had always been fascinated by that kind of thing.

Before stepping on the other side, he held his hands up to the small leaves that sprouted from the vines that covered what appeared to be a concrete wall. 'Nobody gets out by cheating.', he read as he repeated the words that were written on the same sign that welcomed the visitors. A feeling of euphoria pulled an eccentric taste for the difficulty that was presented to him took over his best senses and made him forget about the problems he had already amounted. Any small challenge would spark his most deviant thoughts and an instinct for adventure would arise from within, Jonah didn't even think about those weird dreams or the strange tattoo, he just went for it.

The design of the maze looked different from what he had seen on the balcony. Although most of the path was lit by moonlight, some parts were covered by the vineyards that seem to have been taking over the structure for quite some time, and, the further he would go, the colder the air would get. The landscape was awfully bleak, but that wouldn't scare Jonah away, on the contrary, he was even more keen to go even deeper and discover what was so beautiful about the water fountain that he couldn't see in its complete form from the balcony, as deep down he knew that was just an excuse to continue through the maze and to be able to feel the satisfaction of reaching its end.

Something intrinsic attracted him, more and more, into the deeps of that place.

'I can't get lost in here.', he realised inside his own mind by reasoning that his mental state was not the most propitious for walking around the woods, especially through a maze, a place designed for people to get lost in. Despite being a man driven by reason, Jonah would often let himself be led by the adventurous and irrational side of his brain. He would let his emotions take care of the coherent and avoid seeking a feeling of remorse even if his choices would go awry, however inconsequential they might be.

The mysterious maze did not appear to be anything extraordinary. The corridors were relatively wide and every two wrong passages gave way to a right one. 'Won't be long till I reach the end...', he thought as he let himself go by the momentum again.

'Jonah?' he heard someone's odd voice nearby.

'I'm in here!' he shouted back at the top of his lungs to whomever that was.

The voice was indistinguishable.

'Jonah?'

The same odd weird repeated itself. The intonation seemed to be that of a male voice charged with experience and eager to receive feedback.

'I'm right fucking here' he shouted back.

'Jonah?'

He decided to ignore that for the time being. 'I need to get back to where I came from.', he thought as he realised he would have to leave his amusing stroll at the maze for another time. 'It might be better with some daylight.'

Jonah went back the exact same way he had come in, but his mind seemed to be playing tricks on him as those lucid dreams had scrambled his brain and he now seemed to be unable to find his way out. 'This is no time to panic.', he thought as he tried to ease the anxiety that was kicking in.

Each and every corridor he walked by seemed to look exactly the same. The euphoria was filled with fear as the width between the walls seemed to be getting narrower and narrower. His mind started to project a tapered vision, and his anxiety started to get more and more uncontrollable, which was not favoured by the continuous strange voice that would exhale the same annoying sound.

'Jonah?'

He wasn't particularly polite as he answered the voice once again. He was desperately trying to understand what direction the sound was coming from by the intensity of the voice, but things were not getting any better as the voice would sound the same, in the exact same time intervals. 'One, two, three ... forty-five.', he counted every time the voice would repeat his name.

The more he would walk through the maze's corridors, the more lost he seemed to be getting. And then, his headache reappeared as suddenly as it had been gone before. Sharp twinges took over any strength he might have had to think about anything other than the pain he was felling. He knelt on the floor as he held his own head by the hair, the pain was worse than before, it seemed like he was going to be sick at some point. He clung on one of the vines near him as he felt the blood drain from his hands as one of the thorns in a small pointed branch stung it with tremendous rage, but neither the blood nor the pain caused by the thorns seemed to be more important than what was about to happen.

'Do you think he can understand us?' asked Douglas's distinctive voice, which was echoing in his mind.

Once again, he found himself stuck in the same bed he had dreamt about not more than half an hour ago. The scheme of a situation was the same, he could see the doctor who was speaking towards the same voice that came from behind his head. Giovanni Dartagnan.

'I sure hope so.' said Mr. Dartagnan as he left the place where he was hiding for the first time and appeared in Jonah's field of vision. 'Can you hear me, boy?'

As much as he tried to enunciate, the words wouldn't leave his mouth and the only thing he could think about was how vivid those machines managed to make those lucid dreams. 'If this is even a dream.' he thought as he reflected for the split of a second. He tried to open his mouth and shout out random words towards the two, who now looked at him with an air of curiosity as if he was some kind of circus attraction.

No sound seemed to be eager to come out of his mouth.

'The effects don't seem to be over yet.' said Douglas as he continued to watch Jonah whilst biting the lid off a pen and holding a clipboard with his hand against his own leg.

For the first time in a few minutes, Jonah managed to reason with his own mind. 'Well, maybe this is not a dream after all.', he thought as he realised that this was the time he had taken the longest to get out of that weird trance. The other episode was very short, but the second one seemed to be a tad different. Although he couldn't move his lips and express the anger he was feeling, he was able to smell a strange odor that hung in the air. A distinct, unknown, and newly different odor to his sense of smell.

'Oh, fuck!' he shouted loudly as he realised he was back and had his hand holding, with all the strength he could manage, to a piece of vineyard in front of him.

Blood dripped from his hands, and the pain was tearing.

For a moment he tried to forget the pain and the migraine that was now even more predominant inside his mind. He had to get up before he had another one of those episodes and try to find his way out of that maze.

Jonah was distraught by the fact that he was unable to find the place from which he had come from. He had spent his childhood going to mazes - just like that one - and had always been the first of his friends to find the way out. It did not make sense that the path he had memorised would not take him back to the entrance - his memory was an absolute marvel when it came to things like that. Even if those places could be treacherous and play tricks on people's minds, his was not disturbed to a point that he couldn't find his way back from the few meters he had moved.

The more he walked, the more often he would find dead ends. He tried with all his might to forget the pain and continued to run through the maze.

'Jonah?'

The mysterious voice echoed through the corridors again.

That was quite disturbing as his concentration did not seem to be holding any course other than the search for an explanation for the psychotic flare-ups he had been experiencing for the past hour. He caught himself envisioning the people back at the party having fun whilst dancing and drinking as he was stuck in a personal nightmare. Jonah even remembered hearing Lara Farlet's comment that they would soon return to the Dream Room and experience the incredible thing that was lucid dreaming once again. 'It would be great to be able to try it properly this time...', he thought as he yearned for the strange but incredible experience he had had just a few moments ago.

Jonah was dazzled by how those things would happen to him. It was not the first time that a different experience had gone badly. His friends always invited him to try new things, but he avoided any danger as he knew that the chance of disaster was greater than that of success. He had no belief in silly superstitions neither he believed in luck, which made him even more enraged by the fact that he had to deprive himself of things like that as the feeling of adrenaline and doing the wrong thing gave him some great desired euphoria.

'I will find my way out.', he set up his mind after a few more minutes of trying to find his way back by taking the very same route he had taken before, which made sense in his own head, as finding a point of return should not be so confusing. 'Maybe looking for a different way would be a better option.'

The headache came with no warning once again to disturb his thoughts.

'I'm starting to get worried. He was supposed to have woken up by now.' he heard Mr. Dartagnan's voice as he found himself stuck to the same bed.

He tried to speak, shout, and kick, but the commands he sent to his brain were not answered by the rest of his body. Whatever paranoia he was going through made Jonah realise that it was useless to keep making the same mistake over and over again. Every time he returned to that state of despair, the pains he felt disappeared, which gave him the chance to stop, think, and observe his surroundings.

The room he seemed to have been taken to was tiny, the walls were painted into a dark red, very similar to the room he had been in recently when he visited the doctors, and apart from the light that was pointed directly at him and overshadowed most of his vision, it didn't look like the place was being illuminated by anything else.

'We can only wait.' said Douglas whilst looking at the small monitor that connected some wires attached to his body. 'There is nothing abnormal with his monitoring.'

'Maybe we went to far with the drug...' Dartagnan looked slightly worried.

Jonah realised that the drug Patrick had given him could have been intentionally changed, but he couldn't imagine his best friend being part of any kind of scheme that would harm him in any way. Furthermore, Mr. Dartagnan's tone of concern brought him some comfort. Whatever experiments they were doing on him shouldn't have the purpose of harming him in a fatal fashion, otherwise the conversation between them would be something very different.

In addition to the bed, the monitor, and the strong beam of light redirected straight to his face, Jonah was able to notice that they both were wearing the same clothes as before. Dartagnan was dressed to impress, and Douglas was wearing the same casual outfit from when he had been into his care. He was able to see a small, half-open cupboard that was situated to his left, but the slope of the bed was not favourable for him to understand what exactly he was looking at.

He went on to put together a mental list of things that, until now, could be understood: 'I was drugged wrongfully and intentionally, which is causing me hallucinations and strong headaches; Mr. Dartagnan and the doctor are concerned for my well-being; neither Lara nor Patrick seem to be aware of my situation; I can reason better whilst I am in this situation; I, too, am lost in a maze and no one else seem to know about my whereabouts.'

Jonah took advantage of the fact that the two of them were not speaking anything interesting anymore and tried to mentalize his situation to understand what still did not make sense: 'I do not understand if this is a hallucination or not; if not, what would be the real reality; if I am drugged, when will the effect cease; I need to find the end of this maze and seek for help.'

Nothing but that made sense to him.

As his mind made its way back to the other reality, he ran out through the maze, which now seemed to be an infinite and much larger nuisance that was slowly taking his will to live. Jonah sought to understand why his mind was playing tricks on him and confusing every aspect of his reality. It was obvious that this was some effect of the drug Patrick had given him before they entered the Dream Room, but why had Giovanni Dartagnan chosen him for what seemed to be a mock experiment? Why couldn't he express himself and move when he woke up in that other reality?

The race through the corridors was becoming tiresome and, as much as he tried to ignore it, his headache continued to block his better perception of the path he was taking. Jonah had given up trying to memorize the wrong roads as he searched for his way out of that place, he only tried to find corridors with clear exits, which could give him a chance of finding an exit or any kind of flaw in those concrete walls that would allow him out. 'It was not my best judgment to enter this place knowing my situation.', he reflected as he tried to find the answers to the questions that were consuming his will to go on.

Fatigue finally washed over his body. The exhaustion was not physical, but mental. Jonah had been trying to stay focused despite the headache, whilst the blood on his hands had dried with the cold wind whistling through the maze corridors and giving the place an even eerier atmosphere. As he suddenly stopped he did not seek to observe his surroundings, but to close his eyes and focus his thoughts on a possible solution to all of his dilemmas.

And that was all in vain.

He opened his eyes again and leaned slowly against the vines, adjusting his back so that nothing else would hurt his already bruised body. He stretched his arms and twisted his neck as if he was trying to seek comfort, that's when he stopped to observe the place where he had arrived. A statue stuck in the ground appeared right in front of his eyes, some kind of flying insect, probably a butterfly carved out of some odd kind of black stone, very similar to the one that streaked the backyard staircase.

Jonah could not distinguish the butterfly, after all he didn't live much outside the urban center where he carried away his life, and had never been a frequent visitor of the bucolic scene, but what caught his attention the most was the small saying embedded in the lighter coloured stone that gave support to the distinguished insect: 'Veritas Semper Una Est.'. Hw wasn't a religious person, but he had been educated as catholic and remembered a few teachings he had had during the arduous agony of attending catechism classes in his childhood. 'Truth is always one.' He recalled a painting that hung in the classroom where he slept most of the time whilst an old and confused priest spoke in a chaotic tone. Of course, that made no sense to Jonah, he hadn't thought of god or religion in a very long time. His life had taken a path that, for him, it made no sense at all to believe in any mythological creed that sought a superior being to be its leader as he had never benefited from miracles.

'Veritas Semper Una Est.' he said aloud without knowing if he was pronouncing any of that correctly, but he couldn't find any meaning to the words. 'Mr. Dartagnan must be a very religious man.', he thought as he stopped observing the biblical saying and turned his attention to the butterfly statue.

He was unable to remember the symbolism that the insect's figure displayed within christianity, but that butterfly did not seem to be something that had 'god in its heart'. It had its antennae tied by a knot and its wings cut symmetrically in the exact half, which could only mean something pejorative to the insect's life. His state of mind was in no shape for deciphering puzzles at that moment, much less to give thought to what it might be doing in that maze. He had enough problems as it was.

His head throbbed again with full force. The images of the small statue and the shadowy butterfly were then replaced by the red room once again. His head stopped pounding and he decided to take the time he would be dwelling in that trance to reflect on what he could do to get out of that situation.

'I don't think he's recovering any time soon.' started Douglas as he spoke directly to Giovanni. 'Maybe we should start the procedure with him asleep, I can give him a strong sedative.'

Upon hearing that, Jonah went into despair. As if he wasn't confused enough trying to understand things whilst he was awake, now they wanted to put him in a state of deep sleep. Surely his subconscious would mix reality with the mess of the two state of minds that had been changing places in his head without even asking for permission. Desperation increased when he observed that the doctor, after receiving a positive signal from Mr. Dartagnan, was bringing a needle to his arm. The last thing he remembered before falling fast asleep was seeing the inverted cross tattooed on his left arm. 'This has to be real...', he thought before being sent into the deepest corner of his own mind.

Jonah woke up drooling in one of his own bloody hands, his body shivering with cold and as the vegetation mixed up with the humidity, but, as uncomfortable as it was, the moonlight still lit up the night sky.

He couldn't remember anything he had dreamt, but he had a clear feeling that it was something very strange as he was forced into that state of deep sleep. He was even more confused when he realised that he had fallen asleep on both of his realities, in fact, he had no idea of what he was doing on one of the places whilst his mind was conscious in the other one. His brain could no longer keep up with the reasoning of the whole story that had been going on during the night. 'This must be a very strong drug.', he thought as he tried to keep his calm by convincing himself that what was happening was just a strong side-effect of the drug and that soon his body would eliminate any left-over residues from it.

He got up and tried to force himself to urinate near the statue of the macabre butterfly, the headache had passed, just like when he slept at the party and he was wondering how long he had been unconscious, but he didn't mind to check the time on his phone, as he didn't know what time it was when Douglas had injected him with that sedative. It had been a long time since he had joined his hands in order to pray and, as he did it, he tried to find meaning on something he didn't even believe in anymore. Jonah realised he was talking to the walls as he felt a new sting in the same arm as the inverted cross was drawn.

Before rolling up his sleeves he closed his eyes and pleaded that nothing sinister would magically scar him for life. His mind was about to go crazy and he didn't know if he could hold on to sanity for much longer.

The plea, once again, was in vain.

'Fallacia Alia Aliam Trudit.'. his brain stopped as he read those words aloud - probably with an odd pronunciation - and panic finally overtook his actions.

CHAPTER 6:

His mind halted for a few seconds as he couldn't concentrate on anything other than the madness he was going through and how his life had been completely transformed in such a short spam of time. The reality took over his thoughts again and Jonah tried to bring his attention back to the chaos that had become his mind. He had no doubt the headaches and psychotic episodes would soon make another appearance. Before getting up, he took a photo of the statue with his mobile camera. He did not know nor understood why, but his intuition made him realise that none of those events were at random and he might need to remember every single detail of what was happening.

With his sanity back to the steering wheel, Jonah decided that his primary goal should be that to get out of there. There was not much logic in anything he was doing, so he decided to follow the path and forget about his problems for a brief moment. The ground he was stepping on was damp, and his shoes were already utterly soaked in dirty and grass. He noticed that his white shirt was stained with blood and dirt, and his pants were wet, but that was no reason for him to lose hope.

He took the path back into the maze, running through the corridors that continued to lead him to dead ends. The mental confusion caused by the similarity of the places he passed made him worry that he would never find his way out. 'Perhaps someone will come looking for me in the morning.', he thought without giving much credit to the assumption.

'Fallacia Alia Aliam Trudit.', he repeated the words perpetuated by the unwanted new tattoo that was still smeared with blood. Every time he looked back at the writing and tried to assimilate it or find any connection that it might have with something from his religious teachings from his youth, his memories decided to fail him and not bring any kind of hope or meaning that would help him in his journey. His hands still ached from the cuts caused by the thorns where he had clung, although that was no matter to attract concern at that point. He fished his mobile back from his pocket to see if he could find any reception or internet bars, or any other sort of technological marvel that would help him during those times of havoc. He was curious to look up the meaning of the writing on his left arm as well as anything that would help bring sense to what was going on, but his mobile just showed time. Nothing else.

He thought back to the things he had already understood. It was incredible what he could remember and assimilate between the two realities, and each time he slept, he felt as if his energies were completely renewed, as if he had had a complete and full night of sleep. 'They're putting me to sleep and giving me tattoos...', he added that thought to the list of things he couldn't understand. There were so many doubts that he didn't know what answer he wanted to find out first.

He had been lost in that place for more than an hour now. The cold was getting more intense by the second, and, to make things even worse, he had lost his coat somewhere in the maze and had no idea where.

As he came face to face with another statue in one of the corridors. He suddenly stopped before running out to its exit as it, oddly enough, seemed to lead somewhere for a change. Unlike the stoney butterfly, it showed the shape of a hollow fish in metallic material suspended by a small strut. At one end he could read the saying: 'Laedere Facile, Mederi Difficile.', which came easily to his mind, since the priest who taught his classes always used such a expression to emphasise how young students always sought the easiest way out: 'It's easier to tear than to sew.', he would say whenever Jonah tried to do things quickly so he could leave right away.

Of course, none of that made any sense to his situation. Jonah had never believed in coincidences, and it wasn't then that he would stop to compare the randomness of some weird saying with the situation he caught himself in.

Neither the butterfly nor the fish brought back any memory that could help him at the time. He had never been very interested in symbolism and did not saw how ancient symbols and the outdated idea of slanderous sects could bring anyone any comfort, specially not in that particular time.

He stood up and followed the path past the fish statue and, besides the illusion of that path leading somewhere with purpose, the same scenario came back to present itself, bringing him to another doubtful crossroad as he had to choose his way forward.

'Jonah?'

The mysterious voice called out his name again after a brief moment of silence. The same intonation and volume returned to echo through his ears as he felt his head slowly return to throb. Jonah started shouting random answers throughout the immensity of the maze, hoping that his cry for help would bring some sort of pity his way. He was wrong to think that that place was ordinarily simple. The complexity of finding a way out seemed to be nearing the impossible, and his state of mind was not the best for unraveling puzzles.

He was waiting for another psychotic episode to take over his mind once again so he could think straight before making any rash decisions, but nothing interesting seemed to be happening.

'Jonah?'

Just as Jonah collapsed to his knees on the floor and started crying, he heard a small noise. His mobile emitted some random noise after hours of no response, signalling a message had arrived. As he thought about the fact that cell phone reception might appear at a few fixed points in places with low reception, he tried to remain inert so that he did not lose the only help that was willing to make an appearance. He took the device out of his pocket and realised he had received a text message. 'New message from Patrick Skies.'

He moved slowly, dragging his knees through the floor, when he heard his pants tear apart on the right leg. Despite wearing something that wasn't even his, he did not seek to worry about it right then, he just brought his cell phone to the front of his face and read his friend's message: 'Where are you?'

'Big fucking help...', he thought as he noticed he had no way of writing back. The reception was gone and the phone returned to a relentless search for a network to serve as connection. In anger, Jonah threw his cell phone down hard and shouted in despair for aid he knew, was not on the way.

He was alone.

Jonah got up again, after picking up his mud covered phone, and started walking, now in a slow pace, through the maze. As much as he was jaded from de long walk, and depressed from the path his choices had taken him, he knew that at one time or another he would find his way out. He knew that his plan was not really working for the time being, so he decided to move in a different direction as he tore a wad of leaves from the vines that covered the wall. His bruised hands pricked again in pain, whilst he decided to mark the leaves with the flowing blood. Slowly, and very carefully, he placed one of the stained leaves on a vine that reached the height of his face, removed a good part of the leaves that covered the branch so the mark would stand in evidence so he could see it from a distance and not have to turn the phone's flashlight anymore. The moonlight would have to be enough to light the way.

He followed several corridors doing the same thing. He passed the statue of the butterfly again. 'No need for that here...' he thought as he realised there was no point on leaving one of the leaves in such a unique place, but it also came to him that he was walking in circles and had no idea of how to find the exit from that maze. The corridors were very similar to each other, but now he knew which way to go if he found one of the stained leaves again. The exits wouldn't give him many options to go on, but even so, the chances of making a mistake were multiplied by the immensity of the place and the difficulty of seeing clearly.

'Jonah?'

He no longer paid any attention to the irritating voice that echoed his name. He had finally found a way he thought he could use to beat the maze and was focused on getting out of there as soon as possible. The headaches came and went, but the episodes had stopped for the time being, which was strange, since the occurrent migraines were obviously connected to the psychotic episodes.

Dismay struck as he noticed he was passing through some of the corridors for more than once, probably the paths were interconnected as some of them seemed not to have an end on either of their extremities.

'Try to do your best, priest.' he found himself in the same room that now hosted a third person.

A man wearing a cassock, covering him from head to toe, appeared out of nowhere with a long wooden chain that hung a large metal cross against his chest. He had the features of an old man, nothing but a few hair laying on his head, which seemed to have a dirty and oily appearance, and a grated stubble. In his hands, a bible and some kind of plant that he would soak in some strange liquid before brushing Jonah's face as he murmured a few words no one but himself seemed to be able to understand.

As usual, the headaches were gone. He took the opportunity to concentrate on what was happening as he knew that he would wake up rested as soon as the episode was over. The situation had become even more frightening; he began to feel as he was in one of those terrorising moments where people spent most of the time in clearly dangerous and avoidable traps.

A priest, a doctor, and a rich eccentric old man covered his vision, whilst he couldn't understand anything that was happening. Giovanni observed the recently made tattoos in his left arm, whilst Douglas continued to look at the screen that monitored his vital signs, exhaling sighs of concern.

'The drug he took is still very experimental...' said Douglas, looking directly into Jonah's eyes. 'He seems to be awake, but he should be sleeping.'

'But were you able to program the dream that I specified?' asked Mr. Dartagnan, who did not seem to understand much of what was happening, but was rather anxious to see the results he was expecting.

'You need to be patient with those kinds of things, sir...' replied Douglas with dismay in his eyes.

The priest was back at it, murmuring words that Jonah had no idea of the meaning. It sounded like a fluently spoken Latin, but nothing he could remember from his religious classes.

'Would you do me the favor of keeping quiet?' intoned Mr. Dartagnan to the vicar, who seemed to be startled by the complaint.

'Isn't this the reason you summoned me, Giovanni?' he asked as he lifted his chin and addressed the host.

'I've summoned you to accompany the procedure and protect it by giving it your blessing, I called you for the divine protection of god, and not so that you'd keep hindering the doctor's work.' he replied, seeking to regain superiority.

'I'm just doing my job...'

The priest seemed to realise that Mr. Dartagnan was cautious when addressing him. 'Does he really think this man is an envoy from god?', Jonah thought as he observed the situation. It had been a long time since the idea of believing in a super powerful being had hovered over the minds of instructed people - like Giovanni appeared to be.

Although the priest's presence scared Jonah, he started to find answers in a fluid conversation that seemed to be taking place in that small room. He was fighting to find a reason so the idea of living two realities wouldn't take over his thoughts. 'Is the maze a dream, then?', he wondered before he could force his brain to focus back on the situation that appeared in front of his eyes.

'The tattoos should serve as inspiration in the search for forgiveness, priest.' said Giovanni as he perceived the old man looking at Jonah's arm with contempt.

'I understand.' he said dryly, putting an end to that conversation.

Jonah came back to what seemed to be his reality as he took a deep breath to simmer himself down. His head still throbbed with pain, which got worse with every flare he had. 'There's still more to come.', he thought as he tried to understand the meanings that those words could have had within the context of his troubled life.

'Fallacia Alia Aliam Trudit', he went back to reading the small writing that still pulsated on his arm. The tattoo appeared to have been made abruptly and by someone without any experience or artistic skill. The pattern of the letters was ugly and the handwriting was almost incomprehensible, and he kept trying to look for obscure meanings that could lead anyone to write that on his skin.

He needed to keep his mind busy.

'Veritas Semper Una Est.' he tried to chant aloud, and in vain, before doing the same with the translation he remembered: 'Truth is always one.', that phrase was the one that got to him the most, but it didn't make sense that it had any direct meaning to his life. That maze, and even that statue, must have been there for many years, making it absolute senseless for either of them to have any correlation to any aspect of his life.

Jonah knew he had told lies throughout the years. Lies that affected not only his future, but also that of people he had loved. Lies that might even have hurt others in a physical manner.

He was back at it again.

The priest seemed to be making some kind of promise to his god as he prayed, which to Jonah seemed more like an ancestral ritual than any other thing. He was witnessing something that hasn't been a part of society for a long time. Giovanni was watching him with a worried expression on his face.

Although the host had previously complained about the priest, he seemed to have much appreciation for the ecclesiastical's presence in the room, and did not seem to want to disturb the divine moment that hovered over his eyes. Giovanni knelt beside the priest and put his hands together to get involved in the ritual that followed. The doctor, transparently skeptical by the look on his face, sighed over the two of them with a chaquetic and incredulous expression, he did not seem to appreciate having to go through that kind of thing, but Jonah imagined that he was being very well paid to be breaking so many rules and stretching his ethics to a place he couldn't come back from. 'After all, what was one more clown in a circus like that?', he was starting to believe that the situation could not get any worse.

He was incredulous at the religious devotion that was being shown by the both of them. As he looked at the expression on their faces, he knew they were very likely to believe that they were experiencing some kind of divine

74

connection with their god as they were giving their bodies and souls to that they were doing.

Jonah's imagination went to places he didn't know existed. 'Am I serving as a laboratory rat for some kind witchcraft?', that eerie little thought came and went just as quickly, as soon as he realised that the three men were speaking again, and that was really deserving of his attention.

'You can't really believe that this kind of thing works.' began Douglas by showing his utmost scepticism. 'Sorry but I can't do my fucking job like this...'

'You are being very well paid to be quiet and do as I say!' said Mr. Dartagnan, already exalted. 'Haven't we an agreement in motion, doctor?'

Giovanni did not seem to be expecting an answer from Douglas, who, as Jonah had thought, was being well compensated to go against his ethics like that. He didn't understand much about medical ethics, but that man certainly didn't learn about what he was doing at medical school.

'No more interruptions!' exclaimed the priest, who seemed anxious to continue whatever he was doing.

The three were taken by a sudden silence caused by the discomfort between Giovanni and the priest, the host's face was red with shame after he was exalted, it seemed that the old priest served him as some kind of authority in his own disturbed way. Jonah began to watch carefully and calmly around him, but nothing gave him any hope of deciphering the mystery that had become his life.

'Doctor, when will he be ready for the chair?' asked Mr. Dartagnan whilst Jonah could only imagine he was referring to the same chair he used in the Dream Room.

'I'm not sure yet, but I believe soon.'

The scenario changed again. Jonah returned to the maze, where his head was aching again as his gaze sought the little illumination brought by the moonlight. The experience he was going through seemed to have physical effects. His eyes needed more time to get used to the differences between one reality and the other.

It made no sense that this was not his physical reality. The pain in his hands was very clear and present, he felt the heat as he touched his skin and noticed the wind that ran between the corridors every once in a while. On the other hand, although he was unable to move when he was having an episode like that, the feeling of being there was completely different from a dream, he felt completely awake and lucid, but even so, the feeling was different from the one he had experienced in the Dream Room. Everything was very odd, and his mental confusion was increasing in an exponential way.

'Soon they will bring me back to that one.', he thought as he remembered that Mr. Dartagnan asked about some kind of programmed dream. It seemed strange that Giovanni wanted a programmed dream. Jonah would know exactly what was true and what wasn't, he already knew how the lucid dream induction worked.

The future was a mystery to him, but the headaches were reaching a point where it was difficult to stay upright. He hoped that it was a sign that the episodes were coming to an end, and soon he would wake up in the same place with his body and mind completely rested, as he was before, as it was now his new normal. The only thing he had the strength to do was to fiddle with the phone in his pocket again. It was with the hope that the short signal could return at any time, with the hope that he could call the police or anyone else who could help him out of that nightmare - he also thought about looking for the meaning of his new tattoos in the hope that it would enlighten him with an answer about what was happening to him - but the mobile phone was still useless.

An inverted cross and a Latin phrase that he did not know the meaning: 'Fallacia Ali Aliam Trudit.', he read it aloud again to search for any lost meaning in his subconscious. He couldn't remember when and where, but he had read that before.

There was also the butterfly with the other Latin phrase and the fish embedded in the stone with which he had crossed paths with. As though as it was all a big mess and a very unexpected surprise that those thing were happening, it all seemed to have a very clear common point for Jonah: Religion.

He was certain that Giovanni Dartagnan was part of some sort of backward cult and that the priest was there to conduct some kind of messed up ritual. What he couldn't figure out was what his role could be in such a madness. He had never been a religious man, but he also didn't have the habit of criticising someone else's beliefs, so he saw no reason why anyone would want to do him the harm of being submitted to any kind of ritual. Rich people were used to having one or another eccentricity, however, for Jonah, that already resembled torture, in addition to the fact that he had been kidnapped and drugged against his will. 'This is fucking criminal.'

He didn't have the strength to go looking around again, he just sat in the same place, looking for a minimum of comfort so that he could fall asleep as soon as the episodes happened again. The triviality that came with those ups and downs, brought by the episodes he was suffering, made him look for habits that would make the whole process less painful, and waking up without a pain in his neck or back was showing up to be quite a blessing in disguise.

Jonah, after a sharp sting of pain and a quick blink of an eye, saw the three faces that now brought in him an immense feeling of revolt and anxiety never experienced before. He remembered when he first saw Giovanni Dartagnan that night and how he had admired the elegance of that well-dressed gentleman, who had kindness in his eyes. Douglas had been an excellent professional when Jonah had needed him, but now he joined the eccentricities of a rich old man and an ill-resolved vicar in what seemed to be the end of his life.

The appearance of the room had changed, in fact, what had really changed was the intensity of the place's quirkiness. The bed had been replaced by a chair that was brought from the Dream Room, whilst the few threads from before have now been increased numerously, not only in quantity, but in diversity as well. One of the wires was a small tube that was connected directly to one of his veins through a small needle, whilst his hands were shackled by some kind of leather handles, which made no difference because he still could not move nor speak. Douglas held a syringe close to the small tube, which had been meticulously dosed with some kind of drug.

Jonah had no doubt that the syringe was meant for him.

'The dream is ready.' said Douglas pointing at the monitor, waiting orders from Giovanni.

'Hold it for a little while, I'm still waiting for another guest.' he said.

The thought of a bigger audience tormented him for a second.

If Jonah was going to be induced into a lucid dream, as he had been before, what would change if someone else was present? Was anyone else taking part in that circus? Wasn't three already a good number of people to have in the audience? These, among many others, were the questions that took over Jonah's thoughts.

The priest was still trying to evoque his god in the same ridiculous little ritual he had been for a while, kneeled in front of the chair. He was saying prayers and murmuring chants that Jonah didn't even know existed. The man was clearly catholic, but Jonah was unable to see any characteristic in him that would indicate which of the innumerous strands of the creed he followed. The little he understood, did not highlight any religious symbolism or particularity that defined which sect the priest worked for, but what really interested him, at the particular moment, was to finally grasp his mind on what type of witchcraft he would serve as a guinea pig for in the next few seconds.

'You do understand that what we are doing here is only possible thanks to scientific advances, right priest?' asked Douglas as Giovanni was distracted at the door, waiting for the mysterious visitor.

'Have respect for our good god, doctor. It is thanks to him and Jesus Christ that you have a life.' replied the priest. 'We are already saving this heretic, I don't imagine you want to be next...'

Douglas seemed to have been taken by surprise by the indecent threat, whilst Jonah only managed to panic inside his own brain without making a sound. 'Save?', he thought whilst trying to remember why he was a heretic, he must have had done something that really caught the attention of those people. 'Why does Giovanni want to punish me?', he asked himself as the mysterious person entered the room.

The same arrogant old lady, who had sat next to him during dinner, came in wearing the same dress and looking highly intoxicated. She had an expression of contempt on her face as she saw Jonah lying in that chair, Giovanni even had to hold her by the arm so that she wouldn't jump at him.

'Filthy pig!' she shouted as she spat, pointing at Jonah whilst Mr. Dartagnan kept her in place.

'Calm down now, Monalisa.' said Giovanni as he pushed her into a chair in the corner of the room. 'This is not the time for that. Redemption will not fail, as god is divine and won't abandon us in this time of penance.'

'Amen.' she answered.

The madness of that conversation really scared Jonah.

As Douglas headed towards the small intravenous tube that was connected to Jonah, the priest, Giovanni Dartagnan and the newly arrived Monalisa knelt in front of the chair to join in each other in prayer.

At the exact same moment that Douglas injected the drug into the tube to reach Jonah's bloodstream, he remembered the reason for all that anger against him. He had no idea of how Giovanni could know that about his past, but it was, for him, the only possible explanation for being there.

And it was bad, really bad.

CHAPTER 7:

Jonah woke up with his energies renewed and reached for his cell phone to follow up his strategy of keeping a routine and try and find out how long he had been unconscious, which didn't any make sense, since only a few minutes had passed, and the dream he had was quite long. 'The same thing happened in the Dream Room.', he recalled the effect that induction to lucid dream had on the perception of time.

He was lying with his hands clasped over his chest in a place completely different from where he had had the last episode. He got up suddenly, trying to understand where he had ended up, realising that, finally, someone had taken him out of that maze.

Jonah was at the beginning of a lawn that stretched all the way back to the exit of the maze. He could see a sign that gave space to a large and decorated garden that surrounded the large water fountain, which was no longer pouring water, and had its lights turned off, leaving the moonlight to be the only source of illumination remaining. 'I need to save my cell phone battery so I can call for help as soon as I can get reception.', Jonah intoned aloud. He knew that finding Giovanni Dartagnan again was no longer a possibility, his dream had shown him the problem, and made him understand he was on a path with no return, since all of that religious nuisance would not benefit him in any way possible.

The memory of the dream was vivid in his mind, and he could, now, understand the difference between Lucid and Induced dreaming. That particular induced dream had made him relive one of the most distressing moments of his life.

"Suddenly, Jonah found himself looking at a ten years younger version of himself. Even before he felt the drug entering his system so he could be induced into that dream, he knew exactly what was coming. He was nothing but a young man living one of the happiest moments he could remember. A few months ago he had met the love of his life, and the memory of being in love for the first time made him feel something he had never felt before.

His first love referred to a feeling of anguish and anxiety, at the same time that it released an enormous amount of endorphin and caused him to get out of bed every day with a purpose.

He saw his own bed, still at his grandparents' house in the town he grew up. At his side slept the person he once had thought to be the only one that mattered, to a point where he couldn't breathe as he yearned for her presence. Joana Clemente was the name of his first love, the most beautiful woman he had the chance to lay his eyes on, and who, for some reason that didn't make sense to him, had chosen him to be her boyfriend. He tried not to look for reasons to doubt any feelings that the girl might have as he knew that it didn't make any sense, which was reminded to him on a daily basis by his friends.

Joana had dark hair and green eyes, she was tall enough to fit her head into his chest and short enough so they could spoon perfectly as they slept even if the sweat would break in the middle of the night. It was curious how she had, between her breasts, this little brown spot for a birthmark, laid perfectly where Jonah could match them as they would touch their bear chests. She would often joke around about it: 'It seems that we were chosen by god, separated in paradise to meet again on this plane.', something he had no clue of what it meant.

She came from a religious family and often made spiritual connotations to compliment their relationship. Jonah, despite not having much connection with any kind of religion, found amusement on how Joana's heart could be so pure and honest. In the four years they had been together, he had never thought of anyone else and strongly believed that she felt the same way. The two were incredibly in love, and nothing in the world seemed to have the strength to break that bond.

Throughout the time they spent their days together, they slept, ate, studied, worked, and did anything else they could find a way to do together. As Jonah was raised by his grandparents, he had a little more freedom than people his age would, but Joana's parents always showed concern for their daughter's future. Their love was healthy, but it often hindered her daily duties, which would result in arguments within her traditional family.

Several scenarios occupied his mind throughout the time he was dreaming. All of them showing incredibly happy memories of them together, what made Jonah cry with the nostalgia that washed over him. He hadn't seen Joana since their breakup, but he would often find himself thinking about her. Things would always find a way to trick his mind into making comparisons between an ordinary situation to one memory or another, and, for the most part, it was an incredible thing.

He always thought that one day their paths would cross again, the feeling they had for each other was very strong, something he could never have felt for anyone else. He had several relationships after Joana, but nothing that could be remotely close to what he had once felt for her. All of those memories were there to build the greatest possible nostalgia in his heart, he knew that that couldn't possible be a dream as much as it was a nightmare. He tried to stay strong, without letting his own sentiment of disparage for himself take over his sanity. He was feeling rather good about what he was experiencing , but his brain couldn't seek the self-control necessary to contain the emotion that was about to come.

What he was waiting for had finally come to be. His eyes burst into tears, as his memories came to cross the agonising atrocity he had, for so long, put aside within his own subconscious.

He saw his selfish younger self alone in the kitchen, whilst Joana waited for his return so they could continue the film they were watching in bed. With each step that the image of his own self took, Jonah felt a greater anguish. He wanted to put an end to it, it was one of those moments that, if he could, he would go back in time and change it, but that was a dream, there was nothing Jonah could do to remedy it, and there was nothing he could do to stop his mind from reliving it.

He watched as his younger self crushed a distinguish medicine into a glass of water Joana had asked him for, he knew exactly what was going to happen. He tried to close his eyes so he would not see what was coming, but it turned out that enforced dreaming did not work that way, that scene was recorded in his subconscious, and there was nothing he could do. The scenery changed again, with his girlfriend waking up beside him, weeping as she tried to stop the blood flowing down between her legs. He couldn't do anything back then, and he wouldn't be able to anything inside a dream. His fate was sealed and his life was ruined."

That was the last memory he had from his life with Joana. After that, she was reportedly taken to a hospital where she received treatment and was released after being fully recovered. Joana had never answered any of his phone calls and he was never able to contact her again. Jonah sought to go after mutual friends, but when he learned that she could never get pregnant again, due to mismanagement of the abortion drug he had forced her to take, he completely lost hope to reconnect with her in any way. The girl's solution was to run off to another city, so their paths would never have the chance to cross again.

Although Joana did not press charges against Jonah's crime, he knew that her family thought otherwise. Abortion was still a very sensitive issue for older, more conservative people, but the only thing he thought about before drugging his beloved then girlfriend was his future as a young father. Any alternative that was not an abortion was unfeasible to him. Although they did had an exhaustive talk, Joana had never given him any chance to seek out an illegal doctor to perform the abortion, she had decided to have the baby and still argued that they would be very happy together as a family.

Jonah had never accepted that, and that was the price he had to pay. Live the rest of his life knowing he lost the love of his life.

He had no option but to let himself cry. Tears fell slowly from his eyes as he watched that great white water fountain. Regardless of whatever Mr. Dartagnan intended to put him through, Jonah knew that the purpose of that induced dream was to scare him, which had worked perfectly. The darkness of the place already tormented him, but his anxiety was entangled with the guilt of the mistake that had been reminded to him, thus bringing on a crisis of uncontrollable panic. His vision closed as the infamous headache reappeared. He was very scared and could not find any hope that would get him out of there unscathed. Now, more than ever, everything indicated that the near future had late consequences to bestow upon him. His past sins had come to charge him for what he had done.

He got up from the floor and started slowly walking whilst carefully dwelling on his own thoughts, as he now leaned against the fountain and tried to observe his surroundings to understand where he was.

Something caught his eye as he forced his weary sight to contemplate the whole structure of that old fashioned monument. A metal plate was screwed to the base of the fountain. 'The divine word will be rewritten. We will start over with the last letter.' said the sign, which made him thoughtful, since all those hints throughout the maze seemed to be aimed at him, a fact that now made sense, since all of what was happening had certainly been planned.

'What fucking letter now?', he jadedly thought as he sought logic for an answer to the enigma he now faced, but no answer that made sense came to mind.

'Jonah?' the mysterious voice reverberated again, now with a mysteriously tone of surprise.

His body gave way again as he sat near the fountain, he was already waiting for another episode to come, as his headache was getting more and more acute, which aggravated the fear caused by his insisting anxiety. Jonah closed his eyes for a short time as he tried to gather enough strength to continue and not give up, leaving behind that hell that had become his life.

'I'm not in the mood for fucking games!' he shouted with the certainty that no one was listening.

'Jonah?' the voice sounded again.

He could no longer bear the mystery of that voice, every time his name was called out loud, a new stab of pain returned to torment his head.

'What is formed by letters?' the mysterious voice started a conversation.

'Who's there?' asked Jonah as he jumped back on his feet, startled and hopeful at the same time. He already started to think that he would promptly be on his way home and that nightmare would soon be over.

'What is formed by letters, Jonah?' the voice repeated.

'Words?' he said as he became increasingly anxious seeking to find a face somewhere so he could match the voice to a person.

'Try again. Maybe in a more specific aspect.'

'Would you please just end this torture and kill me!', he thought as he tried to understand the game the mysterious voice was imposing on him.

'The answer is much simpler than you think.'

'What is formed by letters?', Jonah continued to ask himself, trying to find the person who insisted in hiding as if that was a childish game.

'What is formed by letters, Jonah?' the voice said one more time.

'The alphabet?' he replied as he looked at the sky, seeking some kind of divine approval that he knew did not exist.

'Very well, and what was the last letter to be added to the modern Latin alphabet?'

'Z?' he replied incredulously and unable to believe that he was lost and still had to partake in mind games.

'The last letter added to the alphabet was not Z', the voice continued an unwanted explanation. 'But J.'

'Please, stop messing around! Where are you?' he pleaded whilst turning his neck which was already tired from constantly seeking a sight.

'Here, inside this little dome.' the voice sounded lower. 'In the Latin alphabet, the letter I was used with a double phoneme, and the letter J was introduced to end the confusion caused to the less wealthy who started to learn how to read.'

Jonah started walking around the fountain to see if he could finally put a face to the voice that hailed his name for the past hour. The curiosity about the alphabet mentioned by the mysterious voice went unnoticed by the desire to finally be able to draw conclusions about what was happening to him.

He sought to go through the small path that ran from one end to another, it was decorated by rustic stones that gave the ornament an old look. Behind the maze he could finally see the end of that huge property, or at least it was what it appeared to be. A small wooden fence gave way to another field, that was immeasurable by the lack of illumination.

The voice had stopped whilst Jonah searched tirelessly for its owner. As he wasn't able to see anyone, he reckoned the voice should be coming from inside the maze or from another hidden place. 'Don't you fucking think I'm going back there.", he thought before asking.

'I can't see very well, just tell me where you are!'

'Easy now, boy, I'm right here.' he heard the reply that came just after a small wooden knock.

He could hardly distinguish from the image that was beginning to take form before his eyes. The pitch black ambience, mixed with the moonlight, sparked a small glow coming from two small spheres that he could only assume were the eyes of the man who spoke to him, but the face of such person was still a mystery. The voice came straight from inside the fountain, as did the gaze coming from behind a grid that would give the man barely enough room to breathe. The floor must have been made of wood, hence the noise he had just heard.

'What are you doing in there? And who are you?' asked Jonah as he tried not to curse at the only person that seemed to be willing to talk to him as he got as close as possible to the center of the fountain without having to get wet.

'What does it look like? I'm fucking stuck in here.' the voice replied using the curse Jonah spared with an obvious tone as it chose not to answer the second question.

'And who put you in there?' he insisted on starting a small conversation whilst he felt another slight twinge in his head. The pain was beginning to increase.

'The same person who brought you here.' he replied, hoping Jonah would understand the obvious.

'Mr. Dartagnan?'

'Is that what the bastard demands to be called?' the man asked after an ironic laugh.

'I don't know if that's how he demands it, but that's how he was introduced to me.' replied Jonah. 'My night has been a fucking nightmare, would you mind telling me how I can get out of here?'

'Oh really? Won't you even ask if I need some fucking help?' the man replied. His voice had a slight hoarse that indicated a certain age.

'As soon as I can leave this place I will get help and come back for you, I can call the police.' he said firmly and hopefully.

'The police can't help you, boy.' the voice replied. 'But I believe we can help each other.'

'Would you care to elaborate?' asked Jonah as he let out a cry of pain and sat down by the fountain.

'The pain is not over yet? How long have you been having the episodes?'

'How do you know about that? When is it suppose to end?' the mystery surrounding the newest stranger in Jonah's life made him even more uneasy.

Apparently that man had some of the answers that Jonah was looking for, however he could not trust anyone in that situation, even if he was the only one who could help him.

'I'm the man who knows everything.' he replied. 'But first let's find a way for you to get me out of here, shall we?'

'What do you want me to do?' asked Jonah intrigued, at least he wanted to know what he had to say.

'I need you to go back into that maze...' he started to speak at the same time that Jonah already had the answer ready to give him. 'Inside, there's a small statue of a butterfly that has its wings cut off at the exact half, if you join the wings together, the underpass will open and I will be able to get out of here.'

He was, to say the least, intrigued by the engineering of the prison in which that unknown man was cloistered, but as he took a better glance, he could see that the centre of the fountain was very similar to a cocoon, which gave it a lot of sense to its relation to the butterfly.

'And where can I find this statue?' he asked sincerely as had no idea of how to get back there.

'I'll give you the coordinates. I was the one who built this maze, I know every corner and every little detail of it.'

'But who are you, sir? I'm sorry, but I'm not going back into that forsaken maze without even knowing who you are...' replied Jonah expecting an honest answer as his headache decided to pay him another visit.

Before he could hear the strange man's response, he found himself, again, trapped to that horrible chair with those four people who were now watching him with an expression of concern.

Monalisa, who had joined them before Jonah was induced to sleep, was now less agitated and a little more sober, yet Jonah still saw a look of contempt on her face and a fulminating anger that could only be directed at him .

The transition from one reality to another was getting smoother every time. Jonah seemed to have more control over what was happening, but he still was unable to express himself or say anything to anyone. As much as he wanted to scream, get up, and run, his body did not respond to the stimuli in his brain. Despite the static and concern about what would happen to him, his thoughts were focused on the man who had just appeared in the maze, he was anxious for that psychotic episode to be over so he could return to his other reality.

'I can't be sure that everything went well, but the dream induction is over.' he heard Douglas speak.

'We need to end this once and for all.' said the priest.

'What we need to do is to let this wear off naturally. A forced withdrawal can have irreversible consequences.' interfered Douglas once again.

'What would be very well deserved.' Monalisa still showed an inexplicable anger against Jonah.

'All in good time, my dear.' said Giovanni whilst looking directly into Jonah's eyes.

Mr. Dartagnan had an anxious expression on his face, his arms and legs were restless and his mind seemed to be stunned by the events of that night. Giovanni lit a cigarette whilst holding a glass of whiskey in his other hand, Jonah could notice a repressive look from Douglas who was bothered by the smoke in that enclosed room, however, it seemed that he didn't want to say anything as he had already been bothered enough by the man who was paying him to be there.

Jonah saw the fountain again, at the end of the maze, whilst the same eyes that shone in the moonlight continued to look at him with certain relentlessness. The strength of the drug they had given him seemed to be diminishing as the episodes seemed to be drawing to an end, as the distinguished cloistered man had mentioned before.

'What does that saying in the butterfly statue mean?' he asked as he regained his consciousness.

'You mean to tell me you've been to the place I'm talking about...'

'I stumbled upon it whilst I was trying to get out of the maze, but I have no idea how to get back there.' he replied with some concern as he did not want to give out more information than he needed to.

'Veritas Semper Una Est.' sais the old man aloud.

'Truth is always one.' translated Jonah demonstrating knowledge.

'You see, my dear, inside this place everything is a game...' he started to answer. 'I don't know what you did to get into my brother's nerves, but if you're here, it's because Giovanni has some kind of debt to set with you.'

'Your fucking brother?' Jonah was taken by surprise as he got up again from the edge of the fountain to face the old man head on.

'Yes, my brother.' he replied.

'Are you the other Dartagnan brother?'

'James Dartagnan, pleased to meet you.'

Jonah was increasingly confused by everything that was happening. 'Giovanni arrested his own brother inside a fountain? This has to be another one of his tricks.', he thought as he couldn't make any sense of the situation. For a few seconds the small shiny spheres, that gave form to James's eyes, fixed on his and, despite the low light, expressed sadness and weariness of someone who wasn't there by choice.

'And how come you're locked in a place like this?' he asked breaking the continuity of his gaze as he didn't want to empathise with anyone at that moment. It wouldn't be safe.

'I know you may have a lot of questions and I understand perfectly that you see no reason to trust me.' he started as he realised he had lost Jonah's attention. 'But I can't explain anything else before you help me out of here, it's my only advantage at the moment. I hope you understand.'

It was, indeed, an understandable thing. Jonah was stuck in a situation as inopportune as his and would have the same attitude if he were in his place. 'Nothing but a game...', he thought as he got used to the idea that he would have to trust James if he wanted to have any chance of getting out of that place alive.

He needed to accept the conditions in order to improve the situation.

'What do you want me to do?' he decided to give in as another acute headache came with no warning and his eyes went back to face Giovanni.

Jonah felt the words coming out of his mouth as he noticed the astonished expression on the faces of the four people who were still watching him like he was nothing but a zoo attraction. He tried to push words out of his mouth, but the static returned to take control of his impulses.

'What's happening' asked Monalisa when she heard Jonah's voice for the first time.

'The medicine must be wearing off...' said Douglas, keeping calm.

'Then give him another dose!' she exclaimed, trying to find anything around her that could be injected or ingested.

'No!' said Douglas as he tried to impose authority for the first time. 'We can't compromise this young man's life.' the doctor shone a thread of lucidity.

'You are no in power to hinder god's work!' spoke the priest for the first time since Jonah returned from the dream.

'Silence, everyone!' Giovanni had a defiant tone in his voice, and Jonah could see that everyone there felt the same fear when the old man spoke with authority. 'Jonah, can you hear me?'

The question took him by surprise, it was the first time that Mr. Dartagnan addressed him in that environment. Jonah tried to answer, 'You old bastard, what are you doing to me?', but the words echoed inside his head as they never left his mouth.

'Doctor, what can we do?' asked Mr. Dartagnan, realising that Jonah would not be able to answer his question.

He was sweating cold and in constant fear of what might happen, but reality took a turn once again and he found himself lying on that moist grass that surrounded the water fountain where James was still trapped.

'We need to help each other!' said Jonah as he got up quickly.

'What's happening? What are they doing to you?' asked the other Dartagnan.

Jonah rolled up his shirt sleeve on his left arm and showed the recent marks that had been perpetuated on his skin without his consent. James struggled to see something as the distance between them and the lack of light hindered him from seeing clearly.

'A cross and a saying: Fallacia Alia Aliam Trudit.' he explained the drawings on his arm.

'My brother and his religious fundamentalism. Why do you think I'm locked in here?'

'What is he going to do to me? What does this phrase mean?' Jonah seemed increasingly uneasy.

'One thing at a time...' he insisted. 'I really need you to get me out of here so we can help each other.'

'What do you want me to do?' Jonah finally gave in. He had no choice but to submit to James's game.

Before he could hear an answer, Jonah returned to the mysterious smoky room. The priest had returned to the edge of the chair where, resting on his knees, he was praying aloud again as he was clearly disturbing the skeptical Douglas.

'Time is not coming to a halt, doc, I need you to find a solution, we cannot let him return to his senses, there's still much to be done.' said Mr. Dartagnan whilst trying to keep calm.

Douglas nodded as he turned his eyes to the screen that monitored Jonah's vital signs. He had no idea what would happen next as the doctor's look of concern indicated things were not going so well.

That psychotic episode had been the shortest of them all. He finally slept for a few minutes and woke up again on the lawn in front of the fountain where James remained trapped.

'Fast.' he heard the old man's voice as he stood up and became aware of what was happening. 'I need you to go to the butterfly statue before you have another episode.'

'How do you know about these episodes that I'm having? What does your brother's religion have to do with me? What do these tattoos mean? How does the letter J fit into this story?' Jonah had some many questions that he lacked the air to continue. The headache was gone and he was completely rested again.

'All of your questions will be answered, my boy. But first I need you to help me get out of here, I can't do anything whilst I'm trapped in here. Wouldn't you agree?' James sought to show authority in his speech.

'How do I get to the statue?' asked Jonah, showing himself ready to partake in the old man's game.

James described exactly the path that Jonah would have to take to get to the statue, whilst he took his cell phone out of his pocket to type down all the instructions.

'However, the way back should be different...'

'Different?', he thought as he tried to understand how the maze would be able to change its shape.

'Just put the wings together and wait for me to come to you.' said James as he seemed to be losing his patience.

He had promised to never go back into that place, but the situation and the pace of the game had given him no other option. James Dartagnan was his only hope, he had no choice but to trust him.

CHAPTER 8:

'I don't think it was the right thing to do, I'd say he'll get worse over time. ' Jonah could hear Douglas's voice.

Another psychotic episode came to to his mind as he arrived at the butterfly statue. As soon as he had managed to put the butterfly's wings together, he felt an even greater headache than the previous ones, waking up in that small room where those four people continued to observe him and discuss his future.

In addition to feeling alive and lucid, he now felt a great sense of euphoria, an anxiety that seemed to increase by the second, and a desire to get up from that chair to which he was still stuck at. He was still unable to speak or make any sound that could resemble a call for help, all his efforts were in vain and he was terrified about not making any progress.

'I warned you that it could be dangerous to drug him again.' said Douglas, whilst waiting for new instructions from Mr. Dartagnan.

Those words hindered Jonah's ability to think. Fear had taken over his wits and he was not able understand what was happening, but one thing he knew: the situation was only getting worse. He fixated his hope in James, since whatever his plan or idea of solving that situation was, it would be the only thing that gave him the strength to keep fighting and not give up.

'You injected a very high amount of the drug!' Giovanni opened his mouth after staying idle for quite some time.

'Well, I did try to explain it to you! His body is already getting used to the drug, you will need to increase the dosage every time you want it to work properly. It's dangerous!' exclaimed Douglas.

Giovanni ignored the doctor's theoretical lesson. He didn't seem too keen to understand how things worked, he just wanted results.

Monalisa and the priest were leaning against the wall whilst arguing about something that Jonah couldn't really hear. They did not seem to care as much about his health as Douglas and Giovanni, as it seemed that they were there just to seek some kind of punishment that should be inflicted on him for the so called mistake he had made a long time ago. At least that was already clear in Jonah's mind, he already knew why he was chosen to be there. Although the reason was clear, the final goal for his suffering still didn't make sense to him. 'Why won't they just alert the authorities?', he thought of it as an alternative to the torture he had been suffering throughout the night.

Anything would be better than that.

To his own mind, he was experiencing some kind of medieval inquisition, something he thought no longer existed. 'How can such wealthy people like these be so ignorant to a point of being vindictive?', his desire was to cry, give everything up, and just let things happen as they were about. He knew that if he could express himself to those people, he would give up, confess to his crimes and accept the guilt. 'You can punish me, as long as you let me go', he thought before returning to what was most likely his true reality.

James was already there, which made him think that the last psychotic attack had been a long one. The old man was sitting next to him and had a worried expression on his face, he seemed to be intently waiting for Jonah to come back from his mental breakdown.

'Are you alright?' he was finally able to give a face to the voice that had been speaking to him and calling his name for all that time.

James had a rough appearance. The wrinkles on his face gave him a tired expression, despite seemingly almost the same age as his brother, his long beard and long gray hair, ravaged by baldness, made him look much older and closer to the end of his life. Jonah noticed that the old man had crutches propped up on his arms, as one of his legs had been cut off at knee height. 'He must be sick.', he thought as he recalled his great-aunt who had lost one of her legs due to obesity and diabetes, but James's thinness indicated that the reality of his stumped leg could be different.

'I lost it not too long ago, I'm still trying to get used to it.' said James, seeing that Jonah had his eyes fixed on the stomp.

'I'm sorry' said Jonah, realising his insensitivity and that he should try to be a tad more subtle.

'No problem at all, curiosity is one of the attributes I most admire in human beings.' he replied, hoping Jonah would continue the conversation.

However, his headache was coming back again to torment his mind, so he decided to occupy the small frame of time he had before having another crisis with the myriad of questions he had in his mind, to which the old man had promised him answers as soon as he got out of that confinement.

'What do I have to do with your brother's religion?' Jonah decided to go straight to the point.

'Did you do anything that goes against the values of christianity?' James's tone was rhetorical.

Jonah decided not to answer. He still wasn't sure if I could trust that man. 'After all, it's his brother who's doing this to me...', he thought before acquiescing by nodding his head.

'Don't feel bad, I don't condemn you. But my brother is one of those fanatics who see no compassion outside of his belief.' said the old man who tried to stand up whilst leaning on his crutches. 'Are you a religious person, my boy?'

'Not really. I've got nothing against any kind of belief, but I haven't practiced any religion for a long time.' he replied as he got up and went back to helping the old one-legged man who didn't seem to know what he was doing.

'I haven't gotten used to it yet...' he repeated himself, being humble enough to accept the help as he thanked Jonah for his kindness. James seemed to be a very calm person, which was irritatingly contradicting the anxiety of being in that situation.

'How did you lose your leg?' asked Jonah whilst the old man seemed to be giving him an opening to be nosy.

'My brother...' he replied as the expression on his face turned from being kind to a deep sadness. 'He never managed to accept that my religious disbelief was a part of me.'

'How do you mean? What did he do to your leg?' Jonah began to feed the panic into his mind, whilst thinking about what Giovanni would do to him if he was able to cut off his own brother's leg.

James did not answer. Tears welled up in his eyes, which he stifled with a clearing of his throat as he kept his balance on those crutches.

'Shall we we go now?' he asked as he swallowed up his tears.

'Fucking where?'

As the words seemed to come out of old Dartagnan's mouth to build up an answer, Jonah was not able to hear anything he was about to say. Before he knew it, he was back in that small red room. The other Dartagnan stared at him, deep into his eyes, as Douglas punched the television monitor that was connected to him.

'What's happening?' asked the priest, after spending an unusual long time without opening his mouth as he came and went from endless prayers with the same enthusiasm.

'His brain is not responding to the drug's stimuli.' said Douglas.

'Still?' asked the priest at the same time Jonah became more and more frightened. 'What the fuck happened to my brain now?', he thought as he waited for an answer to his unasked question.

'The device is not responding...' said Douglas, looking irritated by the vicar's technological ignorance.

A strange sense of relief began to shake off Jonah's worries, preventing panic from taking over his thoughts once again. For a brief moment he thought his brain was in trouble, which would be nothing strange given the situation he found himself into, but it seemed that trouble was coming from the machine itself.

'Listen here... I am getting tired of waiting for this utopian judgment that you long for! Let's get this over with using the old ways. This kind of penance is proving ineffective, and this boy deserves death!' said the priest whilst shooting an angry expression at Giovanni.

'That's not what we've agreed upon, Father. I thought I was clear that this young man is very important to me and to the entity!' said Giovanni, downplaying the man's tone. It was definitely he who had the final word in that room.

'Entity?' Jonah asked himself as he was relieved that his death was not exactly Mr. Dartagnan's plan.

'Jonah?' he heard James speak calmly whilst looking him up and down.

'I'm back.' he spoke with the certainty of who was already getting used to the coming and going of those psychotic flare-ups.

Jonah stood up promptly, allocating all his remaining energy and cognitive ability to leave that place. His doubts were many, but staying idle would be a waste of time.

The two started walking at a slow pace as James didn't have any practice to handle those crutches. His expression was of tiredness and sadness, something that Jonah could sympathise as he seemed to be suffering from that situation even more than he was.

'I have to say, I feel very relieved, I didn't think I was going to leave that fountain so soon.' he said, trying to balance himself on the crutches.

'Why won't you tell me how you lost your leg? What did Giovanni do to you?' he asked, looking for one of the many answers he wanted.

James did not seem to be very comfortable with the subject. He frowned and rubbed his eyes with an expression of sadness. Silence took over for a brief moment, but the old one-legged man decided that there was no time more appropriate to vent about it.

'As I told you before, I have developed a strong disbelief for religion throughout my life. After many years searching for answers from a superior being, I decided to face reality as it really is. For me, life should always, and will always, be taken as a mere chance. I have never been arrogant enough to say that I know what happens next or what happened before, nor have I ever worshiped anything that seek answers that are impossible to be known. This unbelieving bias has always irritated Giovanni, but a few months ago I became more radical, which ended up causing a very strong quarrel between us.'

'Has your family always been religious?' asked Jonah as he realised that the two had stopped walking, and James was now sat as he sighed at his tiredness.

'Can we stop for a while? I'm feeling a lot of pain in my arms from leaning on these crutches, and, moreover, I have been eating poorly for months now.'

'Do you mean to tell me that it was your own brother who cut off your leg?' Jonah ignored the question and sat down on the damp grass next to James.

'No. Let me tell you the whole story, I'll get to that part eventually.'

Jonah crossed his legs and began to direct all his attention to James, at the same time that his headaches began to return gradually, hindering his wisdom.

'A few months ago, I wrote a column in a local newspaper, nothing grounded or profound, just my opinion about the social backwardness caused by the most recent wave of religious dissemination in current times. You see, recently I have been dedicating a good part of my time to attack religious entities that take advantage of the naivety of simple people who have no specific knowledge on the subject.'

'I have never been arrogant...', thought Jonah as he repeated the old man when he realised that he showed disparage to any kind of religious belief that had the capacity to attract followers.

'But doesn't that go against your religious freedom thinking?'

'As I was telling you, a few months ago I changed my posture. Answering your question from before, my family has always been very religious, and my brother ended up becoming a feverous catholic.'

'I confess that I'm really scared of what might happen to me. Giovanni has already had the courage to do that to your leg, imagine what he has in store for me.' said Jonah without drifting away form James's attention.

'Well, my brother didn't cut off my leg deliberately.' he began to explain. 'In fact, if you stop to think, what he did was even worse...'

A sharp pain returned to Jonah's brain as he felt slightly bewildered and saw Douglas's frightened face again in the smokey room.

'I can't guarantee he will survive...' said Douglas looking directly at Mr. Dartagnan.

'It is not important that he survives...' interrupted the priest.

'Yes it is!' exclaimed Monalisa as the conversation heated up. 'We preach penance, not murder!'

'I need him alive, doctor, even if you have to stop giving him the drug.' he heard Giovanni say before he came back to James.

His energies were again completely renewed, he knew, by intuition, that the psychotic episodes would stop at least for a while. He stood up abruptly and held out his hand so that James could easily lean on his crutches. The old man gave a grunt of pain and, after what seemed like a great effort, managed to get up so that the two could follow their path.

'You were saying?' continued Jonah as if nothing had happened.

'Is the drug over yet?' asked James, showing concern for Jonah's situation.

'I can't say for sure. Sometimes I wake up as if I have rested for hours, without any headache, but then some other times I wake up as if I have a huge hangover.' he replied as they walked.

'Yes, I've been there... Waking up rested means that the drug's effect has passed. The question is whether you will receive another dose or not.'

Jonah decided to be quiet and not mention to James what he had just heard back in the room where he had been having his outbreaks.

'What do you know about this drug?' asked Jonah.

'One thing at a time. I was telling you about how I lost my leg.' he said expressing a level of patience that boosted Jonah's anxiety, whilst holding onto his shoulder so that he would not fall due to the imbalance of the uneven floor. 'I suffer from diabetes, due to old age.'

'So you lost your leg because of the disease.' interrupted Jonah, confirming his previous thesis and feeling a little relieved that his missing limb was not part of the routine of punishments applied by Giovanni Dartagnan.

'I lost my leg because I was deprived of taking my medication. The disease, in my case, is not that serious, but it must be treated anyway. Giovanni put me in that prison and never let me take any of my pills. As soon as my leg started to gangrene, he brought a doctor to a small hut we have close by so he could have it amputated.' he said with a deep sadness behind his eyes that accumulated tears.

That new information really scared Jonah. His anxiety gradually seemed to be making another appearance as it always returned with full force when he discovered anything that could thwart his way out of that place. He had never been a fearful man, he always tried to face life's challenges with courage, but that night was showing a side of him until then unknown.

'But this is fucking torture!' he said, empathising with the old man who limped beside him.

'Or penance, as my brother and his sect would prefer to call it.' he said whilst carrying an expression of comfort to his face.

Each new piece of information in that conversation would bring Jonah even more doubt. The more things seemed to clear up, the more they got confused. He sought to make connections between the reality in which he was able to move and the one in which he had his cognitive ability uninterrupted, but the events did not seem to have a simple logic.

'Why did you decide to buy this fight with your own family? And what sect are you referring to?' asked Jonah as he resumed the previous subject.

'Because I found out what my brother started to do after the death of our parents.' said James as he stopped abruptly in front of a high wall covered by the vines that gave form to the maze. 'We need to focus on getting out of here...'

'You promised me answers!' said Jonah as he tried to understand why they were standing idle whilst they were supposed to be running towards that open field. He was getting more and more irritated by the unanswered questions as he had fulfilled his part of the agreement and was entitled to his reward.

'As soon as we get out of here...'

Jonah didn't have time to reinforce the question.

James dropped one of the crutches to support himself with his own weight on the wall, which gave way to

100

an icy wind that started to cross the small, newly opened edges. The Dartagnan brothers estate seemed to hold several secrets, leaving Jonah even more perplexed as he felt awe and fear at the same time.

James let his body give way to gravity and felt to the ground, where he began to crawl through one of the small cracks that were now part of the maze's wall. He brought his crutches with him and made a sign indicating that Jonah should follow him. 'There is no turning back now.', he thought as he got down on his knees to follow the path indicated by James.

After crawling through the floor for a few minutes, Jonah was faced with the same scenario he had seen less than an hour ago. The two of them were back at the fountain that now spurted water and illuminated the space with twinkling alternating shades of white lights.

'And why are we back here?' he asked, putting the rest of his questions aside.

'Let's go to the hut I told you about before, I imagine we'll be safe there, for the time being.' replied James as he got back on his foot as his weight was supported by his crutches.

He observed his surroundings, looking for any clue that might indicate a house nearby, but he couldn't see anything that resembled the so called hut James had mentioned, as the lights focused on the fountain, obfuscating anything else that could be seen. Jonah just followed the old man's footsteps as he continued to look for any kind of clue that would indicate an exit from that place. His concern was not to find any other home but his own. He reached into his pocket for his cell phone in the hope of having enough reception to alert the authorities about that place.

'No use for that right now, my boy. You should save your battery for when you eventually leave this place. You're going to need it.' said James.

'I received a text message before, inside the maze.' he explained his longing to take the device out of his pocket so often.

'You only receive what Giovanni wants you to receive.' the old man expressed sadness once again.

'I can't see anything that slightly resembles a house, where are we going?' Jonah ignored the warning.

'Not long now, only a few meters from here...'

They followed the stone path that connected one side of the fountain to the other, arriving at the same dead-end wall that Jonah had observed earlier. He was standing in front of the wall, waiting for James to do some other trick that would make way for another type of secret passage, but the old man did nothing but lean on his crutches and follow the path through the grass, going towards the direction which would lead behind the fountain, in the same spot where Jonah had seen the wooden fence. He remained confused, no longer seeking to find any structure that resembled that of a house, but anything that might refer to something unusual, something he could not expect to happen.

'What are you looking for?' asked James with an obnoxious little smile on his face, looking amused by the naivety in Jonah's eyes.

'For you to show me the secret fucking passage!' he replied enthusiastically, whilst alternating his gaze between the wooden fence and the back of the fountain.

'But what a passage, my boy, the hut is there.' said James whilst pointing to a small structure a few meters from the them.

A small wooden house, with a simple and archaical structure, presented itself before Jonah's eyes, he was so concerned with finding something that was hidden that he failed to realise what was right in front of him. He jumped over the fence and held out his arms so that the old one-legged man could hold himself. They walked a few more meters until James could light a small weak lamp before opening the door. The feeble illumination projected the simplicity of the place, which did not match the structure on the other side of the fence. The hut had only one door and one small window, taking up a little more space than the two men entering it could hold. Jonah took the initiative to turn on the interior lights, seeing a small bed and an old wood burning stove that was complemented by a small wooden table surrounded by a sole chair. A small cupboard seemed to hold the kitchen utensils, whilst a desk held stacks of handwritten papers and some books that gathered dust.

'Don't mind the mess.' joked James.

'What is this place?' asked Jonah as he let himself smile for the first time in a long time. Despite being confined within a place from which he did not know how to leave, that hovel provided him a slight feeling of security and hope.

'This is my home, welcome.' replied James.

Jonah put a puzzled expression on his face, not needing to ask the question that was on the tip of his tongue.

'Yes I know. Why don't I live in the immensity of that hotel?' he anticipated the question that would come out of Jonah's confused mind. 'Because I never wanted to have anything to do with my brother's barbarism, and since our parents died, he has taken over the whole state to himself.

'But have you never thought of alerting the police or any kind of authority that might be able to help you? asked Jonah, indignant at the situation.

'I don't have the strength to go against my brother, dear boy. My family's money bought everything, and might I dare say everyone, in this city. We are way too far from civilisation and Giovanni can do whatever he pleases in here. Also, I haven't been to town in a long time, I have lived my whole life confined into this place. Even when I wrote the story for the newspaper I asked some random employee to deliver it in town.'

Despite being frightened by the situation, Jonah came to admire James's simplicity, he knew that modernity had forced most of the population to move to the urban area, even those who worked in farms, gave in to the comforts that only a high functioning city could provide. In any case, there were still older people who dedicated the end of their lives to keeping bucolism alive, refusing to make the transition from rural to urban.

'Are you hungry, thirsty? asked James whilst serving himself a glass of water.

'Oh, I'm parched, so water would be good.' said Jonah as he was too anxious to have any kind of food at that point. 'I haven't eaten for hours, but I don't feel the slightest hunger.'

'It's a side-effect of the drug, just drink some water and you should be fine.' said the old man, handing an ill-washed cup to Jonah and letting his crutches fall so he could sit on the bed.

He let James rest his strength so that they could continue their journey towards leaving that place. There was no tour to be taken in that hut, but what most caught his attention were the old handwritten sheets of paper stacked on the small desk. Jonah glanced at the papers showing no curiosity as he did not want to be indiscreet towards the only man who was willing to help him. He fixed his eyes on one of the sheets, where a particular word made him seek out old memories for a meaning. 'Catharism', he emphasised the word inside his own head, but as much as he tried, he could not find any meaning in his vague memories from his time as a catholic student.

'Does this have anything to do with your brother's entity?' he asked as he took the sheet of paper that was filled in its entirety with incomprehensible handwriting.

'This has to do with history.' answered James, touching the paper lightly and indicating the vacant seat next to him for Jonah to settle down.

He was reluctant for a while before sitting down. Not because he distrusted the one person who was helping him, but because he didn't want to convey any hint of confidence. James could feel Jonah's negative feeling and insisted once again that he let himself relax for a moment.

'Catharism was treated as a heresy in the Middle Ages, a type of belief that still worshiped the existence of two gods, the good and the bad.' he started before being rudely interrupted by Jonah.

'And what does this have to do with Giovanni's entity?' he intoned, as an even greater anxiety started to frighten his sanity.

'These people were persecuted by christians for many years, it was mostly what gave cause to the famous Crusades in the late twelfth century.' he continued, ignoring Jonah's question. 'Which ended up bringing up the so-called Holy Inquisition.'

Jonah knew the history of the church and how christians forced those considered heretics to confess their sins as they were tortured before their god, but he couldn't understand the connection that that could have with what was happening to him.

'And what the bloody fuck have I to do with that?' he asked as he stormed out from the bed.

'None of that has anything to do with you, my boy.' said James with a calming tone.

'Then what am I doing here? Why is your brother torturing me like that?'

'Giovanni's goal is much greater than that! You would be just another example, another offering to his belief.'

Jonah lowered his head and tried to absorve what the old man had just told him, but his mind could only bear to look after himself, he did not have time to seek answers from old and forgotten tales. The only thing that concerned him was to find a way for him to get out of that place alive and go home.

'Do you know how I get out of here?' asked Jonah, ignoring James's history lessons.

'Yeah, of course I know. But the question you should be asking yourself is whether I will succeed on getting you out of here. What I can say is that I will do my best to help you, with great pleasure.' he replied still comfortably sitting on the bed.

'What are we waiting for?'

'Didn't you want to know what is going on with you? What do these tattoos mean?' he tried to instigate Jonah's curiosity.

'I would prefer to get the fuck out of here...'

'Didn't you come here with a friend?

The final question startled Jonah. 'How does he know about the party? How does he know I came to the hotel with Patrick?', he asked himself as he remembered that the old man was confined inside a place even smaller than the one they were at until a few minutes ago.

'I know, it's confusing. But everything my brother is doing has a purpose, which I will explain to you, as long as you help me...'

CHAPTER 9:

A small storm had replaced the starry and bright sky and was hitting heavily against the hut's small window, whilst Jonah hovered his eyes over James. The thing he wanted the least at that point was to be part of a game between the Dartagnan brothers, but the tone in James's voice implied that Jonah had no option but to comply with his request and hope that, in the end, the old man would acquiesce to his request for getting him out of there. After storming out from the small and deteriorated bed, he admired the stacks of books and papers on James's table. He couldn't help but showing a strong curiosity he had been feeling with all that history caused by the feud within the Dartagnan family.

James leaned against the wall behind the bed and began to massage the end of what was left off his leg. He slowly removed the bandage covered by poorly dirty cloths and indicated that Jonah should reach him an old wooden box that was inside the small cupboard above the wood burning stove. The old Dartagnan grasped his hands around new bandages and a small glass that contained an antiseptic; little by little, whilst making a slight expression of pain, he put the bandage back on and covered the stump with a blanket that was crammed on the edge of the bed.

"Could you tell me a bit more about Catharism?' Jonah decided to surrender to the history lesson and submit to the fact that James had a wide advantage over that situation.

'The history of Catharism is beside the point.' he started to answer whilst adjusting himself to give more support to his lower back. 'What's really important is what came from it, as I told you before, the Holy Inquisition.'

'You mean to say that I'm an offering to the Holy fucking Inquisition?' asked Jonah, who thought he was gradually starting to connect the dots of the whole situation.

'I honestly don't know what Giovanni has is store for you, I haven't had an honest conversation with my brother in months, but if you're here, I'm not going to lie, you're part of his plans.'

'How long have you been locked in that fountain?' Jonah realised he still knew almost nothing about James's situation.

'I lost count of the days, but I've been isolated from the world for a long time.' the tone of sadness and the expression of pain returned to his face every time he spoke about it.

'Well then, help me understand why your brother is doing this, what does he hope to achieve by torturing me like this?' Jonah was getting more and more restless.

James took a deep breath, giving the impression that he was tired of that story, and everything that involved his brother's name.

'Why don't you do us a favor and boil up some water to make us some coffee. I'm going to tell you a story about my family.' he said as he fidgeted in bed seeking the best possible position.

Jonah was feeling enthusiastic for a change, which, added to the feeling of anxiety, left him agitated as he searched for everything necessary to prepare the coffee pot. Things in James's hut were not very organised, but at least the wood was stacked in the stove compartment. He remembered that he had kept Giovanni's lighter the last time he saw him, so he reached out for the object in his pants back pocket so he could set fire on the sticks that were placed between the small stumps of wood. The silence had taken over the place, which was not good for Jonah's anxiety.

'You were saying?' he decided to bring the subject back again, whilst pouring hot water from the kettle over a dirty old coffee filter that was decanting in a rusty pot.

'Hmm?' grunted James when leaving what looked like an intense trance, he had a tired expression in his face.

'You told me you were going to tell me a story...'

'Oh yes. So. My family.' he got back to it slowly whilst holding the cup that Jonah had just given him.

"This entire property was nothing but a large open field. My parents were farmers and lived off their own farming, which was passed on to me and my brother whilst we were still very young children, so we learned to grow and kill what we ate. My life has always been like this, for as long

107

as I can remember, and I always accepted reality as it was, that's how my parents taught me.

My mother, Ms. Jennifer Dartagnan, was a very religious woman, one of those people who vehemently followed the words of the bible. She was a housewife, prayed every day, and made sure that her children followed a life devoted to god as she took us to church every Sunday, which, in my childhood, made me feel very comfortable about the simple life we lived, until I changed my mind and my relationship with the family started to grow apart. Giovanni, like me, was always a respectful and hardworking person, never letting anything upset my mother, who always did everything to make sure we had the best possible life.

My father, Mr. Matthew Dartagnan, was a simple man for most of his life. He treated his family like a true patriarch and had never failed to put food on the table. The work was all about the farming, as I told you, but the old man had always had greater ambitions in his life. The idea of building a hotel on the property came from Giovanni, he left home so he could study and live in the big city, and when he returned, he did everything to convince our father to transform this estate into a greater source of income.

Giovanni's initial idea was to combine the hotel with a place of divine devotion, you probably haven't seen it, but next to that main structure there is a humble beautiful little chapel, built by our family with a lot of hard work and dedication, which we shared with the neighbourhood - and by that I mean other farmer that lived kilometres away - that wished to worship our religion the same way we did. Neither my father nor my mother insisted that the world follow their beliefs to the letter, they never tried to impose their creed on anyone who came to stay at the Dartagnan's Hotel. The little church was there, and everyone who wanted to visit it would be welcome.

With the death of our parents, Giovanni decided to give business a different direction. Since he had left home to study, he managed to convince me that the hotel could make a lot more profit. I confess that, despite dwelling on the comfort of a simple life, the extra money always attracted me, but I think that this is some sort of intrinsic instinct to every human being, or at least that's what I tell myself to ease the guilt. Gradually, he began to accept only devoted catholic guests at the hotel, promoting, more and more, orthodox services and imposing his literal interpretation of the bible on everyone who passed by and was inclined to listen to his words. I decided not to pay much attention to Giovanni's delusions. Even though I didn't have much experience in the big city, I knew that the world had changed and people no longer had that urge in taking religious teachings literally.

However, as time passed, word started to spread around, so more and more people started coming to what seemed to come around the church. Many did not even come to stay at the hotel, as they would stay only a few hours locked in praying until it was time to leave. Despite my disbelief, I've always respected my parents' wishes, but since their death, I decided to assume who I was once and for all, and never set foot in that chapel again, so I didn't know the proportion that things were taking, much less what was Giovanni's goal in raising so many devotees to his cause, and that was when I decided it was time to intervene and stay on top of what was happening in my own back garden.

I can't find words to describe exactly what I witnessed the night I decided to attend one of Giovanni's meetings. I hid in his office and watched how my brother managed to catch the attention of all those people using only the gift of speech. I was astonished. The vision of that meeting showed me that there were still many people in the world who could be deceived by abusive interpretations of a book that should be treated more like a fairy tale than anything else. Giovanni was convincing people that society needed to resume the teachings off the church, that heresies needed to be nipped in the bud and that the only way they could succeed in that would be to bring the Holy Inquisition back.

You see... This was the exact moment when I should have kept quiet, followed on with my little life and dedicated myself to my studies. But no. That was when I decided to write that column in the newspaper and express an opinion that was extremely contrary to that of Giovanni and his group of believers. In the next few days, after the newspaper was published, the church was empty. People just didn't want to come back to the hotel and life was getting back to how it was. New guests started to book rooms and enjoy the wonders that this place has to offer, but that started to annoy Giovanni. He was already getting used to having followers and feeling powerful with the presence that those followers were providing him, but they could not bear to have their leader's own brother publicly upset him in the town's largest media source.

My brother went completely mad. He came after me demanding satisfactions and repressed me with all his will. Understand, we have never been best friends, but we've always supported each other and learned to live in harmony in our own separate ways. And I knew it was my fault, I was the one who went after problems that didn't exist, but what I saw that day, in that church, inside my own property, left me disgusted, I would not be able to keep silent. I needed to do something. My first option had been to alert the authorities, to seek help with politicians and law-enforcement officers who could help stop his madness, but many of the sect participants were members of the upper echelons of society, it was when I realised that the only way to stop my brother would be to continue with what I was doing. Alert people of what was going on.

As I couldn't just go on accusing everyone with that kind of status in society of trying to relive an archaic and criminal religious practice, I went out with all I had in the first article I published to try and explain how that kind of thing could be dangerous for society, so then, and only then, in a second article, I could open up the barbarities that were being discussed during those meetings. But it was already too late. Giovanni did not let my follow up article leave the hotel.

As soon as my brother found out what I was doing, he ordered his cronies to arrest me and take me to their meeting, that's when it was over for me. He morally repressed me and made me tell him everything I knew, as he argued that I would never have enough proof to support my accusations and that no one in the world would take my words into consideration and credit me as nothing but a conspiracy theorist. And he was right, you see. I was wrong, because only after my downfall they start doing what they are doing now, the same thing they are doing to you, which, in fact, started with me, and the rest you can see for yourself."

Jonah was numb by the whole story he had just heard. It seemed impossible to him that there were still people capable of imposing their views, based on archaic institutions, through torture. He was getting a better understanding of James's concern, who seemed really frightened by the proportions that his brother's plans could take. The fighting expression on the old man's face began to captivate Jonah's empathy.

'You were the first then... Am I the second?' he broke the silence by asking what was eating him from the inside.

'Probably not, but you are the first one to reach me.' he replied with a sad tone.

'You need to help me understand what's going on, and what would my role be in this whole story!' exclaimed Jonah vehemently, as he got excited by the plot that was being built inside his head.

'I want to help you, my boy. But you need to help me too.'

'What do you want me to do?'

'First of all, you need to trust me, and tell me exactly what you did to be here.' replied James as he tried to demonstrate a calm tone so that Jonah would feel as he was in a comfortable place.

'I really don't know.' he lied again.

'You clearly know... And after everything I just told you, I have to know exactly why you are here. You have certainly done something that goes against Giovanni's ways. You need to tell me what it is, then, and only then, I'll be able to help you.' the old man answered sincerely, hoping that Jonah would stop hiding the truth.

Jonah definitely knew that he was still not fully able to trust James, despite the fact that the story was taking shape and making more sense. He was alone in that place, without friends, without a phone, and without any hope that he would get out of there any time soon. James was his only hope.

'I am trying to connect all the points so I can make sense of this situation. Try to understand, I am being emerged into lucid dreams, induced dreams, guided dreams, whatever it is, since I got here. And the worst thing is that I can't really phantom if this things are dreams or not, reality or not. It's very confusing!' he decided to open up a little more with what seemed to be his only hope. 'But I realised that there is something more to it, such as the tattoos on my arm that I don't remember getting. How is it possible that I wake up from a dream that has such real consequences?'

'Let me see these tattoos again.' said James as he gestured for Jonah to approach the bed where he was still lying.

Jonah rolled up his sleeves on the left arm to show James the still-painful drawings that were recently made by Giovanni and his gang of lunatics whilst he was tormented by those lucid dreams. The inverted cross was already creating a small layer of hard blood on the edges of the poorly and crooked drawing, whilst the phrase 'Fallacia Alia Aliam Trudit.', that was written in a horrible calligraphy, was still red from the recent needles he had taken whilst sleeping.

'They could only have done this whilst I was sleeping in the maze, right?' he asked rhetorically, hoping it that was the only plausible explanation.

'The cross can have two meanings.' started James whilst ignoring Jonah's question. 'This symbol is known as the cross of Saint Peter, which represented, at the time, the humility of the apostle before Jesus.' he finished whilst continuing to enjoy his coffee.

'And what would the other possible meaning be?' asked Jonah anxiously.

'The other came years later, still during the middle ages, when satanic sects started to use the inverted cross to represent the anti-christ.' he replied cautiously.

He felt like he was in a history class, as he listened to that gentleman speak with such passion and congruence about a subject of which he seemed to have enormous knowledge about. Jonah had never been a man who had much interest in knowing things like that, but the new knowledge that was being bestowed upon him during that night seemed to connect very well with myriad of events that were taking over his life for the past few hours. It seemed appropriate that he would understand everything he heard from the old man in order to find a common point with what he had done so that he could understand why Giovanni would find him guilty of receiving any punishment that awaited his call.

'And which of these meanings would fit into my situation?' he asked reluctantly.

'How am I supposed to know?' James frowned and shook his head. 'You do remember that I've been locked in here until you found me right? By the way, you still haven't told me what you did...'

That was an odd thing to say since he knew about the party that was going on and that Patrick was with him before they met. Something about that whole story wasn't connecting the dots.

'Do you know what that saying in Latin means?' asked Jonah, looking to gather as much information as he could from the old man.

'It means: One lie leads to another.' replied James without having to think twice, seeming to have the answers to all the religious questions that Jonah may have.

Jonah instantly understood the connection of that saying with the mistakes he had made in the past. His reluctance to accept what he had done, which came to be a crime, led him to cover his mistakes with more and more lies. The induction to that lucid dream, which showed him the situation from a different point of view, made him empathise with Joana Clemente in that situation for the first time. He had never thought about how his old girlfriend felt when she lost a child, something that for him was nothing more than a future illusion never to be made concrete.

'That has a connection with that butterfly statue, doesn't it?' he said as he was already waiting for the confirmation of his own question.

'Veritas Semper Una Est.' intoned the old man. 'Truth is always one. It does make sense. The butterfly represents resurrection, the acceptance of an error as a form of transformation and rebirth.' he finished when making the analogy between the phrase and the statue.

'Things are starting to make sense...', he thought as he tried not to show any kind of excitement. There were still many things he needed an explanation for.

Jonah had already understood that James wanted his help. He needed him to take his message out and spread it to the whole world, it seemed very important to the old man that Jonah only left that place with the goal of ending Giovanni's plans, which made sense, but Jonah's goal was to go home, away from that madness and everything that could hurt him. Not that he was reluctant to help James to expose his lunatic of brother to society, to draw attention from outside of the city, and to contain all those abuses that the sect had been committing. The Holy Inquisition had been abolished centuries ago, and there was no reason for people to fear the resurgence of such ignorance and cruelty. But that would be a difficult job, since Giovanni held so many people that were important figures to society in his hands, and the mere mention of it in the media would merely sound like another conspiracy theory.

'I can only assume, then, that the letter J means Jesus. Truth is always one, hence one lie has always led to another and Jesus is my salvation by resurrection?' Jonah was impressed with himself. He had been able to absorb the information and transform it into complicated thinking despite the fact he was under the pressure of saving his own life.

'It's a possibility, but I don't think we should stick to only one of those. Giovanni is an astute man, there is always something to read in between the lines.' replied James with a tone of excitement, as if they were getting somewhere.

'And the statue of the fish, what does that mean?' asked Jonah, after telling James about the second statue he had found in the maze, trying to take advantage of the flow of his reasoning.

'The fish statue is nothing more than the representation of faith in Jesus Christ, who is the son of god.' he replied slowly as he tried to drag himself across the bed until he could reach some papers that were hidden somewhere within that mess. 'But here's the most interesting and important thing.' he handed over to Jonah a torn and worn out pamphlet.

114

'There's also a Latin saying on it as well: Laedere Facile, Mederi Difficile.' he continued what seemed to be an endless pool of demands.

'No idea of what that one means.' James's wisdom seemed to have a limit after all.

Jonah grabbed the paper whilst looking for answers to the most diverse questions he still had about that night, but he came across what looked like a draft of an explanatory booklet titled 'C.P.F'. The piece of paper described several conservative and moralistic conducts, aimed at members of what appeared to be some sort of secret society. Torture instructions, to bait preying instructions, and other conducts to be followed by all participants. It was basically a book of horrors.

Small images illustrated archaic practices of torture that were to be combined with several new technological ways of how to deceive heretics and convince them to join the cause. It was all there, most of the answers Jonah was seeking about what was happening to him. A small explanatory chart described the drug he was being injected and how lucid dreams could induce pagans to seek their own penance and accept torture as a form of redemption, or 'divine acceptance', as the little propaganda preached.

Jonah couldn't quite understand how the drug worked. The booklet was limited to mentioning expressions such as: 'psychotic predisposition' and 'depersonalisation', which was enough to illustrate the macabre basis of the organisation formed by Giovanni Dartagnan. At the bottom of the page, another expression in Latin returned to spread doubts in Jonah's mind: 'Ubi Est Cadaver Ibi Congregantur Aquilae', which again made no sense to him, but this time James was there to clear up his doubts.

'C.P.F?' he asked as he looked up and down throughout the sheet of paper and went straight to find James's eyes.

'Christian Pendulum of Freedom.' he replied with a smear smile on his face. 'It seems hard to believe, doesn't it? But the truth is that Giovanni plans to do exactly what is written in there.'

'And the Latin expression?'

'It's their jargon...' said James, reluctantly before translating. 'Where there is carrion, there are vultures.' This is how they refer to what they call heretics, and the metaphor is completed by the allusion that vultures must satisfy their hunger by penance.

'Who are the vultures?'

'They are Giovanni's followers, those who wish to clean society from all evil brought by disbelief. Vultures eat rotten meat. Understood?' James ended the explanation with an expression of admiration on his face. He seemed to take immense pleasure in elucidating the situation.

'How do you have all this information?' asked Jonah incredulously as he realised that the situation he was in was much more complex than it appeared. The small pamphlet illustrated proposals for various criminal practices to be carried on by the C.P.F., the ideas were so deranged that Jonah would take it as some kind of unpleasant joke if he didn't know Giovanni's true history and plans.

'My brother is a very clever man. After locking me in that fountain for the first time - yes I've been there more than once - he presented me with this pamphlet that would be given to members of the organisation.' replied James, showing admiration his brother's slyness, who had left aside family to seek his divine call at the expense of his well-being.

'What does the description of this drug mean? Do they really call it The Cure?' the indignation was such that the questions came out faster than he could think.

'It's exactly what's written there, that's how it works.' replied James as if Jonah was already caught up in all of the nuisances of the myriad of information he had just bestowed upon him, but he did not want to show ignorance and lose the old one-legged man's confidence, besides, he was no longer feeling any kind of discomfort, and Douglas, the hired doctor, had made it clear it would be very dangerous to give him another dose of the drug.

The situation had become extremely complex. Giovanni Dartagnan was not just trying to punish Jonah for the crime he had committed. He knew that drugging someone to have an abortion against her will was not the first rule in the book of good manners, but he couldn't have imagined that his deeds would reach such a controversial consequence. James expressed the speed with which the C.P.F was growing, and how it was essential that Jonah helped him to alert society as a whole of what was to come. It all made sense, and Jonah would have a long way to go until he was safe and sound in the comfort of his own home.

'I understand what you mean now. We must put an end to it all.' said Jonah as he outed the exact words James wanted to hear, but the main plan remained the same: to leave that place alive.

'So you do understand why I need you to trust me?' said James, who had not yet finished his coffee.

'I understand it perfectly.' said Jonah without having to lie. Finally he decided it was time to share everything he knew about his situation with the old man. He was, indeed, part of the team that wanted to hold Giovanni responsible for his atrocities.

The headaches came to dwell inside his mind and take over his thoughts again, he suffered a strong imbalance and tried to hold onto the chair to his right, but a strong sting made him fall over it. Jonah let the cup, still full of coffee, shatter on the floor and lost control of his will once again.

CHAPTER 10:

'I can't really say if he will be conscious or not.' Jonah could hear Douglas's distinct voice.

'I thought you knew what you are doing doc, I need this to work.' said Giovanni, who was deeply staring into Jonah's eyes.

He never thought he would have go through that situation again. Douglas had made it clear to Mr. Dartagnan that he could not guarantee his well-being if he drugged him again, but it seemed that Giovanni's desire to punish him was greater than his desire to keep him alive. Although the air was charged with tension, the situation in the small red room remained the same, Jonah found himself stuck to the lucid dream induction chair, whilst Giovanni argued with Douglas. The priest continued to pray, and Monalisa had returned to her wildly drinking spree. For some reason, Jonah saw an inexplicable anger in her eyes, he had no memory of meeting the woman, much less of having done something that could justify the disparage shown by her.

'I will have to excuse myself for a moment, I have commitments to attend at the party, they must be missing me already.' said Giovanni, looking at the gold watch on his wrist. 'Can you keep a minimum of civility until I return?' he asked rhetorically as he turned his back and left, slamming the door behind him.

'Get me another bottle of champagne.' said Monalisa before Giovanni could shut de the door close.

'I'm certainly inside the hotel.', he still hadn't thought about where he might be, even though he knew that there was no better place where they could torture people, especially after everything that James had told him about his brother. Things happened right there, the Dartagnan Brothers Hotel was the headquarters of the C.P.F. as it was the place where those people had been committing indescribable crimes against anyone who dared to go against their creed. Despite James's recent clarifications, Jonah was still vulnerable to that drug and headaches, which seemed to be getting more acute, despite being faster.

'Why does Giovanni want to keep this boy alive for so long?' asked the priest.

'If you don't know...' replied Douglas without even looking at him. The doctor was clearly there for the money.

'This boy has an important meaning for the sect.' interjected Monalisa as she poured herself another glass of what was left from the champagne bottle she had brought with her.

The mere thought of having any kind of interest towards that lady, or the priest, made Jonah feel terrified. Since the beginning of the evening, when Lara had brought him to sit beside her, he had noticed a certain animosity, something that was incomprehensible to him.

A distinguished lady, with dark eyes, and hair cut by the shoulders. Her wrinkles gave her the appearance of being of old age, probably the same age as Giovanni, but what intrigued Jonah the most was not being sure of what her intentions were to him. It was strange to him that the whole situation involved so many different people and that they did not seem to understand each other very clearly, but, even so, the ultimate goal seemed to be the same, to make Jonah pay for what he had done so many years ago.

Jonah began to feel a slight pressure on his right foot, very close to where the priest had once again knelt to pray. The old vicar was squeezing one of his feet with tender whilst applying pressure to it. That was when he realised that he was barefoot, his shoes were next to the door, with his socks piggy-wrapped inside it. He tried to move and kick so that the priest would stop touching him as the mere touch of that stranger disgusted him and made him shudder, feelings that he could not replicate due to the state he found himself in, however, what was happening in his own thoughts bordered the deepest terror he could possibly imagine.

'What are you doing?' asked Douglas as he noticed the priest's hand.

'None of of your business.' he replied sharply.

'You'll have your chance, priest. Now to stop disturbing the doctor, we need to continue the penance.' intruded Monalisa before the two could do anything else.

Jonah tried his best not to let Monalisa's words startle him, even though he knew she was the one that held the strongest grudge against him.

The priest, like Monalisa, seemed to be very interested in Jonah's penance, but his justification was probably due to his divine particularities. Jonah had not been able to follow any of the sect's sessions, but from what James had explained to him, Mr. Dartagnan was the one who did the preaching at those ceremonies. The presence of a priest probably gave more credibility to less conservative catholics who sought a reason to justify their presence when invited into the Hotel. But C.P.F.'s greatest goal was to recruit as many people as possible so that its premise became valid in an increasing proportion throughout their own territory. It was simple politics applied to religious belief: they had to start slowly, easing their way into the minds of those who were more prone to be convinced, and as the word of their work began to spread, people who wouldn't believe in what they were doing at first would just follow the path set by those who were convinced at the beginning.

'Oh, how I envy Giovanni.' said Monalisa, as she leaned at the wall and made some kind of noise to attract attention, breaking the silence that reigned in the small room.

'Why?' asked Douglas with an ironic tone as he had no interest in knowing the answer.

'I wanted to go with him to the appointment he mentioned. I'm sure he's taking another trip in the Dream Room.' she answered.

'Trip?' Douglas now showed a greater interest.

'It's what we call the lucid dream induction.' replied Monalisa.

'How jovial...' laughed Douglas as he realised that the priest was rubbing Jonah's foot once again whilst praying.

'You old pervert!' he exclaimed, seeking a tone of authority. 'Leave the boy alone! Isn't it enough what he's been going through all night?'

'Listen here, doctor... You are here to carry out orders! The next time you meddle with our private affairs, I will use all my influence to make sure you're the next one in that chair.' interrupted Monalisa.

'Do not startle me, boy!' replied the priest with a loud voice before being interrupted by Monalisa.

'And you, haven't I told you to stop disturbing the doctor? Wait for your fucking turn...' she finished with authority. It became clear to Jonah that she was to be the one in charge in Mr. Dartagnan's absence.

'I need to find a way to communicate with this doctor.', thought Jonah when noticing that Douglas was the only one around that showed him any kind of empathy.

For a brief moment he thought he was delusional. Within a few seconds, Jonah could hear his cell phone announce the arrival of a new text message. The noise was unlike any other that his phone could make, and he could recognise it in any situation. As he opened his eyes, he found James's face staring fixedly at the screen of his cell phone, but before he could say anything, he found himself staring back at the red walls of the small room where he was being held hostage again.

That had been the shortest reflection he had had between one reality and another. He couldn't understand why it happened, but it certainly had something to do with the explanations Douglas was trying to give Mr. Dartagnan and the other members of his criminal sect. The doctor had already warned Giovanni that the continued use of that drug was not safe, however he kept on insisting that Douglas should go beyond the limit.

'Apply another dose of the drug, doctor.' said Monalisa as she finally pushed away from the wall with a small impulse.

'Pardon? I don't think we should, not until Giovanni is back.' replied Douglas with an air of concern.

'He is already in the dream chair and the the cure is already circulating through his veins.' she said as she motioned for the priest to rise from the edge of the chair.

'I don't think it's safe...'

'Do as I say!.' Monalisa seemed tired of needing to raise her voice every time she spoke to the doctor.

Jonah was afraid of the situation. At that moment, he realised that Patrick had not given him the wrong drug, but that, somehow, he had ingested two different types of drugs. The so called cure, which Monalisa had mentioned for the first time in all that time, seemed to have a different effect from the controlling drug that was taken for lucid dreaming, which Jonah had taken with the other guests in the Dream Room. He watched as Douglas approached the chair with another syringe next to the tubes connected to him, whilst he felt the priest prepare all the equipment in the chair so that he was, once again, induced into a dream.

"As soon as he opened his eyes he realised where he was, the first thing that Jonah could hear was: 'In nomine Patris et Filii et Spiritus Sancti'. He did not have to struggle to remember what that one meant 'in the name of the father, of the son, and the holy spirit', it was clear that someone was about to start some sort of catholic prayer. He focused on observing the place he had been brought to by his own mind at the same time he tried to identify a familiar face that would bring him any kind of context.

He was in a place he hadn't been before, what indicated something new as his lucid dreams had, so far, only showed shards of his own old memories. A structure illuminated by torches and crowded with people. The walls had a low ceiling and, although the size of the place itself did not scare, Jonah could not distinguish its beginning from its end; his brain seemed to be trying to trick his eyes. However, he soon noticed that he was in some sort of church, or chapel, or something that resembled to be religious. At first he couldn't recognise anyone as people were wearing a black cloak from head to toe and babbled repeatedly after the priest. 'This must be the little church that James mentioned before.', he thought at the same time he remembered that his mobile had rang a few minutes ago.

Jonah was curious about it. He didn't understand how he could dream of a place he had never been to and how he could be seeing something that seemed so real to a point that everyone's actions made sense and it starting to look like a new reality.

Those people were organised in a semi-circle that faced an altar, where the priest continued to preach words that reflected the spirit of the sect. 'If the priest is here as well, it has to be a dream!', he thought as he continued to observe the space between the altar and the people. Jonah noticed a huge wooden platform that resembled a giant bed. He was not close enough to the object to be able to distinguish exactly what it was, but he thought it might be

122

some kind of monument, like the ones he had found in the maze, which the devotees were worshiping through the continuous sermon given by the priest. The vehemence with which those people outed their words aloud, and the gestures they were making towards that object, was something that Jonah had never had the displeasure of seeing before. He had never been able to see such devotion and euphoria in any other situation in his life.

'I need to get closer to that table,' he thought as he continued to look around, seeking to see a familiar face, but everyone had their faces partially hidden by the gloomy atmosphere. It was then, for the first time since he had awaken into that place, that Jonah tried to move. He tried moving forward, as he would do in the other lucid dreams he had experienced, but that did not seem to be possible in that situation. He tried hard, with all his mighty, but rushing it only seemed to be slowing him down. He was completely paralysed and there was nothing he could do about it.

Before he could start beginning to understand why he was stuck within his own dream, Jonah was pulled by an unknown hand, whilst his body obeyed commands that his brain had not sent it. In a somewhat groggy way, his own self started to follow the person, murmuring incomprehensible words that did not even echoed inside his mind.

The fright he felt, as he realised he had no control over his own wishes, soon turned into a generalised panic. As he passed by one of the church's stained glass windows, Jonah was able to catch a glimpse of his face mirroring, however, as much as the reflection was not clear, he could recognise that face anywhere. Jonah finally understood that he was not inside a dream of his own.

He was in Patrick's body.

There was no time to stop and try to understand what was going on. As he got closer to the big wooden table, he could see that, at its ends, two steel cylinders were fitted into iron pulleys that held two pairs of handcuffs each. He could still see, as he was getting closer, an elaborate gear that ended in an iron crank. The bed had an aged aspect, the wood was old and moulded, and the gears and pulleys were rusted by time, but those steel cylinders seemed to have been changed very recently, giving them an important aspect for whatever that thing was as the members of Giovanni Dartagnan's sect worshiped it.

'Behold, my lord, the divine blessing that these devotees offer you. 'said the priest as Jonah, apparently trapped into Patrick's body, was being transported effortlessly to the large wooden board.

His body was been laid on the table, whilst his hands and feet were being tied at the handcuffs. The priest continued to deliver his sermon, whilst the people in black repeated with enthusiasm the words spoken by him.

'This man.' Jonah readily recognised Giovanni's distinct voice. 'It's here as an offering to god. I ask you to accept his blood and forgive us of all of his sins.'

Jonah was in such a panic that he could do nothing but fight the very barrier that prevented him from moving. 'What did Patrick do?', he asked himself at the same time he was forced to face the ceiling. It didn't take long to understand how that contraption was going to work, he had watched enough films to know he wasn't there to get a massage. He knew that his body was going to be stretched until it would tear apart, or rather, Patrick's body.

'Is this real? Or is it just a lucid dream Patrick is going trough?', he thought, trying to understand what was going on inside the walls of the Dartagnan Brothers Hotel. 'Giovanni wasn't in his room, so it makes sense that he's here, but the priest is here, so this can only be a dream', he tried to analyse the logic behind the situation. He was still trying to understand the dynamics of lucid dreams and it was not clear to him how that scenario could be reflected in his own subconscious.

Giovanni was the one controlling the crank. The gears began to grunt in a forced way, whilst the other members of the cult returned to repeat the incomprehensible sayings that emanated from the priest's mouth. Patrick soon started screaming uncontrollably, whilst his limbs were stretched out on that wooden bed. His voice echoed in Jonah's brain, but the pain that the body seemed to be feeling did not afflict him at all. It was clear that this was a dream, although he could hear bones being broken whilst smelling the fiery odor of blood being spilled from his limbs, but the worst feeling he could have at that moment was Patrick's scream of pain when one of his legs seemed to have being teared apart from his body."

Jonah was feeling as he had passed out after that fateful moment, he just couldn't figure out if Patrick was dead as he had returned from that nightmare. He looked back at James's puzzled face, trying understand if any of that pain was real or if any of his own body parts were harmed by the experience he had just woken up from. The old man was still sitting on the bed with the stump of his amputated leg resting on a small pillow. His expression was of curiosity, but Jonah's horrified look turned his words into enormous concern.

'What just happened?' he asked as he tried to get up to help Jonah, who was rising from the floor he had fallen into.

'Patrick...' started Jonah as he regained his composure and realise that he had his mind in full consciousness. 'How did you know he was at the party with me?' he asked, trying to be neutral on the subject, as he couldn't hide the melancholy out of his voice.

'Giovanni had told me about his plans for tonight, I must confess.' the old man's answer was not very convincing, since he had just told him he hadn't seen his brother for a while.

'You can continue...' he said, as he ignored the white lie, hoping that James would finish his reasoning and explain, once and for all, everything he knew about the events of that night.

'I've already told you, boy.' he started emphatically. 'My brother knows how these things afflict me and always arranges for someone to come and torture me before committing whatever his next atrocity is.'

'So it means that you knew all along what your brother had in store for me? Why didn't you tell me before?' asked Jonah, now standing and ready to extract any information that James could still be keeping from him.

'Simmer down, will you? I've already told you that I'm on your side.' said James, as he moved on the bed and lost the pillow that supported his leg. He seemed to be threatened by Jonah's voice.

'How is that on my side? You know the outcome of my entire near future and are reluctant to let me know about the situation!' exclaimed Jonah, expressing indignation.

'It's obvious that I don't know your entire future! My brother did not share all the details of his plans, he just tortured me with mediocre words, knowing that I am against it and, at the same time, find myself powerless to prevent him from going on with his journey.' answered James, sincerely.

'You lied to me...' Jonah was disappointed. 'You could have warned me about what was coming.'

'I did not lie!' shouted James fervently. 'I've told you from the beginning. I will help you, as long as you help me too.'

Silence washed over the small wooden hut. Jonah could feel that the old one-legged man was being sincere, but he was still very fragile with what had just happened and feared that Patrick could be dead if that wasn't a dream.

'Why did you wake up talking about Patrick?' asked James curiously and remembering that the two had not yet talked about his last psychotic episode.

Jonah told him all the details of his hallucinations and described throughly his last induced dream. He was hoping that James could explain what was going on, since the old man seemed to know more than he let on.

'I have two theories.' he said, appearing way too calm with what Jonah had just told him.

'Please don't hide anything from me...' pleaded Jonah, already tired from the twists and turns brought by that night and that place.

'First of all.' James again stretched what was left of his amputated leg on the pillow. 'I think my brother may have induced a lucid dream into your mind.'

'Care to elaborate?' Jonah was getting tired and confused.

'You told me you were stuck to a chair, didn't you? So these machines, combined with synthetic drugs, have a very strong hold on the human brain, but I believe that this is the least plausible probability. You see, it's very complicated and time consuming to do something like this...'

'So what can it be?' asked Jonah in distress.

'The second hypothesis is that you were not in Patrick's dream, but in Giovanni's dream, or anyone else present at this meeting, as a mere spectator.' said James trying to make himself clear.

'What then? I don't understand...' the dilemma of dreams was getting more   complicated with every new information. It seemed that James knew what he was talking about, like someone who had been studying the subject for a long time.

'If this scenario that you experienced is true, it is very unlikely that you were present in the body of someone who, excuse my insensitivity, is apparently already dead.' the tone in James's voice was serious.

'Dead? Are you telling me that Patrick is fucking dead?' asked Jonah as he let his eyes fill with tears.

'For what you just told me, it's quite possible, isn't it?' he answered frankly.

'But how could I be in someone else's dream and be another someone else at the same time?' Jonah could not find any connection in the theory presented by the old man.

'There is an enormous engineering behind these lucid dreams. The chair, to which you are connected, is equipped with brain wave monitors, and all people who are induced to lucid dreaming share the same type of router, that is, a small universe is created for the connected people, where each one will have the freedom to run through their own dream. However, these brain waves can be programmed to intertwine, which ends up causing what you have experienced now.' said James trying to elucidate things in the best way he could. 'My guess is that you were induced by the drug that causes lucid dreams, but you were living Giovanni's dream, or someone else's, who chose you to relive an experience Patrick had had before.'

'But is your brother's dream something that has already happened?' Jonah could only imagine that the answer was positive. All the lucid dreams he had had until then had been memories taken from his subconscious.

'I believe so. Lucid dreams are nothing more than the reflection of one's subconscious. They are lost memories taken up by the brain itself. There's also the possibility I've mentioned before, where this latter dream of yours was nothing but a very well, and evil, scheme that was designed for you to live. But look, these are all hypothesis, I might be wrong. Do I make myself clear?'

'But why don't I dream something that makes me happy, like it happened the first time? Why doesn't my subconscious look for good memories?'

'That's what I'm trying to explain to you. Your dreams are being modified by the dream chair. And in the case of the latter, I think you were inserted into Giovanni's subconscious, so you came across something you had never seen before.' James seemed to be running out of explanations.

Jonah was stunned by the excess of information. He either had had a dream inside Giovanni's mind, or had dreamed something completely fake and new that was designed for his own delight.

'The combination of these new drugs with the technology of the dream chair is able to take the human mind to the most diverse experiences. It is something new, with little to none experience. It's no wonder it is not allowed.' continued James as he finished his explanation.

'You mean to tell me that, besides being living in a strange reality, I am being inserted in the minds of other people, and in dreams that are not even theirs, or worse, that are not even real?'

James just nodded his head with confusion. The complexity of it all was even deeper than what Jonah had imagined, he could not see a light at the end of the tunnel in face of all that was happening, let alone understand the remote possibility of it happening.

'What can you tell me about this alternative reality? I've been going back and forth for hours from a psychotic state that seems very different from the lucid dreams I've had before.' his curiosity seemed to be in line with the disposition that James, suddenly, showed to explain things.

'I haven't figured that one out yet... But I have a theory about what might be happening to you.' the old man seemed to be afraid to talk about it.

'Another fucking theory? There is no certainty or truth about what is going on here, is there?' replied Jonah, sarcastically, after all he had not alternative but to join the weird little game that everyone around him seemed to be playing. 'What would that theory be?'

'I understand your disregard for the subject, it is very complicated and sometimes difficult to understand.' James followed Jonah's sarcasm.

'Of course, I understand...'

'So... Jokes aside, I believe that these outbreaks from reality that you are having, have already happened.' he stopped whilst Jonah still waited for the explanation to follow.

'They have happened?' Jonah asked himself aloud before he turned his attention back to James. 'But how did I wake up with tattoos I had never seen before?'

'Yes, they have happened, these tattoos are still a mystery to me but I reckon they might have done it to you whilst you were passed out inside the maze. In the other hand they might have done that to you at the same time you were living the memories you just mentioned, but you are never going to be completely sure about it unless Giovanni wants you to. Remember the pamphlet where you read about depersonalisation?'

'Yes.' he remembered what he had read a few minutes ago.

'So, I believe my brother gave you another synthetic drug without you even realising it.' the old man started to talk whilst things started to make sense to Jonah. He soon remembered the sole called cure that he read about in the small pamphlet and was mentioned by Monalisa minutes ago.

'The cure'. responded Jonah.

'How do you know about the cure?' he asked, looking proud.

'It was in the pamphlet you just showed me, and a lady mentioned it in the other reality.'

'Monalisa?' James's question had a distinct rhetorical tone.

'Do you know her?' Jonah showed no surprise, it was quite possible that James knew everyone in that place.

The old man just nodded, again, which seemed to be some kind of nervous tick he had.

'When I woke up from the first lucid dream, I remember your brother mentioning that Patrick had inadvertently changed the pills. Now you want to tell me that I took something else that I don't know about?' Jonah wanted to bring up that topic before forgetting what had happened.

'This is all part of the game, my boy. My brother obviously made a point of misleading you.' he emphasised his speech with a sad tone.

'Let's return to the point, shall we? What's so special about this drug?' asked Jonah before he could digress on another subject without finishing his explanation. It no longer mattered to him how many, and which, drugs he had taken.

'What I mean by depersonalisation, is you preserving the sense of reality and, at the same time, thinking that what you are living is not real, that is, what you perceive, whilst in that red room, has already happened, but at the moment that it happened, you were not aware of it, because your brain was induced to depersonalisation, and that caused those moments to be buried into your subconscious.'

'And now these lucid dreams are bringing this old reality to surface?' Jonah interrupted his reasoning so he wouldn't get lost amid that much information.

'Exactly!' exclaimed James as if he had just discovered fire.

'But how does that apply to me? Is what I see in the room real?'

'Don't you have the feeling of being present in that room? Like you're actually there?' James was trying to spell things out in a way that Jonah could understand.

'Yes. I feel present, but I have no control over my body.'

'It is very likely that this is due to a neuromuscular blocker. Giovanni uses it on his victims to have more control over how his sadistic means of punishment will work.' he explained as he terrified Jonah with the news that he was under the influence of a third drug.

'Three drugs then? So what I experience, when I have these blackouts, has already happened?' he returned to the main subject.

'Yes, but the drug only makes you remember these moments when you have these so called psychotic episodes you've been having. I wouldn't be surprised if my brother was controlling them too.'

'He controls what I can remember?'

'It all depends... If you are connected to the chair, it can induce and monitor a lucid dream, but if it is not, it will control only when you will have the outbreak. He might be able to activate the cure, which is already in your system, through the same technology that controls your brain waves; and from there, he can make you have these outbreaks and remember things that happened whilst you were under the effect of depersonalisation.' James seemed proud of himself for having finished his reasoning with such confidence.

'So he can basically choose what he wants to do with me?'

'Yes, depending on the drug that is active in your brain... It's quite complex.'

'I can see that... And why would he induce me to remember memories of me being stuck into that room?'

James shrugged his shoulders, expressing the same indignation and indicating that the doubt was mutual. At least, the discussions between the people in the small room about drugs and dosages started to make more sense to Jonah.

'Why do they call it the cure?' the more the old man spoke, the more Jonah had questions.

'Some dark and narcissistic reason that only Giovanni can tell you. You don't seem to understand the seriousness of the problem, my brother is willing to go very far to achieve what he wants.'

'I do understand it. I understood that my destiny is bound to a tragic end.' he said, looking unhappy about the direction things were heading.

'We can still turn things around.' the tone of James's voice was very hopeful, but Jonah saw no reason to believe he was going to leave that place alive. 'You need to help me, we need to alert society and bring justice to this place.'

'I'm having a hard time assimilating all of this, I didn't even know anything remotely close to this even existed.' he said thoughtfully.

'I understand. I've spent a lot of time studying and reading about it, and I still can't understand all its complexity, I don't expect you to understand everything instantly.' James's expression was empathetic. He wanted to demonstrate to Jonah that he was not alone in that situation, and that they needed each other to get out of there.

That conversation momentarily came to a halt. Jonah was struggling with his own thoughts to put things back together and understand exactly what was going on that night. He was afraid that his best friend might be dead and that the same thing could happen to him in a very short time-frame. He couldn't remember anything that Patrick might have done that could be considered heresy, on the contrary, he thought that his friend was there to serve, simply, as an offering to Giovanni Dartagnan's eerie sect. 'Imagine what's in store for me...', he thought as he noticed James fiddling with his pockets.

'Did you happen to see where my phone is?' asked Jonah when remembering the brief moment he was awake and realised his device announcing that a message had been received.

'It fell out of your pocket when you were out...' said James, showing honesty as he handed the device back to Jonah.

'Any messages?' asked Jonah, looking at his phone whilst noticing that it continued its relentless search for a single bar of reception.

'You did receive a message, saying that a voice message has arrived.' James looked suspicious.

'I don't know this number.' replied Jonah as he brought the device back to his pocket. It would be useless trying to look for any way that would make it possible to hear the message.

'Well I know the number. Why is Lara calling you?'

'I didn't even know she had my number, how do you know it's her?' asked Jonah, puzzled.

'Lara is my daughter...' James ended his speech with an expression of deep sadness.

CHAPTER 11:

'Your daughter? asked Jonah, finding himself surprised by the news, since only a few hours ago he had seen the beautiful young woman kissing what was apparently her own uncle. He didn't know how to react.

'Yes. Beautiful as she is, she doesn't look anything like her father, gladly.' he said whilst twisting a smirk.

'Sorry, but I'm trying to find a logic in what you're laying on me right now. You know your own daughter is with your brother? I mean in a very intimate way...' he asked incredulous as he took another glance at the phone, hoping to see some reception so he could hear the message.

'It is likely that she tried to call you, but the low network reception at this location must have sent it directly to your voice mail.' James ignored the question.

'Speaking of that, is there any place where I could get reception around here?' Jonah couldn't remember the last time he had to ask that question. Globalisation had reached every little corner of the globe and cell phone towers could be found everywhere.

'There used to be, but my brother managed to end cell phone reception across the estate. I don't think he wants anyone to make contact with the outside world.' replied James. 'But sometimes, some waves can come and go momentarily.'

'Don't you think I haven't noticed this habit of yours.' Jonah brought up the subject again. 'Aren't you going to answer me why your daughter is messing around with your own brother?'

'It's a story that deeply saddens me, and it doesn't really matter if you know about it, it wouldn't make any difference right now. We really need to focus on what we're going to do to get out of here.' said James as he prepared to finally get out of that bed.

'Where are we going?' Jonah was surprised.

'Let's get you back into that party.' said James, who sought to balance himself on his crutches. 'Even better, you will come back and I will make my first public appearance in a long time.'

'Back to the party?', Jonah could not understand what would the old man possibly want in a place where everyone desired his his evil.

'I thought the plan was to get out of here and go as far as possible.' said Jonah whilst sitting in the chair near the small desk.

'And that's the only way out, my boy. Now get up, let's get out of here before Giovanni decides to trick you into having another one of those outbreaks.' said James already standing, as still as he could.

The two went out the door before Jonah could question James's decision anymore. He had already understood the old man's plan, but what he did not like was the ideia of returning to a place full of religious lunatics with a complex of greatness and a very loose disposition to break any law that would thwart their plans. He hadn't stopped to think about it yet, but it did seem like a strange scene. A band of backward and moralistic old people trying to bring back an archaic and sadistic institute to eradicate what they considered heretics from a world that no longer even cared about religion. 'They'll never manage to do it.', he thought wryly, knowing that a plan of that magnitude could never work out in modern society, but the simple fact that those people continued to act for the sect of Giovanni Dartagnan, even if it was in place that far away, in that distant town, made Jonah feel very concerned, considering the consequences that something like that would bring to an entire future generation.

. Rain had ceased to poor and the sky had once again become lit by stars, illuminating the lawn and the maze. The temperature had dropped considerably, giving the impression that winter would come earlier that year. Jonah just watched, whilst James tried his best to move around on those crutches. The old man seemed to be getting tired by the hour, but he insisted on doing things by himself, his pride seemed to be greater than the difficulties he had been facing.

They redid the steps Jonah had done before. The entrance to the maze, which was actually the exit, remained obscure with its poorly maintained surroundings. He still couldn't believe he was going back into the place he had struggled to get out of. 'At least I won't be alone this time.', he thought as he looked to his side and saw that the old Dartagnan knew exactly where he was going.

'I helped build this place, my boy.' said James, as he noticed Jonah's hesitation as they crossed the line that led into the maze.

'How did you find me at the statue before? What passage was that?' he remembered he hadn't had time to question James about the moment he saved him.

'You were unconscious, you didn't see me coming.' James recalled whilst trying to keep a calm expression on his face so that Jonah would not be scared again.

'I remember that, what I want to know is how you got there...'

'This place is very old.' he started to answer before Jonah could insist on the question. 'Our family built several underground asylums to protect us from the atrocities committed by the dictatorship in which we lived at the time. My father was a conservative man, but he had never been a nationalist as he would say: 'The only honor I will protect is that of my land.', he would vehemently say when he heard on the radio new rules that the people were supposed to follow. After this dark period of our history was behind us, my brother and I decided to build this maze to cover all the entrances and possible traps hidden by my father.'

'Were you held prisoner in one of those asylums?' Jonah was curious about the history of the property, but he did not want to let the conversation be taken over by another history lesson.

'The water source was an observation point, in case we were invaded. You see, my father was a tad paranoid about this kind of thing, but in fact we never came close to having our land invaded by anyone. I very much doubt that whoever was the head of government, knew of our existence.'

The surprises of that place would not cease to amaze Jonah. As complicated as the situation was for him, the incredible story of the Dartagnan Brothers Hotel continued to surprise him.

'So you came through one of these passages?' he asked rhetorically.

'Obviously.' replied James, even though he knew he didn't need to.

'But why did we leave there through a secret passage? Why didn't we just go back the way I had come from?'

'Because these corridors are treacherous at night. It involves a complicated structure made of mirrors, mixed with the camouflage of the natural environment, making it practically impossible to get out of here if you don't know exactly what you're doing.' he said as the two went on their way.

'But you can, right?' he remembered the words he had read on the sign before entering the maze that no one would leave there by cheating.

James did not dare to answer. There was no reason for Jonah to be more worried than he already was. The two went on. They passed by the butterfly statue, where Jonah stopped to wait for James to do some of his tricks so that the two could get out of there, but the old man just passed him and entered one of the walls covered by the vines. He could now understand and experience what James had just told him. A mirror, strategically positioned on the other side of the statue, gave the impression that that corridor had no exit for those coming from the opposite direction, but the mere illusion of a closed wall was easily broken by James Dartagnan's knowledge and courage.

'Apparently, you can do it.' said Jonah, again, admired by the charms of that place.

'If Giovanni's goal were not so cruel, this could be a great leisure center.' thought Jonah, as he imagined parents and children exploring each corner of that mysterious place.

'I haven't crossed this maze in a while, my boy. But it is much safer to go over the ground. Someone from the sect may be roaming the undergrounds. You see, this is where they develop their torture plans and even keep prisoners.' said James in a macabre tone of voice.

'And your brother will not see us entering the balcony from the hall?' asked Jonah as he remembered where he left from a few hours ago.

'We're not going there. Trust me, this is the safest way to get to the hotel without being spotted.' replied James.

Jonah had not yet asked himself, until that moment, if anyone was missing him at the party. He had been away for a long time and had not been able to communicate with anyone inside. 'Lara tried to call me, so they probably don't know where I am.', he thought before turning back to old one-legged man.

'Don't you think it's strange that your brother hasn't come after me yet?'

'I don't think you'll like the answer for that one, my boy.' he spoke quietly as the two went through the maze.

Jonah shrugged his shoulders as if he hadn't expected that night to get worse, making it clear to James that any answer would be understood as a yet other mystery to be solved.

'I have some theories on that subject, too.' he replied whilst Jonah showed the expected expression.

'So?' he showed himself ready to hear about it, as if nothing could scare him anymore.

'The most likely is that Giovanni is busy with party affairs. He doesn't have much time to be absent from these events...' replied James when he saw the dubious expression on Jonah's face.

'That brings me to one more question...'

James just frowned. The mood was already beginning to weigh on them. There were way too many questions being made and only a few responses that could be considered concrete answers, but there was no possible alternative so both of them would have to collaborate.

'Your brother said some things that indicated that the party would be happening at the same time that I am in that small room. How is that possible? You told me that the two realities happen at different times.' Jonah's question went against the subject at hand, but at the same time it was very coherent for him to understand the situation completely.

'Didn't you have a moment during the party when you were feeling kinda dizzy and stumbling through the place?' replied James, already seeming to know the answer to that question.

'Yes, but it felt way shorter than it appear to be.' he replied.

'If you were induced to the phenomena of depersonalisation, as I strongly reiterate you were, your memories of that time were erased, there is no way to know how long you were away from the party.' James could see the confusion caused in Jonah's mind. 'Want to know my other theory?'

'Firstly, I need to grasp my mind on what you just told me.' Jonah replied sharply as he couldn't quite understand the whole situation.

He remembered the time he had passed out shortly after the first induction into lucid dreaming, in the Dream Room, which, according to his friend, was just a few minutes. Patrick had even alerted him to look at the clock that monitored the experience. He decided to ask James about that assumption and get rid of all the doubts that the drugs and time differences brought him once and for all.

'Help me put together a timeline. I need to understand exactly what happened.' he pleaded whilst James stopped in front of another of those elusive walls.

'I understand your difficulty, my boy. However, we don't have time for that right now. We need to get out of here before you have another one of those psychotic flare-ups.' replied James as if he was in no mood to explain the facts again.

Jonah went on a kind of autopilot. 'If he isn't going to help me, I can do it myself.' he thought as he started to put the facts in a point of view that made sense. 'I was in the Dream Room. Patrick gave me a pill that Giovanni said was the wrong one, but in fact he omitted the information that I took more than one drug. Psychotic attacks began within the party. I ended up in this maze and had several more episodes. Apparently, the realities are different in time. The real one is the one where I am with James, and the other happened in the brief space of time that I was unconscious in the main ballroom.'

That last part made no sense to him. There had been only a few minutes when he was unconscious, it would not have been possible that all of that could have happened in such a short period of time.

'This thing about depersonalisation. Does it affect temporal perception?' he asked as he returned to reality.

'It does indeed. I've already told you. You cannot seem to understand. All that is happening in this other reality is being induced by the advanced technology of the dream chair.' replied James, looking even more tired when he had to talk and make all that effort to walk at the same time.

'The only thing I haven't understood yet is time.' replied Jonah vehemently.

'Well, time is the only incomprehensible thing in this whole thing, at least for us who don't know Giovanni's technology as a whole. You need to understand one thing: I don't have all the answers to give you right now, but I'm sure that as soon as we unmask my brother, we will have a chance to understand everything more clearly.' James seemed certain that they would succeed in their mission.

He wanted to believe everything the old Dartagnan was telling him, but it was difficult to understand the whole situation in a very throughly way, so the best option would be to continue to believe in the only person who had reached out to him at that time and, together, seek the answers at the source of the problems: Giovanni Dartagnan and members of the Christian Pendulum of Freedom.

The conversation had gone on for so long that Jonah didn't even know where they were. The path continued to be taken over by elusive walls, a cold and gloomy atmosphere, and the noise of unrecognisable animals and insects. James stopped suddenly when Jonah almost ran into one of his crutches, the two of them had reached another dead end within the maze.

'Where's the mirrored image?' asked Jonah, who could already see the balcony lighting over the wall.

'We're not going that way.' said James as he realised where Jonah was glancing.

Before Jonah could question the decisions made by James once again, the old man dropped his crutches on the floor whilst sitting near the wall. Very delicately, he started groping the lawn in search of something. Jonah was curious about the situation, but did not want to disturb James Dartagnan with more questions, on the contrary, he remained silent whilst his new acquaintance continued to look for something that was supposedly there. The vines that covered the wall seemed to be less thick, in addition to being present in a lesser volume. James continued to look for something between the grassy drain and the wall, when his hand came to find some kind of lever that Jonah couldn't see very well. He used all his strength to pull the thing that seemed to activate some kind of trap door, the floor literally started to rise. 'This place is really full of surprises.', he thought, noticing the dichotomy between the emotions he had been having throughout the night.

'Keep quiet.' whispered James as he cautiously put his crutches down at the end of the hole without letting them make a single little noise.

'What the fuck is this place now?' asked Jonah, perplexed by the complexities that the property did not cease to show.

'Quiet!' censored James. 'I told you, these are old shelters built by my father.' he seemed already tired of having to repeat himself.

A little over two meters separated the surface from the ground as Jonah had just enjoyed another of James's surprises. After the old man lit a small dusty lamp, Jonah could see where he had ended up: it was just a small room decorated by shelves, stocked with what looked like food cans and water bottles covered in a thick layer of dust that indicated people haven't been there for a long time. Two bunk beds covered one of the corners, and a small round table, which was not surrounded by any chair, centralised the structure that looked more like a war refuge. As he walked close to the wall, he scratched his elbow on one of those plasterboard covered walls he hadn't seen in years, which made him wonder why would anyone decorate walls like that.

'It's been a while since anyone has come down here, hasn't it?' asked Jonah as he watched James rise from the ground, leaning on his crutches.

'I've no idea, my boy. I can't even tell you that I remember the last time I was here.' the expression on the old man's face was clearly nostalgic.

'Are we going to stay here for long?' asked Jonah already showing a certain anxiety to be confined in such a small space.

James decided not to feed the insisting anxiety attacks that Jonah demonstrated every little while, he just started to move around and examine some of the dusty objects laying on the shelves. He grabbed what appeared to be a bottle of water and, after a strong blow on the dirt, used his other hand to bring up a label for some alcoholic drink that Jonah was unaware of.

'This wine was made by my grandfather.' the reminiscence brought by the image of the bottle had left the old man with his eyes covered in tears. 'You don't happen to have a corkscrew in your pocket, have you?'

'No.' Jonah thought about speeding things up so they could get out of there once and for all, but he didn't want to show insensitivity to the nostalgic moment that James was going through.

He put the bottle back on the shelf and let his crutches guide the way once again. As much as Jonah watched, he couldn't find a way out of there other than the trapdoor through which they had just come from. James surprised again as he pushed with strength a part of the old wall that allowed a slight breeze to enter. Jonah hadn't noticed how thin the atmosphere in the small room was. He filled his lungs with air as soon as he could get out and come across a large corridor with bare walls made of clay.

'Now this?' he was amazed by all those secrets. 'Does this place have an end?

'If it does, I don't know where it is.'

'Where should we go?'

Jonah realised that the exit from the small room led to a crossroads that indicated three different directions.

'You know... I don't actually remember.' James started to think, whilst having one hand supporting his crutch and the other scratching his beard. Jonah was looking for signs that might indicate the right direction.

'The obvious would be to go straight, towards the underground of the main hall, where the party is happening.' started James, whilst Jonah already imagined that the obvious, in that place, did not mean the same as in the real world. 'However.' he continued. 'If my memory serves me correctly, I believe my father built an exit directly inside the church.'

'The church?'

'Yes. You see, my father believed that praying daily was a way to chase the problems away.'

'Hard to imagine that problems could reach such a distant place.' Jonah joked with the bucolic atmosphere of the Dartagnan Brothers property.

The mood wasn't set for jokes and, although Jonah could not observe any apparent danger, James showed an expression of concern.

'Are we in any kind of danger here?' asked Jonah.

'Do you have a short memory problem, my boy?' James was getting sick and tired of Jonah's insisting questions.

'Not usually, no, but I realise that lately I've been repeating myself quite a lot.' Jonah stopped to think and remembered that James had just told him that Giovanni's sect used that underground as some sort of deposit.

'Hmm.' James had a tone of regret. 'It may be that the excess of drugs has affected your short-term memory, but I don't believe this will be a problem in the future, now let's go.' he continued, slowly, looking into Jonah's eyes as he foresaw the advent of yet another question laden with anxiety.

The air was filled with silence, and the two left towards one of the intersections at the crossroad. They definitely did not take the path that Jonah hoped for, but they did take the left path, where James said they would eventually come out into the church itself, where, apparently, the C.P.F. held its meetings.

'We need to go slowly, without making a noise and, preferably, speak as little as possible.' he instructed Jonah as they walked.

James lit a small pocket lantern, since he had left the dusty limo back at the small room, and started to walk close to the clay wall. Jonah's already dirty clothes started to get grimy with mud and wet with humidity, worsening his conditions and making the situation even more uncomfortable.

He wondered what would Lara think when she saw him like that. He also looked for any explanation that would make him understand why the beautiful girl left a voice message on his phone, and how she would have gotten his number. He also took the opportunity to check his phone's reception. He always had a glimpse of hope that when he took the device out of his pocket, he would see a strong reception signal and a flood of missed calls from Patrick.

But then again, nothing.

Jonah had that terrible habit of letting his thoughts put him into a trance and cause him to completely lose his concentration on the situation that was right under his nose. Soon he realised that he was paying absolute no attention to an inch of the path he had taken behind James.

The old man suddenly came to a halt and turned off the small flashlight as quickly as he pushed Jonah against the muddy wall. All the effort he had made to keep himself presentable would have been in vain as he could feel the dampish wall smearing what was still clean from his suit.

'Do not make any noise.' he whispered as Jonah tried to figure out what was going on.

'Is someone here?' he whispered in the smallest volume possible.

'Yes, now shut up.'

After dropping his crutches on the floor, the old man motioned for Jonah to turn on his back as he mounted him like a horse and grabbed his neck to steer guidance, indicating that he should return to the path they had just taken. A few meters later, Jonah saw a small gap inside the wall and soon he could understand that James's intention was to hide in there. He crouched down so that James could stay on the floor and stayed by his side whilst he tried to breathe without letting the mere noise that was coming in and out of his lungs let anyone notice their presence.

More than one person was coming towards the path they were taking. He could distinguish male and female voices, but he was unable to make any sense from the conversation, at least not enough that would make him find a connection between the words that could lead into to something he could use as information.

James motioned for him to lower his head and remain in complete and absolute silence. It was a matter of seconds before three distinct people passed them. Two men and a woman hurriedly walked by. They were dressed in black from head to toe, which made it impossible for Jonah to identify any of them, but the smell from the woman was the same smell that had caught his attention at the beginning of the party. That was surely Lara's perfume. An incredible odor that had marked its presence inside Jonah's subconscious.

James stood up again so that Jonah could carry him back to the crutches left in the gap between the wall and the dirt floor. He continued to make the same sign of silence, but Jonah yearned the urge to speak and ask questions once again. He noticed that James had also distinguished the silhouette of the woman who had just passed by, but for some reason he didn't seem to want to talk about what his own daughter was doing with that group of religious lunatics.

'I think the time has come for you to tell me what Lara's role is in this whole story...' whispered Jonah again whilst James got back up in his crutches.

'What you want to know?'

'Can you start by telling me why is your daughter kissing your own brother whilst you, theoretically, are trapped inside a fucking fountain...'

'My daughter was not raised by me.' he replied, again expressing a sad tone in his voice. 'You see, she doesn't even know she's my daughter.' The old one-legged man's voice seemed to have been suppressed by a lump in his throat accompanied by an urge to cry. 'And I believe my brother has some religious nonsense that explains his incest behaviour towards her.'

'Would you mind elaborating the story?' asked Jonah gently. He didn't want to see anyone cry in front of him, not in that situation.

James lowered his head and sobbed a few times until he managed to swallow the few tears that were successfully leaving his weary eyes. He passed his hand over his face so that the red, which expressed his shame, would not let show the image of a fragile man. The old man was very proud of who he had become in life, and the mistakes of his past were not capable of tarnishing the achievements of such a fruitful history.

'The conservatism of my family had always prevented me from taking my life very far from the world of its religion. From the bible and it's god.' he began an unrepentant and reasoned speech. 'When I got one of the girls who worked on the farm pregnant, my parents did everything they could so I wouldn't be able to care for the child. You see, my boy, I was very young, I had plans to go out into the world, study and live all kinds of things that every young man desires. I readily accepted my father's proposal. Lara would be raised by her mother and would always have a place in our estate, so I could live as if nothing had happened.'

'You told me that you spent your life in that place, that you never went out to study, as Giovanni had done.' Jonah brought back recent information given by James himself, which contradicted his own statement.

'And that was my punishment. My parents used all their power so that I wouldn't be able to disconnect from the farm. They made sure that I couldn't get any jobs or transportation to escape the reality of this place. They were meticulous with the idea that I would have to take care of my daughter from a distance.' James could no longer contain his emotions. The speed with which he swallowed his own crying was slower than that of the sobs.

'And you never thought about talking to her? Tell her the truth and take charge of your own life?' Jonah realised that his question seemed a little too straightforward for the moment.

'Of course I did!' James exalted himself for a little while and soon lowered his voice again. 'But when I had the opportunity to get my hands on a substantial amount of money, Lara was already being educated by my family and very well taken care for. You see, my parents, although conservatives, never lacked to put food on her table or a roof over her head.'

'You only managed to break free when your parents died?'

'Exact.'

'So it's because of Lara that you never left this place?'

'Exactly. You see, my boy, if I wanted to go out into the world with a child on my back, I could have done it, but what future would I have giving her? Would I be a better father for letting my daughter be in need of food and water, or would I be considered a better human for letting her never know about me?'

Jonah came to understand very clearly why such a well-educated and sensible man was stuck in a place like that. He allowed himself to be tortured and live in such terrible conditions just so he could spend time with the daughter he couldn't raise. The dilemma, which he had created for himself, confined him to an isolated, depressing, and distressing life, but his strong character made him stay there and pay for his mistakes in a way he considered fair. He would have to spend his life watching his own daughter being raised in a world he had learned to hate.

'How do you manage to be a mere spectator whilst Lara joins these lunatics?' Jonah decided that James had the strength to put up with a little toughness. Nothing compared to what he had decided to accept in his life, but he knew that he was not there to judge. He was also responsible for a lot of mistakes.

'It's a small price to pay, but Giovanni, despite all our disagreements, promised me that she would always have everything she wanted. You see, he has a great affection for his niece, and he knows that my father's wish must be granted. We were brought up to treat family as the most important thing.' James tried to make Jonah understand some of the complexity of that story.

'That, for me, is an utter and complete madness. Your brother seems to be having an affair with her.' Jonah already seemed to show a certain jealousy for the girl. 'How is it that hindering a father from raising his own daughter something that goes in the way of treating family as the most important thing?

'They were punishing me for having a relationship out of wedlock and with a woman that was supposedly beneath my social standards. There was nothing I could do about it, at least not when the time was right. What comforts me is being able to live with her for part of the day, she is the one who takes care of the place where I'm being held hostage, so I can see her for a few moments during the week.' he replied putting an incredulous expression on Jonah's face.

'You don't mean to tell me...'

'Yes.' interrupted James. 'Lara and those two men were heading towards my room. We need to hurry, soon my brother will know that I have managed to escape.'

CHAPTER 12:

Jonah was still astonished by the story he had just heard from James. The facts narrated by the old man completely escaped the reality in which he had grown up. Despite being orphaned at a very young age, he was raised in an environment full of love from his grandparents and could never imagine a situation like that. He thought, and reflected, on his own situation. 'Wouldn't an abortion be better at times like that?', the question was very poorly resolved in the society he lived in, but he had long thought that freedom of choice would always be the best option. 'Too bad James didn't have that chance.', he thought, whilst imagining that the present they were living into would never have been possible if he and the mystery woman would have had the choice to reach a different decision.

The two continued walking through the humid tunnels that formed the underground below the estate of the Dartagnan Brothers Hotel. Walking underground made Jonah uncomfortable, it wasn't something that brought him any kind of joy, on the contrary, it made him wary and insecure. James seemed to know exactly where he was going, he hardly looked around or thought before following a direction as he came upon a crossroad, although an expression of concern showed that soon Giovanni, and the other members of his sect, would know that he had escaped his prison.

'How do you feel in Lara's presence when she sees you in prison?' Jonah tried to fill the gaps left with each new story he heard from the old man.

'I try not to let feelings get involved in this situation. I just act like someone who is in prison, I show a little anger for being locked up, but I try to make the situation as good as possible' he kept his posture. 'She knows about the fights between Giovanni and me, so she also knows that my future doesn't hold high hopes. Despite her proximity to my brother, I can see my daughter as a good person, and I prefer to think of her as someone neutral within all this chaos.'

Jonah was incredulous at how a family could act that way. He knew that things were different for everyone, but he could never imagined his grandparents would treating him in any way that resembled the one he had just witnessed; and, from as little as he knew of his parents, he was sure that they would never be able to put anything ahead of his well-being. However, that sort of obsession and exacerbated fundamentalism could turn even the best people into unimaginable monsters.

'What will happen when they discover you're no longer there?' Jonah tried not to express his concern.

'How should I know?' James showed sharpness when replying without taking his eyes off the road.

'I thought you might have an idea... Don't you know your brother?'

'He will send his henchmen after me, obviously, but the future is uncertain.'

'Will they suspect that I am with you?'

'One more question I don't know the answer to, my boy.' James seemed to be getting used to the inconvenient questions.

Jonah realised that time would bring him answers, and that James was in no position to make small talk. He needed to stay focused on what he was doing so that the cult members wouldn't find them. It was crucial that they managed to get out of that place without being captured.

He could remember the extension of the maze when he first saw it from the top of the stairs that started his journey. It was true that crossing the Dartagnan family traps had not been a short and simple process, but the place was not so big that it would take them so long to cross its underground. The path was practically a straight line, with some detours directed to the left which, according to James, would take them to the church where the C.P.F. meetings were held.

'Be silent.' whispered James as he suddenly stopped and pushed Jonah against the damp muddy wall one more time.

He tried to open his mouth to ask what was going on, but managed to control himself and wait for whatever the danger was to pass, so that James could explain the reason for getting him even more dirty. He noticed that the old one-legged man put his finger on his lips, making a sign of silence, which showed how crucial it was for Jonah to keep his mouth shut. They could not find any opening between the walls so that they could hide like they did before. They had to rely only on luck so the darkness would be enough to keep them hidden. James quickly turned off the flashlight as he steadied himself without one of the crutches he had dropped on the floor, supporting his balance on Jonah's chest. He kept his eyes closed the entire time they stood still, he seemed vehemently concerned about the situation he expected to happen.

A few seconds after being pushed against the wall, Jonah could hear the trampling of people who were running down the same corridor that he and James had passed. It was the same three people. Lara, accompanied by two men, crossed their path in a great hurry and without looking around.

'They've already found out.' concluded Jonah.

'Yes, and they are going towards the church to alert Giovanni, which means the sect is already in session.'

'But what about the party?' asked Jonah as he remembered Giovanni's promise that the celebrations had no time to end.

'That's not a problem, they take turns during the party. What intrigues me is the possible reason for this meeting. I believe that they are preparing a penance for someone.'

'Someone who's at the party or someone they already kept prisoner?'

'Probably someone they've been holding for some time, they usually study them meticulously so the punishment for a person is executed right.

'Then the session will be interrupted?' asked Jonah, imagining that Giovanni's priority would be to find James.

'I think so, but we can't let them capture us.'

'I understand that we must change course. Where then?' asked Jonah as he reached for the crutch that James had dropped on the floor.

'On the contrary, the church is the best place we can go.'

'Won't there be security? Or people waiting for us?'

'I know my brother, he would never think that we were going towards the church. Even better, I know this place like the back of my hand, I know exactly where we can hide.'

Jonah let James guide the way once again, whilst he could observe the footprints left by Lara's small feet, clearly distinct from the others left by the robust men who accompanied her.

He managed to follow James for a few meters, until he realised that the old man slowed down and turned in his direction, whilst his mouth seemed to open in a slow motion. Despite seeing a clear expression of surprise mixed with fear in James's eyes, Jonah was unable to hear any of the words dissipated by the reverberated sound of his vocal cords.

What was a clear image of a man trying to tell him something, in less than a second, turned into darkness followed by a strong impact that he couldn't see from where was coming.

"Darkness took over the imaginable for a brief period of time, but the scenario that soon spread through his mind was unlike anything he had ever seen.

'Hi love.' said a distinct voice.

He was sure he knew that voice. The subtlety of the sweet sparkle, that spread through those few letters, was the same as he had become used to waking up for a long time. Joana's voice was indistinguishable.

'Good Morning.' said Jonah as he opened a big smile on his face and tried to bring his nose closer to his girlfriend's neck, as he did every day. Her sheer, natural smell, released by a perfect combination of pheromones, made Jonah fall in love every day with the woman who had chosen him.

'Were you dreaming?' she asked as she gently passed her hand over his forehead.

'You know what... I can't remember. I just hope I'm not dreaming right now.' he replied, always trying to be the romantic one.

Joana let her hand slide over Jonah's chest, seeking to meet the small birthmark that mimicked what she used say was a link between the two.

'Have you heard about Plato's Myth of Soulmates?' she asked as she fixed her gaze on the small spot, lightly circling it with her fingers.

'No, but I have a slight impression that you can explain it to me...' replied Jonah as he opened a sincere smile, whilst admiring the stunning beauty of his passionate girlfriend.

'Of course I can!' she said as she suddenly jumped underneath the sheets and wrapped her arms around Jonah.

He knew he needn't say anything, all he had to do was just watch as the love of his life did another one of her demonstrations of knowledge, which impressed Jonah more than any beauty she might have had.

'Plato describes in his book, The Banquet, that men, in the beginning of time, were complete beings: two heads, four legs and four arms.' she began to explain, whilst Jonah began to focus all his attention on the fascinating story that was about to come. 'However, these men began to feel so powerful that they decided to face the gods in paradise, trying to take it for themselves. I believe you know where I'm getting at...' she finished as she turned on the bed, pointing her bare chest upwards.

'No, obviously I don't know... Can you finish the story?'

'I love it when you get curious!' she met Jonah's gaze again whilst expelling passionate and admiring laughter.

Jonah just rolled over his eyes as if he was ashamed, hoping that Joana would return to her story as it had finally caught his attention.

'Obviously, the gods won the fight and decided to exterminate all men from the land, but Zeus decided to give them an even more cruel fate, and the men ended up cut in half and thrown back into the land, as a form of punishment.'

'Why is it a punishment?'

'Besides being cut in fucking half?' she laughed. 'Because men, and now women, began to feel an unknown desire. Something they didn't know where it came from. That's what, in my opinion, the feeling of missing someone means.'

'So men lost their half forever? Is that what soulmate means?' Jonah tried to interact with the little of the story he was being able to follow so he wouldn't appear so stupid.

'Not really. Today's men, in fact, have forgotten that they were once a complete being. They don't really understand what missing someone means, but Plato explains that the fact that we were full in the past, makes us search endlessly for an unattainable love and for the intangible meaning of feeling full again. At least that's what the story means to me.' the depth of Joana's reasoning made Jonah completely lost whilst admiring the bright blue color of her eyes.

'And why is that story going through that little beautiful mind of yours in this particular moment? What drives this beautiful and brilliant brain to seek such profound answers?' asked Jonah, unable to contain the smile that suddenly appeared in his mouth.

'Do you see this mark here?' she said as she ran her finger over Jonah' chest as she brushed away the hair that covered the small brown spot.

Jonah was admiring the birthmark that he hardly ever noticed.

'I have the same one!' she said as she reached for Jonah's hand and took it to her chest in the exact opposite of his. 'If we face each other, our birthmarks meet. Do you understand what I mean now?'

'Yes.' he said as he blushed in a mixture of passion and embarrassment.

'I am sure that today I feel whole and full. I found the meaning I was looking for in love as it had always been a mystery to me.' Joana had an incredible way with words. She knew exactly what to say to completely hold Jonah's attention.

She hugged Jonah tightly again, making the two marks meet at the exact same point.

'Can you feel this energy?'

'What I feel when I'm with you is something so strong that I couldn't possibly measure with words, at least not the way you do it. I don't have that ease to describe love.' Jonah tried to reciprocate the gesture.

'Love is not a strong enough word, nor perhaps a feeling of such magnitude, to describe what I feel for you.' she said whilst leaving a light kiss on the small mark and resting her head on Jonah's chest.

Jonah felt an immense lightness in his body. Life seemed to have a complete meaning at that very moment, exactly as she had just described the myth of soulmates. The love of his life was lying in his arms, and time no longer made sense as eternity seemed to have a definite destiny. It was all he could ever imagine, but he could never think that he would feel anything that intense for anyone in the world. Everything about Joana was perfect to him, and the love he felt for her could not be better described than how it had been.

He felt his eyes were slowly beginning to blink, but the light sleep that was taking over his mind, and the comfort he felt at the proximity of the woman he loved, were suddenly replaced by an exuberant cry of agony. A high-pitched scream, so loud that it started to echo in his numb mind. Joana no longer had the same expression of happiness, and the scene before his eyes was no longer the comfort of his bed.

'Why Jonah, why did you go do this to me? Were my words of love worthless? Did my devotion to our relationship mean nothing to you?' Joana's words tore the imperative feeling of calmness apart whilst the expression of happiness on her face was taken by one of pain and anguish that Jonah so much hated to infringe on those he loved.

The scenario was completely different. The room with the soft bed had been replaced by a dank underground that stank off faeces and urine. Dirty water was pouring from between her legs as the sole image of her sobbing face flooding with tears reflected through his mind in a terrifying way.

She was no longer naked, but covered in a white nightgown with a badly knotted cloth over the neck that covered every part of her body, even beyond where his vision could reach. The bottom of the nightgown was covered by a mixture of fresh blood and the sludge created by the sewage, whilst the upper part was gradually touched by the tears of blood that Joana spilled from her eyes.

'Why Jonah, I loved you so much' she exclaimed as Jonah tried, and failed, to reach to his girlfriend for comfort.

He started to cry at the same time that despair overcame sobriety, because nothing he tried to do to control the situation had any effect. The more he tried to touch Joana's body, so that she could explain what was happening, the less he felt he was able to get close to the woman. Jonah began to feel a new wave of water crossing his half-opened legs, hot water, almost fervent, with a stark red color that he could only define as blood.

His body was petrified, and his wishes were repeatedly rejected by his brain. He even tried to turn his face away so that he no longer had to face the truth that was before his eyes, but every side he turned to, his eyes would forcibly open and show the image of Joana screaming and bleeding.

'Why Jonah? WHY?'"

Jonah could see that he had returned to reality as that definitely felt like a dream, a situation he had never experienced in his life. He could remember learning about the Myth of Soulmates, by Plato, at school, but he had never had that conversation with Joana, much less been with her trapped in a sewer. The scenario that terrified his mind had left room for the old situation he was in before returning from that trance, and Joana's pleading cries were drowned out by the silence that reigned within the underground that was overlaid by the maze of the Dartagnan Brothers Hotel. His head throbbed with pain, but now the pain was physical and it didn't come from inside his head like the one caused by the drugs he had been taking all night.

He ran his hand over his head, trying to clean the blood that was dripping from the blow he had taken. He had no idea of how much time had passed since he was there. He ran his hand towards his pocket, after drying the blood on his dirty pants, looking for the phone that would tell him the time, but he was not able to find it.

He tried to open his eyes widely and began to whisper James's name in search of any sign of life, but he did not receive an answer nor he could identify any remaining vestiges that would spot the his presence.

The marks left by the footprints indicated the presence and the direction taken by James, along with those off the members of Giovanni's sect. A distinct step of an old slipper marked the unique step of the old one-legged man who, clearly, had left that place against his will, but what caught his attention the most was the same footprint he had seen before, on a clearly smaller and feminine foot, which indicated that Lara had been there.

Jonah was unable to understand why he was left behind. It made no sense that they would leave him over there, after all, he was the one being chased that night. 'It may be that this is part of Giovanni's plans for me.', he thought as he sighed with tiredness. He had been walking all over that place for hours without finding any indication that he might soon be able to leave.

'Focus!', he said to himself as he realised he was, once again, alone. He had to get up and get out of there as soon as possible. The dirt that was taking over of his body no longer mattered to him, he didn't even bother to shake it off as he got up from the damp floor.

The logic to be followed was that of the footprints left by James and those who took him by force. It had become clear to him that soon the old man's distinct footstep had stopped following the others. The members of the sect must have carried him over so that they would not waste time on James's slow limp, since his crutches had been abandoned in the same place where Jonah had last seen his face.

He went on to follow the strangers steps to another crossroad. The clear image of the footprints indicated that the path taken was the one towards the left, the same way they were following to get to the small church, the infamous place that James said he knew like the back of his hand, the same place where they could seek a way out.

Jonah continued to follow, but the physical pain in his head began to give way to the pain he had been feeling before. He could clearly feel that he would soon have another one of those psychotic episodes. That would not be the best time for him to fall into the ground; the footprints on the damp ground were already starting to dry. The pain came in full force. A pain that he had not yet witnessed.

'Stop doing this to me!' he shouted haphazardly, remembering that Dr. Douglas had warned Giovanni that it could not be done that way, and the effects of the wrongdoing were beginning to appear.

His body rocked forward and bounced back as he tried to maintain his balance, which was in vain, since only his mind had left his static body to return with force. The image of the wet mud with dry footprints began to become distorted. Its sharpness left room for a sequence of meaningless images that intertwined between each other. Although his headache was now stronger, it was unable to bring him down at this time. He continued to walk after the tracks that were now getting difficult to see.

He halted and looked back, trying to find the marks he had just passed, but there was nothing there anymore. The damp mud floor had given way to a clean white tile surface, it was so clean it looked like it had been polished just a few minutes ago. Jonah closed his eyes tightly again, trying to dispel that distinct attack he was starting to have. He even sat on the floor, waiting for the other reality to come and take control of his body once and for all as the drugs would take over his brain and put a stop to the shuffling of his thoughts.

His effort was in vain.

The footprints were completely gone. The floor continued to change color, now less frequently, allowing the white tile to become more and more prevalent. He got up again and started running in the same direction he was before.

'Jonah?' he heard mouthless voices again.

'Enough, please, enough!' he pleaded as he stood still.

Each time he closed and opened his eyes, he felt a sudden change in the way he perceived reality. The humidity and cold that prevailed in the underground of the Dartagnan Brothers Hotel, combined with the loneliness that old James had left when he was kidnapped, was giving place to the comfort of a mild climate and the feeling of cleanliness in his body carried by the touch of a warm hand on his arm, but the soft and delicate skin, like the voice that called his name, had no owner.

He shook his head and opened his eyes seeking to come back to reality once and for all. His dirty, bruised, and aching body returned to feel the pains left by the events of that night, but the feeling that something was not right was latent. Jonah sought to find any remnants of concentration that he might still be able to sustain. He looked around, searching for the best way to situate himself to what was happening.

It no longer interested him if his whereabouts were known to Giovanni and the other members of the sect. If he was still there, it was because they wanted him there, well and alive.

'Anyone here?' he shouted betting on the chance of someone coming about and rescuing him out of that place.

The silence was imperative to muffle the sound of any response that might have been propagated, which was interrupted by the intense headache that returned to torment him.

His mind went back to transit between different realities, the floor turned to white tiles again, which made no sense to him, since he had been lying on a bed in that small room for a long time and could not see its colour.

'Can you hear me?' another unowned voice echoed in his mind as his eyes saw only the transition from the white floor to the muddy one.

The feel of the soft-skinned hand had been replaced by a tightening of his wrist. He tried to move it, but the force was so great that he could barely move his hand.

'Am I able to move?', he thought warily, as until then he had been unable to make any movement whilst he was having one of those psychotic episodes. He felt that, although his wrists were tightly attached, he could now slowly move his fingers. What looked like another one of those outbreaks, came to be perceived more and more as a reality.

'Who's there?' the words thought inside his mind reverberated through his mouth, giving voice to what was previously just an appeal for sound.

His headache started to fade as his consciousness could take control of the situation. Gradually he managed to open his eyes and notice that his neck moved as it answered to the orders given by his brain, his mouth opened, and his eyebrows frowned whilst he managed, little by little, to understand the situation and analyse what was happening.

His wrists were still trapped to the well-known dream chair. Despite being able to slightly move his neck, Jonah felt that his head movements were still limited by two side plates that prevented him from fully seeing what was going around him, which was a quite odd as he had no memory off seeing the floor on that room. 'How can I know the these are white titles?', he asked himself as he tried to move his neck around.

'Stay calm. We are waiting for you to wake up completely, we will soon unshackle you from the chair.'

The voice was clear. Lara Farlet was there, he smelled her perfume again whilst trying to attach a face to the voice he heard, but the only thing he could see was the door to the small room where he had been having psychotic outbreaks.

As his head was freed, he then tried to find bottles, dirty glasses or cigarette butts that he remembered being left there by the people that were tormenting him, but there was no sign from Giovanni, Monalisa, Douglas, nor from the perverted priest, just the white of the floor that gleamed the dark red of the walls and the voice of Lara Farlet.

'Or is it Lara Dartagnan?', he thought as he waited to be forcibly removed from that chair and dragged into some kind of medieval structure where they were going to torture him until his eventual death could sufficiently serve the penance established by Giovanni.

Jonah sought to remain calm, despite knowing who those people really were. He was still treading in unknown territory and did not think he would be able to get out of that place by the use of force.

He was lucid. His thoughts surfaced inside his mind as the flood of drugs inside his veins had not let it happen for a long time. He was able to remember everything that happened during that night and he knew that this was not his true reality. He knew he was having a psychotic attack like the many others he have had whilst wandering the most distant paths of that state. He knew the whole truth about the Dartagnan family, and he knew that his goal was still to get out of that place alive.

What he didn't know was why this outbreak was different from the others. Why was he able to move and talk now? How long before he could get back to reality?

'Finally! Welcome back, Jonah.' Giovanni's distinct voice echoed through the room, as he stormed through the door, causing Jonah to lose his composure and start to cry.

CHAPTER 13:

The more Jonah tried to understand what was going on, the more agitated he became. The sensation he was feeling was too real for it to be a dream or one of those psychotic episodes, he hadn't cried with that intensity since he ended his relationship with Joana Clemente.

Giovanni Dartagnan's face took over his field of vision, and his head was outlined by the strong light that previously hindered his vision. He tried to find any other known face, but the one of the man who was trying to ruin his life was the only one that would stand out.

'I need you to stay calm, my friend. You've been pretty much out of it for quite some time.' Giovanni's voice sounded with an ease that aimed to calm Jonah's mind.

Gradually, Jonah managed to stop crying and tried to make sure his thoughts made sense. 'That was not a dream...', he thought as he sought all the care in the world so he wouldn't say anything that had happened with him to Giovanni or anyone else.

'Where am I?' he finally managed to say.

'You're under my care.' Douglas's voice followed as he came to be a part of Jonah's point of view. There was still no sign of the priest or Monalisa, but Lara was around there somewhere.

'What happened to me?' he started with the most obvious question, trying to get into the game as he knew he had to.

'You don't remember anything?' asked Giovanni with an expression of curiosity.

'I do remember. I remember many things, but what I want to know is why I am tied up to this chair?' he asked as he raised his voice. Jonah, even though still dizzy due to to being recently woken up, couldn't remember having had that kind of confidence before.

'Sorry, we were worried that you might get hurt.' replied Giovanni, nodding in Douglas's direction se he would release the bonds that held Jonah's hands.

Everything seemed to be developing very easily, Jonah did not expect that he would be able to speak to Mr. Dartagnan that way and still be answered. It went against everything that had been going through for the past few hours, but he knew he couldn't get carried away by the cult leader's false kind impression, he needed to gain his trust and thus use it to his advantage.

'Wow, wow. Easy now!' exclaimed Giovanni as he jumped back when he realised that Jonah went to meet him as soon as he had his bonds loose. 'What's going on with you?'

'You! Don't play dumb with me!' shouted Jonah whilst being held by Douglas.

'Jonah, what happened?' he saw Lara's beautiful face.

'Where am I?' he asked, once again, without exhaling trust to anyone around. He knew he needed to be smarter than the others if he wanted to leave that hotel unharmed.

'You're in a recovery room, under my care.' Douglas repeated himself.

'Can you remember anything that happened in your dreams?' Giovanni asked once again.

'How long have I been stuck to this chair?' Jonah wanted to make sure that the time in that psychotic attack was the same as the reality he hoped to return.

'A few hours. We were worried.' Lara sounded sincere.

The three of them made a startled look towards Jonah.

He shook his head from side to side, trying to seek answers in the small room. He kept looking around for Monalisa and the priest, but there was no sign that they were anywhere to be found. 'Soon I will return to reality, but now I must take advantage of my lucidity in this place to find answers.', he thought as he realised that soon his head would hurt again.

'Do you remember what you dreamed of?' Douglas repeated Giovanni's unanswered question.

'Dreamed?' Jonah began to be frightened by the sense of reality that the conversation was giving him, letting the emotional start to override reason and spoil the brief moment of confidence he had just had.

What do you think you were doing in this chair until now?' asked Lara.

'I... I don't know? You tell me!'

'You got sick after some time at the party.' she started to answer.

'We brought you here so that Douglas could help you regain your consciousness.' interrupted Giovanni, who was looking at him with a worried expression.

Obviously, none of that made any sense to him, since that situation was just the result of a misunderstood lucid dream, something he was just beginning to understand, but the lucidity with which he could think, and the concreteness of the events that were taking place around him, started to scare him. Before, he couldn't even move inside the small red room, but now he was fully aware of everything that was happening.

He promptly went off to check his new arms tattoos. That moment startled him. Despite feeling a slight discomfort in his arm, the two tattoos were completely gone. He tried to strongly rub against any makeup that might have been put over them, as he noticed that Giovanni and Lara glanced at him with a certain concern, but he knew exactly what they were looking for. His body was sore, as if she had just been doing hours of physical exercise; he could see some scratches on his legs and arms, but nothing that matched the state he was supposed to be in according to what he had just lived so vividly.

His clothes were clean and hung on a hook that was nailed to the door, whilst he was wearing a white t-shirt and short pants off the same color, which he couldn't remember ever seeing before.

But those were just some petty problems, and he knew that he could not let his fear be shown, but rather extract as much information as possible so that he could leave that place alive.

'Can I talk to you alone?' he finally broke the silence when he met Giovanni Dartagnan's eyes.

The charming old man nodded indicating that Lara and Douglas should leave the room. He started walking with his hands crossed behind his back as he watched Jonah looking for something different throughout his body.

'Of course I wouldn't be a fucking mess in here, this is just a dream...', he started to think. 'But the tattoos should be here, I remember seeing Giovanni watching them before.',

164

he concluded so that he could turn his attention back to Mr. Dartagnan.

'Why don't you explain what is happening to me?' he asked trying to look as sane as possible.

'Which part you don't understand?' asked Giovanni, giving him a surprised look. 'It seems to me that we were very clear about what just happened here, right? You were sick during the party because you used the wrong drug before using the dream chair.'

Jonah waited for Giovanni to say something more before he could start asking questions again.

'Don't you remember when you passed out in the middle of the main hall?' Giovanni asked before giving enough time for Jonah to organise his thoughts.

'I do remember that, yes.' he replied dryly to relive himself of the memory of his first psychotic attack that night.

Jonah decided it would be better not to tell Giovanni everything he remembered, but he did went through a step by step of what he had in his mind up to that point so he could see the expression on his face and activate his memory so that he could remember any other details that might be useful to him.

'And it was at this very moment that we brought you here. You fell on the floor, waking up just now.' said Giovanni whilst looking seriously at Jonah. 'Do you remember anything else after crumbling into the floor?'

'I remember dreaming several things...' Jonah tried to get into Giovanni's game without giving out information. 'Actually, I remember this situation here being the dream.'

'How do you mean?'

'I remember being in this room, with you.'

'But you've been knocked out all the time.' Giovanni started to become more defensive.

'Short moments...' Jonah didn't want to define what those moments were, because the new information seemed to have made Giovanni uneasy.

'And the rest of the time?'

'I remember dreaming, and if you are telling me that this is my reality, I dreamed a lot.' said Jonah trying to establish a leading role into that game.

'And what exactly were these dreams?'

'Why don't you tell me?' Jonah's tone was outrageous.

'What are you implying?'

'Nothing, despite the fact that you were controlling my dreams through this chair' he said as he pointed to the place where he had been previously held.

'We were monitoring your life signs, that's all.' Giovanni defended himself.

'So why was I tied to this chair? Isn't it like one of those in the dream room?' Jonah noticed he was managing to put Giovanni in a difficult situation.

'Listen here, boy. We are here to help you, I do not understand this accusatory tone of yours.' Giovanni was starting to get startled. 'You were stuck to this chair because this situation was unprecedented, we had never had anyone who took the wrong drug before being connected to one of these chairs. We monitored your vital signs and your brain waves for your own good!'

Jonah could feel that Giovanni was losing his patience to that accusatory and demanding intonation as the two looked at each other with unfriendly expressions. Jonah knew it wouldn't be easy to win that fight. Whatever the situation was, dream or no dream, Giovanni had the advantage, and Jonah needed to be smart so that he would not be fooled by the theatrical rhetoric that Giovanni was posing with his elegance and good manners.

'So, why don't you tell me more about these dreams you had whilst recovering.' said Giovanni as he walked slowly in front of Jonah.

He was really trying not to say more than he needed to, but the situation was not the best and the atmosphere of the conversation did not seem to favor him. 'If this is a dream, I have no reason to be afraid.', he thought logically as he realised that the reality would not be influenced by that conversation.

'It is a bit weird for you to tell me that these dreams I had whilst recovering were not induced by the chair.' began Jonah with an ironic tone, already bringing an angry expression in Giovanni's face.

'And why do you say that?' Mr. Dartagnan was clearly trying to keep himself calm.

'Because I never met your brother in my life, and there he was.'

Jonah finished that sentence knowing that he could not return from that point in time. Either that was a dream or his true reality, that information would tell Giovanni everything he needed to know as the owner of that immense property would already be aware of everything that his brother would have told Jonah about him.

'My brother? That is, indeed, very strange.' he said with a really confused expression.

'Strange how? Because he manage to get out of his confinement?' Jonah was defiant again.

'Don't let these dreams make you lose track of where you are young man, I have every right to defend my honor in my own house.'

Giovanni continued to keep a confused expression, but he didn't want to give the impression that Jonah might be leading the conversation.

'But tell me more, what did my brother tell you?'

'You know what, I can't really remember it very well... But I do remember talking to him for a long time at the end of the maze that runs through this land.'

Giovanni pulled a smirk. He could see that Jonah wouldn't be stupid enough to contradict himself in his own speech, not in a moment of tension like that. The pompous man could clearly see that Jonah was hiding much more than he let on.

'Well then, Jonah...'

Mr. Dartagnan began his speech as he cleared his throat and lit a cigarette. Jonah had already noticed that the man only smoked when he seemed to have something important to say.

'What do you mean to tell me with all this?' he continued as he blew smoke through his reddened nostrils. 'Let me help you, young man. Show me what's going on in that head of yours. Do you really think that I'm here plotting some evil crazy nonsense and that my supposed brother appeared in your dreams to warn you about it?'

Jonah realised, in that very second, that he had never mentioned any 'evil crazy nonsense' in any of his words. Giovanni had just blurted out that something was wrong there and that Jonah wasn't as crazy as he wanted to make it look like. However, if his theory was right and that was really a dream, he could not waste more time with that pointless conversation. He had Giovanni right where he wanted: curious and uneasy.

'What happened to James?' he went straight to the point.

'James...' Giovanni replied with a nostalgic sigh.

'So I'm right then?'

Giovanni did not answer.

'Why don't you put your suit back on so we can get back to the party. I have a few things that I want to show you.' he said as he took another drag off his cigarette.

'Isn't the party over yet? What fucking time is it?' Jonah was surprised that people still could catch their breath after all the time they had been partying.

'A few minutes past six.' replied Giovanni, looking at the shiny golden watch on his wrist.

That was kind of what Jonah had in mind. Whatever reality he was living in, time had passed at the same speed. He wasn't sure of the right time, but he knew dawn was about to come.

'Have you seen my phone?' he asked when he remembered that he could find some answers if he could get his hands on the device. 'And my friend, Patrick, do you know where I can find him?'

'I have no idea of where your phone might be. And Patrick is likely to be at the party, your friend is a very exciting person.' that sounded exactly like Patrick.

Giovanni turned his back and went out the door, after putting out his cigarette inside a glass nursing a warmed out drink that was perched on a small wooden bench close to where Jonah's clothes were hanging.

Jonah got up from his chair and started changing his clothes so he could accompany Giovanni to the party. His suit was clean, smelling good, and perfectly pressed, showing no sign that it had been dirty by clay, mood, or any of the other weird fluid he had encountered whilst he was inside the maze. He looked again at his bare arms to search for the tattoos that were so vivid to him before, spat on his fingertips and rubbed the exact spot where the small inverted cross had been marked on his body in the hope of washing off any sort of makeup. The pain was definitely there, or at least some kind of placebo effect, but there was no sign that his skin had been pierced by needles.

His shoes were polished and his socks stretched over them. Jonah removed the glass containing the cigarette butt and placed it on the floor so he could sit on the bench to put on his shoes on. He felt that his feet were a bit sore, but that didn't tell him anything, as his shoes were not that comfortable and he usually got blisters on the soles of his feet after standing up or walking for too long.

He stood up sharply, ready to face whatever was waiting for him behind the door that Giovanni had just closed after himself. He collected the clothes he was wearing just a few minutes ago, and pushed the small wooden bench towards the wall. A sharp noise of splinters crashing on the floor caught his attention after giving him a small fright, it was when he realised that he had not yet completely recovered his attention and dexterity, he was still a little dizzy for having spent so much time sleeping on that chair.

He crouched on the floor to collect the small pieces of glass and place them inside the larger part of the glass that had not been broken by the short fall. The cigarette butt caught his attention as it was still burning. It seemed that Giovanni's intention was to put out the ember, but the cigarette was completely dry as it had not reached the liquid. He kept collecting the small pieces until he could notice a small detail in a shard from the glass that had broken into a 'V' shape. The marks of a dark red lipstick intoned the shard and gave it the shape of a small lip that quenched its thirst there before the glass was tucked away.

For a brief period of time, he thought the mark would be Lara's, but even though he was still a little stunned by his newly awaken state, he could still analyse the beauty of that radiant woman to the smallest detail. 'If she was wearing a lipstick like that, I would have noticed.', he thought before concluding that another woman had been around there whilst he slept.

Monalisa. 'Of course I'm not going completely mad, that woman was here.', he put those words into his mind so he could remember to observe which lipstick that eerie old

169

lady was wearing. He knew that as soon as he arrived at the party he would find her, more than explicitly, she was the one who flattered Mr. Dartagnan the most.

Jonah went through every possible pocket, but his hands couldn't find the telephone he needed so much, even though it would probably be useless right then. He tightened and adjusted his tie, which was probably tied by Lara, before closing his jacket and going out to meet Giovanni, who was waiting for him on the other side of the door he had stared at for hours whilst dreaming without being able to reach it. 'Whatever that means, it is an advance.', he thought before turning the knob to face Mr. Dartagnan.

'Shall we?' asked Giovanni as he motioned for Jonah to start walking beside him whilst their slow steps were syncing.

He softly sighed before following Giovanni's footsteps. His shoes were grunting from the freshly washed rubber and his eye-lids were still heavy from long lasting sleep. Giovanni smirked and softly ran his hand over his face as he scratched his well-groomed beard, his walk was sturdy for a man of his age, but Jonah could see that the distinguished Mr. Dartagnan was already beginning to suffer from the mishaps of ageing.

'How old are you?' asked Jonah sharply.

'No one has asked me that question in a long time.' said Giovanni, laughing at Jonah's lack of sensitivity.

'I see that people are afraid of you.'

'I prefer to think that what you call fear is respect.'

'Is it that bad? Letting people know your age?'

'No, but it's a little dowdy. I'm sixty-two years old, which means I deserve a little respect, don't you think?'

Jonah didn't want to answer that. He always thought that people would be worthy of respect when the attitude was reciprocal, and not simply because of their age difference.

'Can I stop by my room? I would like to speak with Patrick before... Before what again?' he asked as he realised he didn't know where they were going.

'Jonah, you are not a hostage here, you can do whatever you want. But I already told you that your friend must be at the party, if you want to check, the room is right there in front of you.' replied Giovanni, pointing to a door just a few meters away. 'As for what we're going to do, I have something I want to show you.'

Jonah followed up the path and stopped in front of the door to Patrick's room, which was next to his own. At least now that idea of interconnected rooms would do him some good. He fumbled through his jacket pockets until he found the magnetic key that would open his door. His room was clean, as he had left it, and there was no sign that anyone had passed by it. He tried to open the door that connected his room with Patrick's, but it was locked. He knocked loudly and intoned his friend's name even louder, yet his voice reverberated through his own room without making any substancial noise that would invite an answer from behind the door.

'As I told you before, your friend must be at the party.' Giovanni made the same gesture with his hand so that Jonah would accompany him again.

The two went on walking down the narrow corridor as silence had taken over the lack of conversation. Jonah realised that he did not know the age difference between the two Dartagnan brothers, but decided to leave that question for later on; he was very curious to know what the head of the sect had to show him.

They walked on and opened the door to the main hotel hall.

People were still dancing and chatting away. The music was calmer and the tiredness was palpable, although the windows were open, Jonah could smell the alcohol that emanated from the crowd that had been drinking tirelessly for hours.

'Don't these people ever get tired?' he asked when thinking that if he, at that age, no longer had the same energy to endure that much party time, the elders should be exhausted by then.

'When you went to the Dream Room, didn't you feel your energies renewed?'

'Don't you remember that you gave me the wrong drug?' he was trying to reply to every question as if he didn't know anything he had learned in the time he spent inside the maze with James. It would be wiser that, for everyone around, he was experiencing that reality, and that Giovanni was speaking the truth.

'It is true. But now you woke up well, didn't you?'

'Yes, but it was because I slept, wasn't it? You said it yourself that I was not being induced to lucid dreaming.' Jonah frowned to show a certain irony in the rhetoric.

'Exactly! We had to put you to sleep so that the effect of the wrong drug would wear off and your brain would function properly once again. As I told you before, this is the first time this has ever happened.'

Giovanni's premise, once again, was valid. 'He has a fucking answer for everything.', thought Jonah, as he noticed that it would not be that easy to get information from Mr. Dartagnan, but he knew exactly what they were injecting into his body and also what Patrick had wrongfully given him in.

'Patrick must be here then?' he asked as he carefully passed his eyes through every corner of the room.

'Most likely, but this place is too big for you to find him now. I really need to show you something so that we can clear up all those thoughts that are going through that young mind of yours.'

Jonah really wanted to see his friend. The last time he saw him, he was being dismembered whilst laid into a medieval torture bed. However, the curiosity in what Giovanni had to show him was greater than anything else at that moment.

They made their way trough the same door that had taken him to the maze before. Jonah became more and more anxious as he could see what that place was like in daylight. Anxiety started to mix with a feeling of anguish and fear; he had promised to never set foot in that place again. The dew gave a beautiful color to the lawn in front of the maze and the morning cold made Jonah shudder and close the first button on his jacket.

'It's beautiful, isn't it?' said Giovanni, leaning on the porch that supported the two huge granite stairs.

'You have a property that can make anyone envious. In fact, why don't you advertise and open this place to the public?' he asked, knowing the exact answer.

'Are you a religious man, Jonah?' he asked admiring the immensity of that place and ignoring what had just been said.

'I was raised by catholics, but I never preached about it, to be honest.' he replied without having to lie.

'I like to think that all of this is a divine work, a blessing from god, the creator of everything.'

Giovanni spoke as if Jonah was not around. It seemed that he was an inanimate figure, an object for which Mr. Dartagnan was venting and telling stories.. The host continued babbling words related to religion and his beliefs without being able to hold Jonah's attention. He was more concerned with admiring the astonishing maze that could be depicted as his worst nightmare just a few hours ago, and now took all of his attention with its beauty.

Things became much clearer in the daylight, he could clearly see the entrance and exit at the bottom of the maze. The water fountain was there, now empty and without the presence of the already caught old one-legged man who had tried so hard to help Jonah out of that place and, even further, he could observe the small hut that had sheltered them for a short period of time. The place where James told him about the C.P.F.

'Would you mind?' Jonah heard Giovanni say as he emerged from the trance that had taken over his attention.

'Hm?' he replied without any parsimony.

'I asked if you would mind accompanying me to a place nearby, I want to show you something, remember?'

'Oh, sure, but do we need to go through this maze? I don't feel very well in closed places.' he lied as it there was no chance he would be alone with Giovanni in his own future grave.

'No, no.' he said with a brief laugh. 'It is just around the corner from the hotel, I have a small chapel nearby, please follow me.'

Jonah shivered. 'Now there is no turning back.', he thought as he made sense of it, feeling that it would be useless to say no to Mr. Dartagnan. If he wanted to force him to do something, it would be as easy as a simply invitation. The logical reasoning was simple: better to go willingly and loose, than forced and tied. Besides, Jonah was still not convinced that this was nothing more than another of those lucid dreams, but with an extra touch of reality. The symptoms of the so called depersonalisation had made a real number on his mind.

'What are we going to do in this church?' asked Jonah as the two descended one side of the magnificent stone staircase leading to the garden.

'We are not going to the church, but to a place nearby. You seem very anxious Jonah, just wait and see.'

Jonah started walking next to Giovanni once again, he was really curious to know where the old Mr. Dartagnan was taking him. If the church was not the destination now, surely he would come to know the rooms of Mr. Dartagnan's sect, which he imagined to be the ones he had experienced whilst taking on the role of Patrick in what appeared to be one of his own lucid dreams.

They continued to walk until they turned the corner of the base of the Dartagnan Brothers Hotel. Jonah wondered what was stored inside that huge basement surrounded by a wall of huge stones and covered with sparse vegetation. In fact, he wondered about the underground plant where he was and whether old James would have been taken to some old torture room that Giovanni and his troupe of fanatics certainly had down there.

Jonah was able to see, from a distance, the small church that James had mentioned so much in his stories and that Giovanni had just called a chapel. The building was short in stature, with thick pillars, and a few windows with rounded arches, what was a clear representation of Romanesque architecture from the early Middle Ages. Although small, that church had nothing simple or any resemblance to a mere chapel. It was robust and full of details, surely the Dartagnan family would have spent a lot of money to make sure that structure would take such a beautiful shape. The church gave an idea of heavy construction, stuck in the ground and practically impossible to be felled. It really was a temple of worship, and it was very likely that Giovanni Dartagnan would not let anyone get in without being invited.

'Splendid, isn't it?' he stopped suddenly and started admiring the architectural work as if he had never seen it before.

'A beautiful structure indeed. You calling it a chapel doesn't really do it any justice.' said Jonah.

'It was built by my family many years ago. Wait until you see the inside.'

'Is that where we are going?' he asked again.

'Not yet. Follow me, please.'

Giovanni and Jonah started walking again, but in the opposite direction from the Dartagnan family church. They approached a small structure with low walls, which must have been less than a meter high. The entrance was signalled by two high iron gates - more than twice the size of the walls - which were marked by the Dartagnan family crest.

'You wanted to know about my brother.' said Giovanni after crossing the gate and stopping suddenly. 'There he is.'

It took Jonah a few minutes to realise where he was, as he could see the corner of the maze where he had spent the last night lost. It was only when he read the words embedded in a stone right in front of his eyes that he realised where Giovanni had taken him: 'Here lies James Dartagnan. Rest in peace.'

CHAPTER 14:

Jonah's eyes were taken by a momentary surprise. He read, and reread the words on the tomb several times until he could be sure that his mind was not playing tricks on him due to the mental confusion he had been suffering all night; and, as it seemed, that was the tomb of James Dartagnan. 'Born: September 7, 1954; Dead: December 7, 2019.', the dates were engraved just below the small phrase that symbolised what was once someone's existence.

'You mentioned my brother before. I have no idea of how he could have appeared in your dreams, but there he is.' said Giovanni, pointing to the tomb that Jonah was looking at very closely.

'That proves nothing.', he thought, knowing how easy it would be for Giovanni to build a fake tomb within his own land.

'He died not long ago...' said Jonah whilst looking at the small inscription of the tomb. 'How did he go?'

'He was sick, diabetes.' replied Giovanni, making the a cross sign whilst turning his back to the tomb.

'There's no photo.' it would be a relief to see a face different from what he was used to.

'None of the tombs here do.' Mr. Dartagnan was now walking among the other several tombs scattered throughout the cemetery.

'Now that I come to think of it, Lara did mention that the party would be introduced by the two Dartagnan brothers, why do you continue to maintain an illusion of your brother if he is already dead?' asked Jonah without any parsimony.

'When someone holds a favourable position in society, it is sometimes necessary to keep up appearances.' Giovanni answered lucidly.

Jonah was trying to find a way so he could confirm the events he had experienced a few hours ago. He needed to understand what was the reality he was living. He started walking in the opposite direction from Giovanni to look for two names: Matthew and Jennifer . Surely the Dartagnan brothers parents would be around somewhere in that graveyard. 'It would be impossible for me to dream

176

something so distant from my own reality.', he thought at the same time that he realised that those machines had the latest technology and could surprise his expectations.

'Are these your parents?' he asked when he came across a double tomb right next to James's.

'Exactly. I haven't been here in ages.' replied Giovanni as he stopped beside Jonah and, once again, made a sign of respect for the names of Matthew and Jennifer .

'And these other people?' asked Jonah, knowing that the property had started with the generation before his.

'Just some other people who lived here and were close to the family.' he replied whilst adjusting his coat as he started to head back to the iron gate that signalled the exit of that place.

Jonah didn't think twice about following Mr. Dartagnan; in addition to hospitals, cemeteries were within the places he detested the most in the world.

The two started to wander around the property. Giovanni did not speak anymore, he seemed to be reflecting on the moment he had just experienced, his expression was that of someone who had many nostalgic thoughts knocking at the door of his mind, which could lead his peace of mind to oblivion among a tangle of existential questions and doubts. Jonah was no stranger to that feeling, he had spent hours wondering what he had done to deserve to be there, but deep down, he knew exactly what it was, despite not thinking that he deserved to be punished in such an extreme way.

'You've told me you are not a religious man, do you have a particular reason behind your disbelief?'

The young man was startled by a brief deja-vu that, for a fraction of a second, took the reins of his mind. He felt as if he were in the presence of James, who had just asked him the same question. He had not yet stopped to notice how similar the Dartagnan brothers were; the voice, as well as the way of speaking, could be confused even if the two weren't in the same place, and the pride with which they spread themselves before people left no doubt that those two gentlemen were brothers, offspring of the same father and mother.

'Nothing in particular. The idea of an all powerful super-being doesn't make any sense to me.' he replied without trying to deceive Giovanni. He knew that a sudden religious redemption would not save him from whatever fate the old man had prepared for him.

'That's the problem with your generation.' he said whilst chanting sadness and shaking his head in a negative way.

'Or maybe...' started Jonah already regretting it and knowing it was too late to go back. 'The problem was the excess of religiosity in yours.'

Giovanni was vividly trying to repress his feelings, but he started to show an anger so strong it was palpable. Despite the old man showing tremendous subtlety in his ability to hide his expressions, Jonah could see that what he had just said was bothering him deeply, but Giovanni kept his composure and decided to continue the matter as a civilised man.

'What would make you say that?'

'Wouldn't you say that if people stop believing in what they cannot see, the learning of reality would become somewhat more tangible?' he replied as he implied something that seemed to be confusing Giovanni.

'What I think...' he started with an ironic tone. 'Is that the excess of useless information that people receive today replaces real values that were preserved with more kindness in the past.'

'So you believe that today's values should not behave in a way that combines mistakes from the past with intellectual advances?' he decided to enhance his own vocabulary when he realised that Giovanni wanted to clash with extraordinary words.

'I believe that god and all of his wisdom are present in every moment of mine, yours, and every single life on earth; and the day will come when we will all be held accountable for the mistakes we've made.'

Giovanni now seemed more devout than ever. 'Maybe the old man is finally showing his true colours.'

'So you believe that we will all be judged for the mistakes we made during our lives?' he asked when thinking: 'Whilst he seems to be completely sure that he is

178

doing some divine service with all those atrocities, he doesn't seem to realise that his own speech puts him in the same judgment as his victims.'

'And rewarded for the services provided.' he completed Jonah's sentence at the same time he stopped walking and started to face him with mystery behind his eyes.

'Are you hungry?'

Jonah was stunned by the sudden change in the conversation.

'Let's have breakfast. I doubt anyone at that party will miss me at this point.'

He was as hungry as he was tired. He realised that he hadn't eaten anything for hours and that nothing would please him more at that moment than a well-served breakfast. It was one of those rare situations where a person feels a little hope in a legitimate turmoil of despair.

He followed Giovanni's footsteps, curious to know where the host would take him that time. He could see that as they walked, they were going back in the direction of the main building of the property.

'This maze is incredible.' said Giovanni as they reached the grand staircase. 'If you want I can show you some secrets later.'

It seemed like a joke, but Jonah couldn't laugh. The mere thought of walking into that place again made him shiver.

'Now you believe that what you experienced was nothing but dreams?'

'But how do you explain that I dreamed of something I never experienced?'

'This part is quite difficult to explain, but I believe it has something to do with the fact that you were connected to the dream chair without the right drug in your system. If you want, we can go see the doctor.'

'It wouldn't be a bad idea, why don't you invite him for breakfast?' replied Jonah knowing that Douglas would be the only person in that place who could feel any remorse to the point of helping him.

James was no longer a reality. Even if what he was experiencing was another one of those weird dreams, the old one-legged man would have been locked back in the water fountain or, in the worst case, killed by his own brother's henchmen.

However, Jonah was increasingly letting himself believe that he was living that new reality. He did not know how to explain it, but with every minute he passed in there he felt as if he were more and more alive, in the exact same way he felt whilst he had been with James.

He really needed an explanation.

As they passed the main ballroom, Giovanni ordered one of his servants to ask for doctor Douglas. So they went on their way up stairs.

They passed through two huge doors at the end of the corridor and entered the largest room that Jonah had ever laid eyes on in his life. The place was very well decorated and furnished. Various works of art, such as paintings and sculptures, were distributed in order to harmonize the field of vision of whoever laid their eyes in there. Although the place was shaped like a room, it was more similar to a huge apartment, except for the fact that the rooms were all interconnected. The place was also complemented by a door separated what Jonah assumed to be where Giovanni's bed was, and another one that gave way to a small bathroom.

Giovanni sat at the end of a grand dining table that stretched across a extremely clean and polished floor. He motioned for Jonah to settle wherever he pleased. 'I'm inside the lion's den.', he thought when he realised that Mr. Dartagnan could have him wherever he liked without putting any effort to it. He had to be sure that any stories or statements told by Giovanni, or anyone else there, would be taken into consideration and analysed thoroughly by him. All the care in the world would not be sufficient until he could perform the miracle of finding James or any other way that would take him far from that place.

'Could you send any of your employees to find Patrick? I need to speak with him urgently.' he pleaded Giovanni, whilst buttering his bread as he was eager to start filling his empty stomach.

'Of course.' replied Giovanni, making a sign with his eyes to one of the servants who was standing by the door. A short time lapse crossed his mind when he remembered the dream where his friend was tortured by Mr. Dartagnan's sect. He shook his head and blinked his eyes hard to chase away the bad thoughts so he could focus all of his attention on the conversation that would follow.

'Doctor! Join us.' said Giovanni, without bothering to get up.

'How can I help you?' asked Douglas politely refusing to sit down, giving the impression that he was not there to stay.

The doctor had a depressed and worried expression. Jonah could feel that Douglas was not enjoying being involved in that situation. 'A job like any other.', he thought when empathising with the situation of earning some extra money without asking how. He had his head down and rarely looked Giovanni in the eyes to answer; his voice was tired and held a deep tone of regret.

'Our illustrious guest here has some doubts about what happened to him.' said Giovanni as he began to make use of the grand banquet that had been set at the table.

'You spent hours unconscious, but now I believe that there will be no more psychotic episodes.' the doctor said dryly as he continued to aim the floor.

'But what happened to me? How can you explain these dreams I had?' Jonah knew that the answer would not be the most honest.

'You already know what happened. You took the wrong drug, which led the lucid dream induction to have unknown effects.' Douglas was facing Jonah now. 'But, unfortunately, I cannot tell you what happened in your dreams, that is beyond my control.'

'I am sure that a doctor with your reputation can eloquently clarify the doubts of this young man.' Giovanni dropped his cutlery on the plate.

'As I mentioned, I can clarify any aspect of a medical nature, but I do not have the ability to guess why anyone dreams what they dream.' the tone in Douglas's voice had clearly changed; sarcasm seemed to challenge Giovanni Dartagnan, making it clear to Jonah that the doctor was trying to tell him something.

The three were silent for a while, allowing the chewing and splintering of the dishes to be responsible for the soundtrack of that uncomfortable situation. Douglas continued to stand in the same spot, where he had looked down again without wanting to reveal anything that might put his security at stake. Jonah knew, and understood, very well that it would be risky for anyone there to disrupt Mr. Dartagnan's plans.

'Anything else?' asked Douglas as he started to move his feet, indicating he was about to leave.

'I am not in the mood to think about questions that have no answer.' said Jonah, realising it was a mistake to ask for the doctor. It was certain that Giovanni's employee would not be babbling truths in front of his own boss.

'If I may, can I have a private word?' asked Giovanni before Douglas could get out.

'Certainly.'

The two left the Mr. Dartagnan's room. Jonah was restless in his chair, yearning to be alone in Giovanni's room. He knew that the boss's quarters would be monitored by cameras, but he had to take risks if he wanted to find a solution to get out of that place unharmed. He ran over to where the bed was and tried to go through the drawers with the hope that he could find a working phone or anything else that might help him.

There was way too little furniture in that place. The bed was surrounded by works of art and had a nightstand on each side. 'This can only be the side he sleeps on.', concluded Jonah when he noticed a small statue of a saint he did not know and remembered that the other side of the bed should be occupied by Lara Farlet. He closed his eyes and let out a grunt of disgust at the thought of how that woman had been deceived her whole life and had no idea that she slept with her own uncle, whilst her father was being tortured.

He tried not to misplace things, let alone break anything, but his backside didn't seem to follow the same instincts and caution as his brain. Before he could even realise what was happening, he heard the splintering of the small statue shatter across the tile floor that covered Mr. Dartagnan's rooms. The noise was intense, and he could only hope that Giovanni was having a warm and loud conversation with Douglas on the other side of those giant doors. Jonah looked like a table tennis referee, looking from side to side without knowing what to do. He tried to control his nervousness and find a quick and temporary solution so that he could think clearer about what to do with the mess that was at his feet.

He knelt on the floor and tried to collect the remains of porcelain into his pockets and, not before he managed to make a small cut in his hand, he came across a small piece of paper with one of those stamps made with candle wax melted and branded by the well-known Dartagnan family crest. 'Ubi Est Cadaver Ibi Congregantur Aquilae', said the front of the small card. 'The jargon of Giovanni's sect!', he thought as he remembered the small pamphlet he had read in James's hut, realising, with excitement, that he was not going crazy after all. He quickly put the small piece of paper into his jacket pocket.

He managed to go on collecting the small ceramic pieces and rubbed his hand on the back of his shirt. He tried to hide that he had cut himself, but it didn't look like his palm was going to stop bleeding anytime soon. He cleaned the floor close to Giovanni's bed as well as he could and ran back to the chair where he was supposed to be sitting. At that time, he knew that it would not be good enough to hide that cut, he would have to come up with some random excuse so that Giovanni would not suspect his misfortune around the room. He took a slice of bread and the butter knife and let the blood stain it red, then reached for his cloth napkin, which was on the floor, and wrapped it around his hand.

'You cannot be left alone, can you?' said Giovanni as he sat down at the table once again.

Jonah just twisted the corner of his mouth and made a negative sign.

'Do I need to call the doctor back?'

'It won't be necessary, it's just a small cut and this piece of cloth should suffice.

'If you need it, don't hesitate to ask.' Giovanni went back to eating his meal whilst he stopped paying attention to Jonah.

The piece of paper he held in his pocket was the only thing he could think about. He needed to find some excuse to be alone with his thoughts and try to organise a strategy that would take him away from that hotel.

'I haven't been to the bathroom in hours.' he said pointing to the amount of food he had devoured. 'I think I'll go to my room and take the opportunity to rest for a while.'

'Don't be silly, you can use the bathroom here. Before you can get back to the party, I need to show you one more thing.' said Giovanni as he pointed to the closed door that gave access to the bathroom.

'Show me one more thing...', that was starting get tiresome. Jonah had already made a mental note that Giovanni wanted to keep him out of his own room for as long as possible, he knew he wouldn't find Patrick. If all the things would fall into place and align with his recent memories, it was obvious that his friend had had some trouble along the way.

It was not the time to contradict who was holding all the cards. He got to his feet and headed for the door Giovanni had pointed to. The bathroom, to his surprise, did not match the rest of the room, it was a simple and functional toilet, in fact, just everything he needed.

The candle wax seal was broken; obviously, no one would hide a not yet opened piece of letter inside a statue, and Jonah was certain that the information there was extremely important, information that had already been read and reread.

Jonah made sure he was making some gruesome noises as he opened the lid of the vase as he sat down the patent with his clothes on so he could open the little note quickly.

'By spending a few minutes in this dirty and abominable bar, I can confirm that heresy has long been taking over the space left by the constant growth in religious disbelief. I regret to say, but we must fight evil with evil; there is no more space or time for us to face reality by standing idle. If our leaders are no longer able to deal with the growing problems we face, it is time to put aside hypocrisy and literally practice what we preach. The word has been given. There is no turning back.'

The macabre tone of the newly read words no longer scared Jonah, who was already beginning to make peace with fate that had brought him there. The note insinuated that someone had been researching people and some sort of superior order had been given, making it look like there were more people involved into that situation besides Giovanni and the members of his sects.

Time had begun to drag on since he entered that bathroom, and Mr. Dartagnan might had begun to get suspicious of his late absenteeism. He turned on the sink faucet and ruffled his shirt so he could rub his arms with soap and water. He knew those tattoos were there, covered with something. He felt they were real. His arm bruised from the strength he used to rub it, but there was no sign of ink.

'What else do you want to show me?' he asked as he sat back in the chair.

'Finish eating...'

'I'm already satisfied.' intruded Jonah before Giovanni could deliver yet another thrifty speech about how his old age made him better than everyone else.

He kept thinking about that note and any mysterious hidden meaning that those words might hold, but there was no much more he could understand from the message besides the points he already knew: the importance that all that crazy inquisition and religious fundamentalism held to Mr. Dartagnan. The only thing that could bring him a little peace of mind and calm was the certainty that what he had lived during the distant hours he had been with James was not a lie. He still couldn't quite understand what it all meant, but at least he was sure his mind wasn't running a mock about the things he had experienced.

At least, not completely.

The two took the same path they had taken before, but this time, instead of heading towards the cemetery, they turned right and, to Jonah's surprise, started to head towards the beautiful church built years ago by the Dartagnan family. A sudden fear came to take over his feelings; he was sure that this was the place where he had dreamed that Patrick was being tortured. The place where he would probably receive his much-acclaimed penance. His mind had been drawn to memories that were not his own, memories of a dream Patrick had had and that he was not yet able to understand. The grotesque landscape that took over his imagination brought back the anxiety he thought he had learned how to control, but his biggest problem was the imminence of what was about to happen.

'Why are we going there?' asked Jonah, trying not to show any concern as they approached the building.

'I want to introduce you to someone. A friend of mine.' replied Giovanni.

'What friend?'

'You don't really know how to be patient, do you? Wait and soon you'll see.' he replied as the two approached the church.

Jonah was already hoping to find the same stained glass window that mirrored Patrick's face in his dream, and, despite the fear being emphatic in signalling that his body should run away as far as possible from that place, he was more than curious about what was to come. He couldn't understand what he was feeling; he seemed to have a fear of not having slept well, which resembled a regret of spending an entire night at a party and not being able to sleep the next day. It was a hangover feeling, without him actually being hung over.

He felt very strange.

'Do not worry.' started Giovanni as he realised Jonah looked worried. 'A visit to the church will do you some good.'

The moment Giovanni opened the heavy wooden doors, a dense air-wave eager to escape from inside that place, gusted through the doors as if it was fleeing from an enraged animal. Jonah could notice that the 'little chapel', of which James was referring to, was neither macabre nor hunted, it was a church like any other, and its right foot was much higher than Jonah could remember from the lucid dream. The windows were large and clean, allowing sunlight, which was now beginning to warm the dew left by the cold night, to illuminate the poorly decorated and dirty stone walls.

His attention was quickly taken up by the silhouette of a man walking through the bank aisles towards the simple altar that ended the small building. The man wore a simple cassock and carried a cross intertwined into his fingers. He followed the familiar path whilst humming something indistinguishable between his lips.

'Jonah, I would like to introduce you to a friend of mine.' said Giovanni as his steps approached the man who stopped paying attention to whatever he was doing.

The introduction was not necessary. Jonah knew exactly who the clergyman was.

'Father Mark, pleased to meet you.' the remembrance brought by that voice made him shiver, as the priest held out his hand so Jonah could return the gesture.

CHAPTER 15:

The sight of that unwanted familiar face made Jonah shudder. Only a few hours before, the same man was helping Giovanni torture him with those dreams, and now, he held out his hand as if nothing had happened. His appearance was much cleaner than Jonah could remember. The few strands of oily hair were now properly cleaned and combed back, whilst the thin, stubble beard had left room for the priest's features to further intone his old age. He was carrying the same old bible under his arm, and had the same devoted spirit sparkling through his eyes as if there was nothing worthy or bigger than his faith.

'Pleasure.' he said whilst the priest looked at him with a curious expression after spending a long time with his hand outstretched.

'Please...' the priest replied pointing to a small container engraved into the stones of the entrance of the church that contained water.

'No thank you.' Jonah refuted, knowing that the priest was pointing to something they called holy water.

'Giovanni told me a little bit about you, welcome to our humble church.' said the priest as he turned towards the corridor that stretched between several wooden benches until it reached a small altar at the end of the structure.

That place was completely new to Jonah, which made him think that maybe he was really hallucinating about what he had experienced in his lucid dream about Patrick. The place where he had seen his friend being tortured bore no resemblance to the one he was now visiting.

They continued their walk around the church as Jonah tried not to say too much so he wouldn't let out anything that might take the small advantage of knowing the real intention of Giovanni and his sect. Although he was still not sure of what was the reality he was living in, everything that had just happened taught him to be meticulous with his words, and his time with James had made him understand that trust should be handle with care inside the environment he was stuck in.

'Several loved ones have passed through here.' said Giovanni whilst himself and the priest alternated in history lessons.

He had no idea of what was going to happen. Giovanni and the priest seemed to be happy that he was around, but he was sure that something bad was already planned and set for his near future, but the uncertainties were still a majority at that exact point in time.

Little had caught his attention within that place, until they suddenly stopped walking and Father Mark started to point to a distinct inverted cross raised into the stone wall. The priest watched the surprised expression on Jonah's face, as it was already clear that the situation was some kind of test.

'Do you recognise this cross?' asked the priest, realising Jonah's singular interest as he fixated his glaze in the object.

'Not really.' lied Jonah, trying to be short with his words, remembering the little history class he had received from James a few hours ago.

'Most people confuse St. Peter's cross with some kind of satanic symbol, which is normal.' said the priest, running his old fingers through the cross.

'Saint Peter's Cross?' Jonah tried to be curious about the version of the story chosen by the priest.

'Yes. The cross that represents humility, love and respect.' replied the priest whilst Jonah laughed internally with the hypocrisy that exuded through the pervert priest's mouth.

'But why is this cross inverted?' Jonah decided to show interest in the story told by the priest, maybe he could buy some time until any kind of help could miraculously come to his aid.

'Saint Peter, when condemned to crucifixion for burning Rome, asked for his cross to be placed upside-down, saying he was not worthy to die like his master Jesus.' replied the priest with great enthusiasm.

'But what was so important about Saint Peter?' Jonah wanted to get to a point where he would irritate the man.

The priest sighed loudly and smirked at him. He seemed to be appalled by Jonah's lack of knowledge, but he was not going to dismantle the tension he and Giovanni were building up just for the sake of satisfaction.

'He founded the church of Rome, he was the first bishop of the city. He was one of Jesus's great apostles.'

'Hmm... I always thought he was that gentleman who welcomes people in paradise.' Jonah decided to turn up his debauchery and see if he could extracted anything that could help him.

The expression in the priest's eyes changed abruptly. The simple animosity that reflected Jonah's play turned into anger. He could now see it in his eyes, the real priest who harassed him in the room where he had been imprisoned for hours and hours was right there, ready to come out and play. He was on the verge of exploding and grabbing Jonah by the neck, sentencing him right there to whatever penance he sought fit.

'Should we go back to the party?' interjected Giovanni before things reached an irreversible level.

Jonah didn't answer, he just looked away from the priest so Giovanni wouldn't suspect that he might know anything. The conversation was definitely interrupted and the three went to the door through which they had entered in silence.

'Feel free to return whenever you want.' said the priest in a forcedly calm tone.

'Thank you!' he replied by chanting sarcastically and sticking both hands deep into the small bowl of holy water and rubbing them together.

He felt Giovanni's haste as the host pushed him towards the exit. The old priest blasphemed whilst Jonah was engulfed by Giovanni's swing.

'What the fuck was that? Why the lack of respect?' he asked as they walked sharply away from the church.

'Sorry, but I don't think your priest treated me well...'

'Didn't treat you well? He was nothing but nice!'

Jonah was silent. The priest had really shown himself to be more than sympathetic, and he was the one who sought to show animosity.

'Where are we going now?'

'Back to the party.' Giovanni's reply was dry.

Jonah was already regretting the direction his audacity had taken. He wanted to hurt the priest, but he didn't expect that anything he might say was going to make Giovanni angry like that. He wanted to gain time and seek advantage over the information he held, but he did not want to speed up the process of his penance.

'It was not my intention to offend anyone.' he said as the two started walking in less haste. He was so hot by that upscaled conversation that he had to take his jacket off so he wouldn't sweat.

'You didn't offend anyone.' he replied whilst emphasising the last word. 'But rather an entire ancient institution that houses a multitude of devotees!'

Giovanni's tone was one of anger. Jonah realised he was over the top and his apology was more than necessary so that time was still on his side and he could find a way out of there. He had a huge belief that James was still alive. 'That situation was too real to have been just a dream.', he thought as he waited for Giovanni to calm down again.

He was already certain that Mr. Dartagnan would take him somewhere from which he could no longer escape. 'Is he finally going to do to me what he did to the others?', that was the question that prevented his brain from thinking clearly.

At the same time that his mind started to speed up, Jonah noticed a slight stain on the sleeve of his shirt. His mocking gesture, with the so called holy water he had used to wash his hands in the church, had wet the inside of his shirt and seemed to be revealing spots of ink between his skin and the piece of cloth. He knew he couldn't be wrong about that. He had felt his skin hurt. He just did not understand how the soap and water, which he had just rubbed on his arm, had not exposed the still fresh wounds on his skin. 'It is ridiculous to think that, in some way, the so called holy water would have cleaned the makeup that hid the tattoos.', he thought before he could start raving about the subject. He needed to calm Giovanni's spirits and hide from the old man that his marks had reappeared.

They were approaching the strenuous staircases that led from the garden to the ballroom when Jonah saw that he could no longer remain in that situation.

'I hope everything is alright between us. I believe that you have misunderstood me as I did not mean to offend you.' he said without any confidence.

Giovanni lowered his eyes and looked at Jonah up and down. He noticed that the young man crossed his arms over his belly and hid the wet sleeves of his shirt.

'You got wet...'

'Nothing major.' he replied as he decided to put his jacket back on.

'Why don't you go to your room and change your clothes... I'll send someone to bring you a clean shirt and have that one washed.' said Mr Dartagnan with certain authority in his voice.

'No need to bother... The sun is already high and soon the heat will dry off the water.'

'Nonsense. You are my guest and you will not roam around like a rag.'

Jonah decided to stop contesting Giovanni, even though his insistence on getting him to change his clothes was very strange, he knew that he had already bothered him too much in the last few moments.

'Who knows, maybe I'll find Patrick on my way there...'

The two climbed up the stairs until they reached the door that opened to the ballroom, as Jonah headed towards his room. He had already lost hope of finding Patrick since, apparently, that lucid dream had shown him a reality that he was not willing to believe. The door that connected the two rooms was still locked, but even so, he uselessly knocked again and called out his friend's name.

Several clean and well ironed shirts were at his disposal in one of the wardrobes inside the room. Giovanni, of course, knew that, as he plead to send Jonah to his room and ask him to wait for someone to deliver him clean clothes.

He started to hear strong footsteps coming from the corridor. He imagined that whoever Giovanni had sent for him with would be coming, but the pace of the steps and the numerous of different soles that touched the floor made him believe that perhaps it was not clothes that were about to arrive.

He glanced at his arm and realised that his black tattoos were contrasting with the almost transparent white of the wet shirt, making the so called marks more than visible again. He knew it was ridiculous to think that the church water was different from the soapy one he had tried to use a few minutes before, there would certainly be an explanation to how that had was happening, but if Giovanni and his gang were coming to meet him, that wouldn't be the best time to unravel another one of the puzzles that hung over the state of the Dartagnan Brothers Hotel.

As he could hear the footsteps approaching his door, Jonah forced his brain to think of a way to escape. He needed to be alone and sort off his thoughts before he could be captured again, he had no idea of what would be the next item on Giovanni's list of horrors, but he was sure the old man had noticed the sudden appearance of the tattoos and that would speed up whatever the future was holding for him.

Jonah went around every corner of the room, trying to find anything that would help him get out of there. 'Of course...', he thought as he approached the windows and found bars behind the glass. He even tried to look under the bed and think about hiding there, but he knew that was the most ridiculous option he could think of at that moment, despite being the only one that came to mind.

Quickly, he went back to the bedroom door and locked it so he could buy a little more time before Giovanni's henchmen could capture him.

'Open the door!' a distinct voice sounded with angst.

He went towards the door that connected the rooms again, but no matter how hard he tried, he couldn't even move the handle down. That was when he suddenly remembered he still had his card-key inside one of his pockets, but he still couldn't find anywhere that the key would fit and open the door. His mind went into auto-pilot for a while, as he decided to drag the card-key around the door, hoping that it would trigger some sort of mechanism that would open that door.

He knew it was his only chance at the moment.

As desperate as his actions were, the card-key turned out to be useless. There was no purpose for it whatsoever.

Time was running out for Jonah, and he knew that as soon as he was captured, there would be no hope for him to get out of that place alive.

As his hands were impatiently shaking, he dropped the card-key on the ground and let his knees give in so his body could crumble after it. He was still shaking as he noticed that of his knees felt a great amount of pain as he felt into some kind of lever on the floor. It was stuck in the gap between the floor and the door, something so small his eyes wouldn't be able to see if it wasn't for the pain he had just felt.

One simple switch and he was able to extend his freedom for a little longer.

He then entered Patrick's room, which was exactly the same as his, and went directly to the window to see if it also held the bars that had recently prevented him from running out into the garden. Before opening the curtain, he already knew he shouldn't have had any hope that this room would be any different from his, but his mental confusion, mixed with a brief excess of anxiety, did not allow him to save the little time he had. Jonah confirmed what was expected at the same time that he heard people shouting after his bedroom door, making a big fuss and opening it up against its will; he knew he had a few seconds before Mr. Dartagnan's henchmen realised that he would have crossed the door between the two rooms.

He quickly opened the door that locked Patrick's room and walked out without looking back. 'If I'm quick enough, I can disappear from their view before they realise I'm not in the room.', he thought as he imagined he would have a minute or two before Giovanni's troupe searched the room; the stupid idea that someone was going to hide under the bed had just given him a short and valuable span of time.

Jonah knew he couldn't go back to the main ballroom, as he had no doubt that Giovanni and some of his henchmen would be waiting for him. He went in the opposite direction looking for a door or a window that would help him, but the corridors that connected the rooms were private to the point of having no opening to the outside world.

'Jonah!' the henchman shouted again.

He knew that he should now think quickly. His seconds of advantage were already catching up with him, and he would soon be discovered if he couldn't find at least a place to hide.

He continued walking through the corridors hoping to find any door that could be open. He tried almost every handle he could find - pushing them both up and down - whilst he felt the footsteps of Giovanni's henchmen approach him.

Nothing seemed to work.

He remembered - when he saw a huge mirror superimposed on one of the walls that made one of the corners in the corridor - the wise words that James had spoken to him a few hours ago, whether that was a dream or not, it seemed that the excess of information he had absorbed throughout the night would serve him well after all. 'This place is full of surprises.', he thought as he recalled the words of the old one-legged man. He began to run his hands around the mirror in search of any sort of lever that would open a magical passage to another place that no one could even imagine existed. His hopes were crushed with the same intensity that it had been built.

'Do not move!' the faceless and mysterious voice sounded from afar as he held his head down, pretending he didn't hear it.

Both time and space were getting shorter by the second.

His brain had to think very sharply as he noticed what his eyes had just seen. The sturdy man who strode towards him pointed a flashlight so close to his face so that the beam hindered him form seeing anything else, it was when Jonah turned to face the mirror and was able to see that the flashing reflection of the object mirrored itself on the opposite corner, revealing that the wall held a fake facade.

He started to run, before the stranger could reach him, going towards the wall that resembled the one he had seen in the maze, when James had passed from one side of the wall to the other without making any effort except to rotate the object in the opposite direction. He had finally found one of the big surprises by himself.

The mirror rotated one hundred and eighty degrees, allowing Jonah to end up in a small confined space held between the mirror and a wooden door. He could hear the footsteps of the henchmen, who continued to chant his name at random, as they followed running after him through the corridors of the hotel. Everything seemed to be fine. He had succeeded in dodging those who wanted to impose harm on him as he began to feel safe, even if confined in that small space between the corridors and the mysterious door.

He did not know why, but something told him that door wouldn't open so easily, and that some kind of mysterious crap would be necessary so that he could escape from that confined space without having to return to the main hall. It wouldn't be long before Giovanni's faithful men came to him with the information that Jonah was missing, and even if they didn't know about that passage, Giovanni would certainly narrow down in his own mind the few places where Jonah could be found.

However, the surprises continued to present themselves to Jonah. The door was not locked at all.

It seemed too simple to be true.

The opening of the door revealed a simple wooden staircase that would take him downstairs. He knew that his time was short and that he should thread very carefully down those steps, he was entering unknown territory and had no idea what he was going to face at the bottom of that staircase. He went down the stairs very carefully as not to make any noise that might attract any attention.

The place was pitch black and Jonah no longer had his cell phone to light the way. He tried to feel the walls so that he could walk without hitting anything along the way; the uncertainty was a surprise and the disadvantage was imperative, he could not make any mistake before he knew where he was. The stone walls were damp and Jonah could feel the moss that had grown there due to the lack of light; an icy air seemed to cross his face little by little, and his shoes came up against an uneven path with poorly fitted and slippery stones.

He spotted a small clearing a few meters away. 'Yes, of course.', he replied to the very thought which whispered that was the direction to be taken. He did not have many

196

choices for what would be his next step, so he decided to follow his instincts and look for a path that would take him out of there.

The dimmed illumination came from a lantern hanging on the wall and as soon as he was able to grip his hands around it, Jonah confirmed what his mind imagined about the architecture of the place. Stone walls everywhere. He still couldn't see much further ahead of his own nose, and taking the unattached object from the wall allowed him to run the risk of being spotted whilst continuing to take new steps down the unknown.

The silence was filled with brief and indistinguishable whispers, and the pitch black gave way to a weak and symbolic illumination that wouldn't reveal much ahead.

'We can't start until we find him!' exclaimed a female voice, which Jonah was able to suddenly attribute to Monalisa.

'That indigent is extremely important for the event, Giovanni.' said an unknown voice as he left one of the dark corridors.

'My men are looking for him. We will start without him, we cannot postpone the ceremony any longer.' the leader of the sect replied without waiting for anyone to contradict him.

The three started walking through the corridors as they were followed by more people who remained silent and obedient. Jonah had already quietly and slowly placed the small lamp in one of the corridors walls before it could spoil his presence amid those people. He felt that if he kept a good distance from them, he could take an advantage of the poor lighting to follow their footsteps to wherever they were going.

It seemed like his only option.

The unraveling in front of his eyes began to take on a shape that seemed very familiar to him. As soon as that small wave of people had passed through what appeared to be an entrance to a larger room, Jonah decided to hide between one of the corridors and observe - or at least try - the situation before he could make any decisions about what he would do next.

He still could not see exactly what was happening, which required him to sharpen his hearing and try to pay attention to the words proffered by the troupe of madmen who were part of Giovanni Dartagnan's sect. They all wore some kind of black robe that covered them from head to toe; having their head wrapped by a hood that barely showed any of their features.

'We meet again, my dear friends...' Giovanni's distinguished speech intonation started to reverberate through what seemed to be a great structure.

His voice continued to chant words of devotion and divine promises. The more he spoke, the more people worshiped and applauded him with tremendous admiration; Mr. Dartagnan really had the gift of speech and knew exactly how to attract the attention of the people around him. The induction was delivered with fancy words and sayings in Latin. Jonah tried to understand everything Giovanni was saying, but the distance between that small space that he was confined to, and the place where the devotees met did not allow such clarity.

'I need to get closer.', he thought as he got down to his knees and started crawling like a frightened child at the damp and dirty corridors. His brain was startled at the information his eyes were giving him.

From a distance he could see the same stained glass window that he saw whilst playing pretend in Patrick's body. That was, of course, the fateful horror room where he had seen his friend being tortured in one of those crazy dreams he had had. The members of Giovanni's sect were positioned in the same way as before; as their chief stood up pretentiously on that altar with the priest posing besides him, who now took the reins of the situation and was beginning to babble fictitious blessings in a dead language. It seemed that history was repeating itself inside Jonah's mind, but he was now sure he was there. That had to be his real reality. Even if what he had lived with James could be true, the situation before his eyes was too real to be a dream.

The torture bed, which once occupied a primordial position in front of the altar where the priest prayed, had now been replaced by two large polished and varnished wood trunks. The structure looked even more macabre than the previous one; the two trunks were interconnected by steel cables, which extended from top to bottom to form some kind of fence.

The ceremony continued as Giovanni spoke in an imperative way once again; the other people continued to follow his words as if they vehemently believed that man to be an envoy from their god.

'Bring me the offering!' he exclaimed after babbling another half dozen words that were blessed by the priest with an amen.

Jonah tried to find a better position to observe what was going to happen next, but if he continued for a few more meters he would be completely exposed to the public eye. He was the only one who didn't wear one of those black robes, what made him prone to attract attention very easily. He was certain he was supposed to be there, so his absence in such an offering should have already sharpened people's attention in a way that any sign of his presence would cause an alarm.

A chant started to sound as soon as two huge iron doors parted with the crossing of several of those people in black carrying a completely naked person right above their heads. The body was hung on several supports and had its arms and legs dangling through the air as if it was dead - or at least unconscious.

'Let us receive our guest with a round of applause, ladies and gentlemen!' intoned Giovanni as he raised his arms in awe.

Everyone there followed his cue and accompanied each other in what seemed some kind of greeting. Everyone raised their hands as if they were waiting for a divine force to take over their own bodies and lead them into ecstatic worship. They were slaves to an archaic indoctrination and made their own lives an object that should belong to their god.

'Let us give a warm welcome, ladies and gentlemen...' continued Giovanni as the troupe approached the structure with steel cables. 'Let us receive the one who sinned and will receive his penance. Let us receive the one who will be offered to god as a vote of confidence to his plans.

Giovanni sighed, filled his lungs with air, and exhaled.

'Let's welcome Patrick Skies!'

CHAPTER 16:

Jonah's eyes couldn't believe what they were seeing, as his ears could not believe what they had just heard, as his mind was trying to fit in the pieces of the memory that was being made inside his head. Patrick was still alive, but about to be used as an object for the eccentric satisfaction of Giovanni and his followers. His body had reached the end of the corridor where the altar was set, which was surrounded by people and that medieval torture object that Giovanni would use to seek redemption from his god at the expense of others. He could conclude - if that was really his reality - that he had experienced a lucid dream induced by Giovanni a few hours ago, confirming James's theory of what had been happening to him during his psychological episodes. Patrick had his two legs properly attached to his body and still seemed to be breathing.

'Fuck! I need to do something, I can't let them do this to him!', he thought as he started to get up, but not before being pulled back down and avoiding being seen by all of those people around his friend.

'Be silent, or you'll be next.' the voice seemed familiar, but the intonation of the whispering made him think harder before he could assign it to a name.

Someone was hindering him to turn around. 'If you want to live, stay quiet...', the seriousness in those words seemed to be something that Jonah should not ignore; whoever was behind him should have an interest in keeping him as a secret, as it would be very easy to simply disclose his whereabouts for the rest of Dartagnan's sect. It was clear that the person behind him was part of Giovanni's cluster of lunatics. Jonah could clearly see part of the black robe, whilst being immobilised by whoever was crouching on the floor.

'Who the fuck are you?' his voice was loud enough to draw attention from one of those people in black who turned away from the sermon preached by the priest and Giovanni.

'Quiet!' the voice whispered loudly as his arms were pulled back into the small corridor.

Jonah wanted to get up and run towards his friend; he knew that something very bad was about to happen and Patrick needed his help.

'If you want to stay alive, I need you to listen very carefully to everything I am going to tell you.' the voice continued to whisper without Jonah being able to recognise it.

The most sensible thing to do was to obey whoever was leading the situation. Jonah had learned to play the game using logic in the past few hours, as he knew his position there never would be one of superiority; he did not know the territory nor the people, he was not part of any of the groups and his only friend was about to be tortured. But worst of all, he couldn't do anything to help him. His desire to jump, scream, and go out in his direction was beyond anything he had ever felt before, it was greater than any other impulse he had ever felt in his life. But common sense should prevail over emotion.

There was nothing he could do.   .

'There is nothing you can do...' the voice whispered, echoing his own thought.

'Who are you?' Jonah repeated the same question.

'What difference does it make?' the person made sure he understood his identity would not be revealed.

'Why are you helping me then?' he wanted the voice to keep talking so he would be able to recognise it.

'Here...' said the voice as it put a key in the palm of his hand and closed it tightly, indicating that it was imperative he did not lose it. 'You will know exactly when to use it.'

'Please, no more games... Just fucking help me out of this place.' his voice rose again.

'Silence!'

Jonah tried to turn his face around again, but the hands that held his waist lifted and lightly hit him in the face. The gesture was more symbolic than aggressive, hardly making any noise or implying any pain.

'Take these directions and you will arrive at exact place that will help you solve all of your problems.' said the voice as it handed him a small piece of paper.

'Solve my problems? I just want to get out of here and go home, please.' he said when he let tiredness take over common sense. It no longer seemed to matter if Patrick would survive or that the word of James would be spread outside that place as he had promised him. 'It doesn't even make sense to keep a promise made in a dream to someone who's already dead.', he thought as he finally convinced himself he was living his true reality, most likely being that James was really dead and that Giovanni had induced him to all those memories through lucid dreams programmed into the dream chair.

'Please...' he started to plead as he realised he could finally turn his neck around to look for a person who was already gone.

Jonah was, once again, alone as he noticed his hand was beginning to throb in pain. He was holding that key so tightly that he didn't notice that his recent injury left by the shard of the statue dropped in Giovanni's room was starting to bleed again.

'Shit!' he exclaimed as he tried to control the tone of his voice for the first time; he knew he should be cautious, after all a light of hope hung over his fate for a change.

He didn't understand why, he had no idea of how, and it didn't matter that the situation didn't make any sense. He just wanted that help to be real, that someone, among all those terrible people, really wanted to help him.

'Having us, the divine will of the lord god almighty.' Giovanni's voice was loud and pretentious.

Jonah understood that the atrocities of Giovanni's sect continued to take shape in the great underground hall. He fought against every instinct that made him even think of crawling back to watch his friend's slow and horrifying death, after all, how good would his presence be there? He had made peace with the idea that there was nothing he could do; this was a real situation, not a dream in which he was in charge, his life was at stake there, and no matter how much he liked the person he was supposed to save, for Jonah, one thing was certain: his life always came first. He knew he was self-centred, narcissistic, and that other people's opinions were of no use to him, his animal instinct was very clear in that particular situation. His well-being would not be hurt by the possible salvation of anyone else.

Even so, something slowly made him crawl back to the end of the corridor and observe what the sect was doing to his friend Patrick.

The scenario was not looking good.

'Look my lord, how devoted are those who follow you! How sorry are the ones who have betrayed you! And how mighty is your word to all of us!' said Giovanni in an almost incomprehensible voice, looking up as if he was waiting for a light to shine on him.

'My dear Jesus, in recognition of all the benefits you have done to me...' the priest followed Giovanni's voice with what seemed to be a prayer.

Mr. Dartagnan held the same red staff he had used a few hours, before presenting himself to the public at the beginning of the party. The red object did not seem to have any use other than aesthetics, but the old host posed as if he was doing some kind of ceremonial dance around it. He swayed to the opposite direction of the staff as he raised himself with one arm to one of the trunks so that he could stand tall and continue to attract everyone's attention. A real show, a presentation worthy of a leader; every move he made was synchronised with whatever he was saying. He offered himself to his god as if he knew him personally, as if he had invited him to his local coffee shop. However, the most incredible thing of all was how people longed for it and seemed to want to be him. Each word was followed by the most diverse and attentive ears present; and each step was observed and praised as if he was floating among the myriad of people lined up in front of that torture machine - which was about to receive its offering.

'Bring him on, my dear. Let our guest contemplate the beauty of what we have prepared for them.' Giovanni seemed to have taken a strong dose of adrenaline. He was euphoric. The mere idea of what was going to happen had left him bouncing like a child about to enter a roller coaster for the first time.

Patrick was being carried by two people holding him by the arms. He had his head suspended in the air as if he was anaesthetised by a large amount of drugs.

'I believe everyone here is already familiar with Patrick Skies's story. Even so, I insist that a brief summary should introduce him to our humble meeting.'

'I offer you my heart...' the prayer continued.

Jonah needed to control all of his instincts so he wouldn't jump and throw himself into an inevitable failure to save his friend. He returned to seek comfort in logic. Saving himself was the priority.

'Patrick Skies, ladies and gentlemen, is one of those people who thinks it's appropriate to take advantage of an unfavourable situation and reward himself with the lack of people's sobriety.' he began his speech as he paced back and forth smoothing the medieval structure of torture with his hands. 'It was not once, nor twice or even trice. This man was the protagonist of countless occasions where he took advantage of defenceless women. Whenever he was presented with an opportunity, he managed to ignore the fact that his unwilling partners were completely inebriated, as he would let himself take advantage of them.'

Jonah knew exactly where Mr. Dartagnan was going with that conversation. Patrick was a man who did not ask permission when approaching a woman, even if she was drunk. However wrong something like that could be perceived in some people's eyes, he didn't think his friend should be judged like that, there were laws regarding acts that could be considered violent, and Patrick, if deemed guilty, should be held accountable that way. Although, he could understand why Giovanni and his followers believed that they were suited to deal with matters like that by their own hand, and their god.

'Today is the day that Patrick will have the chance to redeem himself! Pay for his mistakes.' he spoke as if he had rehearsed that speech for hours in front of a mirror. 'As you well know, everyone here has the power to choose, no one is forced to ask nor accept god's forgiveness. However, choices have consequences, and we, as protectors of our lord's kingdom on earth, will give Patrick Skies a simple choice to be made.'

'All for you, most holy heart of Jesus...' the priest seemed to shake his legs with the pleasure he felt in each sentence he prayed.

It didn't make any sense that Patrick had to make a choice; he was in a deplorable state and was certainly unable to measure the consequences of the actions that would follow that moment, even if his body was starting to regain a pinch of control back. The people who were holding him by the arms started to distance themselves, and Patrick, as confused as he was, seemed to be starting to understand what was happening to him. He tried to cover his nakedness with his hands and shrug his shoulders to avoid the light breeze that ran through the four corners of that enormous room.

'And do not allow me to fall into sin in all my life, amen.' that seemed to be the end of the prayers. Giovanni looked at the priest very calmly until it was time to make the cross sign and turn his attention to the audience that awaited for him.

'You are here today because you've made mistakes.' started Giovanni whilst directing his gaze into Patrick's eyes. 'You were chosen by the members of this assembly to have the chance to redeem yourself.'

The expression on his friend's face was of confusion, and a lot of it. Clearly, he didn't understand why he was there. Jonah was sure that Patrick had spent hours during that party making new friends and talking to anyone who stood in front of him. The young man was the soul of any party he attended and was always very well received by everyone who knew him. But now he was surrounded by a sea of lunatics who circled him, hiding their faces, and watched him like he was some kind of circus attraction. That was certainly the most vulnerable point of his entire life.

Giovanni's henchmen grabbed him and began dragging him towards that strange wooden memorabilia. Patrick tried to fix his feet on the ground to make a force towards the opposite direction, but his body was so fragile that his wishes were nothing more than misinterpreted movements; his body was completely exposed and all of those present had their eyes fixed on him.

Jonah was still uneasy when he observed his friend, who had his destiny traced to a path of no return. He knew exactly what was going to happen. All his experience during those lucid dreams, and the time he spent with James, started to connect the events. Patrick was hung on the steel wires that connected one wooden trunk to another. The torture tool still seemed to be off, as Jonah couldn't see anything there that resembled what he had seen in his dream; those cables did not seem to be able to stretch, and the varnish that enveloped the wood seemed to give it a new and modern appearance, unlike the old medieval aspects that formed the bed that had supposedly torn one of Patrick's legs whilst Jonah seemed to be living his worst nightmare.

'What the fuck is going on?' spoke Patrick for the first time, realising that his arms and legs were tied to the steel cables.

'Look, ladies and gentlemen, how this pauper offends us with blasphemy by interrupting our sermon.' said Giovanni as he laid his hands on a remote control.

'You imbecile old man, what in god's name are you talking about?' Patrick seemed to regain control of his own thoughts.

'How dare you say his name in vain! How galant can this young man be!' Giovanni had a huge smile on his face, whilst he swan around his red cane.

'Who are all these people? What the fuck do you want from me?' he tried to convey authority in his voice, but clearly his mind was tormented by the surprise he was being exposed to.

Giovanni continued to ignore Patrick's questions and requests as he turned his attention to the device to which Patrick was now properly attached. In one hand he held a remote control with two buttons, whilst in the other he held the red cane that he did not seem to let out of his sight. He lifted the object and approached Patrick's body; the young man now closed his eyes in disgust and frowned in fear at what was about to happen. Mr. Dartagnan lightly passed the cane across Patrick's naked body as he continued to squirm through the few movements he was restrained to.

'Stop, please!' tears started to run down Patrick's face.

'Are you ready to receive your penance and redeem yourself before god?' asked Giovanni without looking the young man in his eyes as he still sought the attention of the audience.

'What did I do?' Patrick now had his expression taken by fear and sobbed with every word he managed to complete.

Giovanni just stared at him.

'Ah!' he shouted as he squirmed as little as his movements allowed.

Jonah was about to have an outbreak with what he had just seen. Giovanni pressed one of the buttons on the remote, whilst the torture paraphernalia had started to emit small electric shocks.

'Look, my friends. Now he seems to have feelings in his heart.'

'What are you talking about? Please stop this!' Patrick sobbed with his head down as his eyes shed more tears than he thought possible.

Jonah stood up from the floor when he heard another cry of agony from his friend. He had to hold on and just stand idle whilst he saw Patrick letting weakness take over his body by urinating himself as he shuddered at the visibly strong shocks he was receiving.

'There is nothing you can do.', he thought repeatedly before he could hide his own body as he was within sight from anyone who might have lost even a second of attention from the stage set up by Giovanni's sect. 'You made your choice. Your life.', he followed his new mantra, crossing his arms and laying his head on his lap so that his vision would not interrupt that moment of lucidity. Real life had knocked on his door.

Buying a fight by himself with all those people didn't make any sense. The result could only be one.

'Ah!' Patrick had raged again as he continued to writhe within his wet body.

'You see, my friends. Even in pain, this man is not willing to ask for divine forgiveness. He's a heretic by profession!' Giovanni sounded a giggle that was followed by laughter from all around.

'Ok! Fine!' Patrick started to speak when he realised that the old man was pointing the remote again at him. 'I apologize, I'm sorry.'

'You ask for forgiveness, I see. And what would that be for?' Giovanni had switched from his machiavellian laughter to a tone of extreme seriousness.

'For what I did! I promise I will never do it again!' Patrick returned to sound words whilst trying to swallow the weeping that prevented him to reason.

Before Giovanni could respond and continue to torture Patrick, Jonah was able to understand exactly what Mr. Dartagnan's true nature was. That was not an opportunity for redemption, the leader of the sect had no intention of allowing Patrick to escape from that place alive. He was supposed to apologize for something he had done without clearly knowing what it was. As torture in the old inquisition had never been proven to work, precisely because of the incongruence caused by the effect between cause and consequence. Patrick was already willing to apologize without even knowing what he had done to deserve to be there, but that would not be enough for Giovanni and his sect, the sole fact in which words were expressed in the form of excuses wouldn't suffice their thirst for revenge. They wanted more, they wanted to see the young man suffer, without even knowing why he was there. That was worse than what was done in the holy inquisition. It was torture in its most basic form. It was a simple exchange between agony and pleasure, where Patrick would never have a chance to know what was happening to him.

'And what exactly did you do?' Jonah finally heard Giovanni's voice sound like someone who was immensely happy; someone who had just satisfied his most sordid desires at the expense of an innocent.

Patrick simply stared randomly at the horizon. He didn't seem to have any idea of what he had done to deserve to be there; his conscience did not seem to find anything that found a logical explanation between acts committed in his past that could terrify his present in that way.

Another shock caused a high-pitched scream to exhale from his lungs, whilst his mouth began to bleed as he had bitten his own tongue.

'Tread carefully, my dear, god gave you a tongue so that you can speak. I will give you one last chance to confess your sins before this assembly, otherwise I will have no option but to force redemption out of you.' Giovanni passed the red cane over Patrick's body as he shivered with fear at the mere touch of it.

Jonah knew he should expect the worst. He had made the decision not to interfere with the situation so that he could save his own life, but he did not know if he would have the courage to stay there and watch what was about to come. His hand was still dripping blood and his head was growing tired of thinking; for a brief moment he thought he was going to have to go through lucid dreams and psychotic episodes once again, but it didn't make sense that everyone in the sect was there and he would be stuck in a chair with no one to take care of him. Perhaps he had been left in the care of Douglas, yet Jonah had realised that Giovanni would not be able to entrust such responsibility to someone who did not share his beliefs.

'Maybe they won't kill him...', he thought, trying to redeem himself of the responsibility he was putting aside as he decided to wait for the outcome of that circus with the hope that he could free his friend when the sect members were gone.

'I'm losing my patience!' shouted Giovanni when the priest came to his encounter, placing his hand on his head and babbling some kind of religious nonsense that was supposed to calm him down.

'I've already said I confess!' Patrick tried to express himself lucidly, but his mouth was bleeding faster than he could spit.

'Confess what boy? I told you that I'm not in the mood for child's play.' he replied as he gently pressed the button on the remote control. He seemed to want Patrick alive.

'Whatever you want.' he mumbled whilst crying.

'That's enough.' Giovanni ignored Patrick's words once again.

The audience of subjects continued to watch closely every step that Giovanni took. The red cane was once again making subtle movements between the audience and Patrick's trapped body, who now let his head hang over whilst he continued to sob and spit his own blood.

'My dear people, you know me... And you can say whatever you want about me, but you will never say that I am not a sensible man. A fair and honest man who keeps his word. I promised to give this man a chance to redeem himself before god, our lord almighty. However, he keeps avoiding the truth and is no longer able to look us in the eye to admit he is wrong. Wouldn't you agree?'

That made Jonah think about what his penance would be. He knew very well why he was there as Giovanni had already shown him in one of the lucid dreams, which would make it easy for him to apologise and leave that place with his hands in his pocket as if nothing had happened. Of course, he knew that nothing would be that easy, and the mystery surrounding what would happen to him only increased, which made him even more anxious and scared.

Giovanni's speech was coveted by the audience and the question was followed by a nod of agreement that Jonah had never seen in any other situation. He even thought that he was about to agree with Giovanni, before he could switch back his mind to a lucid state.

'You also know how much I admire democracy and I've always made sure to listen to everyone's opinion. Does anyone here have any reason to prevent this man from now answering for his actions before this assembly and its devotees?'

Jonah felt an impulse telling him to get up and say something, but he soon realised that Giovanni was not speaking to him.

Silence reigned in that instant. No one there was brave enough to stand between Mr. Dartagnan and his relentless desire for revenge.

'Very well. May god's will be done.'

The priest ended Giovanni's speech by making a cross sign, which was followed by all the other members present there. Jonah closed his eyes, which filled up with tears, and let out a brief sob as he wiped his face with his shirt sleeve.

Giovanni raised the red staff again and hitched it to a small rope that was next to one of the wooden logs. A gust of water fell on Patrick's shoulders and head, who just shuddered at the shock of the unexpected shower.

'This holy water will allow you to reach god's kingdom with a clearer conscience.' said Mr. Dartagnan as he made another cross sign and was followed by everyone present.

He brought the red staff back to himself and, with finesse and calmness, came to unveil a beautiful and shining sword from underneath its sheath. He removed the entire thing out, what revealed precious stones embedded in the object that formed an inverted cross at its base. Jonah soon remembered the story that James had told him about the saint Peter cross, however he couldn't distinguish what those stones would mean, even if that sword could have any symbolism for the present moment.

'Your last words, young man?' Giovanni looked deeply into Patrick's eyes as he raised his head again to face destiny head on.

'Tell me what I did!' he pleaded whilst Giovanni showed a smirk on his face and turned away to face the crowd.

The leader of the sect raised his gleaming sword and brought its point towards Patrick's face. For some reason, Jonah's friend was not reluctant; he let Giovanni do what he wanted and end that suffering once and for all. Jonah could see the tiredness on his face, he could see that his expression of weeping and reluctance had given way to a feeling of acceptance and sadness. However, Giovanni's mysterious sword did not cut anything. He opened Patrick's bloody mouth as he raised the steel tip between his teeth and with his hand he pulled his tongue out as far as he could.

Giovanni let the sword return to its sheath as he went on looking for the remote control that he had lost in one of his pockets. As soon as he found it, Mr. Dartagnan did not hesitate to press the fateful button, causing Patrick to bite his own tongue so hard that it fell to the floor after a fraction of a second, covered with blood.

Patrick started gasping for the air he couldn't find; his lungs begged to be contracted by the oxygen they needed so badly to function again, but his mouth was choked with his own blood that was pouring from the newly opened wound caused by the bite he had taken on himself. It was only a few seconds before Patrick drowned into his own blood and stopped breathing.

Jonah was stunned. He didn't know whether to run, cry, scream, or go to straight to Giovanni and avenge his friend's death. The audience remained silent, not everyone there seemed to agree with the atrocity they had just witnessed; it was when the leader of the sect pulled the sword from its sheath and raised it towards the sky as if he was trying to offer something to his best imaginary friend: the death of an innocent man.

Some people sang a cry of adoration whilst others just looked at each other with bewilderment from the situation they had just witnessed. The priest dropped to his knees, raising his hands in the air, babbling prayers and words of adoration.

Jonah had no idea of what to do, except that he should get out of there as fast as he could. His brain was able to control the impulse he had when jumping from the ground and trying to go to Giovanni, it was less than a second before he would have ran off to meet his own death. He took over his own conscience again and started slowly walking back to the confusing wet corridors that took him there.

The feeble noise of metal coming in contact with a stone on the floor was not enough to draw the attention of the people who were still contemplating, or frightening, at Giovanni's recent act, but it was enough for Jonah to realise that he had left the mysterious key that had just been delivered to him fall into the ground. He stepped back sparingly until he could crouch on his toes and reach into the damp and grab the key stuck to the clay with the tips of his nails.

The flat sole of his shoe slid into the damp clay right after he managed to get his hands on the key, which was enough for him to hit his head into the wall and make it slide through the floor.

'Who's there? another unknown voice started asking inconvenient questions.

Jonah needed to run.

CHAPTER 17:

The image of Patrick drowning in his own blood still dominated his thoughts, as he ran and made his shoes slide around every corner that turned down the corridors of the Dartagnan Brothers Hotel underground. He had no idea where he was going, but he was sure he couldn't stay there; he did not wait long enough to see whether the mysterious man had noticed his presence or not.

Jonah was not going to wait to find out.

He kept running at random without knowing where he was going. The place was bigger than expected, but like every corner in that hotel, he would find an exit sooner or later. He tried to be attentive so that he could spot any corner where he could hide, he had a key and instructions in a partially wet paper in his hands. He wasn't sure if he could trust the person who had given him those things, but he had no option but to risk his own future.

The further he went, the more that place started to look like the underground where he thought he had been with James. The damp walls and the mud floor gave the place the same dark and icy air that he clearly remembered experiencing. 'That was too real to be a dream.', he thought as he tried to slip between two walls at a dead end.

Before he started to unfold the small piece of paper, he was already aware he wouldn't understand its contents, which came as no surprise, as the written coordinates were given from the point of view of where he met the person who gave it to him. A drawing would have been more useful to him, but the piece of paper contained only written instructions as to where he should turn and how far he should go. 'First corridor on the left. Second on the right...'. That information would only be useful if he could return to the starting point, but he no longer had any idea of the path he had taken. The fright and fear that someone might capture him made him run without thinking about where he was going, and, no matter how hard he tried, he could not remember it.

'As soon as you turn into this last corridor, you will need to clean the mud-covered wall so that you can find the lock. Do not try to clean the entire door. Only the middle part will be enough.' It was no surprise to Jonah that the paper contained information like that as he just started to think of a way that he could make sense of the information and get to the last corridor.

After a few minutes waiting for someone to reach him, Jonah got up and started walking down the corridors that, despite being shorter, became wider; he was more and more sure that he was heading towards the underground he had been before. He still could not perceive with certainty any corner he had been with James, but the place became to look more alike.

For a moment, he took his attention off the corridors he was walking and tried to find in his pocket the key that the mysterious person had given him. The object was heavy and completely covered with gold; it had the usual shape of an old key, like everything else in that place, and should probably open one of those heavy wooden doors that were no longer found anywhere else. The base of the key contained a few gems that he couldn't quite know how to identify. 'A beautiful reflection of possessions...', he thought as he remembered that the catholic church still boasted immeasurable wealth all around the world. However, a small detail in the key caught his attention; embedded in red stones he could see the shape of a fish, the same he had supposedly found within the maze a few hours ago.

'And how do I get back there?', he wondered as that key would certainly have some connection with the small statue. He tried to remember seeing any sign that might indicate a lock on the statue, which made no sense, since he already knew that the key should open the door covered with clay, but all of that symbolism should have some kind of meaning. He wished that he were in the company of James, the old one-legged would certainly have a long and profound explanation of what that could all mean.

The incessant search for such a door would have to wait. Jonah dropped to his knees on the dirty floor as he realised that his head was throbbing in pain once again. 'What the fuck...', he thought before he could be taken back to one of those psychotic attacks.

"'My dear. You need to recover and go back to living normally. You've been like this for months. Your father and I don't know what else to do.'

Jonah soon realised he was in another one of those induced dreams that were nowhere in his subconscious. The voice that spoke was familiar to him. Joana's mother watched her daughter huddled in bed with tears; she had a lean appearance, to the point of being scrawny. Her face was practically unrecognisable, clearly she hadn't been taking care of herself for some time. He recognised where he was, but he had no recollection of having lived through that situation. Certainly someone was controlling his thoughts in one of those dream chairs.

'Joana?' the voice took on a greater tone of concern.

As much as Jonah tried, he couldn't get close to the body of his old girlfriend. It was as if he was floating around a large impenetrable bubble that presented him with a story he didn't want to know about. He knew little about Lais Amon, Joana's mother, but he knew she was fond of him, at least during the time he had made her daughter happy. Jonah was fascinated by the story behind his old mother-in-law's name. 'My grandfather had a great appreciation for life and gave my mother the name of the god of fertility.', she would tell everyone who asked with curiosity about the uniqueness of the name.

Jonah always found it contradictory that such a catholic family would use a pagan name to honor someone, but Joana's grandfather had always been a man ahead of his time and saw no problem in using life as a way to mirror the past.

As he rambled on about silly memories, the story portrayed by his dream had suddenly changed. The scene was filled with people he had never seen before, all dressed in black and crying tirelessly; in the center he could distinguish Lais Amon, his former mother-in-law, as she wore a black veil over her face and tried not to show the weakness that plagued her thoughts through crying, but it was visible that her expression showed anger.

Jonah tried to talk to people - which he already knew would be in vain - whilst trying to find a sight that would explain to him what was really going on; that's when he was able to see the lid of an open coffin and realise that he was experiencing Joana's funeral. He was soon able to recognise other relatives of his former girlfriend, but the rest of the people had their faces covered and could not be identified by him.

It was not the first or the second time that he had one of those attacks, he already knew enough to differentiate an induced dream from a lucid one. That scene had never happened, he knew that Joana was alive and well. He knew that, surely, someone from the sect was trying to scare him and urge him to seek his redemption by repentance.

Jonah wanted that dream to end once and for all, he was lucid enough to know that he still had a lot to do in reality so that he could get out of that place whilst he was still alive.

'Love?' Joana's voice rang in his ear as the funeral's macabre tone started to get more and more threatening.

He tried to look inside the coffin to find the voice that spoke to him, but Joana's body was now giving way to a newborn child who stirred and cried. His mind spun as he tried to make any sense off the situation, but it seemed things were getting worse by the second.

'Love?' an unknown voice repeated Joana's saying.

One of the hooded people had started walking towards him, whilst new voices started to repeat the same word.

'Love?'

In a few seconds all the people who were present at the funeral started walking towards him, whilst the newborn child was lifted from the coffin by Lais Amon, who started to squeeze its neck until the baby was asphyxiated. One by one, the figures began to remove the black hood and reveal their faces. Or rather, Jonah's own face. All the people depicted themselves as him, all the hoods revealed his own face; some wept and sobbed, whilst others smiled broadly until they began to salivate as if they had no control over their own actions.

Jonah tried to take steps back so that he could get away from all those people who were marching towards him, but the more he felt his body regress in space, the more he felt himself approaching the coffin where the distinguished child had its head hanging by the hand of his former lover's mother.

'Love?'

That was the most horrifying scene he ever thought he could imagine. The baby had lifted its head from Lais Amon's arm and started to repeat Joana's saying in a suffocating voice."

That had certainly been the worst dream Jonah had had in his entire life, whether it was programmed or not, which made him think of what kind of person could have such a sordid mind as to imagine anything like that.

He woke up covered by his own cold sweat. His head still hurt and his concentration was escaping him. He needed to turn his attention to the door he was supposed to find; he was already used to coming and going from those dreams, which made him able to recompose himself quite quickly. He couldn't understand how was still be having those episodes, he really thought that after waking up in that chair, where he had spent most of the night deliriously wondering about, he wouldn't have any more problems with psychotic episodes. However, he was trying to see the positive side of it all; he sought to find useful information in each dream and use it to his advantage, but that last dream had been pure evil, something really disturbing and meaningless. 'It doesn't really fall into Giovanni's personality to want to torment me like that, for no reason and without any hidden messages.', thought Jonah before going back to the path ahead of him in search of the infamous door.

The subterranean spread to the horizon at a distance that Jonah couldn't phantom. He had definitely returned to the place where he wandered with James; he realised that, in fact, he was taking the opposite path that the old man wished he had taken.

That place was no longer an untapped map for Jonah. He tried to remember where the small room where he had entered with James through the maze was. If he could find it, he might be able to go the other way and get to the fish statue. It was certain that the object had something to do with the key that dangled in his pocket.

His head hurt again, but this time in a way more similar to the time when he had lost himself in his own steps before waking up in bed surrounded by Giovanni and his followers. The image that propagated the wet and cluttered floor was, little by little, alternating with that of a dry, soft grass. The pains came and went steadily, in addition to being so weak as not to hinder his concentration; it seemed that someone was trying to show him something, perhaps indicating a specific path or place. 'But how do I get there?', he thought as he returned to what seemed like his own reality.

The small psychotic break that had just shown him a short path that seemed to take place just above from where he was, in the maze of the Dartagnan Brothers Hotel. Something simple and devoid of any surprises or mystery that might involve secret passages, but the last image had not been clear enough. He did not know exactly what he would find at the end of the path that had been presented to him in that strange moment of depersonalisation, however it did not seem that he had any alternative but to follow the way that was given to him.

He went on, trying to find the small room he was once with James, as that was the only real clue he could grasp his mind around, but the corridors and walls of that place were very similar, which made it very difficult to find anything that would resemble a door. 'Maybe looking for a way out would be wiser than finding a door.', he thought as he tried to make sense of where he was. He knew that the underground contained several secret exits that would lead into the maze, but he had no idea of how to find them. 'Why don't these hallucinations show me how to get out of here?', he wondered whilst looking for a positive side in the fact that someone was controlling what was going on in his brain.

He continued to wander the underground at random, having no idea where he was going. His mental state was not the best, his mind was confused and his thoughts took turns between what had just happened to Patrick and the fact that he should save his own life. The similarity of those corridors confused his mind, whilst he waited for another one of those short psychotic breaks to give him a hint of what he was supposed to do.

However, the lack of attention, and the anxiety, made Jonah realise where he was. What he had been looking for, but had already given up on finding, materialised in front of him before he could understand how he got there. Perhaps his mind had been following the opposite path that he had previously taken with James, or perhaps his lack of attention had caused him to find a place that he was no longer looking for, or he could have been wandering in circles for all that time; what mattered now was that he was in front of the door he had been looking for and could soon leave the underground and return to the maze so he could look for the fish statue.

As he managed to find and clean the doorknob, before he could use the key and turn it, he realised that he was entering unknown territory. The place had the same dimensions and was practically organised in the same way, the only difference being the lack of the small hatch that would take him out of the underground. James had told him that many rooms like that could be found in the underground, as that was where Giovanni and his henchmen kept the people they had captured.

To his surprise, the room was mostly empty, containing the same amount of supplies as the other. He sought a bottle of water to quench his thirst and soon turned his attention to find something that could indicate an exit. 'Maybe I'm on the opposite side of the underground.', he thought as he looked across the room seeking for the same lever that could open a secret passage that would lead to the maze. Each and every part of the ceiling was sealed by old rotten wood, where cobwebs indicated that no one had set foot in there for a long time.

'Push the holy book.'

He heard a voice whisper as he tried to understand where it came from.

'Who's there?' he asked without holding the volume of his voice.

'Silence!' the voice exclaimed after making a hissing sound.

'Holy book...', he thought as he turned his attention to look for a bible. Those words could not mean anything else inside that place. His eyes went over the wooden framed shelves whilst his mind continued to pay attention to the voice that had suddenly gone mute. All the books were turned paper forward, leaving no indication of what any of them might be. Jonah figured that hitting just one book would be useless at that point and decided that pushing everything at once would save him some of his precious time.

'It won't work like that, you must find the right book.' the voice said at the same time that he used the entire part of his forearm to push a series of books at once.

'But how do I know which book to push?'

His question was followed by silence.

Jonah then tried to push the books one by one. 'There is an easier way for everything.', he thought to himself as he tried to contain all his attention on the task that had been assigned to him. One of the first books he took in his hand contained the words he longed to find: Holy bible. He already knew that was the one book to be pushed against the shelf, however, after performing the act proposed by the unknown voice, nothing happened.

'It's not working.' he whispered, hoping the voice would answer him before he could go into despair.

Silence reigned.

Jonah removed the book and pushed it again, looking for a different effect to a repeated mistake. Again, nothing happened. He took a deep breath and calmly returned to shelve the book in the same place; with just two fingers, he slowly pushed the bible back onto the shelf, hoping that some mechanism would be activated as the bottom of the wall was reached. He did the same thing for several times, now with anger, anxiety and speed, trying to find different results in the same action that was not getting him anywhere. He leaned on the bookcase and put his other hand on his head; what appeared to be the return of psychotic attacks proved to be only his impatience towards things that didn't work. He had always been like that, he had no patience for flawed acts that resulted in a waste of time.

As he was losing his patience with the lack of results, Jonah allowed his body to slide against the shelf until his knees rested on the floor; he no longer wanted to unravel the mysteries of the Dartagnan Brothers Hotel, his only wish was for it to come to an end. He started to look at the objects that were placed at the bottom of the small wooden bookcase. Several strange objects were exposed in there, as if a particular person had spent a considerable amount of time living off the scarce amount of supply that was already rotting. The objects were very strange; wooden skulls pinned by nails and small coloured decorative boxes - the kind that annoyingly had no space to store anything in it - in a deteriorated state by lack of care. It really felt like nobody had set foot in that room in a long time. 'Perhaps the mechanism activated by the bible has some kind of malfunctioning.', thought Jonah as he got back on his feet so that he could try to find a way that would get him out of there.

'You're doing it wrong.' the distinctive voice whispered again.

'Would you just fucking tell me what to do?' Jonah raised his voice in anger as he was already tired of that game.

Obviously, the voice did not respond.

His utmost desire was to drop everything on that shelf, go out the door, and look for another place that would take him to the ground floor, he even thought of going back the way he came from and try to leave the place where he had just seen Patrick being murdered in cold blood. The brief reflection of what had just happened made him shiver, as he still had in his memory the sound emanating from his friend as he choked on his own blood as he gradually lost his life. However, he retained the urge to look for answers in his anger and decided to focus his attention on a small book that leaned between two of those wooden boxes.

The few old and dirty pages showed nothing that Jonah did not yet know. In fact, he could recognise the small explanatory pamphlet from the C.P.F., the same he had found in James's old hut whilst living the two realities. 'Maybe this is the holy book...', he thought whilst trying to make sense of the words that the distinct voice had given him, but he couldn't understand that anything other than the bible could be defined as something sacred to those people. Anyway, as much as he tried to put and take the booklet off the shelf, nothing different was happening.

Jonah lost his patience and dragged his hand across the shelf where the objects and the pamphlet were. The skull fell heavily on his foot and the small wooden boxes crashed across the hard floor. He didn't know whether he would get down on his knees so he could pick up the mess he had just made, or if he would just kick everything in front of him so he wouldn't have to deal with that problem anymore, which was clearly the easiest choice.

'Collect the objects with attention.' the voice came again before Jonah could calmly put his knees on the floor.

He went on to collect all the small objects as he looked for anything that could catch his attention; in a few seconds he could already see that the small boxes, now slightly ajar, had each a button inside.

'Which button should I press?' he asked anxiously and tearfully.

'Just one of the buttons opens the passage through the bookshelf, the other will lock you in that room until someone realises it and come to your rescue. Pay close attention to what you are going to do. The answer lies within you.'

To his surprise the voice decided to give him an explanation that time, he really did not expect that he would get any sort of specific instructions that could help him at that point, but the riddles continued to cause him problems and his desire to unravel more mysteries was over. 'My rescue...', he thought, knowing his sole alternative was to press the right button.

The buttons inside the boxes looked exactly the same. Jonah tried to find any detail in one of them with the hope that anything would signal what the mysterious voice had just told him, but the objects were also identical and, apart from the marks of time, had no distinction.

'The answer lies within you.', he started to repeat aloud the sayings of the voice in an incessant loop, trying to make sure that any information he had absorbed in all that time could indicate a hint of how it should work. 'Well I do

223

have a fifty percent chance of getting it right...', he started to think whilst giving up on finding any answers, but the opposite would bring the error, and with the error would come his confinement and eventual capture.

Fifty percent was a chance he couldn't take. He didn't have that privilege and he needed to think in order to find the right way out, but he had no idea of how to do it.

'The answer lies within you.'

The words of the unknown voice returned to sound like a song in his mind as he fixed his thoughts on anything that could bring him a solution to his problem.

The only thing he could think of was his tattoos. The famous St. Peter's Cross still had two different meanings to Jonah, but none of them brought any coherence to that particular situation. 'Fallacia Alia Aliam Trudit.', he read aloud the words of the small letters that marked his forearm. The meaning behind that sentence had not yet been completely clear to him, except for referring to the mistakes he had made in the past. But what he definitely couldn't understand was how someone would have tattooed him tips, which he would eventually need, on his arm so that he could escape a situation that had not yet happened. Even if it didn't make sense, he tried to use everything in his power to search for any meaning in those words.

Jonah sat down on the floor once again, lifting his knees so he could support his head and concentrate his thoughts on what he was supposed to unveil, when he heard the sound of a metallic gleam hitting the floor, bouncing until it stopped.

'The answer lies within you.', he repeated the words aloud as he remembered the key he had received and that it, more than likely, would have something to do with all that mystery.

His eyes started to run over the key he now had in his hands. Jonah had already observed almost every detail of the object; the little fish symbol continued to shine through the red stones, which told him nothing about how the key that could help him at that moment. That was when a brief moment of wisdom came to his mind and reminded him of the little phrase placed under the fish stuck in the nearby maze: 'Laedere Facile, Mederi Difficile.' That brought his mind back to a place that was dormant.

'Easier to tear than to sew.', the translation soon came out of his mouth when he took the booklet that was being held between the two boxes and began to tear it without any parsimony, and, to his surprise, the answer came with immense ease; the cover of the booklet was the only sheet that did not tear, locking itself as he put on a little more strength before realising that something was stuck in there. A flaccid metal tape was attached between the front and the back cover; Jonah took all the care in the world so that he wouldn't break the little shard of metal. Little by little he managed to pull the object out, which was exactly what it appeared to be: a mere piece of some kind of mouldable metal. He tried to analyse it before he could give it any purpose, but the small object did not contain any writing or anything else that could indicate a solution to the mystery he had been unraveling, which came to be quite unsettling, as he did not have any idea of how to connect the metal thread to his problem.

The first, and simplest, solution was to lay the metal strip on the boxes, but nothing happened. He also tried to touch the buttons, being very careful not to press them by mistake, with the newly found object, something that also had no effect. Obviously, it wouldn't be that easy, but Jonah was already tired of unraveling mysteries and simply rested his hands on his thighs and decided to wait for the voice behind the wall to give him another clue. Another sudden act of mystery came to happen when he tried to dry his sweaty hands on his shirt and realised that the small metal had been stuck to his trousers. Apparently, the object contained some kind of magnetic force that had worked when coming in contact with the key in his pocket.

The small metal fillet fit exactly on the side of the key that was opposite to the one containing the small red stones. As soon as Jonah allocated one object to the other, the magnetic field did the rest of the work by perfectly covering the gap in the key. 'It still doesn't make any sense...', Jonah thought as he noticed that none of the boxes had any entry for a key. He brought the key close to the boxes, one at a time, looking for any kind of surprise that would solve his problems; as soon as he approached the box on his left, a faint, short red light flashed inside the button, which made him suddenly think that it would be the button to be pressed, but his momentum was broken by wisdom, causing Jonah to approach the key to the box on his right very sparingly, hoping that nothing would happen and that the mystery would end right there.

As he was expecting, his luck had not kept pace with his wishes and a green light decided to bring torment to his mind as it slightly blinked as the key got closer to it. 'Green or red?', he thought when he reasoned that the logic would be: green goes, red stops. However, logic had not been helping him in his unexpected and unwanted adventure at the Dartagnan Brothers Hotel. After all the effort he had spent to unravel all those mysteries involving the key and the boxes, Jonah had arrived at the same point where he had started; he had a fifty percent chance of getting it right, as the green one still gave him a slight advantage if logic was his starting point.

He could no longer wait for time to pass. His options were limited and logic would have to be his ally from that point on.

He was ready to press the green button when he saw the red stones on the key turn black, as he approached it towards the box. He then realised that everything was keening towards red. All the stones engraved into the objects he find or saw that night were red; Giovanni's staff was red; Patrick's last words were red - he really thought that situation had nothing to do with what he was about to decide, but his mind couldn't stop returning to the sight of his friend bleeding to death.

Without further dwelling over the idea, Jonah approached the key to the red button as he saw the stones sparkle again. He then closed his eyes and pressed the red button, leaving logic aside and hoping that his life would not be confined within those four walls that surrounded him.

A crackle sounded from behind the bookcase, pushing it forward and causing a small passage to be exposed into a dark direction and with no sign of anyone being around.

'Did it work?' he asked, waiting for the unknown voice to come to his rescue, indicating the next steps to be followed.

A figure surrounded by a dimly lit silhouette began to run in the opposite direction. Apparently the person was not prepared to receive Jonah that soon, which indicated that his actions had taken the right direction at the presented crossroads.

'Wait, please!' Jonah hissed with a certain intensity that he still had from the adrenaline given by his latter choice, realising that the unknown shadow wasn't paying him any attention.

'Follow me.' whispered the voice as it took an even greater distance.

Jonah followed the straight path ahead of him, unsure if he was even following the mysterious person who was guiding him. His hope was that he would not be led into a trap and that the unknown voice was really on his side. The path was really dark, as well as damp, which made Jonah slip every time he tried to speed up his pace to get closer to his newest guide.

'Keep your distance and be quiet!'

It wouldn't do him any good to upset the mysterious person. Jonah followed the orders he was given and continued to walk slowly, hoping that, sooner or later, he would reach an illuminated place where an enlightened soul would be ready to save him. The space covered was short. A beam of light opened when the mysterious person slowly climbed a wooden ladder and opened a hatch that led to the ground floor.

Jonah couldn't believe what was happening. He was back at the place he had fought so hard to get out of. The events that had unraveled throughout the weekend made him go back to the exact same spot where he swore never to go back to.

Daylight lit the face of the person who had been helping him. His eyes startled and his brain was more confused than ever. It made no sense that Monalisa was leading him away from the sect of which she was a part of.

'You?' he asked aloud, jumping backwards as he stood firmly on the grass that shaped the maze.

'Yes, I'm your only chance to get out of here. Now keep silent and help me with this fucking thing.' Monalisa's voice was back to its normal intonation.

'No, no, and no!' he replied trying to contain the volume of his voice.

Monalisa ignored the audacity of the man who was in one of the most vulnerable points of his life and pointed to a place on the floor. Jonah followed the movement of her finger and saw the small statue of the fish that had previously made him confused as he circled the maze. The questions were so many that his mind could not focus on a single point, but the presence of the small statue in front of him made him realise that he had reached the destination that had been imposed on him. He was sure that this would not be a favourable situation, but if Monalisa wanted him dead she wouldn't have taken him to a place where others would hardly be able to find him.

'What do you want from me? Why are you helping me?'

'The last thing I want in this life is to help you.' replied Monalisa angrily. 'Now do as I say and be quiet!' she finished by pulling a gun from behind her waist and pointing it at Jonah.

He raised his hands after controlling the shock that had made his legs tremble. His desire was to close his eyes and let Monalisa end that suffering once and for all, but he felt, deep down, he still had a chance to save himself.

'What do you want from me?' repeated Jonah as he kept his head down.

'You really don't know who I am? Can't you recognise me?' asked Monalisa with a tone of anger that increased with each word.

Jonah tried to find that old, wrinkled face in some forgotten place inside his mind, so he could at least have some idea of who he was talking to, but nothing he could remember made any sense. He had no idea of who Monalisa could be, his only memories of her was that she had recently haunted his dreams, whilst he was made prisoner inside that red room with threats of torture.

'Let's refresh your memory then, shall we?'

CHAPTER 18:

Monalisa took out from her jacket's pocket what appeared to be a small round device that resembled some kind of smartphone. She looked deep into Jonah's eyes and showed a smirk before she could touch the screen of the device. Jonah felt a strong headache, even greater than the previous ones; he knew he would be immersed in another of those lucid dreams even before he felt the first strain of pain, but what surprised him was the ease with which Giovanni's accomplice had transported him into chaos.

"Jonah soon realised that he was induced into one of Monalisa's dream. He could see a woman, with her back turned to him, leaning on the edge of a bed, whilst crying and trying to control herself at the same time. A small hand, from the person lying on the bed, stroked her head and said that everything was going to be okay, the voices mixed and the faces were completely hidden from him, and as much as Jonah tried, he couldn't move to get a better view of what was going on.

'You need to help yourself, the worst is over.' said Monalisa, still showing the back of her head as she sobbed.

The person was silent, and Monalisa's little sobbing was replaced by a simple image. Jonah was still watching her from behind, but the thin and awkward posture of the woman he had met a few hours ago already showed him her identity. The old lady had an old tic on her neck; little by little she twisted her head to the right side for a small crack in the bones, it seemed like a simple gesture, but it was one of those things that would become a nuisance for the rest of the day if it weren't soon calmed down.

The scenario changed, and Monalisa found herself watching television, going from channel to channel without giving the device time to show her what was being broadcasted. She looked like a tired and anxious old woman. Beside her, on a small side table, was an ashtray completely crammed with cigarette butts, as well as several bottles of alcohol that rested on the table already empty or near the end; on the opposite side a small metal pipe reproduced what, until that moment, Jonah had never seen before, the object was used to smoke strong drugs, such as crack or methamphetamine. She whimpered and sobbed, as she lit one cigarette on the tip of the other, as if she was trying to prevent the flame from going out. With each butt she squeezed between the others, she took a huge sip from one of the bottles. There was a large, dirty glass there, but the old woman no longer bothered to pour the drink on it. The floor, which she seemed to avoid putting her feet on, was filthy and full of garbage, which included broken bottles and cans of food that created life within themselves. The scene was not scary, but rather disgusting and sad. Jonah was creating an urge within him, but he tried not to let his emotions steal his attention. He needed to seize that moment. 'If she is making me experience this, there must be a reason.', he thought as he shook his head and returned paying attention to the woman's movements.

For the first time, Monalisa stood up and faced a direction that allowed Jonah to get a good glimpse at her. Her face looked a little younger, more alert and less wrinkled, but she still carried an ugly and uncared desire for appearance, the exact look that someone would carry for choosing such a lifestyle, which was shown to Jonah deliberately. He was watching that scene for some reason, Monalisa wanted to show him something.

The scenario changed again. The woman no longer looked so old, much less destroyed by drugs. The various bottles of cheap and strong alcohol had given way to a beautiful and full glass of wine, while cigarettes had not yet accumulated and the metal pipe was not present. The house where she was staying was organised and her hair still looked clean. Her face was still filled with the strong bonds of depression as her catatonic sight indicated trauma, and her lack of haste for the simple things that surrounded her gave it a clear indication that life had not been fair, if such a thing even existed.

Jonah realised that Monalisa had been spamming some kind of her own timeline in his mind. That dream was there to show him something. The image of her sitting on the bed with someone indicated some kind of illness, and her deteriorated state before that could only mean that the situation had been deteriorating for some time. The next image propagated by Monalisa already showed a happier life, but her face was no longer showing.

A beautiful garden surrounded by toys, swings and seesaws brought the image of a bouncing girl who came and went from side to side turning around in the wind whilst letting strands of hair mess up her vision and hiding her face from whatever problem the world could lay at her feet.

Jonah suddenly recognised those feet.

As soon as he realised where he was, his heart was taken by another shock. Not because it was the garden of Joana's old house, but because he was trying to understand what kind of connection that Monalisa might have with her ex-girlfriend. For Jonah, it was frightening that all those people, who he did not know, knew so much about his life and the details that had spoiled his relationship with Joana. But that was a matter from the past. Jonah knew he had never experienced that particular situation, he had no memory of seeing Joana skipping around a garden like that, as if she was a child waiting to go to a toy store. Obviously, Joana's joy and willingness to live brought contagious happiness, but that particular situation was being imprinted in Jonah's dreams as something that had been real in someone else's past.

'Here, Joana, come and see!' the voice exclaimed as the former love of his life allowed her hair to flick back and showed the stunning beauty of her perfect face.

She came running towards Jonah. The voice came from behind him, but he had no way of turning his attention to the person who was acclaiming the name of his beloved, he could only feel that he knew that voice, and he knew it very well.

A whirlwind changed the mirroring of his vision again. The old woman went back to look like as she was wearing a mummy costume, with wrinkled skin and a bag under her eyes that sustained insomnia and a huge variety of mixed drugs that seemed to ease her pain. Monalisa's face now looked into Jonah's eyes, as if the person knew he was watching her, but Jonah was not intimidated. He looked deeply into the eyes of the lady who was trying to scare him with all those deceptive propagations and did not hesitate to speak:

'Whatever you want, come and take it from me...'"

After his face was crammed with a punch, his mind woke up and came face to face with Monalisa's, who was still resting her hand in the air with a sign that she would soon lower it to hit him again.

'I'm here, I'll take everything I want from you!' she replied whilst letting the arm, which held the gun with the grip pointed down, fall over Jonah's face.

His head started to spin. His attention was lost by the pain that hung over his already swollen eyes as his lips started to slowly bleed. That weapon was heavy and made him feel a strain of pain so strong that it was able to hinder him from thinking.

'What the fuck did I do to you?' he asked with the little air he was able to grasp and still hold in his lungs before he could cough and sharpen the pain in his head.

'You really don't know who I am?' asked Monalisa.

'I've got no idea of who you are.'

'The dream I just showed you!' she exclaimed vehemently, hoping that Jonah would be inspired by his wits and finally realise who she was.

'How do you know about my story with Joana?' he demanded an explanation as he came back from the buzzing in his head, trying to understand why that woman knew so much about his life.

'Your story?' the gun's grip beat his face once again. 'Look at my face, look into my eyes and tell me that you still don't know who I am!'

Her face did seem familiar, but his mind was failing to make sense of who that person might be. Jonah sought to look deeply into her eyes with the hope that his memory would bring a moment of clarity to his mind that would indicate the identity of the woman who tormented him.

'You tortured my daughter!' she exclaimed as she wiped the tears that were falling from her face.

'Lais Amon?' he asked incredulously. He could never imagine that that woman could be Joana's mother. Her face was disfigured by the constant use of drugs and alcohol.

'Yes, Jonah. It's me.' she replied whilst resuming her composure.

'What are you doing here?' he asked as he tried to get up from the floor and walk away with his hands raised. He didn't want to give any reason for the woman to fire that gun at him.

'You have no right to ask me questions!'

'What do you want from me?' he ignored the order.

The grip of the weapon struck his the face one more time, causing Jonah to fall before he could even completely getting up from the last hit. His face was throbbing with pain and his right eye started to swell, impairing his vision as he spat out the blood that accumulated in his mouth.

'Please stop...' he pleaded as he put his hands over his head with his knees deep on the grass.

'Listen very well to what I'm going to say. I am not here to help you, quite the contrary, you are the one who will help me. You will do everything I say, without questioning anything, and then maybe, and only maybe, you can still leave this place alive. Understood?' Monalisa did not expect an answer, but Jonah decided to contradict the woman who had him at gunpoint.

'No. You will tell me exactly what you are doing here and why I have to help you. And before you threaten me again, know that I am more than tired of this whole situation and I am no longer afraid of what may happen to me.' he finished, still on his knees, holding Monalisa's hands, which were pointing the gun at him. He brought the object so close to his own face as he closed his eyes and waited for his fate to finally catch up with him.

Monalisa seemed to be surprised by Jonah's reaction; she certainly didn't expect that to happen. He felt very confident as he realised that she had stopped to rethink the situation as she needed to readjust her plan to that new reality. He had never had a close relationship with Lais Amon, but that person in front of him was no longer the sweet and carrying woman he had known. Not only because of the appearance that had made her unrecognisable, but also because of the expression on her eyes. A dark and injured soul bearing many problems that had been deteriorating her will to live. He could feel the vengeance that came with each glance the woman gave him, he knew that his courage should have a limit and he could not let his emotions let him lose control.

The two continued looking at each other without making a single sound. The air was dense and any step outside the curve could trigger an unfavourable reaction for Jonah. 'If she wants me alive, I must have some use to her.', he thought as he searched for the right words to say so Monalisa would give him some credit and tell him what she was planning to do.

'Think again Lais.' he started before being interrupted.

'Monalisa! If you call me Lais again I will pull this trigger without thinking twice, do you understand?' she emphasised her words.

Jonah just nodded as he swallowed the saliva that fear had produced in his mouth. 'There are lines that I must not cross.', he thought whilst resuming his reasoning.

'I'm sorry, Monalisa. I need you to include me in your plan. There is no way I can do exactly what you want without knowing what your goal is.'

'Where's the key I gave you?' she asked as she lowered the weapon and held out a hand towards Jonah.

Soon Jonah could see that he had an advantage over Monalisa. If he was there, alive, she must have had a purpose for him. The key didn't matter at all, she was the one who had given it to him, but if she had risked helping him get there, going against Giovanni and all the other members of the sect, it was because he held a certain importance to her plans. That made Jonah wonder what those plans were, and why she didn't just take him to Giovanni and let Mr. Dartagnan have his way with him and go on with his torture plan.

'What do you want from me?' he asked again as he took the key out of his pocket and handed it over.

'Are you fucking dyslexic or something?' she frowned as if she wasn't expecting an answer. 'I told you, I want you to do what I tell you, without asking questions.'

Monalisa took the key and put the gun on the strap that tightened her dress as she slowly moved away from Jonah until she could reach for the small fish statue. She bent down carefully and inserted the key into a small lock

234

that Jonah hadn't seen before. The statue made a small crack, causing a drawer to open at its base, the compartment was too small for her to remove anything significant from there, but the surprises continued to captivate Jonah's eyes. Monalisa tugged on, very gently, a cylindrical object that appeared to be larger than the compartment that held it; its appearance was simple, despite the dark red color that gave him an elegance worthy of being owned by Giovanni Dartagnan.

'I imagine you won't tell me what that stick is for?' asked Jonah as he tried to open the eye which was getting more and more swollen due to the blows he had been receiving.

Monalisa sighed heavily, trying to ignore the voice that plagued her concentration, as she seemed to be having some difficulty following her own plans.

'You disgust me!' she said as she crouched down next to Jonah's face. 'And this is the object that will get me out of this place.'

Jonah closed his eyes and swallowed the vomit that formed inside his mouth. Monalisa exhaled alcohol through all the pores of her body, and her breath smelled like a mixture of ashtrays with a lack of appetite. She went back to the statue, taking out from underneath her dress an object similar to the one she had just removed from the statue, replacing it, and turning back the key. After making sure that the small drawer was properly locked, she stretched her arm all the way back and threw the key with as much strength as she could at a random place. Jonah let his eyes follow the path to the key, thinking of a future situation that he would need to find it, but looking for an object in the middle of that maze did not seem like a sensible thing to do.

As the woman tried to recover from a sudden lack of balance, Jonah began to think about the remote-like object that he had just seen in her hands. The small round device should mean something that could answer the questions he still had about his psychotic episodes. The depersonalisations that followed each and every movement of his life, without being invited, seemed to have some kind of remote control for it to be activated. He had lost sight of the object, but he was sure it was still there, as Monalisa put and removed things from the bust of her dress as if it was a bottomless hole.

Something inside his had was telling him he needed to get his hands on that device.

'How long have you been part of the C.P.F?' Jonah's question put an intriguing expression on Monalisa's face.

'How do you know about that?' she asked as she untied her dress.

'I have my ways.' he said as he got up, thinking she might not be as important to Giovanni's sect as he thought she would.

'Let's get out of here. I need to hand you over to Giovanni.' she said as if that was the most normal thing in the world.

Jonah fell back hard on the floor and started to laugh wildly as he felt an enormous amount of pain in every single cell of his body. Once again, he was all dirty and embarrassed, but he knew that this time his appearance would not cause any suspicions.

'What's so fucking funny?'

'The fact that you think I'm going back to Giovanni.'

'That wasn't a request... It was an order!' she said as she wielded the gun again towards his head.

'I thought it was already clear that I'm not afraid of you!' exclaimed Jonah whilst looking at the woman from the bottom up. 'You've already showed me that you can't kill me, you need me.'

'Well, it's time for you to rethink this little theory of yours.' she said as she cocked the gun. 'I need you in front of Giovanni, dead or alive. Delivering you alive would give me a greater reward and satisfaction, but I will not hesitate to drag you around whilst you bleed through the hole I put in your head.'

Monalisa's voice sang in a psychotic tone. For the first time, Jonah was afraid of the wrinkled old woman. Ever since he learned that she was Lais Amon, he had thought that he could persuade her to get him out of there somehow. He thought that the sweet lady he had once known was asleep within that sordid mind that accompanied Giovanni in his tortures; he thought there was a way to awaken that soul who was covered with hatred and desire for revenge; he thought Monalisa was his passport out of there.

'How long have you been doing this?' he asked as he got up and started walking beside Monalisa.

'This what?' she asked ironically, implying that Jonah hadn't seen her in a long time.

'That, you know... Part of Giovanni's sect.'

'I met Giovanni a few months ago, but I'm not part of any sect.'

'Then why are you here? Do you want me to have the same fate as the other heretics?' he asked wryly.

'You need to learn to follow the development of things quickly, boy. Why do you think I helped you get out of where I want to take you back? What sense do you make out of that?'

Jonah began to think with what was left of his wits. It really didn't make any sense for the old woman to take him there. She held the key before he ever did and had him just a few feet away from Giovanni, it was never so easy to hand him over to the head of the sect and receive whatever reward she was due.

'Maybe you needed me to complete what was missing in the key...' he argued after eliminating any other hypothesis.

'Very well. But I could have gone to the room that I, myself, told you about and get what was missing from the key. Why would I need you?' she continued what seemed to be some kind of trivia contest.

The experience he was having talking to Monalisa was more intriguing than any other he had ever had. Both the Dartagnan brothers had made him a fool with their answers, causing each puzzle to have more questions than answers. 'Maybe I can find the answers I am looking for so much if I play this woman's game correctly.', he thought as he left his wandering thoughts and returned to the real world.

'A bigger impact, maybe?' he asked himself, raising his eyebrow and feeling stupid at the same time.

'That would be a ridiculous reason, wouldn't it? Let's just say that such an assumption is part of a larger motive.'

she turned her attention to him as the two continued walking through the maze towards the great stairs.

Jonah couldn't quite understand, but it seemed that Monalisa had been letting herself create some kind of bond with him. 'She seems quite drunk, maybe I can take advantage of it.', he thought as he remembered how charismatic he was when he was drunk. He decided to put a charming expression on his face and pretend that he no longer understood anything.

'You need to understand that you ruined my daughter's life. I feel disgust, anger, and aversion every time I look at that dirty face of yours...' Jonah completely changed his expression; what seemed to him that was creating a bond was nothing more than another kind of mental game. He had never felt so offended in his life.

He understood that that woman was not playing around, much less letting her drunkenness hinder her plans. Her manipulations were making Jonah comfortable with the situation, something that would make it easier for her to hand him over to Giovanni without any scratches.

'All this because of the abortion?' he dared to ask.

'Beg you a pardon?' she exclaimed aloud as she removed the gun from her holster and pointed it at Jonah again. 'Give me a reason, you useless piece of shit, so I won't end this right now.'

'Do you really think we would have been good parents at that age?' he asked without showing any fear towards Monalisa's action. 'Do you really believe that it would have been a better option to ruin our lives with an unwanted child?'

Monalisa was not pleased at all with that story, but she seemed to have a very strong motive within herself that prevented her from shooting Jonah, which made her lower her pistol and concentrate her forces on keeping calm.

'You've never spoke to Joana again after what you did, have you?' she asked rhetorically. 'Do you know what happened to that poor girl after you left?'

Jonah didn't want to answer. If those dreams that were induced into his mind during the last hours had any chance of being real, he already had a feeling that Joana's life did not took a turn for the best.

'And you reckon that giving me to Giovanni will fix the mistakes of the past?' Jonah knew he could beat the old woman if he brought out his sentimental side; he could be cold when he needed to.

'My goal is not to fix the mistakes of the past Jonah, but to make you pay for what you did to my daughter and our whole family.' she replied, drying the tears that started to fill her eyes.

'And for that you want to feed this archaic sect and satisfy the sordid desires of repressed old people?'

'You don't understand...' Jonah seemed to be touching a sensitive spot.

'Why don't you let me see Joana? I know that I cannot bring back the days lost by my mistakes, but perhaps I can bring better days for the future.'

He realised, as soon as he finished speaking, that he had exhausted any possibility of getting into Monalisa's head. It was clear that the woman was in no condition to respond to his emotional blackmail, and the way he had spoken was so palpable and so insensitive, that she was never letting him go. Jonah had loved Joana, really, and very deeply, but that was already a turned page in his life, and now his only goal was to get out of there alive so he could disappear into the world and never have to see those people again; he didn't even want to go after the police, nor the media, so that he could satisfy the wishes that James had laid on him, he just wanted to forget all of that and move on with his life.

'Do you want to see Joana?' asked Monalisa, sarcastically, as she put the gun back on her belt.

'Yes...' he replied with tiredness.

She made a brief signal, indicating with her hand that Jonah should follow the path that was right in front of him. He stopped to think that he had paid no attention to anything within the maze. Monalisa seemed to have memorised the path as they did not have to return even once and were getting closer and closer to the stairs that led to the main party hall, where Giovanni would certainly be waiting for him surrounded by thugs, making it impossible for Jonah to escape. He felt that his end was finally about to come, soon he would have to face the consequences of his actions and endure the penance that was saved for him.

'And what would you like to say to my daughter, if you could see her today?' she asked with a slight smile as her shaking hand reached for a cigarette from inside the bust of her dress. 'Come on.' she pushed him after taking the first drag.

'I would apologize.' Jonah said after holding his weight back.

He had no idea of what he would say to Joana if he could see her at that moment. He hadn't seen her in so many years. He didn't even know if he still felt anything for her. Perhaps she was still the greatest love of his life and would be the one for him forever, as he had never loved anyone again. However, he didn't think much about his old girlfriend, although he still dreamed about her every once in a while, what made him wake up depressed and homesick. He always tried to think that he missed the feeling he had for her, the intimacy they shared, and the good times they spent together, but he did not have hopes and dreams that one day they would meet again to follow up that troubled history.

'As if apologising at this point would make any difference in my daughter's life. Don't be a fucking asshole.' Monalisa tried to speed up the pace as they approached the exit of the maze.

Jonah was quiet, but trying to slow down the pace as they were getting closer and closer. He knew that nothing else could save him from the situation that was about to come, but it brought him a certain comfort to know that he was extending his life span for a few seconds.

'Why didn't you just gave me to Giovanni when you saw me in the cult hall?' he insisted to the same unanswered question, still not believing that this was all to make a bigger impact.

'The goal, Jonah.' she changed the tone of her voice as if she were talking to a child. 'It's using you as a bargaining chip. Understood?' she spoke as she gave two light slaps on the top of his head. 'That's why I had to get you away from there, so I could bring you back as if you were on the brink of escaping. It needs to look real!'

'How do you want to use me as a bargaining chip?'

'Joana is alive, and Giovanni holds her hostage in the rubbles of this estate. Nobody knows that she is my daughter. Giovanni would never free her from her penance just for that particular reason, but if I am the person who brings him his most glorious prey, I may be able to exchange one life for another.'

CHAPTER 19:

'Wait a minute!' exclaimed Jonah before Monalisa could push him out of the maze. 'Let's look at this again, shall we?'

'Look at what now? It's time to face the consequences of your actions like a man! Come on!' she exclaimed as she pulled Jonah back towards the exit of the maze.

'No!' he exclaimed. 'Please wait...'

'You've got one minute.' she said as she returned to point the gun to Jonah's face. 'I've already told you. You can go dead or alive, up to you.'

'What makes you think that Giovanni is going to give you Joana like that? Think about it, he can only see it as a betrayal. You infiltrated his sect to try to get your daughter out of there.'

'It doesn't matter anymore, I've spent months with this man, I know exactly what he wants, and that's you.', she replied, throwing her shoulders up as if she had all the answers on the tip of her tongue.

'But why does he have Joana? What did she do wrong?' Jonah wanted to understand exactly what was going on over there.

'She had an abortion, you absolute idiot... How slow are you?'

'But it was me who did the abortion, she didn't know.'

'And with all that conclusion you still can't understand why I want to use you as a bargain?' Monalisa seemed appalled by Jonah's lack of logic.

'That won't work! I knew, or lived, or whatever it was, I still don't quite understand what happened with my mind, but the deceased James told me things that don't imply that Giovanni will have all that disposition to make an exchange.'

'Deceased?' asked Monalisa. 'James is alive and well, as far as I know. I've never met the man, but Giovanni speaks about him all the time. What did he tell you?'

The facts continued to surprise Jonah, or at least they began to answer certain questions he still had. If James was still alive, what he had experienced for all those hours had been real, which brought him some comfort, although he still couldn't explain how it all happened at the same time. 'One thing at a time...', he thought as he turned his attention back to Monalisa.

'Where is James? He can help us.' was the first thing that came to his mind.

'How the fuck am I supposed to know? I spent the whole time with you in that room, don't you remember?'

'Finally answers...', thought Jonah as his eyes shone towards Monalisa's.

'So that was real? But what about the time I spent with James? When was that?' he asked trying to finally make sense of all that chaos.

'What are you talking about? We only induced you to some lucid dreams, and none of them involved James.' she answered sincerely. 'I don't even know how you know James exists...'

'Back to square one.', he thought again and decided to refocus on convincing Monalisa not to take him to Giovanni. As much as it made sense to leave that story as a hero who had saved his ex-girlfriend by handing over his own life to the psychopathic villain, he still held the idea that what mattered most at that moment was his own life. It was like that with Patrick and he was sure it would be the same with Joana. If he could save himself, he would.

'The time has come... Come on now.' she said as she lit another cigarette.

'Please, let's rethink this situation and find a better solution.'

'Enough Jonah! You did wrong, and now you are going to save my daughter with your life. I would think of it as a moment of redemption.' Monalisa seemed more out of her mind than ever.

Jonah needed to find a way to get Monalisa out of the way. He thought about running out into the maze, but despite the woman's drunken state, he knew she would be able to find him in no time as she knew that place much better than he did, and it wouldn't be long before he could find himself lost in one of its dead ends again.

'Stop trying to find a solution. If you met James, then you know what Giovanni is capable of, you must understand that there is no shortcut to any of his nonsenses. Be a man once in your life and make up for your mistakes!' Monalisa took him by the arm and started to force their way out of the maze.

'I can take responsibility to any mistakes I've made in the past, but I am not obliged to give my life to a bunch of lunatics who believe they are guardians of their own imaginary friend!' he exclaimed as he forced himself to stay where no one could see him.

'I suggest you use those same words when you meet Giovanni again.' she said with a sarcastic tone. 'It will make it much easier to convince him that way.'

Monalisa raised her pistol as she waived it through the air and repeated the phrase she had been saying to Jonah for the last half an hour: 'Dead or alive.'

It was already going through his mind that giving his life there, quickly, would be the easiest way to end all that suffering, but something inside him made him accept that his life should not end there, and, besides everything, he would have the chance to see Joana once again.

The two started walking slowly towards the stairs. Jonah still admired the beauty of how that structure had been built in such a harmonic way and complained internally that beautiful things like that were wasted by mean and old-fashioned beings. He was about to start climbing the stairs, but Monalisa pulled him by the arm and brought him to the front of that stone wall that supported the main hall where the party was taking place. He was already thinking that the old woman had regretted what she was doing and that his destiny was about to change, however Monalisa started to feel the wall like she was looking for something.

'Another secret passage?' he asked wryly.

'I lost count of how many I've found.' she replied with a strained expression.

Jonah was sure that she was not a person that wanted to impose evil. He wished he could fix the mistakes of the past and convince her that the two could get out of there together and seek help to rescue Joana still alive from whatever trouble she was in; even if James's speech made him believe that Giovanni had influence over the most powerful people in the city, there would still be someone who could help them.

'Are you sure you want to do this? We can get out of here and get help...'

'There's no help, Jonah. This place has a life of its own.' she replied as she blinked lightly. 'There's so much more to it that your feeble mind cannot even begin to understand it.'

All the anger that Monalisa seemed to have towards him was sort of calmed by the fact that she had captured him. Jonah knew he could not step outside the line, as the woman still had a gigantic rage towards him. All those induced and lucid dreams and everything he had witnessed when he was in the red room made him sure that she was not to be trifled with. 'She must have taken something to calm the nerves.', he thought as he waited for Monalisa to find the secret passage she was looking for.

'Sorry for the delay, but I'm a little tipsy.' she said laughing as she wobbled across the grass.

'No rush...' replied Jonah whilst waiting for a miracle to come to his way.

She was not in her best condition, but she was still the one who held the gun.

She soon found what she was looking for and managed to open what appeared to be a false door built into the stone wall.

'Pull it.' she ordered, making a motion signal whilst swaying the fire arm through the air.

Jonah had no choice but to do what he was told. He started to pull the door with all of his strength. The stones added an enormous weight to the passage that should lead to the hall where he had been before, where he had seen his friend Patrick being killed.

The door opened and he found a narrow stone staircase, which made sense, since the room he had been to was in the underground. They went down through the short space to meet the already known damp stone floor that Jonah traveled through in order to never return, but there he was, once again, about to face what fate had in store for him.

The room was in the same way that Jonah had left it, with the small difference that now all the men dressed in black, led by Giovanni Dartagnan, were kneeling around

Patrick's body, which was still dripping blood on the floor. Jonah was able to distinguish Giovanni as soon as he saw him beside the priest, bearing that same red staff over his shoulder.

Monalisa entered the room very calmly and sparingly, she looked like she was dancing on the top of her toes, avoiding not to disturb anything that was considered to be sacred; Jonah soon realised that she wasn't one to believe in any of that fanatic nonsense, at least not in the same way as the members of the sect. She seemed to be only interested in recovering Joana from Giovanni's clutches and getting out of there without leaving any trace.

'Are you sure you won't change your mind?' whispered Jonah, who was beginning to tremble with anxiety. 'I'm telling you this won't work...'

Monalisa just ignored Jonah's fear and kept going until she was as close as possible to the people who now began to notice her presence, interrupting the words of adoration from Giovanni and the priest.

'Where were you, Monalisa, and what can be so important that you missed the last offering?' asked the priest, unable to observe the presence of Jonah through the pitch black that covered the entire place.

'Giovanni.' began Monalisa with an informality that did not seem to be welcomed by those who were present. 'I bring you your greatest wish, what no one else here was able to do.'

She already seemed to be delivering her intentions even before showing what she had brought; the harshness and dexterity with which Monalisa had been dealing with the situation, as well as the calm that she had been maintaining so that she would not give up who she was, seemed to be leaving room for a worry surrounded by anxiety and sadness. The old woman was showing herself to be vulnerable, which would not go well in a place like that; those people did not have an ounce of compassion when it came to maintaining order within the sect. Monalisa let her shadow give way to Jonah's face, which brought expressions of surprise and admiration throughout the room.

Jonah was trying to stay calm, but anxiety had completely taken over his ability to reason, he was inside the lion's den and surrounded by dozens of them. His only option was to hope that Giovanni would keep his mercy in the future, but that was uncertain and his fear-tormented mind seemed to know that panicking would be the only solution for him as a defense mechanism.

'Oh, now, who do we have here, ladies and gentlemen.' Giovanni got up from his knees with surprise and admiration. He pulled Monalisa by the hand, kissed her on the forehead, and patted her head as if he was poking a spoiled child.

Jonah was impressed with the situation. The Monalisa he remembered, inside that little red room, was cunning and vehemently imposing her will, whereas that Monalisa, in front of him, looked like Giovanni's little pet, ready to fulfil whatever was asked from her.

'Jonah, my dear! We were looking all over for you. You are a hard man to find.' he said sordidly whilst showing a smirk.

'You disgusting old man! What did you do to Patrick?' he asked, already knowing the answer.

'Well, I didn't want you to miss the show, and I swear we waited for as long as we could, but not to worry, you've arrived just in time for the next one.' said Giovanni, knowing he was hurting Jonah with every word he exhaled from his lungs.

'What kind of sordid mind have you to believe that crimes of this nature can be justified by fanciful and fanatical nonsense?' he asked as he had his swollen eyes burning with anger.

'Crime? Did I hear you right? Is the same man who believes he lives by his own laws who is here to preach me about crimes?' he laughed and was instantly followed by everyone present.

'There's nothing I have done that compares to what you just did to Patrick.' he said, looking at his friend's lifeless eyes as he still had his mouth wide open and filled by his own blood.

'Ah, but that's where you're mistaken, young man.' Giovanni started walking towards him whilst he spoke.

Monalisa was quiet as she listened to the end of Giovanni's speech. Jonah knew that she was waiting for

Joana to come from that same narrow hallway that Patrick had recently been brought in, and as soon as that happened she would be there to seek her salvation.

'And where was it that you found him, Monalisa?' Giovanni turned his back to Jonah and to looked into the woman's eyes, which seemed to be lost in its own little world.

'I found him in the maze, sir.' she was now showing the upmost respect towards the head of the sect.

'You know you will be very well rewarded for this.' he said as he motioned for her to join the other members.

Two people, completely covered by black robes, approached Monalisa and covered her with the sect's uniform; they turned to kneel around Patrick's body whilst continuing to watch Giovanni's every movement.

'So, Mr. Jonah Albuquerque. I know you don't know how it all works here, so we'll make an offering for you to watch. Then, when your turn comes up, you will have the chance to seek your own redemption. Does that sound fair to you?'

Jonah decided not to contest. Giovanni did not know that he had been there and had witnessed everything that happened to Patrick. Such a chance for redemption was nothing but something those lunatics found to clear their sordid conscience of what they had been doing. In the end, no one stood a chance to escape that place, at least not alive.

'I've saved a special place for you, I am sure that this offer will catch your attention.' he said without looking at Jonah. 'Monalisa, why don't you sit with him and make sure that he won't interfere with the ceremony; and give me that weapon, you know very well this is a sacred place.' Giovanni finished another one of his little speeches, without having to impose it as an order.

He nodded to two of the men in black who got up and went over to Jonah. They put his hands on his backs and fastened them with a pair of old and rusty handcuffs, then they put his legs together and wrapped a thick piece of rope around his ankles, tightening it as much as they could to keep his legs still.

'Be quiet, don't say a word.' she whispered as she sat down next to him, away from the rest of the sect.

'You know that I have no incentive to help you, right?' replied Jonah emphasising the obvious.

'Just follow everything I do, there is a chance that you can leave this place alive.' she said whilst giving him hope, but Jonah had a feeling that it would be the end of him if he did nothing to stop it.

'Well then, my friends. Please, help me welcome the next offering, and may this soul have the humbleness to ask for forgiveness.'

The master of ceremonies, Giovanni Dartagnan, raised his arms, praising at his favorite imaginary friend, whilst the priest, again, started to babble the same old prayer that he had previously used for Patrick's entrance. Monalisa was tense and apprehensive, she knew exactly who would come through that door, and she also knew that she could not let her emotions take the best of her senses as she depended on her self-control and on the sensibility of Jonah, who was there to save his own life, taking with him whomever might cross his way.

The huge iron doors opened again, and from behind it, four men, properly dressed, entered through it carrying an enormous iron pot. They positioned themselves in front of the altar, where the priest was, and placed the object on a support that had already been installed; soon, other people came to their aid with a pile of thick wood and small sticks, placing them under the boiler. Jonah could already feel what was coming, but he avoided thinking that Giovanni was capable of such a thing, preferring to give hope a chance and not make assumptions before he could be sure of what was going to happen.

'So, ladies and gentlemen...' Giovanni positioned himself in front of the big pile of wood, addressing those who were present. 'Our next guest broke god's laws a few years ago, but she never had a chance to pay for her mistakes. Today, we will give her that chance!'

Mr. Dartagnan held his red staff high and, by activating some mechanism through a small button, made the object ascend a small flame launcher at its edge. Slowly, he lowered his staff and set fire it, making it clear to everyone present that his intentions were sordid to a level never imagined before.

249

'Please join me so that we can welcome our next guest'. he said with elegance.

The image that followed Giovanni's speech terrified Jonah's eyes. The large iron doors, already open, gave way for two thugs to parade as if they were part of a martial band; they carried a huge wooden cross, apparently extremely heavy, that held Joana's naked body. His former girlfriend had all of her intimate parts exposed, only her eyes were covered by a dirty rag, and her mouth was gagged by a piece of cloth. Jonah felt that Monalisa was about to panic, but the woman seemed numb from the drugs she had taken and managed to hold the air she was trying to scream out of her lungs. He had never had children, but he could imagine what she was feeling; moreover, he did not want to believe his own thoughts, but old feelings blossomed again through nostalgic memories that came disturbing him in a moment that could not be more inopportune.

'Your life is a priority.', he thought as he spoke to himself. He couldn't let his emotional override his rational thinking at that moment; even if Monalisa had mentioned that she could save him as well as Joana, he couldn't have that as a support, but rather he should look for an alternative so that he could get rid of those bonds and leave that place without being noticed, since Giovanni and all the other members of the sect were very focused on the scene that was taking place before their eyes.

'Joana Clemente!' exclaimed Giovanni whilst taking off her blindfold. 'Welcome to our humble congregation.'

She seemed to be trying to scream, but the gag in her mouth seemed to be preventing her from even breathing; her nose was completely congested from the crying she couldn't hold. Jonah remembered exactly every detail of her body, including the birth mark that was printed in her chest in the same place as his own, but seeing her like that made him want to explode in anger and jump towards Giovanni Dartagnan's neck.

Giovanni continued to vomit mystical bullshit through his mouth, whilst the priest followed the rhythm of a broken record player as the same prayer sounded out loud from his lungs. Monalisa pressed her fingertips with such force that Jonah could see her skin giving way to small cuts; there was nothing he could do but wait.

Once again, he made a brief sign with his red staff, which led his helpers to undo the bonds that held Joana on the cross. One of them picked her up from the floor and started to caress her as if he was trying to comfort a young child and, very sparingly, deposited her inside the boiler now full of warming water. Giovanni removed the cloth from her mouth and started to look it into her eyes whilst her crying drowned out any other noise that could be heard throughout that room.

'Please...' she started to plead, seeming to understand nothing of what was happening. 'Let me go!'

Joana continued to plead for clemency and, little by little, tried to grab the edges of the pot she was in and pull herself out, but Giovanni used his red staff to push her back, providing entertainment for everyone present in the audience who expected her to drown herself from being so tired or boiling with the water that was already heating up.

'This beautiful girl, Joana, will have the chance to save her soul before god, seeking his divine forgiveness.' Giovanni started the explanation whilst continuing to tire Joana's arms with his shoves. 'A few years ago, she committed a crime against god and all of his followers by killing a poor and helpless life she carried inside her body.'

'But that wasn't me!' she screamed in tears.

'You're off to a bad start, my dear. The first step to redemption is acceptance.' Giovanni continued whilst keeping his staff pointed at the boiler in case Joana tried to escape again. 'A crime is a crime, whether it's committed directly or indirectly by you. You may not have taken the main action that led to the murder of that child, but you bear the blame for having acquiesced with the main practitioner.' he stopped his speech and pointed the red staff at Jonah.

'Jonah?' she shouted confused as she was surprised by the presence of her old boyfriend. 'What's happening? Please help me!'

Jonah could feel Monalisa's anxiety exhale from her pores; she pulled the hood down so that her entire face was covered, leaving no chance for Joana to recognise her, whilst

Jonah, immobile, found himself unable to do anything to help.

'There's nothing he can do, Joana. But make sure his turn will come and Jonah will also pay for what he did.' Giovanni spoke again, at the same time that he swayed along the damp stone floor, swinging the red staff up and down.

'Tell them Jonah! Say I am not to blame for anything!'

He wanted to speak. Something inside him made him realise that Joana did nothing to deserve what was happening to her. He was the sole soul to blame for all that, and all the feelings he once had for her came afloat; he wanted to hold her in his arms, he wanted to save her and apologize for all the bad things he had done whilst they were together.

Giovanni turned his gaze back to the audience that was watching him. He took a huge container of gasoline from somewhere near the cauldron and started to feed the yet feeble fire that heated Joana's newest dwelling.

'Listen to me carefully and don't say a word.' Monalisa started to whisper without looking away from her daughter, having her mouth practically static. 'I put a letter in your pants' pocket with instructions for you to follow if you can get out of here. I thought this would be unlikely to happen, but I am increasingly certain that my words will not convince Giovanni. I also placed the object we retrieved from the statue in the maze and the device you saw me use before you were induced into that lucid dream. The instructions are clear and must be followed precisely; if I fail, please have the decency to do the right thing at least for once in your life.'

Monalisa stood up and left towards Giovanni without being invited, still having her face completely covered by the black hood, which drew the attention of the other members of the sect; no one there seemed to have the courage to do something even remotely brave as that.

'Monalisa, my dear friend, is there something wrong?' Giovanni stopped the ceremony suddenly and started to focus his attention on the woman who had interrupted him.

'I'm curious, Giovanni.' she started to clear her throat and put a different intonation into her voice, walking calmly around the boiler. 'Actually, I am trying to understand why this poor young woman is being judged.'

A whispering noise came over the ceremonial hall. Giovanni showed an expression of surprise as he wasn't used to being contradicted, especially in front of all his followers.

'I see no problem in discussing the matter, after all, this is a democratic institution.' he spoke knowing that he would always be supported by the majority of his own people. 'Would you care, however, to elaborate?'

'Let's see. Both I and several others here believe that a person who has been misled should not be judged to be primarily responsible to a crime. It would be unfair to anyone, especially for a woman.' she tried to emphasise that part. 'To pay for the mistakes made by a man who believes he has control over a body that is not his.'

Jonah had been surprised by Monalisa's argumentative ability, especially considering the state she was in, drunk and drugged; he could never imagine that she would have the courage and the audacity to face Giovanni like that. Mr. Dartagnan was, at least, curious to listen to the rest of her speech; he even put his staff on the floor, which he had not done since the beginning of the ceremony, and seemed to be thinking deeply about it, even inclined to accept her arguments. He started pacing back and forth, sometimes implying that he was about to start a speech; at times, he seemed to be experiencing a particular situation inside his own mind whilst he softly laughed and shook his head. His gaze came and went to meet Monalisa's, even passing by Jonah, who was restless with his feet dangling with the little movement he still had left in his legs.

'You bring us an excellent point, Monalisa.' he finally spoke as he picked up and pointed the red staff at the woman who seemed to be relieved. 'You know that from the first moment we met, the day you came here looking for comfort for the mistakes you made in your life; for the abuse of alcohol and other illegal substances, I've always thought that your redemption was possible.'

'And I appreciate everything you've done for me, Giovanni.' she interrupted his speech showing a feeling of relief.

'Who else here thinks like Monalisa?' he suddenly turned to the audience that was static since the moment he started to speak. 'Hmm? Anybody?'

Some people even tried to open their mouths to support her speech, but before anyone could say anything, Giovanni took back control of the situation.

'Most of your speech captivated me, and I am sure that other people here think the same, mainly because the one inside that boiler is a woman. However, what would be the reason why she did not alert the authorities about the unlawfulness of Jonah's act?' he asked as he pointed the staff at him.

'Well, you know how oppressive society can be towards delicate matters like this, especially for a young women.' she kept trying to appeal for female support whilst Giovanni gave her penetrating looks as if he knew exactly what she was trying to do.

'Monalisa, please.' Giovanni seemed to have lost his temper. 'You've spent months with these people. Be courteous and tell them the truth!' he exclaimed, raising his voice as he approached her until he was close enough to remove her hood.

'Mom?' Joana exclaimed when she recognised Monalisa's face and started to climb the boiling cauldron edges as it left small burns on her hands and arms.

Giovanni used the staff again to push her back into the water that was already getting too hot for her to withstand.

'I confess that it took me a while to find out about your true identity, Ms. Lais Amon.' said Giovanni very calmly.

'What's going on, mom?' asked Joana, who was clearly beginning to feel the effects of that cauldron heating up.

'Be calm, my love, and be quiet.' said Monalisa without taking her eyes off Giovanni.

'I don't need to tell you what's going to happen now, do I?' asked Giovanni as he focused his attention on the old woman.

Three men came to her and held her by the arms so that she had no chance of getting in the way of what would follow in that ceremony. Giovanni followed up with his sermon, adding a brief speech about loyalty and how traitors should be treated as Jonah remained completely still, waiting for his turn.

'Now, ladies and gentlemen, we will give this young woman a chance to confess her sins before god, seeking her divine absolution.'

'I confess, please forgive me!' Joana was keen to come out and exclaim her forgiveness, without letting Giovanni finish his speech.

Jonah felt a slight presence behind the bench where he was sitting. A hiss caught his attention, but his mind was sharp enough not to let other people notice the presence of whoever was there. Beneath the bench, two hands cut the rope that held his legs and, as soon as he was free, the same pair of hands came to free his wrists from the shackles behind his waist.

'Keep calm and quiet, as soon as you hear the signal, run towards the exit that leads to the underground of the maze, where you had been with James.' he could soon recognise Douglas's voice giving him instructions.

'What signal?' he asked before realising the man was already gone.

Even though he was hands free, Jonah sought to maintain appearances so that no one would have a chance to realise what was going to happen. He continued to observe the outcome of Joana's situation, each time more eager to get up and go towards her, however, Douglas's sudden appearance gave him a small hint of hope that he could leave that place still alive, making his eagerness to save his own life reign over his emotions once again.

'What are you doing here, doctor?' asked Giovanni as soon as Douglas spontaneously appeared through the front door.

'I have an urgent matter to discuss with you. Can you follow me?' he asked as he approached the cult leader.

'I'm a little busy right now.' said Giovanni sarcastically. 'Why don't you take a seat and I'll be with you soon.' his tone was carefree; he seemed to be ignoring Douglas, thinking there was nothing that could be more important at that time and place.

Douglas sat in one of the chairs next to the audience and kept his eyes fixed on the spectacle of horrors that spread in front of his eyes. Joana started to have difficulty breathing and every time she touched the edge off the boiler, her hands burned, leaving a peal of her skin behind, which made her fight again so she wouldn't drown in the boiling water. Monalisa wept and pleaded for Giovanni's clemency, even though she knew that the old man would never let her out alive, but all that she wanted was for her daughter to have a future far away from that place.

Jonah felt he should do something. 'Wait for the signal...', he thought over and over as Douglas's words repeated themselves inside his mind whilst he swung his legs anxiously. He was feeling sorry for Monalisa as he could see a genuine feeling of concern in her eyes.

'I apologize, Lais Amon, but I must continue the ceremony.' said Giovanni without thinking twice as he returned to speak towards the public that observed Joana's future taking shape.

A loud noise was followed by smoke and screaming. Jonah had a ringing in his ear and could not see more than two feet in front of him. People were scared and running from side to side until the dust settled and his vision became clear again. Someone had blown up the large iron doors leading to the hall of ceremonies, disturbing the order of Giovanni Dartagnan's sect. The old man was furious and huffing curses everywhere as he ordered his henchmen to go after whoever had the audacity to disrupt his service.

'That's your cue, Jonah!' Douglas had to shout for him to come back to reality and stop watching the despair of others.

'I need to help them.' he said as he got up and started running towards Joana and Monalisa.

'There is no time!' shouted Douglas as he left towards the exit to the underground.

Jonah did not let Douglas dictate the orders and went out to meet Joana. He couldn't understand why he decided to do that, maybe it was the euphoria projected by the tense situation he was experiencing, but his mind could only think of Joana and the fact that she was the woman of his life. All his faulty acts from the past started to haunt his mind at once, he wanted to fix everything he had done, he wanted to save Joana and he wanted to apologize to Lais Amon, and that was his chance.

As he was able get close to the cauldron where Joana was almost boiling alive, Giovanni was there to prevent him from doing anything. The red stick came against his chest, pushing him to the ground and causing him to be exposed and vulnerable. Mr. Dartagnan quickly took the sword off its red sheath and pointed it at Jonah's chest.

'My plans for you were very different, boy; but apparently, your story ends here.'

Giovanni started to press the sharp blade of the sword towards Jonah's chest, when two bursts, separated by a short time, caught his attention and freed Jonah from his death.

His sight went into some kind of tunnel-vision, and the space-time of the events around him brought up an immensity of feelings as the two bursts became two fire bullets. Each of them hit a person's head. Joana and Monalisa had their eyes opened, but their bodies no longer signalled any presence of life.

'Jonah!' a shout echoed and any other noise was drowned out by his concentration being focused in a particular person.

James Dartagnan was near the exit to the underground, sitting in a wheelchair, holding a long-range rifle that he had just fired. Jonah failed to spot Douglas, but it was more than clear that it was the doctor who was pushing that chair.

'Fast!' he shouted again, signalling for Jonah to come towards him.

CHAPTER 20:

Jonah was in a hurry, he just didn't know what for. The first thought to cross his mind was to jump on James's neck and end the disgrace that was his petty life once and for all, but he knew that the old one-legged man would be his only chance out of that place. As soon as he reached James and Douglas, they started running through the underground corridors until they could reach yet another of those secret passages within the state. Jonah was crying and screaming. He was terrified about what he had just witnessed and couldn't think clearly what to do from that point on. He did what he thought was the most sensible thing, following the footsteps of Douglas and the tracks of the chair that was pushed by him. The chair that carried James. 'Nothing but another murderer.', he thought angrily when he realised that he would never have the chance to apologize to Joana.

She was dead, forever.

They soon reached one of those rooms that Giovanni's sect used to hold prisoners who would eventually take their turn in one of those ceremonies. Jonah was still trying to make sense of everything that had just happened, but his body was shaking inexplicably and his mind was spinning without being able to keep focus on a single idea.

'Why the fuck did you do that?' he asked aloud as he put his hands around James's neck.

'It was either them or you, my boy.' replied James with an air of sadness.

'Why didn't you just shoot your brother?'

'I've already told you that I have plans for Giovanni. My brother will not have such a merciful ending. You see, my dear, he will pay for everything he has done, and it will not be that simple.' replied James by raising his voice as he took Jonah's hands off his neck very calmly.

'So you chose to kill two innocent people instead of shooting your brother? A killer!' he replied without restraining the volume of his voice.

'You need to stop this sentimentality! The goal here is much bigger than the simple choices that you assume we have.'

They started looking at each other whilst keeping the silence. They were not yet completely safe and needed to continue their journey as far as James's new plan wanted to take them. Jonah continued to watch every move that either of them were making, he didn't want to let anyone have any advantage over him at that moment.

He put his hands in his pockets aiming not to show any sign of aggression, when he came across the objects that Monalisa had put in it. He felt what appeared to be the piece of paper containing the message she had written and the two objects that were supposed to help him in the near future. A cylinder, which he imagined to be the object Monalisa had just fetched from the statue, and another that was shaped like a smartphone. Jonah kept his quiet and did not show any sudden expression that could give away the new information he had just found. He took his hands out of his pocket and continued the conversation as if nothing new had happened.

'How do you two know each other? And since when?' he asked when he realised that he had no idea of how that unholy union had came about.

'Doctor Douglas is an old acquaintance of the family. It was very fortunate that our paths crossed again.' said James, whilst massaging the stump of the amputated leg that still seemed to hurt.

'Old family acquaintance? I thought you were working for Giovanni.' Jonah decided to confront him, not forgetting the apprehension he saw on his face whilst he obeyed Mr. Dartagnan's orders to administer the drug on him during the time he was imprisoned in the red room.

'You should know by now that, most of the time, there's no choice in this place.' replied Douglas with dismay.

Jonah just nodded as he tried to put his thoughts in order. He reckoned his mid was clear enough for him to define that situation as his real reality. All those induced and lucid dreams couldn't be as real as that, and the way things were going, he knew Giovanni was way past playing mind games, as his reality no longer seemed to make momentary exchanges and the episodes of depersonalisation had already seemed to have ceased.

'I need some answers.' he started as he noticed that that would be the most appropriate time to ask questions. He had not been satisfied with the vague answer given by them, but the story of how they met did not matter at that moment.

'You see, I've already told you everything I know during the time we spent together, but maybe Douglas has some more specific answers that I can't give you.' said James, reaffirming that the situation that Jonah had lived with him in the past was actually real.

'Well, this would be a great starting point.' Jonah began to wonder how that whole time-frame issue could be explained. 'How did I experience two different realities at the same time?' he asked as he addressed Douglas.

'The key for you to understand what is happening to your mind, is the phenomenon of depersonalisation.' Douglas started to answer whilst Jonah tried to settle in the small refuge they were now hiding.

'James did mention that before, but I still can't understand how I could have lived two reality at the same time.' his eyes went back to stare at Douglas very carefully as he waited for an answer.

The doctor hired by the Dartagnan family approached him and ruffled the sleeve from his left arm as he began to run his fingers gently in the places where Jonah had his recently tattoos still healing.

'Can you feel that?' asked Douglas as he reached for Jonah's hand and placed it where his was.

'Yes.' said Jonah, felling a mixture of fear and excitement.

'Giovanni made me implant two nano-chips inside your skin.' he followed his thought as he continued to run his hand over Jonah's arm, which was already making him uncomfortable.

'And why the tattoos?' thought Jonah, wanting to understand why that additional nonsense would be necessary.

'That I can't tell for sure, but by now I believe that you've already understood that Giovanni likes mind games. In addition, you may have already found different meanings for these drawings, as well as for other myriad of symbols that you saw in dreams or wherever.' explained Douglas as he walked away from Jonah.

'And what do these chips do?' he asked.

'Each of them releases a different drug.' replied Douglas as he began to go through the shelves in the room, searching for something. 'One is a synthetic drug that causes you to be induced to depersonalisation, which gives Giovanni the power to put you in situations that you do not remember having lived.'

'But I had never met James before...'

'Not that you can remember!' Douglas now turned his attention to him, whilst holding a small wooden box in his hands.

'How do you mean?' he asked as he tried to remember anything that he could have lived that resembled the memories that had been induced by the so called depersonalisation.

'Have you got the habit of going to bars or any other public places?' that question was obviously rhetorical.

Jonah thought about the countless times he would go out, and there were many nights that he and his, now deceased, friend would drink so much that neither of them couldn't remember anything in the next morning.

'So my best guess would be that during one of these occasions, Giovanni must have made someone drug you and then took you to one of his facilities.' Douglas did not seem surprised by anything he was saying as Giovanni's atrocities seemed already normal to him.

'Why didn't you say something in the time we spent together?' he asked as he looked at James.

'And how would I know? You see, my boy, that happened months ago!' said James, turning his face so that Douglas would follow his explanation.

'Months?' he asked incredulously.

'You were kidnapped by Giovanni and his peers and you spent a few hours in here, when you met James and made those memories; then you were taken back to your house and those memories were erased from your memory; and now you have been prompted to recall those facts. This is the most clear that I can make things.' said Douglas trying to be as specific as possible.

'That doesn't make any sense. You and I spoke, in my dreams, about things that were happening at that very moment, whilst I was stuck in that red room with Douglas.' Jonah continued to make all the questions he could whilst putting his ideas in order as he found holes in a poorly told story. 'What about the time I lost in my own house? Wouldn't I have noticed that?'

'You see, Jonah, these are dreams. Although you have relived a memory of yore, Giovanni has the power to control all of your thoughts and even insert new memories inside your brain. Your questions were answered in a way to make you understand the facts in the exact order he wanted. Not everything that you lived during the time we spent together was relived whilst you were dreaming and, likewise, not everything that you dreamed happened exactly in reality, understand?' James seemed to be showing more of his knowledge than before. 'As for the time you say you've lost in your house, that was no more than a couple of hours, so you were probably asleep...'

'And how can I have spent months with these tattoos on my arm without having noticed them?' he asked as he started looking at the drawings covered by a crust of blood.

'Stop focusing on the tattoos, they were clearly done today, most likely at a time when you were knocked out by the effect of depersonalisation.' replied James. 'Giovanni induced them into the depersonalisation moment you were living with me through the dream chair you were attached to. Got it?'

'Yes. This memory was suppressed in your subconscious until the moment Giovanni decided to activate the second nano-chip.' he said whilst passing a lighter through some scissors he had found in the wooden box in order to cauterize it.

'The lucid dream drug?' he asked as he pulled Douglas's arm away.

'Exactly. That's what they call the cure.' said Douglas as he approached him once again. 'Be quiet, I'll remove the chips from inside you.'

'Wait...' said Jonah as he had something going through his mind. 'I need to know when it happened. Is there a way for you to induce me to that moment? Through a lucid dream, perhaps.'

'If we had one of the chairs, yes, but we don't.' Douglas was ready to cut his arm, using the scissors.

'What if I tell you that I believe it is possible?'

Jonah's question had been followed by the movement of his arm going into his pocket and removing the two objects from it. He decided to leave the letter inside as he wanted to have a moment alone to read it as it wouldn't be a smart thing to share it.

'Where did you find this?' asked Douglas as he fetched the objects from Jonah's hand before he could hold on to them.

'Monalisa...' said James as he held out his hand for Douglas to pass the technological devices to him. 'She must have put them in your pocket as soon as she saw how Giovanni was treating Joana.'

'She did indeed, she told me as she was doing it. What are they, exactly?' asked Jonah, giving Douglas a disapproving look. He didn't like the way he reacted at all.

'This cylinder has something to do with that staff my brother carries up and down.' said James when returning the object to Jonah. 'Now this one...' he finished his speech and handed it to Douglas indicating that the doctor should follow the explanation himself.

'This is a device that controls the chips that were implanted into your arm...' said Douglas whilst moving his fingers through the device.

He then recalled the lucid dream he had when Monalisa simply pointed that device in his direction.

'Why did Monalisa do that?' asked Jonah when he realised that the doctor was putting the scissors back in the small wooden box.

'Why don't you read it? The answer is probably inside the letter in your pocket' said James sneakily.

Jonah wanted to answer it with another question, but it would be best to focus his attention on Douglas. He had been fiddling with that device for a few minutes now, which didn't exactly calm him down as he knew exactly what was going to happen.

'Do you remember the exact day you met Jonah, James?'

'I do.' said the old one-legged man when fetching the device to put on the date.

'I don't think that what's coming next is going to be a surprise for you, Jonah. I hope you find the answers you are looking for.' said Douglas as soon as he touched his finger on the screen.

Sharp pangs of pain came galloping towards his head as he tried to sit up and find the most comfortable way possible to have one more of those psychotic episodes.

"The Black Hole jutted out of his mind as soon as his eyes closed against his will. The smell of alcohol exhaled through the air, whilst strangers danced and pushed from side to side. The bar was practically empty, occupied only by the well-known attendant and a strange woman that had her back pointed towards him.

Long, blond hair laid down her back that was uncovered by the neckline of her dress, whilst her hand, bent over the glass, played by swirling the little spoon that was there to stir her drink. He could observe himself approaching the mysterious woman as he came to have a brief moment of pride for himself.

Lara Farlet flashed him a smile as soon as Jonah caught her eyes as he hunched over the counter.

'Whisky, no ice.' he told the barman that did not seem to appreciate the harshness on his command.

However, Jonah was not shaken by the old man's lack of charisma, as he tried to get closer to the beautiful woman who was still contemplating the boredom that surrounded her.

'Would you like another one?'

'Hm?' she replied without seeming to have heard the question.

'Your drink has been over for some time. Would you like another one?' he asked again when he realised that her hand had finally stopped stirring the remaining off the ice in the glass.

'Who are you?' asked Lara as she finally turned to face him.

Jonah knew he was living one of his own dreams, but he had no memory of meeting Lara that night. He remembered that day exactly, because he hardly repeated his shirts when he went out, and this was a special occasion, he was there to celebrate the day of his parents' death, something that seemed strange to everyone else, but he saw death as a inevitable path, and instead of feeling sorry for himself, he had decided that he would always celebrate the few good memories he still had from their time together.

They continued to talk, until the image of Lara kissing his lips made him angry for not remembering that moment. He felt that he knew that woman, but he would never have the ability to remember that if it weren't for the dream that made him relive what was seemingly forgotten.

'Shall we?' he heard himself ask at the same time he held out his hand so Lara could get up from the stool.'"

His mind woke up again in the same room in which he had fallen asleep. He found himself fantasising about Lara's presence whilst watching James and Douglas observing him with a fairly confused look.

'Why did you bring me back?' he asked knowing that he could find more answers within that dream.

"I didn't. You just don't have any more memories from that moment.' said Douglas as he held out the device that showed an error signal.

'I found a note in your brother's room a few hours ago. I believe that the C.P.F. is trying to purge what they consider to be sins from all of those people.' said Jonah, trying to make sense of what he had just observed. He figured that the Black Hole would be a good place for Giovanni and his sect to gather heretics.

'Tell us what you just saw, my boy. You see, this device is not a television.' said James, who was waiting impatiently for an illustration.

Jonah put the two devices back in his pocket and told them everything he had just witnessed in the lucid dream that he had been induced to.

'You don't have to be a genius to guess what happened after that.' said Douglas, looking at James.

'I'm sure Jonah is thinking about something else, but yes, it is obvious.' he replied, hoping that Jonah would soon join the team of experts.

'Of course I got it, what I didn't understand is why I don't have any memories of the situation that followed. Wouldn't it be my subconscious? Can't even the rubbles of my mind remember it?' he asked, ignoring James's inappropriate hints.

'It is very likely that she drugged you before you left the bar, the obvious guess would be that she slipped something into your drink.' said Douglas upon receiving a positive sign from James.

'I was very keen on that detail during the dream, I didn't see anything that could resemble such a situation.' said Jonah wanting to appear aware of the situation.

'My brother, and his money, can be quite influential, my boy. You see, your dream will never show you that man behind the bar poisoning your drink.' James seemed to have everything figured out.

The excess of information in such a short space of time made Jonah rub his swollen eyes and shake his head. He tried to understand the order of events and clarify all of his doubts through his own experiences, however, what he needed most was to leave that place before it was too late and his future had the same fate as that of Joana and Patrick.

'What should we do next?' he was ready to obey orders and help with whatever was needed.

'First we need to remove these nano-chips from inside your arm, otherwise Giovanni will still have the power to induce you to lucid dreams and, even worse, to control them.' said Douglas as he went back to fetch the old scissors from the small wooden box.

'Well, actually, that brings me one more question doctor, if I may... Why were you injecting drugs directly into my bloodstream if I already have this things inside my arm?'

'I was just giving you a neuromuscular blocker so you wouldn't be able to move and interact with the real world.' the doctor's answer did not convince Jonah about all the nuances that were going on inside that room, but that would have to do, for the time being.

Jonah reached out his arm towards the doctor. The procedure was quick and virtually painless; the tattoos were now just a messy design distorted by the new scars that would be formed by the stitches given by Douglas. James stood up again, thinking very carefully about what would be their next step.

'What will we do now?' asked Jonah impatiently.

'Not much to be done, young boy.' said James that now expected Douglas to give him some kind of ointment for the scar on his leg's stump before covering it again with bandages. 'It will be the three of us against them all.'

That was not the best idea that the old one-legged man had had. There was no chance that they could face Giovanni and his entire troupe of lunatics by themselves. They were smaller in number, strength and resources; a mercenary doctor, an old man, and a stunned young man who faced a reality he had never thought existed.

'And what's the next step?' insisted Jonah, ignoring all his instincts that told him to get out of there as soon as possible.

'Douglas, did you get access to Giovanni's agenda before you could escape?' asked James.

'Yes. Thanks to Jonah, who helped me without even knowing.' he replied, referring to the moment he was in Giovanni's room.

'What makes you think that he's not aware that you had access to his own personal agenda? I believe he must be missing you already.' asked Jonah as he established the obvious.

'Do you really think I would risk my life if I hadn't taken the necessary precautions?' asked Douglas incredulously.

'How am I supposed to know? I still don't understand how the two of you ended up together...' replied Jonah trying to revive one of the many unanswered questions he had made.

'I've already told you that Douglas is an old friend of the family. He's been helping me for some time now.' replied James when trying to reassure Jonah.

'Giovanni believes that I am programming your last lucid dream.' replied Douglas. 'So I'm sure he won't miss me, much less realise that I have a digital copy of his agenda.'

'My last dream?' Jonah was curious. 'What would that be?'

'I expressed myself wrong. I wouldn't be the one to program it, but rather calibrate the chair and adjust the dosage of the drug.' replied Douglas, putting a disappointed expression on Jonah's face.

'Really? You are curious about that...' asked James, who seemed not to understand what was going on inside Jonah's head.

'Let's go back to the ceremony hall. I have images that prove the farce that is my brother.' said James without seeming very confident in what he had planned. 'If we can unmask him in front of all of his followers, we may be able to make him lose strength and, for fear of being framed, let us out of here.'

Jonah noticed that Douglas lowered his head as he heard James's words. It was clear that he was lying, but he saw no other choice but to accompany the men to a place that would be as close as possible to the exit. 'My survival is my only goal.', he thought again as he repeated in his own head the mantra that had kept him sane during all of that chaos.

They went out the door before anything else was said. The underground corridors seemed to be empty, which made no sense, as Giovanni's henchmen should certainly be looking for Jonah. 'Maybe they went straight to the wooden hut.' he thought when he remembered James's address. That path was already becoming an old acquaintance of Jonah, which did not bring him any feeling of solace nor made him more comfortable with the situation he was experiencing. He had James in front of him with Douglas pushing the wheelchair.

'How did you get this chair?' asked Jonah, intriguing suspicion and showing himself willing to be aware of the whole situation.

'Lara convinced my brother that this would be useful for everyone involved with my care.' he replied with a slight smile.

'Lara, your daughter...' Jonah brought up a subject that clearly touched James's inner peace. 'Have you spoken to her? Did you tell her the truth?' he asked when he realised that James wanted to turn around to face him.

'I suggest that we put aside the emotional side of this whole situation and focus on what really matters, is that alright?' he said, ignoring the questionnaire that Jonah was starting.

The rhetorical tone of the question was enough for them to remain silent; James sought to use the same tactic that Jonah had lived in his depersonalisation, they were walking the path close to the wall and always hurried when they came close to any kind of crossroad that could serve as a hiding place. He could see that the place was unfamiliar to Douglas, the doctor watched every corner of the underground as if he was mentally mapping the place for future use.

'Were you really stuck in that fountain?' asked Jonah, who was trying to understand better what was and wasn't true in the dream he had.

'Yes, that part was true. By the way, I think I never thanked you for getting me out of there.' said James, seeming genuinely sincere. 'Thank you.'

'I'm just trying to understand what was really real in that situation.' said Jonah, feeling inconvenient.

'I believe that everything was real, except that you seemed to be experiencing that situation at a moment it was not happening. That's why the conversations seemed so real and reliable in a space-time point of view, but don't worry about that now. I'm sure everything will be clear to you at the right time.'

James's response did not please Jonah. He wanted an explanation at that very moment, he had no patience for that kind of thing and he did not find himself in a position to be taking up any comfort on not seeking answers.

'My tattoos...' he started as he saw a look of despair in James's face. 'There was some make up covering it up, and it only went away when it came in contact with the holy water in the church. Please tell me that is not possible...'

'Of course it isn't...' started Douglas as he glanced over his shoulder. 'One more time, my friend, these people know exactly what is going to happen before you even know it's possible. That was probably some kind of chemical product in the water that made whatever was covering them up disappear.'

'Fair enough' he thought, thinking that details like that wouldn't matter anymore.

His mind went into a state of deja-vu when he realised that James had made Douglas push him into a hole between the walls as soon as the noise of people running became more and more noticeable. Jonah had not been pushed this time, but he did imitate their movements, trying to be as quiet as possible. James motioned with his finger so that no one would make any noise, whilst Jonah watched, from one of the corners, the people who were quickly approaching them. Lara seemed to lead the search group, her close relationship with James indicated that she would always be present when the old man was involved in the affairs of her brother's sect.

As soon as Lara and the rest of the henchmen passed by, Jonah realised the mistake he had made, causing his anxiety to stir up his thoughts and take over the rational part of his mind. He had let the note, left by Monalisa, fall into the ground, perhaps because he was fidgeting in his pocket to make sure that he had not lost any of the objects he had collected during his journey through the Dartagnan Brothers Hotel, or for the simple fact of not being completely aware of what he was doing.

The expression on James's face, as soon as he realised Jonah's mistake, was of extreme disappointment; the old one-legged man was very attentive and willing to end his brother's plans, but now everything he had achieved would be wasted because of such a futile error.

'I'm sorry.' whispered Jonah at an extremely low volume.

James closed his eyes with sadness, as soon as he realised that Lara had spotted them. She seemed to be in shock, surprised that she had three people in her vision that she never imagined seeing together. However, the old Dartagnan's despair proved to be unnecessary as Lara placed a foot on the paper envelope with Jonah's name written on it.

'Giovanni is asking me to come back.' she lied when taking her phone out of her pocket and pretending to be writing a text message in response, what made Jonah think that his telephone was the only one being blocked by some sort of signal.

James frowned so that his state of confusion was clearly visible to everyone who could see him - including Lara - but the old Dartagnan's bastard daughter just ignored any sign that might compromise whatever it was she was trying to do. She passed through to the place where they were hiding, without looking around, and followed the path that led back to the hall where the ceremonies were taking place.

Jonah waited for James to take the lead and follow Lara wherever she was going, after all, the woman would not take a risk like that if she didn't had a purpose, and Jonah couldn't wait to find out what it all meant. However, James remained static, completely paralysed. He seemed to be in shock and not knowing how to react to what he had just witnessed, because, despite the distant relationship he had acquired with Lara, she had always been faithful to Giovanni and the sect .

'Aren't you going to do something?' he asked as he looked at James's catatonic glance. 'Doctor?' he turned to Douglas who was also waiting for instructions.

Their lack of reaction made Jonah take the lead and leave in the same direction as Lara, and he soon realised that Douglas followed his momentum and started to push James's chair.

Jonah soon spotted Lara entering one of those small rooms that were scattered across the underground, but he was afraid of being the first to meet her, after all he was Giovanni Dartagnan's number one outlaw, but his choices were limited due to the momentary intellectual disappearance of James, who had his wits coming back to its normal, but was still partially confused by everything that was happening.

They followed the direction to the room where Lara had just went inside. Jonah didn't want to think twice and leave chance to his brain to make wrongfully assumptions, he opened the small wooden door and entered without even looking around, making the last thing he saw, before passing out, to be Lara's arms raised as they carried an iron pipe that would hit him in the head.

CHAPTER 21:

"His mind was taken by the image of his own living room, back to when life was still normal and bearable. Lara was sitting on the sofa whilst he poured two glasses of wine and prepared a tray of snacks on his kitchen counter. She wore a black dress and had her legs crossed, sustaining a jealous posture, but what caught Jonah's attention the most was the way her face kept a mysterious and charming look. He had always found it easy to understand people, but Lara's expression was a mystery to him, and that was something that would always intrigue his most profound senses.

He was clearly out of his mind. He had spilled wine all over the counter, and the way he had arranged the tray of appetisers made no sense what so ever, but the expression on his face showed a sheer feeling of happiness, something he couldn't remember feeling in a very long time.

'So, what do you do for a living?' he asked as he joined her on the couch.

'A little of this, a little of that.' she replied keeping the mystery.

'I'm sure you can come up with a better answer.' he said, showing a glance of awe.

'I work in a hotel outside the city.' she replied, trying to end that subject as quickly as possible.

'Hmm.' he realised her obvious lack of interest in the matter. 'I've never seen you in that bar, do you come to town often?' he was trying to find common ground so they could have a conversation that both parts would take in.

'I rarely leave the place.' she replied dryly.

Lara seemed to be impatient, waiting for something to happen, but Jonah wanted to keep the conversation going, to get to know the person who was sitting next to him better and, eventually, to do whatever came naturally.

'Can I use the restroom?' she asked as she got up from the couch.

Jonah led the way to the restroom and watched as she walked in so elegantly. He thought he had won the lottery at that moment, a woman like that rarely appeared in his life, which brought out his superficiality and made him wonder about how they would be together forever and get married in a few days. His anxiety made his first impression on a woman take the best of him and led his mind to run a mock throughout a future that would never exist, which was never a good thing since his eccentricities would end up driving women like that out of his life extremely quickly.

She was taking longer than usual to get back from the restroom, when Jonah decided it would be a good idea to check on her and see if everything was okay, or if she maybe needed something that his man fashioned bathroom would not supply. He staggered to the bathroom door, making more noise than he wished to, and as he was about to knock on the door to offer help, he was able to hear Lara talking on the phone in a low voice.

'But what do you want me to do?' she asked.

He felt bad about eavesdropping on the woman's conversation, but that was his own home and he was way to drunk to care about it that much.

'I'll need help.' she said whilst pushing down the flush and turning on the sink tap.

Jonah sprinted out from the bathroom door and returned to his place on the couch. He arrived panting, trying to get back to normal, and make it look like he had never left. Lara soon came back from down the hall with a smile on her face, as if her trip to the bathroom had brought her answers to questions he didn't know she had.

'More wine?' she asked rhetorically as she headed for the kitchen without looking at Jonah, making herself at home without his consent.

That was when Jonah felt that his mind was sending him a myriad of red flags. A sign that he had had too much to drink and it was time to rest. He was feeling dizzy and seemed to have trouble breathing normally; his mind was spinning and he couldn't focus his thoughts on a sole thing. Looking at Lara's face no longer gave him any feeling of awe or admiration, he was actually concerned to what he had just witnessed, as if his instincts were screaming for him to flee his own home and get as far as possible from that woman.

'I think it's getting late.' he stammered, unsuccessfully trying to get up from the sofa. 'Why don't we try this again some other time?'

Lara ignored Jonah's request and went back to the couch to sit beside him. That beautiful smile he was so keen on looking at was back on her face as she seemed relieved of any distress that had previously troubled her mind. Jonah felt that he was increasingly letting his fear and anxiety be shown through what was about to happen; what he had heard in the bathroom did not seem normal, and all of his instincts screamed for him to get out of there, but he was too weak to do anything.

'What's happening to me?' he asked as he realised that his mind was playing tricks on him. His vision swirled and distorted the image of things around him.

'Relax, let yourself go.' she said whilst stroking his head, forcing him to lie down on a pillow.

'I'm not waiting for anyone, ask them to leave.' he stammered again when he heard the apartment's intercom ring.

His will was promptly ignored as Lara got up and let whomever it was inside the building by pushing the button that opened the gate. Jonah's mind became more and more fragile and his attention could not be locked in anything but the reverie of his thoughts.

Within minutes the doorbell rang. Lara ran towards the door to let in the person who had come at her call, but Jonah could no longer distinguish the voices that were uninvitedly speaking in his own living room, much less shape the movements that dangled in front of him. The person's silhouette indicated a big, strong, young man, but he couldn't be sure of anything else by then. His mind could only think of resting and his eyelids could no longer keep his eyes open.

Gradually, his body let himself be carried away by the hands that swayed him from side to side, and his eyes watched one last image before they let themselves close, causing Jonah to fall into a deep sleep."

He woke up in the chaos that cluttered his mind; he did not know if his headache came from the mental confusion that had been created by the dream he just had or by the throbbing left by one of the countless blows he had received on his forehead that night. Jonah was sure that he just had a dream, something that was hidden in his subconscious and he was finally able to access. He no longer had any of those chips inside his body that could release the drugs he had been receiving for hours, so the only alternative was to think that his own mind had come to his rescue, helping him remember something that could be useful in the situation he was.

The last image he had seen was a clear depict of the mysterious man injecting the nano-chips, that Douglas had just removed, into his arm, but what had caught Jonah's attention the most was that he was touching that same cylinder that Monalisa had captured in the garden. After a brief reasoning, he concluded that that object must be of great importance to Giovanni, which explained the fact that it was hidden in a place that no one could find, or at least that was what Mr. Dartagnan thought.

'I need to read what Monalisa wrote in that note.', he thought, making sense that he could find the answers he yearned for on the letter Lais Amon had left him as an inheritance. However, his desire to search for it in his pockets was hindered by the ties that held all of his limbs. His mind was so focused on what was just showed by the dream, that he had not yet stopped to observe the situation he found himself in after the short time he had been away from reality.

He realised he was the only one inside that room that was somehow tied up. He found himself lying on the damp, mud-covered floor, whilst Lara, Douglas and James met in the other corner of the room, talking in such a low volume that Jonah couldn't understand what was going on. His arms and legs were tied by a weak and rudimentary rope, obviously the resources there were limited and insufficient for everyone to be detained, but Jonah was not thinking that he had been chosen at random.

'Hey!' he exclaimed aloud when he received a warning from all three to keep his voice low.

'I told you! This asshole will be the end of us...' Lara's words confused Jonah in order to practically erase everything he had understood until then. She was now covered, from head to toe, by the black uniform that Giovanni made everyone in his sect wear.

The three returned to talk abruptly, completely ignoring the presence of Jonah, who was trying to understand how that implausible alliance had came about, but as much as he tried to connect the dots, he couldn't make sense of anything that explained it.

The fact that he was ignored didn't bother him so much. What really made his blood boil with rage was the image of his belongings stored on the small table beside the bed. The device that controlled his dreams was accompanied by the mysterious cylinder and the unread letter that Monalisa had left him. Jonah felt that every step he took towards a possible exit from that situation was surprised by an intense push that took him back to square one.

'Can someone explain to me what's going on?' he whispered when he saw James and Lara embrace, bringing even more doubts to the mystery that spread before his eyes.

James spun the wheels off the chair and approached the corner where Jonah had been laid. The expression on his face contemplated a mixture of happiness, concern and anxiety. His will clearly fought against a mysterious dichotomy that dwelled in his mind and his eyes seemed to hide a very important truth for the outcome of Jonah's future.

'What do you have to tell me?' he asked when he realised that the old one-legged man had his words choked in his throat.

'I followed your advice...' he said, smiling and shrugging his shoulders like a child who didn't know what he had done.

Jonah forced his memory to go back so that he could remember any advice he had given James. The recent past events were clear in his mind, but the priority of how things were organised in his brain held no recollection of what the old man was talking about.

'I spoke to her. I spoke to my daughter!' he said whilst his eyes seemed to fill with tears.

He did not remember that as an advice, but as a mere remark he had made to the weeping man who had told him a sobbing story about his past. Actually, he didn't think that was such a good idea, quite the contrary, he thought that any cloistered feelings that might arise at that time would hinder his plans to get out of that place, but due to the direction the situation was taking, his survival did not seem to be a priority for anyone but himself.

'Why am I tied up again? It's really frustrating to wake up like this all the time.' he asked as he showed no interest in the story of that unholy reunion.

'Unfortunately, the plans have changed.' replied James, who seemed genuinely saddened by the situation he had imposed on Jonah.

Instead of freaking out and letting his anxiety take over all his impulses, Jonah calmly showed interest in James's latest turn of events and tried to empathise with the the old man's situation, who had just confessed to his daughter about the evils he had done throughout his life.

'Good, it seems that you're happy now.' he said, smiling and glancing at Lara, and then resting his eyes on the objects that had been confiscated from him. 'So, what's the plan now?'

The three exchanged glances as if they had not yet decided who would deliver the bad news. Douglas had been quiet for the entire time since Jonah woke up, which seemed to further accentuate his supporting role in that chaos. However, even though he was tired of playing games, Jonah realised that a mystery was being hidden behind all that indifference that was presented to him. 'I need to get my hands on that letter...', he thought as he returned his mind to his main goal.

'We can't afford to waste any more time.' Lara finally spoke. 'We must take him to Giovanni, it's the only way to get out of here.'

'Come again?' asked Jonah as he let his serenity escape.

That conversation was spiralling out of control as it continued without Jonah being included in it. Lara, Douglas and James seemed determined to give segment to their new plan, which did not included him. Jonah felt betrayed, but he already understood the rules of the game; he knew that he couldn't trust anyone, and the mistake of having followed Douglas and James in that trap was no one's but his own. Deep down he knew that the terrible plan James had just told him was nothing but a diversion to get him willingly involved.

'You see, my dear. A few months ago, when we had our little adventure, I had the courage to speak to Lara and tell her all about my past and finally tell her who I really am.' James seemed to be willing to include Jonah in the conversation that was supposedly deciding his future. 'We've spent some time getting to know each other until we decided to give ourselves a chance to start a life out of here, as father and daughter.'

'Really? After all he got you through? That's just lovely...' Jonah fixed his gaze on Lara's face, who seemed to raise anger with every word he left out of his mouth.

'In the end, my dear boy, we'll do what is best for ourselves, won't we?' James moved forward without letting Lara interrupt him.

'What about you, doctor?' Jonah was willing to appeal to anyone who could help him. 'I thought Giovanni didn't know you were involved in my disappearance.

'I play for the winning team, Jonah, nothing personal.' he was not at all surprised. The mercenary doctor answered as expected. 'And by now, Giovanni already knows everything, and all points of entry and exit of this property must be covered by security.'

'None of that makes any fucking sense!' exclaimed Jonah, trying to get rid of the bonds that held him. 'You just risked your life to get me out of Giovanni's hands, why this sudden change?'

'I needed you out from that place so I could deliver you myself. Things changed during the two hours you've slept...'

'Two hours?' he asked aloud, thinking he hadn't been out for what seemed more than ten minutes.

'Lara was finally able to speak to my brother.' James made his voice predominant once again. 'And he has agreed to let us go if we hand you over to him.'

'There must be a way that we can all get out of here together.' Jonah was about to beg.

'Unfortunately, there isn't.' Douglas looked genuinely disappointed.

'I was also surprised by the proposal, I thought Lara was looking to hand all of us over to my brother, that's why I was inert when I realised she had spotted us.' James seemed keen to explain the situation in a way that would make sense to Jonah.

'And all that talk about saving the world and freeing people from the psychopath that is your brother?' Jonah was getting angrier by the second.

'I want a chance to fix the past, young man.'

Clearly, Lara had outwitted Giovanni's henchmen in order to convince James and Douglas that this would be the best way out for everyone. Jonah was really surprised by the sudden change and still did not believe that everyone there was in the same page. It did not make any sense that James had abandoned all of his plans to follow up his sudden heartfelt episteme to mend his wrongfully doings from the past. But Jonah was the one who was tied up and he would have no chance of getting out of there safe and sound unless he could not get his hands on that mysterious cylinder and the letter left by Monalisa, which were now very safely guarded by James in his wheelchair; his only hope was to wait for any of them to make a mistake so he could take his chance to just run away from everyone.

'Let's go now! I do not want Giovanni to think that we have given up on fulfilling our part of the agreement, I haven't made contact for a long time.' Lara seemed very eager to go back to Giovanni.

Jonah's most haunted thoughts were about to happen. They went out the door and took the path that led to the C.P.F.'s ceremonial hall as he didn't even bother looking around to plot an escape plan. He knew enough about that infamous path he was walking on to know that he would have no chance of escaping Lara Farlet's clutches, mainly because he still had his hands tied and was being guided by her at gun point.

'Do not try anything funny, I will not hesitate to shot you.' she spoke as if she had no intention of losing sight of him.

That path seemed to get shorter and shorter every time Jonah went through it; that back and forth between the underground and the ceremonial hall was starting to get old, and the time it took to get to where Jonah had lost not just one, but two loved ones, was getting stripped of any scape possibility.

The place was practically empty. Some people were cleaning the blood waste left by the recent deaths, whilst others were picking up the rest of human entrails that decorated the floor. Giovanni was sitting in a chair on the altar beside the priest who held a cross in his hand and prayed without opening his eyes. Mr. Dartagnan had an expression of sadness on his face and he did not seem to exude the same enthusiasm he had held whilst applying his backward methods of torture and penance.

'Where is everyone?' asked Lara, when she approached and kissed Giovanni on the cheek, causing James to curl up in his chair in disgust.

'The few that are left, are already upstairs.' he replied, indicating that the place where Jonah would suffer his penance had changed.

Giovanni jumped out of the chair, wielding the red staff and changing the intonation of his mood as if he was skipping a television channel. He put a smile on his face and started to spin the mysterious object as if he was playing a part in a play; he walked among his new found guests without meeting Lara's eyes, just pointing with his staff so that she would clear the way and leave his sight.

'Well, well, what have we here.' he started humming. 'My old brother, it's been too long!'

'I see you've made some changes... No longer using the church, are you?' he asked referring to the fact that those meetings used to take place somewhere else.

'We've moved around since we last spoke, brother. Looks good, doesn't it?'

James tried to agree with a smile without having to defer a single word. The old one-legged man did not seem at all happy to be in the presence of his brother, who he had learned to ignore and hate over the years, his patience was explained only by the fact that he wanted a chance to make amends for the mistakes he had infringed upon Lara during the first decades of her life.

'Lara told me you have an offer to make.' he replied dryly. 'We are here to accept it.'

'Easy now, dear brother. You know I don't like to haste things up.' he replied whilst walking around James and passing his hand over his shoulder as he looked at Douglas with disgust.

The doctor was, without any doubt, the strangest figure in that place. His mercenary status gave him an advantage in that unique situation, but, as logic would dictate, his options got more and more limited by every choice he made. He observed every aspect of what was happening very carefully and measured his words with ease before compromising his situation.

'I didn't think I would have the honor of your presence so soon.' said Giovanni without slowing down.

'You know very well who I am.' Douglas intoned a mystery as he raised his voice confidently for the first time.

'Indeed I do. Let's talk later, you and I.'

Giovanni finally got close to Jonah. His face showed a mixture of happiness and concern, which made no sense for Jonah since Mr. Dartagnan, finally, had him exactly where he wanted.

'You have been a complete fucking nuisance in my life, young man.' said Giovanni as he started to show anger. 'All of your little misadventures and willingness to avoid the inevitable did a lot of damage to my organisation.'

He was obviously referring to the emptiness of the room they were standing in. It was no surprise that gunshots and bombs on doors would drive away those who did not have the same level of insanity as Giovanni. Sticking around to see what was coming next was suddenly not appealing anymore. Jonah, after all, had managed to fulfil one of James's wishes; even if unconsciously, his random acts had led him to disperse Giovanni's followers. Only a few people stuck around the ceremony hall; some security guards, obviously there for the money, and some other sect members remaining from the illusions promised by a deluded old man with no sense of limits on what power could bring him.

'You didn't think that this kind of madness was really going to go on for much longer, did you?' asked Jonah as he felt another blow in his face, which was already completely disfigured by the excessive amount of strokes he had been taking during his time of captivity.

'The human being is nothing but adaptable.' Giovanni seemed to be changing his mood every few seconds through a sharp bipolarity. 'We will continue the ceremony with the few remaining faithful, those who truly believe in the power of god, which, by the way, only strengthens our cause.'

'Your brother told me the whole truth about you... Be sure that you will never get away with this.' Jonah tried to be aggressive so that Giovanni would not let his overconfidence put him on an even higher position.

"Oh he did, didn't he? Tell me then. How did he explain to you about the dream you had where your friend Patrick was quartered? How did he know all these details before you even knew this place?'

'This has already been explained to me, you goddamn lunatic! I know very well that you've programmed these things into my mind...' Jonah seemed to have an advantage over Mr. Dartagnan at that very moment.

'I bet he failed to mention that he already knew everything that was going to happen, didn't he?' said Giovanni as he looked back at his brother. James had an expression of anger and regret hidden behind the sadness in his eyes.

'Would you care to explain?' Jonah let his voice collapse along with his naivety. He knew he could never have believed the words of a person he never met before.

'I've already told you, my boy. This is all part of a much bigger thing than you can possibly comprehend.' he replied without showing remorse or any feeling that expressed guilt, contradicting his bigger plan ideas as he had recently chosen to abandon everything and go play house with his new found daughter.

He finally understood that the lies were coming from everywhere, realising that Giovanni had been, in a somewhat contradictory way, the person who had been most honest with him.

Jonah wanted to throw up every time Giovanni opened his mouth to boast about the crazy things he called a divine cause. The man he had met during the weekend seemed to have a lucid and wise expression about everything that happened around him, as well as showing great enthusiasm and intelligence in each word he'd spread, and tremendous appreciation for all life around him. However, what Jonah saw before his eyes, at that moment, was a desperate, confused, and partially abandoned man. Even Lara, who had spent her life with him, was about to leave him to resume a non-existent relationship with the father she had never truly met.

'Giovanni...' said James, who seemed in the verge of losing his patience. 'We've fulfilled our part of the agreement, now I need you to let us out of here.'

'All in good time, brother.' replied Giovanni without taking his eyes off Jonah. 'Soon Lara will be back.'

'Where did you send her?'

'Be patient... you'll soon understand everything.' Giovanni seemed really mysterious with what was about to happen, which seemed to confuse James, who already thought he was getting to the end of that conversation. He wanted his brother to fulfil his part of the agreement and put aside those games that seemed to give him so much pleasure.

Jonah, as usual, in situations like that, tried to remain silent and hope that the outcome would give him any opportunity he could take advantage of, but the more he expected, the stranger Giovanni's actions became.

'You need to fulfil your part of the agreement!' shouted James, finally losing his patience.

'You do not give me orders!' Giovanni countered without letting the loud volume off his brother's voice overcomes his.

Tension was starting to build up between the Dartagnan brothers. James seemed to be afraid that Giovanni would not fulfil his part of the agreement and, even worse, that he could use Lara to take revenge for the mishaps he had been causing him; he knew exactly that there were no limits to Giovanni's cruelties, but his actions were limited by the situation in which he found himself. Giovanni's advantages over him were countless as he couldn't even move himself without someone else's aid; the place, which he had once called home, was strange to him and the people there present saw him as a confused old man, not even willing to call him a threat.

'We should put aside our disagreements, for now. I promise you that you will get what you seek, my brother.' began Giovanni. 'Now, please, will you accompany me to the ballroom.'

The main hall, where the party had been taking place, was now completely empty, indicating that most of the people had already left. They, however, followed the path to a place that Jonah had forgotten he had set feet on. Mr. Dartagnan's artefact museum was partially occupied by some of the sect's members. He soon noticed the presence of Catarina, the distinguished lady he had met in his sole visit to the place, who no longer behaved as a mere maid, but as another member of the C.P.F., dressed and polished as one of them, which was no surprise at that point. 'No explanation necessary.', thought Jonah, connecting the dots between the place she was supposedly guarding and the man she worked for.

'Catarina!' exclaimed Giovanni as they entered the room. She still held that same mysterious, empty look of someone who barely had any contact with the outside world.

Whilst Catarina and Giovanni talked about what seemed to be something of extreme importance, a different structure was being set up around there, something that was no longer new to him. 'The return of the chair...', he thought when he saw the object that had started his unexpected journey that weekend; he knew that things were shaping up to surround him as the main attraction. He was the one who was going to be tied up to that chair against his will, whilst the rest, smarter than him, would go on living outside that place as if nothing bad had ever happened.

The chair had been placed in front of a large television as it was surrounded by Giovanni's subjects, whilst the priest was preparing himself to start the next ceremony which was about to, as it would seem, bring the end of Jonah's path in that place. James, who was still supported by Douglas, became increasingly uneasy and, little by little, used words - the only weapon he had - to imply that his brother did not deserve to carry the name he had for not honouring his word.

The old one-legged man, however, suddenly fell silent when he saw the return of his daughter who had suddenly entered the back door of the small room. Lara Farlet seemed to be the center of attention; she appeared completely different from when she had left them. She was fully dressed in nun clothes: a tunic covered by a scapular and a veil that would shadow her own face as she carried a heavy cross hanged in a necklace around her neck. She kept her head lowered, glancing at her clasped hands, walking on a straight line until she could meet Giovanni.

Jonah did not seem to believe what his eyes were showing him, whilst James appeared agitated and desperate in his chair so that he could take Lara's arm, shake her, and have common sense brought back to her head, but he was incapacitated of doing anything as he was very well surrounded by Giovanni's henchmen; Douglas had already left the post at his side, when he realised that the game was swaying to the opposite direction. The mysterious Catarina had her mouth open with her teeth exposed, showing a smile so yellow and dirty that Jonah came to shiver with disgust.

Giovanni had changed his expression from apprehension to one of extreme satisfaction, realising that James was taken aback by the image that spread in front of his eyes.

'My dear and loved Lara.' Mr. Dartagnan began to speak. 'I present you to our companions, followers of god, as the most courageous and brave offering that this group will ever have the pleasure of knowing.'

Those words seemed to physically hurt James, but on the other hand, Jonah, at that point, couldn't expect anything other than a surprise like that from those people that seemed to live inside their own little world.

'Lara, ladies and gentlemen, even though many of you don't know, is the result of a broken relationship. My heretic brother's bastard daughter.' he spoke those last words as if he was taking a dagger from his chest. 'Yes! You heard me well.' he followed, noticing that some people were startled by the fact that the two were always in public showing an affection that would not be normal amongst people that shared the same blood. 'This beautiful young woman, today, decided to set aside all her disagreements with her father who had once abandoned her. Today she will make peace with my brother and ease the burden he created before god.'

The last words seemed to have calmed James down as he presumed that his brother would keep his word by adding a little more spice to a situation, that was already embarrassing and humiliating enough, in front of all those people, but as long as he could have a chance with his daughter, none of that mattered. However, Jonah knew that all of that sweet talk was certainly carrying a mystery that was not so simple.

'My niece Lara, ladies and gentlemen.' he continued as the whispers about his private life had ceased. 'Offered her own life to our cause.'

CHAPTER 22:

Giovanni's last statement made James even more restless in his wheelchair, no longer having someone at his side who could offer him any comfort. Jonah tried to observe the development that things were taking, and how the game would be played henceforth.

Whilst tensions within the small medieval museum of the Dartagnan Brothers' Hotel were getting higher, several were the reactions in people's faces. The few remaining seemed to have disagreements about what was going on. Some seemed to be perplexed by the situation that had just being presented to them, mainly because they discovered that Lara was Giovanni's niece and the two were supposedly maintaining some kind of intimate relationship, what was aggravated by the fact that the less deluded members had been having doubts about the true purpose of all that fanciful circus and Giovanni's exacerbated fundamentalism. Others, with a more fervent belief, were enthusiastic and excited about the myriad of possibilities that were opened by the new information that was just presented to them.

'Lara?' James decided to break the silence, realising that his own daughter was walking towards the dream chair mounted in the middle of the room. 'What's happening?'

Whilst the old man distress demonstrated - for the first time since Jonah had met him - stagnation and lack of answers, Lara just ignored her father's call - who tried to go towards her - and went towards Giovanni as if nothing more in the world bore any meaning to her.

'My dear niece.' said Giovanni, kissing her outstretched hand. 'How delighted and honoured you make us as you freely and spontaneously offer yourself.'

'I'm doing nothing more than my duty before god, Giovanni.' she said as she held him by the neck and touched his lips with intensity and tenderness.

'I know, ladies and gentlemen, that there are many questions that come to mind right now. However, I ask you to be patient and give me a vote of confidence. Everything I've done here is for all of you and all those who pray for god.' said Giovanni, knowing that his late actions had been putting doubts in the minds of those who saw him as a leader.

Giovanni was still very well protected by those who stood by him, especially by his armed and well-trained security guards, but his greatest fear was the voluntary fleeing of those who held such an option. The sect was founded on the principle that no one would be forced to remain there against their will, and those who had already abandoned the sinking boat would not have the courage to fight what was going on that place, since they were more than complicit in countless crimes and feared that divine justice itself would reach them long before any manmade's justice would reach Giovanni.

'I know that the schedule for this amazing weekend has not been following exactly what was promised, but I am sure that, with the understanding of everyone here, we can save the time that we still have and make this the best meeting we've ever had.' Giovanni was determined to use his oratory gift to convince the remaining people that that was the right thing to do.

James continued looking for a way out so that he could get close to Lara, impatiently rubbing the stump of his leg, as he knew he did not have any chance against his brother in that place; Jonah saw, in his eyes, the regret of having accepted Lara's proposal, but he understood that the ease with which he had been deluded came from feelings that had long been repressed and desired, feelings he was just having a few moments before when he saw Joana for the first time in years.

'Please, Lara, remember what we've talked about.' James continued to plead as his words seemed to squander through the air before they could reach her ears.

Lara passed by James and spat on the floor at his feet until, finally, she sat in the dream chair in front of the big television that was set for all of those who were present, whilst William, who appeared to have taken Douglas's place, passed by and connected the cables that would induce her to lucid dreaming.

'Without any further ado.' Giovanni was speaking again, ignoring his brother's pleas. 'I'll let Dr. William explain to you what will happen. Please, doctor.' he finished his speech by casting a contemptuous look towards Douglas. He still didn't know what he would do to punish him for his betrayal, but for now the doctor had been left out of his plans.

'Lara will be connected to this dream chair, where, through a deep analysis and reconstruction of brain frequencies, she will show us a glimpse of one of her memories.' said William as if he was talking to a bunch of children in a classroom. The second doctor didn't seem to have much of a way with words.

It was then that the beautiful woman, who Jonah had spent the night watching and raving about a future together, closed her eyes and let the drugs take over her body, bringing her mind to the deepest secrets buried in her subconscious, letting all that delusional people observe her vulnerabilities and learn about a past that was not welcome; the television began to drizzle contorted images from an unknown location, apparently those brain frequencies were being transported in a way to make a connection with the devices that connected Lara's mind to the dream chair, and then to the television that would allow all that madness to be watched. Jonah tried to keep his eyes fixed on the screen, but his curiosity caused him to shift his glances between Lara's expressions and the annoying hiss that was broadcast on the television.

As soon as the signal between the brain frequencies and the television was well established, the first image showed up on it, being received with awe by everyone present; even Jonah, who was appalled by how much his life had changed during his time in that property, let out a breath of admiration.

"Lara was walking on a tall, green lawn that, despite being poorly cared for, gave rise to a bucolic and serene feeling about the moment she was reliving. Around her, the Dartagnan family's property was in the process of being built, still missing the enormous structures that gave it the extravagant aspect at present time. Her eyes looked at a simple and plain woman who was working on the farm plow, wearing simple clothes and devoid of anything that would indicate vanity.

'Mom! Look, look!' said Lara, sitting on the grass whilst pointing to a dandelion that she had grasped between her little fingers, and was blowing with the feeble air she could hold in her lungs.

The woman held a sad and lifeless look, accentuated by the lack of will she showed in practicing her craft. The marks on her arms were diverse, indistinguishable from the struggle form the labor, or from other obstacles presented to her by life, but what most called Jonah's attention was her unwillingness to live and the tears that filled her eyes without never spilling.

The scene changed and brought up the image of an old kitchen with wooden furniture and a wood burning stove. The same woman worked tirelessly to provide the food that was about to be consumed, not by herself, nor her daughter who had her hands busy carrying the pots and pans she would put on the table, but rather to serve a crowd of people who started to sit by the table.

'Here, Lara.' the voice of a young Giovanni Dartagnan sought the attention of the small child, reaching out a handmade rag doll made by someone who obviously did not know that craft.

Little Lara had a smile on her face and went to meet another person sitting on the opposite side.

'Look what he gave me, uncle.' she said when seeking the attention of a young James who ignored her and then startled her by tackling her with his foot, pushing her as far away as it was possible.

The image on the television changed again, after a brief interruption of the same drizzle that preceded each connection made between brain frequencies and technological equipment.

She was now standing and surrounded by unknown people, with the figure of an already mature Giovanni Dartagnan at her side. In front of him, perched on a wooden table overlaid in the garden of the already built hotel, was a cake that held small candles that indicated her eighteenth birthday.

'Happy Birthday.' said Giovanni as he wrapped her around his arms with a hug. 'Let's go for a walk, shall we?'

Lara accepted the invitation with a feeble smile, indicating that Giovanni was the only person who held any meaning to her, considering that neither James nor her mother were present in that scene.

The walk took them to the well-known graveyard, where Giovanni made the cross sing and held Lara's hand whilst praying respectfully to the tomb that held her mother's remains. Lara cried and hugged Giovanni tightly after rubbing her eyes so that the shirt of the only person who seemed to care about her well-being would not soak.

Once again, the scene changed, showing now a small and simple room that could only be Lara's little refuge inside the Dartagnan brothers property. Giovanni was lying on her bed, whilst she lifted a decanter full of wine in order to fill two glasses that were set on the table.

'Now that you know your father's story, what do you think about me?' he asked as he swallowed his tears and covered his naked body with the white silk sheets he had given her as a gift.

'About you?' she replied confused. 'How could the tale of my father abandoning me change my opinion about you?'

'You understood that I'm your uncle, didn't you?'

'And what difference does it make?' she seemed hopelessly in love every time she met Giovanni's eyes. 'My mother is dead and my father is reclusive in that hideous hut. You were the only person who, in my entire life, showed any kind of affection and took care of me. I couldn't care less if you're my uncle. All I care about is the only love that I've ever felt in my whole life'

'It is very unlikely that one day we will be able assume this relationship publicly, Lara. Society sees this kind of thing as an abomination.' Giovanni seemed much more lucid than he was in the present.

'Since when do we care about what society thinks?' she lied down beside him and started to stroke his hair. 'All I care about is what god says. Isn't it true that the old testament approved of family relationships?'

Giovanni's eyes shone with joy, causing any worries that haunted his mind to cease its existence at that very moment; he kissed her tenderly and said he loved her for the first time in his life.

'Maybe this is something we should keep in mind, Giovanni. Society's values have changed way too much throughout the past decades, perhaps we should focus on recovering some of these values within our social circle.' she said with wariness as she wasn't one to speak her mind with such ease.

The television image changed and began to show a large wooden table, covered by a banquet that served the most diverse people seated around it. Giovanni sat on one end with Lara on his side as his hand rested on hers. The guests smiled and talked, whilst Lara watched with pride the place she had arrived within society, which made the fact of her father's absence and mother's death insignificant when compared to the brilliant future she had ahead.

Giovanni waited for everyone to finish their dinner so he could address all those people he trusted and explain his ideas, plans, and desires. His words were applauded by everyone present, which included the most diverse niches in the entire local society. Lara got up from her chair and, with a smile on her face, thanked everyone for their presence.

'Be absolutely sure that your presence here is essential for the future of this organisation. The future holds a path full of success to all of us.' she said, whilst raising her champagne flute for a toast."

The reactions throughout the audience were the most diverse. Some people, mostly those who were new to the sect, showed immense surprise at the story they had just witnessed. On the other hand, a lot more people seemed to be aware of the unholy relationship that was taking place between Giovanni and Lara, and they did not seem to care too much about it.

James sobbed with tears after being reminded of scenes about a past he was trying to leave behind; he knew exactly how he had treated his own daughter all those years and there was nothing in life that he wanted more than to apologize and make up for the lost time. Lara's betrayal seemed to have shaken him intensely, after all he was there, exposed, and ready to forget all about his brother's atrocities, in order to build a relationship that would bring him back to a meaningful life. As for Jonah, nothing that came from that family surprised him anymore; he remained focused on looking for any flaws within Giovanni's security scheme. Something was bound to give way so he could take advantage in order to get out of that place. 'These people get crazier by the second...'

'So, ladies and gentlemen. Do you understand, now, why I appreciate you staying?' Giovanni broke the silence as soon as people started to comment on the newly information that was just bestowed upon them.

Whispers and murmurs reigned again as Giovanni stood up on one of the benches, leaning on his faithful red staff as he admired the perseverance of each and everyone of those who still remained. Doctor William started to remove the cables that connected Lara to the dream chair so that she could return to reality, whilst Douglas 'had approached Catarina to start what seemed to be an exhausting conversation.

'The Christian Pendulum of Freedom, my friends.' it was the first time that Jonah heard the name of the sect come out of Giovanni's mouth. 'Is much more than a simple organisation where we apply divine penance to those who let themselves be carried away by the countless temptations placed on this plan, but rather we seek to defend the word of god and bring back principles and values that have long been forgotten by society.'

All the members of the sect kept their attention on Giovanni, whilst Lara approached to intertwine her fingers with his, making James squirm with rage. The priest continued to preach from the altar without being accompanied by anyone else, leaving his presence to resemble some kind of background white noise to Giovanni's words.

'Our next event would be the enforcement of Jonah Albuquerque's penance.' Giovanni pointed to the place where he was sitting. 'However, his capture was conditioned to a deal between my niece and my brother, and that will lead us to an interlude in our programming.'

Jonah did not expect his turn to be delayed once again, as he was ready to face Giovanni and try to assume his guilt so that penance would not lead him to his death, but apparently, he was given a little more time to organise his strategy.

'Lara offered to show us the most intimate scenes of her life. Scenes that bring her pain and sadness.' he said again, waving the red staff back and forth. 'Now, Lara will pay for what her father did.'

That announcement took everyone by surprise. That was not common within C.P.F., as people should pay for their own mistakes.

'Giovanni, no!' exclaimed James, who knew exactly what his brother had in mind and tried, unsuccessfully, to wheel his chair towards him. 'That was not the deal we had.'

'And what did we agree upon then, brother?' Mr. Dartagnan seemed to have all the answers on the tip of his tongue.

'The deal is the delivery of Jonah in exchange for our freedom!' he exclaimed vehemently, meaning for his pleas to seek effect on the few members of the sect who believed that a man's word was sacred and should be kept.

'Very well.' Giovanni now started to approach his brother. 'And all of you will be released.' he got so close that James had to throw himself back in the chair and move his face away. 'Released by the truth. Released by the opportunity to apologize and pay for your mistakes.'

James projected forward again, grabbing the collar of his brother's shirt and pulling him as close as possible. The sect's henchmen soon came to his aid, but Giovanni interrupted their movements with a brief raise of his hand.

'You know this wasn't the deal, you piece of worthless shit. Now keep your goddamn word in front of all your followers and let us go.' the old one-legged man showed a rage that Jonah had never seen before.

'Circumstances change, James.' said Giovanni whilst getting rid of his fists and straightening his posture, fixing his collar, and adjusting his tie.

The anger James felt for his brother at that moment showed his most intimate vulnerabilities, which were emphasised by his clear inability to fight Giovanni and his well set congregation.

'Lara, my beloved.' he said when he met his niece again. 'We will continue with our schedule.'

'Yes my love. I'm ready.' she replied harshly, intertwining her hands over her chest.

'Unfortunately, we didn't have enough time to elaborate something worthy of our time, and recent events make it impossible for us to use the ceremony hall and the altar.' he said as Lara got down on her knees in front of him, with her face pointing the opposite direction.

She raised her hands towards the sky and began to pray with her eyes closed, bearing an expression of serenity worthy of someone of extreme coldness and confidence. The situation did not startle Jonah; the woman had been raised in that environment by people who really believed in everything that was happening. Lara had no knowledge of the world outside that place, and the religious belief was the only thing that made sense to her; that being the only aspect that pointed out the ethics and morals to be followed so that her life was valid, and had meaning, from a divine point of view that had been forced on her throughout the teachings of a life-time. She seemed very comfortable with everything, which made Jonah think that it was just an introduction to something bigger to come. However, that time, he couldn't be more wrong, and the situation that followed would be forever embedded to his memory.

Without an altar or any other elaborated symbolism, Lara stripped off the top of the black habit she was wearing, leaving her chest exposed as she kept knelt in front of Giovanni and prayed eloquently whilst holding back the fear that, little by little, showed through the tears that she couldn't contain.

'Don't be afraid, my dear.'

Those were the last words heard by Lara Farlet before Giovanni pulled the sword out of the red sheath that disguised the staff. He murmured a few inaudible words and slit his own niece's throat right there, in front of everyone, allowing blood to flow from her neck on the floor that covered the grounds of that small museum of torture.

The public's reaction was one of complete euphoria. People started shouting and applauding the gesture that was still taking shape in Jonah's head as he couldn't believe the atrocity he had just witnessed. The screams completely drowned James's crying and despair; the old one-legged man had his arms crossed as he scratched his skin with such force that his pores began to bleed slowly.

'Silence! Respect this moment as if you were praising god himself.' shouted Giovanni, wanting to prevent that the death of a relative of his would have that kind of connotation. He was clearly wounded and his heart was aching with tearing pain, but he couldn't show any weakness if he wanted to keep being leader of all those people.

James forced himself out of the wheelchair and, with nowhere to lean, fell to the floor with the knee that was left to him, starting to crawl towards the body of his daughter who lied in a lifeless pool of blood.

'What did you do?' screamed James, crying aside the body.

His position was pathetic and everyone there seemed to feel sorry for the situation in which the old man found himself.

'You are sick, Giovanni.' he said, holding Lara's head over the stump of his amputated leg.

'Pathetic...' he replied whilst turning his face without letting James take another mere second of his attention. 'Take this man back to his quarters.'

James was taken by the arms and started to be dragged as if he was a sack of wheat; the strong man, full of ideas, and with a strong ideology, that Jonah had briefly known, was now in a deplorable state with no trace of dignity. His mind seemed to have entered a catatonic state, causing his eyes to look at random towards the horizon, taking as a last sight his daughter bathing in her own blood after accepting her own death as gift to her god. His body was placed back on the wheelchair, which was then pushed by one of Giovanni's henchmen into oblivion.

Jonah soon realised the opportunity he had been waiting for was posing right in front of his eyes. The way of which James was thrown in the chair, made the objects that once belonged to him become visible. The rest of the people had gathered around Lara's body, whilst Giovanni was talking about how that sacrifice would be an important step forward to the sect in order to garner more support and new members. Apparently his mind had taken his ego to a state of extreme narcissism, causing his subjects to see him as a divine super-being that was there to be worshiped and followed. Jonah took advantage of the situation and managed to recover the cylinder, the smartphone, and the note left by Monalisa without letting the man who was guiding James's wheelchair notice. He had already wasted a lot of time on escapes. Realising that it would no longer be the best strategy, Jonah decided to open the paper quickly, after putting the cylinder in his pocket, and reading what Joana's late mother had left him as inheritance.

"Jonah, this object that you helped me recover is the only way to stop Giovanni. Look inside your own mistakes for the answer that will lead you to opening it.

Remember what you did in life and look for your own redemption. Do not let my daughter's life be wasted again."

The last sentence of the little note made his mind search for every good memory he could find from Joana's life, tormenting the fact that he would never be able to see her again.

He expected a bigger note with at least a few curses and a little more instructions, but Monalisa didn't seem to have had enough time to worry about the situation that Jonah would be going through when he managed to get his hands on the much-hailed object.

Risk was his only option at the time, which made Jonah take the object out of his pocket and just hope that no one noticed it. The object he had seen from a distance, in the hands of other people, now seemed to have a clearer purpose; several were the buttons that came down from a sensitive touch screen, some with clearer functions, others less so. The most obvious was an on and off button, which he thought was the most useful to him at the moment, even though he didn't know exactly what he would be turning on or off, but his future would not be made easier by just the touch of a screen.

The touching came to nothing.

'Giovanni.' he heard doctor William's distinct voice announce. 'I think you would do well to speak to Jonah.'

Mr. Dartagnan turned to Jonah and caught him on the spot. His hands shook and pressed the myriad of buttons that the little cylinder held, but nothing seemed to have an effect.

'Well, what do we have here...' he said as he approached Jonah and took the smartphone from his hand as he managed to hide the cylinder away in his pocket 'Someone's been learning secrets for the past few hours, isn't that right, young man?'

Jonah stood still, not knowing what to say.

It was clear to him that that would be his end, but Giovanni's face indicated a certain pride in the fact that Jonah had gone so far as to discover secrets that no one else there even seemed to know existed. He swirled the object between his fingers, finally holding the smartphone up as he rested his body on the red cane.

'Do you want to know how this works?' he asked as he watched the fear in Jonah's eyes.

Jonah remained motionless. He knew that this would be another way for Giovanni to prove that he was better than him, that he held all the keys to the mysteries of the Dartagnan Brothers Hotel, and that he would always be one step ahead of him.

'Whoever helped you to find these objects, young man, will pay for it.' as soon as he said those words, Giovanni rolled his eyes to find Douglas's face.

Jonah still had a little hope for the mercenary doctor. Perhaps the situation would make him help him again, which, although unlikely, was the only option he had at the moment. Perhaps, if he demonstrated himself as one of his ally, it would open a door for him to help him get out of that place once and for all.

'Monalisa left me the smartphone, along with this note.' he did not hesitate to snitch on the already deceased woman, after all, Lais Amon was rotting somewhere inside the ruins of what seemed to be the projection of an endless nightmare.

Giovanni calmly took his eyes off Douglas, without letting his expression of suspicion change. Douglas's response was a simple and sincere understanding that his reputation was hanging by a thread.

'Monalisa, really?'

Jonah nodded even though he knew that Giovanni was not waiting for confirmation. Douglas showed a sign of satisfaction and relief when he met Jonah's gaze, not letting it appear that he had chosen a side, which was more than understandable, considering the abomination of the situation in which they found themselves. 'Every man for himself.', he repeated that mantra as he understood once again that he was the captain of his own fate, and help would only come to him if it was also beneficial to the other party.

'Well then, Jonah. Do you want to know what this one does?' Giovanni insisted with the question, holding the smartphone as he tucked the note away without reading it and looked for Jonah's glance, placing himself in front of him.

He kept looking away without letting Giovanni realise how anxious he was, but he couldn't hide the obvious; he had no escape, and no one to help him. James and Douglas had brought him hope, but the closer he got to an exit sign, the more he seemed to be moving away from it.

'This object was designed to control you.' started Giovanni whilst Jonah still had his mind in a distant place. 'Do you want to see how it works?'

Jonah tried not to lose the rest of his hopes. Monalisa had left two things: one of them was now useless, since Douglas removed the nano-chips from his arm; and the other, which he had no idea of how to use, seemed to have more value and was safe and sound inside his own pocket.

Giovanni took the smartphone close to his arm and made him aim at the small touch screen, placing his finger on the button that said 'Start lucid dreaming.'

'William!' shouted Giovanni angrily, realising that his action didn't held a reaction. 'Why isn't this working?'

Douglas's fellow doctor came up to Jonah and pushed the button again, which only irritated Giovanni even more.

'Do you think I don't know how to press a fucking button?' asked Mr. Dartagnan.

'I have no knowledge of how this works sir.' he said, lowering his head.

Giovanni reached for Jonah's arm and rolled up his sleeve so that his skin would be exposed; the place that once gave space for his poorly made tattoos, now connected stitches of recent cuts. Giovanni's reaction, which followed the brief moment after being aware of what had happened, would not please anyone.

'Douglas!' he shouted when throwing the smartphone on the floor causing the object to shatter into countless pieces.

CHAPTER 23:

Douglas knew exactly what he had done; he seemed to be waiting for the moment where Giovanni would find out about it and come to him, demanding satisfaction. The brief moment that preceded Giovanni's shout of his name caught Jonah's attention as Catarina shook Douglas's hand, which was not a simple handshake, but an exchange of something very small. The slight twitching of Douglas' fingers, as his hands touched hers, implied that the mysterious lady had left him something before leaving for one of the doors at the small torture museum at the Dartagnan Brothers' Hotel.

'What the fuck is this?' asked Giovanni as the doctor approached him far enough to observe what he was pointing out.

'It was James, Mr. Giovanni, you know how persuasive your brother can be. Being kidnapped by him was not an easy time.' Douglas seemed to have an incredible gift for telling unreasonable lies.

Jonah knew that Giovanni did not have the knowledge that Douglas had switched to James's side of his own free will, but his story was simple and strongly unrelated so that it could be easily credited. However, it seemed that Giovanni had an even greater gift in believing that his money would actually buy the truth at any point in tie, or perhaps he was simply letting the lie be a temporary answer, something that could bring Douglas back to his side. It was certain that Mr. Dartagnan would have a future in mind for those who had betrayed him, but apparently, the moment was not auspicious enough for creating disagreements that could be used as a temporary alliance.

'You know very well that these nano-chips are indispensable so that I can finish what I have planned.' Giovanni said as he was seemingly calming down.

'Yes, sir, but as I told you, it wasn't my fault...'

'It doesn't matter who's fault was it.' he cut off Douglas's answer without wanting to give space for other lies to be raised in a place he considered sacred. 'If I pay you enough, can you solve the problem?'

Jonah soon saw that Giovanni knew exactly who Douglas was, and even better, he knew, from the start, how to persuade him.

'Yes sir.' he replied simply when lowering his head and leaving the small room.

'It looks like you'll have to wait a little longer, Jonah.' said Giovanni, who already looked tired of how wrongfully things had been going with Jonah.

Jonah did not think it would be appropriate to answer right then, in fact, he hadn't opened his mouth to say a word for quite a while. All he could think about was looking for a way out from that place. However, the premise left in the air by Giovanni, that his plans would only be successful if those nano-chips were implemented again in his arm, made him wonder what would the mighty Mr. Dartagnan have in store for his future.

'Why do you need those things inside me?' he asked as he broke his long lasting silence.

'You already know too much about the things that happen here Jonah.' said Giovanni as he stopped running his fingers over the small scars that were beginning to heal. 'I must confess that I am surprised by your reaction. I didn't expect to have so much trouble making things work with you.'

'Is there a chance you'd let me go?' he asked, having nothing to lose even though he knew he wouldn't get an answer.

'The same chance the child you killed has to return to life.' Giovanni replied, looking deep into Jonah's eyes.

'I killed no one! You have to agree that the matter is hugely debatable...'

'Not in here, it is not.' Giovanni interrupted without giving way for Jonah to follow that reasoning. 'Here we follow the word of god and the teachings of the bible, this is how things have been since the beginning of humanity and this is how they should continue to be. Society increasingly forgets family values, and traditions are set aside so that perversity takes hold of those who are vulnerable within the christian society.'

'Family? Perversity? Do you hear the words that come out of your mouth?' Jonah had let fear turn to anger.

'You just killed your own niece and your brother has been tortured for months at your command!'

'And who put you in charge to decide who lives and who doesn't? You are nothing but a disgusting worm that have been placed in my path and will be extinguished the way you deserve!'

'Then report me to the authorities!' Jonah sought to plead for his life from any possible argument. 'May the laws determine my destiny, and not your fantasies about an outdated book.'

'I'm the justice here!.' Giovanni raised his voice and showed even more aggressiveness to show who was in control.

Mr. Dartagnan was letting his serenity and coolness be overcome by rage. He was sweating and itching like someone who was going through abstinence, like a person who was uncomfortable and out of his natural habitat, which made Jonah think that maybe that game could turn to his side. However, he knew that the conversation they were engaged into would get him nowhere; he knew that there was no dialogue with people like that, extreme fanatics were never to be contradicted in their on turf, and whatever he said would be countered by sordid and outdated ideas from someone who had not let his mind evolve with age.

The silence reigned for some time. Both Jonah and Giovanni seemed to hold thoughts that were taking them away from reality, but the intimidating looks continued to wander across both fields of vision, implying that the battle was not lost on either side.

'Whilst we wait.' said Giovanni. 'There is one thing about you that I could never understand...'

Jonah did not expect to have any kind of elaborate conversation with Giovanni, he had already given up trying to convince that lunatic that he deserved to be absolved from his mistakes and be freed from that place alive, but curiosity was never successfully confronted by common sense within his mind.

'Tell me, then.' he replied without thinking twice.

'I've watched one of your dreams several times without understanding what it means. Maybe you can elucidate me about the meaning that such a situation has inside your subconscious.' Giovanni looked really curious.

Jonah knew exactly what dream Giovanni was referring to, which, for him, was never a dream, but an endless nightmare he had had since he was a little boy. He had never been able to understand it.

'And may I ask how do you know about such a dream?' he asked, feeling that his privacy no longer held any sovereignty.

'I reckon we're past that stage, young man. You must have understood very well how things work around here by now.' Giovanni was aware that Jonah was fully keen on the functionalities of the dream chair technology. 'I'm sure James and Douglas thoroughly explained to you how the drugs work within your system.'

Jonah was even more surprised to learn that Giovanni already knew about Douglas's betrayals; even so, he continued to somehow want to keep him under his wing so he would remain an asset to his fanatical ideas. The mercenary doctor should hold a tremendous importance within Giovanni's plans as to operate that technology and all of those drugs.

The invasion of his privacy, however, did not prevent him from being honest and seeking empathy with the old man. After all, he was nothing but human and seemed to hold a curiosity just as strong as Jonah's.

'I'll answer that if you tell me something I haven't been able to understand myself...'

'Why not...'

'As you were inducing me into depersonalisation I found myself inside Patrick's body when he was attached to that weird bed that stretched him to his death. What was that?' Jonah was incredulous as he finally let something like that come out of his own mouth.

'You even know about depersonalisation, I'm impressed.' said Giovanni as he stared into Jonah's eyes. 'That was a programmed dream, not depersonalisation. I made you feel like you were Patrick. It was just something to scare you.'

'That's really messed up... You should really see a doctor about that...'

'I do, and he's called god.' Jonah knew exactly what Giovanni was going to say. 'Now, answer my question.'

'I do not know.' he replied.

'Oh come on...'

'Really. I've got no idea of what that means, it's just something I dream about since I was a very young boy. Never got to know what it meant.' he answered sincerely.

'Odd. I have something similar in my mind that I've also never managed to decipher. No matter how much I am devout or how much I do good for my community, god continues to play the same trick on me, over and over again.' Giovanni seemed to be in a moment of self-reflection, and really involved into a conversation.

'Fancy knowing my theory?' asked Jonah as he observed a breach that might create a bond between them.

'I think I still have some time, so why not...'

'I think it is not possible to understand all aspects of life. Take, for example, our differences. We will never be able to reach a fair consensus between us. But we do have, within the same society in which we both live, established rules that allow us to live in harmony.' he said, showing emotion.

The metaphor used by Jonah came to hold Giovanni's attention for a brief period of time, the old man seemed really intrigued by the meaning that Jonah had found for his dream. The fact that he never managed to get to the floor of the building, and never managed to know who was waiting for him there, had an interesting connotation about how he was guiding his own life.

'This is one of the most crucial differences between you and I.' said Giovanni whilst putting a smirk on his face. 'I would never accept a theory that limits me as far as not reaching my goals, on the contrary, I prefer to leave this plan before my ideals are blocked by renunciation.'

Jonah did not expect Giovanni's response to be that deep, which left him without reaction for a moment, leading him to seek a break in the matter and bring back what was his biggest concern.

'You seem, at times, to be such a lucid and intelligent man. I can't understand how you can justify killing me or anyone else in this madness you call organisation, based on mere words written in a fantasy book, thousands of years ago.' Jonah knew he had offended Giovanni, and that was his intention.

'And maybe you will never understand it.' he replied dryly when he realised that Douglas was making his way back from wherever he was.

The doctor carried in his hands a closed suitcase that Jonah could only imagine contained the nano-chips that would be re-implanted into his arm, but the expression on his face did not seem to match the fact that he had returned bearing good news.

'I hope the expression on your face is not consistent with what you carry in that briefcase, doctor.' said Giovanni, who let Jonah on the care of the guards once again as he made his way to meet Douglas.

The two began to exchange words in a heated and dubious argument; Giovanni exuded anger and disappointment, which made Jonah think he might have a chance after all. Catarina reappeared behind the same door that she had disappeared before and tried to calm the situation before the two came to take more drastic measures between themselves.

She took Giovanni by the arm he had been scratching and gave him what appeared to be a pill. Perhaps a medicine or any other type of drug that would calm the anger that was putting fear in everyone else. Douglas held on to his position as soon as he noticed the way Catarina treated Giovanni, which further intrigued Jonah about the whole mystery behind the distinguished lady who, despite not always present, always seemed to have a solution to every little problem she would come to face. The two exchanged words for a few minutes until they found a solution to the apparent obstacle hindering what was supposed to come.

'Very well, ladies and gentlemen. Let's go back to the main hall. I believe that everyone is going to be surprised by what my fellow people have prepared for us over there.' Giovanni promptly stamped a smile worthy of the leader he was, leading the way to be followed by everyone else.

The circus was fully set in the hall that previously gave way to the big party that Jonah took part in. A small and simple altar had been quickly assembled in the center of the room. The table Jonah had sat during dinner had given place to one of those dream chairs, as an audience was starting to build up in front of it. The priest, who had disappeared since Lara's death, had returned to show his tragic appearance, looking like someone who had spent the past few hours drowning in a bottle of christ's blood, causing Jonah to shiver every time their eyes met.

'Please put him in the chair.' said Giovanni to two of his henchmen, bringing torment to Jonah's mind. He was feeling that his time was getting closer and closer to the end.

Two men held him tightly, which was not necessary since he was not fighting it as he felt pain to the even slightest movement his body made against his will, and sat him in the dream chair, holding his feet and hands so that he would be completely still until they could tie the extremities of his limbs.

The anxiety came with strength. Jonah hadn't had any hope of getting out of there for while now, but it was only then that it hit him, making him realise that his future was unavoidable. In one night he could account for the death of his best friend, his ex-girlfriend and her mother, as well as other atrocities he had witnessed against people he had just met. His mouth was dry and his mind was unable to focus; several were the insanities that his brain had been propagating behind his eyes, and few were the possibilities in which he could survive.

He had no idea what Giovanni had programmed to be his long-awaited penance, but he couldn't get his mind off all of those medieval torture paraphernalia the sect had recently used against others. Whatever Giovanni had planned for him, it was still a great mystery, and it caused his mental state to depreciate more by the second.

'Giovanni!' Jonah let his mental stability escape him and started to scream desperately. 'Let me out of here!'

His plea was ignored and, soon after, drowned out by the handkerchief Giovanni carried in the pocket of his jacket. The piece of cloth filled his already battered mouth so deeply, that he couldn't even spit out the blood that had not yet stopped flowing from his wounds.

The stage was set and the main attraction was already present. Giovanni Dartagnan had finally succeeded in organising his final plan; not in the way he had imagined, and with a much smaller audience than he thought he would have, but he was going to have the satisfaction of having Jonah exactly where he wanted.

As soon as Giovanni began his usual speech, the priest came down from the altar to meet Jonah. He was so drunk that he could barely keep his balance. He could feel from afar, before the priest got remotely close, the terrible smell left by the misture of alcohol and cigarettes, which exhaled from his open and full of crooked teeth mouth. The old priest's hair was no longer straight as it had been when they met in the church, the priest now looked more like the one Jonah had met in the small red room whilst he was being tortured with lucid dreams and depersonalised memories.

Jonah broke out in a cold sweat when anxiety, once again, hit a new peak. The moment the priest got close to him, he could see the dirt accumulated within his teeth.

'Now it's just you and I.'

The old man began to rub his recently stubble shave on Jonah's face, whilst sniffling his enormous nouse in his ear. He even threw up in his handkerchief-covered mouth when the priest stuck out his tongue and licked the side of his face from top to bottom.

'You are mine now.' said the priest as he slid his hand over Jonah's chest until he reached his groin and squeezed his testicles with such force that he let out a cry that was muffled by the handkerchief.

Giovanni just turned his face away with a sign of disgust taken by the priest's meddling, preventing the old pervert from continuing to do whatever was in his sordid mind.

'Now I need your utmost attention, my people. For all this time that you have been with me, I have omitted from you, ladies and gentlemen, something of extreme importance to our organisation.' Giovanni caught Jonah's attention, who could still feel the repugnance as he exhaled by disgusting smell from the priest. 'The reason that we are all here today, alive and ready to move on, is this woman that I will introduce to you. Please, a round of applause for my dear sister, Catarina Dartagnan.'

The announcement didn't just take Jonah by surprise, but everyone in attendance who began to whisper and comment on the newest arrived news they had just heard. After a brief moment of awkwardness, one of the guests encouraged the applauses requested by Giovanni, which was followed by a loud wave of clapping and cheering that came to an end when requested by Mr. Dartagnan himself.

'Thank you, thank you.' he said, looking pleased with the general reaction. 'Now, in a very brief moment, I will explain to you the role of Catarina, and how our next offering, Jonah Albuquerque, relates to the cause.'

Jonah's mind began to imagine all kinds of possible scenarios, trying to understand what his relationship to that woman would be, but his energies were completely depleted and his thoughts could not dismiss the idea that he was there to die.

The time-frame was too short to follow the surprises that appeared in the main hall of the Dartagnan Brothers Hotel, which now made more of a full sense by how its given name was settle, since James was not very welcomed in there. Giovanni stopped giving explanations and started acting as if everyone there was following his line of thought and understood everything he was doing. The same opening in the floor, that had swallowed the dining table Jonah had sat on before, opened to bring yet another dream chair; the extremely advanced technological paraphernalia had Giovanni's initials engraved in extravagant golden letters. Giovanni's chair seemed to have some increments that the others didn't have, a technology that seemed to be really advanced when compared to anything else that Jonah had ever set his eyes on, but what most caught his attention was the lack of cables and monitors who accompanied its peers.

'I will show you something that is very personal to me. Something about my family that I've never showed anyone else, something that only a select few know about.'

Giovanni's words seemed to be sincere and held an immense meaning for him. Jonah managed to focus his attention on what was about to happen since the priest had left him alone and was now nursing an empty bottle of wine whilst lying on the floor by the altar.

Giovanni said nothing more, letting only his gestures show what was going to happen. Douglas appeared at his side to help him lie down into the dream chair, not needing to do anything else as things became to work themselves completely automatic from then on. The shape of the chair started to change so that Giovanni would be as comfortable as possible, his head was already the target of some laser-like-lights that made him sleep immediately. A large projection screen appeared over Giovanni's head, causing the murmur to reign among the guests who continued to be surprised every little detail that would come to amaze.

"Two young adults, who were talking to what looked like a young Giovanni. They had the appearance of simple and humble people, but at the same time they held an expression of conviction on what they were about to do.

Next to Giovanni sat an elderly woman, perhaps a little older than the young adults, but with an aspect of much greater experience; her clothes were beaten up and her hands were callused by the hardness that life had imposed on her. She was crying tirelessly and rubbing her face with her hands so she wouldn't let her sadness affect the child in front of her.

'Son, do you understand that this person will bring you a sister?' asked the woman, Jennifer , matriarch of the Dartagnan family.

He replied with a negative gesture and a confused look. Maybe he was too young to understand how anyone could relate to him without coming from his mother's belly, or maybe he didn't even understand how children came into the world in the first place, but he certainly didn't seem happy that his parents were giving him that news on in front of a stranger.

'I thought you were my mother.' he said whilst swallowing his weeping. 'Is she my mother now?'

'No! I am your mother and this is your father.' she said whilst pointing to Matthew. 'But this lady carries a gift from god, and unfortunately she won't be able to take care of the child in her tommy.'

'And why do you want to take care of this child? Am I not enough for you?' young Giovanni seemed to be about to explode amid the confusion created by his parents.

'You will always be the greatest love of my life, but you will have to share our attention with this girl who will be born in a few months.' said Jennifer , pointing to the belly of the mysterious woman and leading the boy's hand to touch the life that was being formed inside her womb.

'Enough, Jennifer . When he grows up, he will understand the reason, there's no need to explain ourselves to a child.' said Matthew, already fed up by that conversation.

'Why don't you go to your room and play with James?' she said whilst rubbing the boy's head and insisting that he got up at once.

Giovanni left the place where the adults were talking and pretended to make his way up to his bedroom, where his brother was already lying in bed, but he, surreptitiously, hid behind the half-open door that left room for him to eavesdrop the conversation that followed.

'I told you it wouldn't work.' said Matthew, letting his back lean against the chair.

'And what do you want me to do? Do we let this woman commit the crime she intends to? What would we be, before god and his final judgment, if we have this dwelling into our consciences?' Jennifer's questions were so many that Matthew just shook his head as if he were there just to obey orders.

Jennifer held out her hands on the table so that the woman could find the comfort she was offering.

'Now... I want you to give me those home remedies that the man offered to take off the child.' she said passing a feeling of confidence through the look in her eyes. 'I promise you that I will take care of you until the day of delivery, and I will care for this child for as long as I breathe.'"

As soon as the projection disappeared from above his head, Giovanni promptly rose from his chair as if he had no hangover left by the experience he just had. Jonah knew that if the drugs were taken in a rightly fashioned way, people would be good as new after experiencing a lucid dream.

'So, ladies and gentlemen, this is another story about my family that I share with you tonight.', he said as he rotated the red staff around his fist whilst he climbed back

312

up in the recently assembled altar, becoming evident to everyone to follow his steps.

Giovanni's audience was a very strange one. People whispered as if they were in a play that was being shown for their sole entertainment, but for Giovanni it seemed to be a moment of sadness combined with a feeling of relief and satisfaction. For the first time, he let himself sat down in one of those ceremonies, as he crossed his legs and started looking at the horizon as if all his problems were solved. That was when his eyes met Jonah's, sitting in that chair and ready to suffer the long-awaited penance that had been awaiting for him.

'So, ladies and gentlemen.' he repeated the jargon he had being tireless repeating throughout the whole time after clearing his throat and getting back to his feet 'I believe that those with the sharpest minds among you have already understood exactly why this young man is tied to this chair.'

Jonah felt that his time had come when all eyes inside that place started focusing on him. Catarina had taken the position at Giovanni's side and Douglas followed her closely without letting any of his movements come to attract attention. Jonah couldn't help believing that he still had a chance to leave that place alive, and he saw that possibility only and exclusively in Douglas. Every time their eyes met, he tried to indicate the sadness contained inside of him so that perhaps he could stir emotions out of Douglas, and encourage him to conduct some majestic gesture that would get them out of there safe and sound, but as it seemed, the doctor had already returned to Giovanni's good side and he had nothing to offer that could change his mind.

'Everyone knows exactly what Jonah did to deserve to be here, and now you know why this subject is so delicate to me. I know very well that this organisation was not created to satisfy personal desires, and I promise that this will be the only time that I use my position for personal gain.' the members of the C.P.F. held their words and acquiesced with their master. 'We will then proceed with the evening's events.'

Jonah was so frightened to have finally come to his final destination that he had not noticed that dusk was beginning to fall through the big doors leading to the balcony where he had previously observed the maze that had tormented him for hours, which was now clear to him, actually happened a few months ago. Giovanni started to approach Jonah slowly until he got so close to him that his body shivered with fear that came and went from the most haunted places in his mind. Unlike the priest, Mr. Dartagnan smelled very nice and always carried grace within him, and he would never be able to forget that. It was what made him think, in that instant, of what the end would be like, what death would bring him, and that he would finally discover what awaited him in the after life, if such a thing even existed. He, the skeptic who did not believe in any of the fantasies adored by all those lunatics, would be the first among them to know what really happens after the end.

It so happened that thought of divination came to his mind. 'Is it too late to ask for forgiveness?', he thought as he tried to remember a prayer that would absolve him os his sins and grant him save passage to a possible heaven. 'Or maybe my place in hell wouldn't be so bad.', he ended his line of thinking before he decided there was no point on dwelling on that matter.

It was too late for him, and hell couldn't be worse that what life was at that point.

'You must be really scared.' whispered Giovanni in his ear as soon as he got close enough.

Jonah went into despair and started to project out screams that were still muffled out by the cloth lodged into his mouth. His body was already used to the constant pain he felt due to the blows he received throughout all that time.

'Let the man speak his mind, provide him with a worthy ending.' said one of the men in the middle of the audience that Giovanni could not recognise.

'Let him speak, Giovanni.' to Jonah's surprise, Catarina had come to put a little common sense in her step-brother's ear.

The leader's morale was no longer at the peak it had once been. He decided that satisfying a small desire from one of his subjects wouldn't be the end of the world and would demonstrate that his seriousness with the sect had never been more imperative.

'So speak then, boy.' he said as he removed the bloodstained cloth.

'I really don't know what I did to make you hold such hatred towards me. I know very well that I made a mistake and I know very well that my attitudes cannot be repaired in a way that brings back the lives that were lost, including those that you ended yourself here today.' he tried to appeal to the logical sense of anyone who could get him out of that chair. 'I have nothing to do with anyone in your family, and I never wished anyone any harm. Please let me go.' he certainly still had a lot to say, but he didn't find the strength to allow his voice to be heard. He was trying to find clemency amid the people in the audience, but no one there seemed to be willing to risk their own well-being in order to save him from the hell he was living.

'You see, ladies and gentlemen, he doesn't know what he did to deserve what is about to happen to him.', Giovanni turned his attention to the members of the sect who also seemed to expect a slightly more logical explanation of the facts, which brought an unexpected discomfort to Giovanni.

'Whatever I did, I don't deserve to go like this, without a chance to fight!', Jonah said his last words before Giovanni spoke again.

'Didn't you understand what happened to Catarina, even before she was born? It is because of people like you, my boy, that many lives are denied even being tried! My sister is the purest consequence of avoiding such acts of evil, she is a godsend creature and is here to prove that people like you do not deserve to have the life you waste, you don't deserve freedom! You don't deserve to live among us!'

'You and your family did the same to Lara! James showed me how you made him leave her behind so your family would not be ill-spoken within society!' he was trying to make a point, trying to appeal to he other member's willingness for forgiveness and sensibility.

'That's what that imbecile told you? James wanted her abortion, the same way you did with your unborn child, and after that was denied, he wanted to give her up for adoption, to a family so far away he would never have to hear about that child again!' Giovanni's words were sadly deep as he held the tears that were trying to make their way out of his eyes. 'My family sought the only solution they could so that girl could have an honest life!'

'For what? So you could kill her in front of her own father?' Jonah knew he was throwing away every chance he had of turning Giovanni's senses around. 'You are nothing but a murderer.'

'Don't you dare use that filthy mouth to disrespect Lara's memory, she was more than you could ever be...' he was reaching an extreme point of angst. 'You have no right to speak ill of people like her, that once set foot in this sacred place.'

'So then I deserve to die? Then you hold the right to kill me?' he asked as his anxiety returned to torment his mind.

'Die? Who said you're going to die?' Giovanni didn't even bother to demonstrate the rhetorical tone of his question before shoving the bloodstained cloth back into Jonah's mouth, and continuing the ceremony. He was tired and had enough from Jonah. He knew he held all the keys to his own kingdom and no one in there could stop him from fulfilling his wishes.

He waved his red staff through the air and Douglas soon came to meet him as the two began to discuss warmly without Jonah being able to distinguish exactly the words that came out of their mouths, but one thing was certain, the doctor was not comfortable with the situation that was to follow.

'I've told you that so many times...' said the doctor between one sentence and another.

Jonah could remember the exact meaning of those words from the time he had been trapped in the red room and the warnings that doctor Douglas had given Giovanni about the harms that the excessive use of that drug in Jonah's body could bring him, but Mr. Dartagnan did not seem to be concerned with the consequences that would be coming henceforth.

'I'm truly sorry.' said Douglas as he approached Jonah with the suitcase he had been carrying since he returned from wherever he had gone.

He opened the case and withdrew a large syringe containing a light-blue liquid. Giovanni came to his side and started rubbing his hands anxiously, hoping that the moment he had been waiting for would finally come.

'Jonah used to have two nano-chips in his body that allowed me to control his lucid dreams and the depersonalisation effect.' he turned to the audience to explain. 'However, my brother managed to remove the objects that I struggled to put inside him.'

Jonah shook his head in fear and trembled with intensity as Douglas would approach him with the filled up syringe.

'According to the doctor here, it will not be possible to make new chips so quickly so we could return them to Jonah's body. However, we found an even better solution.' he seemed really satisfied with the conversation he had had with Douglas and Catarina.

Catarina arrived at Douglas' side, showing him a pinch of support that only a very intimate person would.

'My initial idea was to make Jonah relive his own past, and experience the crime itself, with a few increments, of course.' he said referring to the possibility he had to change Jonah's dreams. 'But doctor Douglas here will enable us to inject a new species of the drug into his system. Something that, if I'm not mistaken, will never leave his body.'

Jonah soon gathered the ideas presented by Giovanni and realised that his plan was not to kill him, but to torture him for who knows how long. He sought to bring comfort to his own thoughts so that his end would come without pain, he knew he had no regrets in his life and he was sure that he had done nothing wrong, at least not to a point where he deserved what was about to happen to him. He had no idea of what was really going to happen in the next few seconds, but he knew he would never be able to have a normal life again.

Douglas injected the syringe into his bloodstream with a certain rush in his eyes. Catarina, after fiddling inside Jonah's trouser pocket, held Douglas by the hand and comforted his shoulder as if he were the one about to have his life ended in a tragic way.

Before his mind went into a complete reverie and left the conscious plane he was so used to, he was able see

Douglas embrace Catarina, as she shoved what she had just taken from his pocket into his hand, and whispered words in his ears without letting Giovanni see it. The doctor then walked out the door, having the infamous cylinder Jonah had carried for hours without knowing its purpose, without letting his eyes look back.

'Sweet dreams, my boy.' said Giovanni as soon as his eyes started to close.

"The tall building made a new appearance in Jonah's mind. That thirty meters high monstrosity brought an immeasurable adrenaline back to his mind before he could jump to meet whoever was waiting for him down there. He closed his eyes and began to feel that energising wind before he could open them again and realise that he had returned to the top of the building, where everything would begin again."

The End.

Made in the USA
Columbia, SC
11 August 2022

GRACE
UPON
GRACE

Mary Lou Erickson

Xulon Elite

Xulon Press Elite
555 Winderley Pl, Suite 225
Maitland, FL 32751
407.339.4217
www.xulonpress.com

Paperback ISBN-13: 979-8-86850-216-3
Ebook ISBN-13: 979-8-86850-217-0

To my incredibly supportive husband, my family, friends, and prayer warriors, who have continually encouraged me every step of the way, May you be blessed beyond measure as you have so blessed me.

TABLE OF CONTENTS

ACKNOWLEDGMENTS

I AM INCREDIBLY thankful for Andy and Karen Ill for stepping into our lives as Sheltering Trees. Your willingness to be obedient to the call of God in stepping into our lives in our time of need and guidance is beyond words.

Laura Spencer, from Christian Life Church in Mount Prospect, Illinois, Thank you for your wisdom beyond your years, your courage to speak and teach the Word of God, and for being vulnerable, honest, and kind to all of us ladies in Bible study. Your exuberance was exhilarating and refreshing. Thank you for being a willing and faithful vessel of God; I will be forever impacted by your creative and tangible illustration reminders through smooth rocks in a jar as all the altars (miracle moments) of God's grace in my life.

I would like to thank my dear friend Amy Joob for being a faithful prayer partner and encourager.

INTRODUCTION

GOD'S GRACE IS boundless and reveals itself in many ways. It has no limitations, expirations, or stipulations attached. You can't earn His grace by doing all the right things. He gives it freely and in the measured portions He deems necessary. His grace can range from minuscule, to big, to sufficient, to extravagant! He picks the exact moment you need it.

We all have knowledge of grace or how to be gracious at least, but do you have spiritual knowledge of grace? I first thought it was only when I truly needed it. I tried to do all the right things. I had always believed in God, but it wasn't until I had given my heart to the Lord when I was in seventh grade that I experienced Him in a much deeper way and on every level; I have followed Him ever since. It was only within the last ten years that I have developed a deeper revelation of God's grace.

You will read how the Lord began to reveal many instances where His grace was given, how His grace rushed in, and how His grace was lavished over me. It was when I had to give grace to someone who hurt me that I prayed He would give me His own grace for them because I couldn't muster up any myself. He whisked me through a collection of life experiences and biblical experiences, and I felt His grace move and work in my life. There were times when He was right by my side, and I didn't see Him; He was and is infinitely faithful!

I confidently profess that experiencing His grace upon grace is life changing. Now I am on the lookout to see Him moving. I am elated to see His handiwork in others' lives as well, and I love the opportunity to point it out to them. He never leaves our side, is madly in love with us, and is waiting for us. He has so much to show us and do for us in our lives if we let Him. He never tires of us or has had enough of our messes, and He is never wringing His hands with worry over what to do next. He knows our hearts and sees us as He created us. He is a forever forgiving God, even if it takes a million chances to realize it.

May you be open to journey deeper with Him. May your curiosity stir your heart to see what God has in store especially for you. May you have courage to allow change to catapult you into the magnificent wonder and adventures of following Christ. As you read this book, I hope you will see instances in your life where His grace is present and evident. May you experience His abundantly extravagant grace upon grace.

Grace upon Grace

> For out of His fullness [the superabundance of His grace and truth] we have all received grace upon grace [spiritual blessing upon spiritual blessing, favor upon favor, and gift heaped upon gift].

> John 1:16 AMP

May you savor this verse. May you ponder on His fullness, grace, and truth. May your eyes be opened to His grace in your life, favor upon favor, and blessings upon blessings. Though the gift of grace might come in different packaging than we envisioned, it is perfect, timely, and oh-so preciously intimate to our individual needs. Worthy we might not be, but we are lovely and just as He created us to be. Though troubles have come, He is faithful and true. Though we may run from His love, He is patiently waiting to cover us with grace. May you not tarry too long, for freedom and a fantastic adventure awaits you. For His Word says God can do exceedingly and abundantly above all that we ask or think according to the power that works in us (Eph. 3:20). Therefore, we can't out-imagine, ask too much, or be too far gone for His power to work in us. Step out and step into His arms.

Chapter 1

GRACE LOVES

....

MAY YOU SEE with eyes of wonder the keeper of all our hopes, dreams, aspirations, desires, weaknesses, secrets, and innermost thoughts as He weaves a beautiful tapestry out of our lives. His timing is perfect, and His grace is extravagant. Grace upon grace, He will show you His faithfulness. Grace upon grace, He will pick you up and dust you off. Grace upon grace, He will show you wonders and stir your heart. Grace upon grace, He will show you how He sees you and how much He so passionately loves you.

The grace of God is without limits. There are no boundaries around His love for us; there are no stipulations, nor fine print to trick us. We can't earn grace; He gives it as a gift. Receiving the gift of grace is so special, tender, and specific. It is a surprise; it comes in many sizes and shapes. It is an expression from the giver, a salutation of a moment, and a celebration to the beholder. It is special because it isn't an expected occasion like your birthday, anniversary, or a holiday. Sometimes you don't even realize it was given—you received it before you knew you would even need it. It was a foundation built up to hold you high and provide strength, yet it gives insight when chaos over-whelms you.

God's grace has so many avenues and manifestations of His love. Yet at the same time, we know it to be the pardon that Jesus paid for our sins. It sometimes shows itself as a change of heart in a situation. It can be an insight or a new perspective. It can be in humility or extra confidence. It can be protection or unexpected provision. It is between you and God; He knows your intimate thoughts and what is best for you. He sees what's coming down the road and maneuvers you in the right direction (Deut. 1:30; 31:8; Isa. 45:2; 52:12; Ps. 139:5).

He created us and knows each hair on our head and every freckle or wrinkle on our skin. He created each heartbeat, designed our identity, and is pleased with His good work in you!

Grace is the immense expression of God's love.

His love is expressed by one act of grace upon another. God's foremost motive and desire is our heart. Every action is out of love for us to win our hearts. He constantly aware of the condition of our hearts. He waits patiently; He stirs our hearts and fulfills our desires.

It is God's love that calls us out of the darkness and into His presence. Because of His unconditional love, He relentlessly pursues us no matter how much we mess up.

The chorus of "Never Too Far Gone" by Jordan Feliz[1]:

> *There's no distance too far that I can't*
> *reach you*
> *There's no place that's so dark that I*

can't find you
Anywhere that you are, if you need proof
Take a look at these scars, and know
I love you
Doesn't matter, doesn't matter, doesn't
matter what you've done
You are never, you are never, never
too far gone.

His love for you is infinite and unchanging! What a reassurance and an everlasting promise. We are never too far gone, and we will never be separated from Him.

> For I am convinced that neither death nor life, neither angels nor demons, neither the present nor the future, nor any powers, neither height nor depth nor anything else in all creation, will be able to separate us from the **love of God** that is in Christ Jesus our Lord. Romans 8:38–39 NIV

To hear the words "I love you" sends our hearts soaring. My heart is joyful when my children and grandchildren say they love me. We giggle and say, "Love you more and love you most," "Love you to the moon and back," "Love you deeper than the sea and more than the stars," and "Love you bigger than dinosaurs and more than Swedish fish." Just imagine hearing God say, "You are the apple of my eye, and I will never stop loving you!" He will love you to eternity and beyond.

"If God had a refrigerator, your picture would be on it."²

—Max Lucado

He is the shepherd, and we are His sheep. He will care for us, and if needed, He will carry us. He will search until He finds us when we are lost. He will groom, prune, and lavish over us. He goes before us and makes our path straight. He will guide us to green pastures and still waters. He will protect us and mark us as priceless.

You might be going through some tough times; know that God is aware. You might feel lonely; know that God is there. You might be hurt; know that God cares. He knows every detail of who you are, right down to the number of hairs on your head. He had you in mind when He created you, and that is indeed what He sees. His view of you never changes; our mistakes do not diminish His love for us, and the world's opinion of us holds no weight to the thoughts of our mighty God!

Because the creator of the universe said so, God is the embodiment of love. He is love and has thus created us to love. Love is the driving force and representation of His character. He created everything and everyone for love and relationship. His only instinct is love, no matter how many times you have messed up and no matter the severity of your sin. Even in disciplining, He loves us enough to bring the flaw to the surface and lovingly smooth it out to reveal the beauty He designed in us. He has your best interests at heart, for we **are** His heart!

There is nothing you can do that would make Him stop loving you. I will repeat it; you can do NOTHING to make Him stop loving you.

I have loved you with an everlasting love...

Jeremiah 31:3 NIV

Give thanks to the Lord for he is good. His love lasts forever.

1 Chronicles 16:34 NIV

What is love, you might ask? Well, God made sure to write it down so we would always know:

Love is patient; love is kind. It does not envy; it does not boast; it is not proud. It does not dishonor others, it is not self-seeking, it is not easily angered, it keeps no record of wrongs. Love does not delight in evil but rejoices with the truth. It always protects, always trusts, always hopes, always perseveres. Love never fails... (1 Cor. 13:4–8 NIV).

While listening to the radio, a song by Jesus Culture called "Fierce"[3] came on.
The chorus:

Like a tidal wave
Crashing over me
Rushing in to meet me here
Your love is fierce
Like a hurricane
That I can't escape
Tearing through the atmosphere
Your love is fierce

Imagine a hurricane, tidal wave, or tsunami. We have all seen pictures of different hurricanes over the years. Mass destruction. I was born and raised in Kansas, so I truly know the power of a tornado, which is only semi-comparable. His love is so fierce that change will always happen—some redecorating is required. He might have to obliterate our old life to rebuild and reveal his splendor.

He loves us with immense intensity, more than an "F5"/250-mph-wind devastation, simply beyond our comprehension. His love is deeper than the Mariana Trench, the deepest part of the world's ocean known to man. His love is more expansive than all the galaxies collectively. His love is infinite.

He is crazy about you! Truly, that statement isn't just an endearing phrase; it is the Gospel Truth. He gave His Son for you, formed you in your mother's womb, and is like the shepherd who would drop everything to find His one lost lamb. You matter to Him, and He will spend a lifetime pursuing a relationship with you.

"There is no pit so deep that God's love is not deeper still[4]" —Corrie ten Boom

Chapter 2

GRACE PROTECTS

··

You are my hiding place;
you will protect me from trouble
and surround me with songs of deliverance
(Ps. 32:7 NIV).

I HAVE SEVERAL experiences with His protection. For example, I was delayed getting home by an obnoxious car that blocked me in behind a semi-truck and wouldn't let me move around them. I was fussing and stewing when the Holy Spirit came over me and said, "Just stay put." I turned my radio on and chose to chill out behind the tractor-trailer as instructed. A few miles later, we slowed down and saw a car accident; I could have been involved if I had gotten my way. I said a prayer for those involved and a prayer of thanks for making me slow down.

While driving to Nebraska from Illinois with my kids to meet with my husband, I was totally unaware that a tornado was crossing our path. I am from Kansas and know well the warning signs of a tornado, and this was eerie looking. Up ahead, I saw the other side of the storm line:

sunshine with rays coming down. I picked up my speed and outran the tornado. Once we were in the clear, my daughter, who was five-years-old, said, "Mommy, look at the angel with curly hair sitting in the clouds."

When Moses led the Israelites out of Egypt and a life of slavery (Exodus 14:15-31), the Lord told Moses to stretch out his staff over the Red Sea. The Lord held back the sea with a strong east wind and turned it into dry land. The waters were divided, and the Israelites went through the sea **on dry ground,** with a wall of water on their right and their left. Moses was instructed to stretch his staff back over the Red Sea when the Israelites had crossed to the other side. The water flowed back and covered the chariots and horsemen—Pharaoh's entire army that had followed the Israelites into the sea. Not one of them survived. What a protection of epic physical proportions!

Shadrach, Meshach, and Abednego were pro-tected because of their obedience and alliance with God (Daniel 3). They would not bow down and worship King Nebuchadnezzar. The king then had them thrown into the fiery hot furnace. Only the three men went in, but there were four men seen inside; an angel of the Lord was with them. When King Nebuchadnezzar saw this, he knew their God was saving them. They came out without a single hair singed; their garments weren't scorched, nor did they have a remnant smell of fire. They were completely untouched.

God's grace is supernatural protection. The naked eye does not see it; it is felt and beyond the mind's imagination. Nothing is impossible for God! It is written in God's Word, the Bible, of three instances in which the Lord "took" His faithful servants to Heaven. Of them were Elijah, Enoch, and Moses. Elijah was taken in the plain sight of Elisha by a chariot and horses of fire in a whirlwind (2 Kings 2). Enoch lived to be 365 years of age and walked faithfully with God. Enoch was the great-grandfather of Noah and the father of Methuselah (the longest living man-lived to 969 years of age). Enoch was taken to heaven without dying (Gen 5:21-24). The Lord took Moses up to Mount Nebo above the Moab plains to show him the land the Lord had promised to Moses's descendants. Moses died and was presumed buried; however, no grave was ever found (Deut 34:1-12), and Moses was present with Elijah at the Transfiguration, standing beside Jesus (Matt. 17:2). The Bible is full of mysteries and wonders.

He sends His angels as a hedge of protection to surround you. He has saved you from many near misses over the years, near misses you never even knew existed, and ones that will forever be etched in your mind.

Recently, I applied for two promotions at my grocery store job. I had all the qualifications, drive, and customer service skills. I was the assistant manager and completed all my management training, with ten years of prior restaurant management experience to boot. It was the natural succession to step up. I knew the first possible promotion would probably be filled within that store. I understood it would be a smooth transition and promote employee morale and client recognition. I still tried for the experience, because you never know, right? They decided to go with my original thought; I wished them the best.

The second promotion I thought for sure I had in the bag; I had worked there previously, had great sales-building ideas, am a team player, and everybody loved me. A few days before my notification, I started feeling uneasy about it. "Um, excuse me, God, I am not feeling Your peace about this job right now," I said to Him.

I have learned from our relationship that if I don't feel His peace, then it isn't right or not supposed to happen. It is crazy how fast I went from "Yeah, I will be department manager and make more money" to "I don't think I am supposed to do this; I don't think I want it at this store."

I woke up two days later and felt peace flow over me, and it was going to be okay that I didn't get this job. I got the call that day, and to no surprise, I wasn't upset when I did not get the job. It was the most excellent "no," and while sometimes my mind would try to justify that they made the wrong decision, I would snap right back and lean on God, whom I trust. God's protection was revealed a few months later. He knew what He had in store for me; I had to stay humble and open to what He had in mind for me.

My very good friend Amy Joob, mother of two, Christian author, speaker, and model, told me a phrase I believe and cling to. "Rejection is God's protection." Every time it has rung true in my life. Every time, God is faithful! The answer no might not be the words I want to hear, but better now than later and having regrets or harmful consequences. You can trust God. The relationship between God and me is growing stronger. He stirs my heart and shows me His heart. He gives me strength, confidence, and a dose of humility when I need it. He sends provisions, encouragement, and those I can love in His name. And faithfully, He sends rejection to protect me. He sees what I don't see, knows the outcomes and consequences, and knows His plan for my life. If He says no, then that is good enough for me. Why? Because I can trust my heart and my life in His hands. I know He has the best in mind for me. I know He will open another door or give me the strength to endure till it is the right time. Because of this powerful phrase in my life, I have seen His protection in others' lives and an opportunity to share my experiences to encourage them. Hang in there if the answer is no, for an even better yes is coming.

If I hadn't been told no, I would have settled and sold out. I might have gotten too bogged down to hear God's voice. You never know what you might be missing if you don't consult God. I now am pursuing another new adventure in my life; one I might not have had if I had been given the job. "Let's go, Lord. I am ready." Believe and trust God; He wants to provide you with the delights of your heart, as long as they are the best thing for you and line up with His will.

Chapter 3

ALTARS OF GRACE

....

ALTARS ARE MEMORIAL stones erected in significant places to mark where God was faithful and triumphantly gave grace. There are many memorial stones resurrected in honor of God in the Bible. They marked the site where the grace of God rushed in, a time of revelation and transformation, a season of near misses, answered prayers, and long-awaited healing and fertility, a milestone of minuscule or epic proportions.

The memorial, God of miracles: In Joshua 4:1-24, the miracle of the Lord stopping the Jordan River for the twelve tribes of Israel and the priests that carried the ark of the covenant. He commanded Joshua to have one appointed leader from each tribe:

> Go over before the ark of the LORD your God into the middle of the Jordan. Each of you is to take up a stone on his shoulder, according to the number of the tribes of the Israelites, to serve as a sign among you. In the future, when your children ask you, "What do these stones mean?" tell them that the flow

of the Jordan was cut off before the ark of the covenant of the LORD. When it crossed the Jordan, the waters of the Jordan were cut off. These stones are to be a memorial to the people of Israel forever (v.5-7).

When Joshua and the nation of Israel, carrying the ark of the covenant, stepped into the Jordan, the Lord caused the waters to be cut off, and they walked on dry land in the middle of the Jordan. The Lord instructed Joshua to have twelve men, each representing their tribe, gather a stone from the dry section of the Jordan and carry it to the place on the other side where they would stay the night. They were to build a memorial to remind them forever that at this place, the Lord cut off the Jordan for the ark of the covenant.

Wow! Can you even imagine such a sight? What a "seeing is believing" moment. How tremendous to witness God's protection and provision at that exact moment. You would think you would never forget it for the rest of your days, but this miracle was not only for all the tribes of Israel; it was for all who would pass by that exact spot to see and reflect on the significance of the way God stepped in to save the Israelites. The stones would last forever, just like God's love for us is never-ending; it will last forever.

The memorial, House of God, the gate of Heaven: In Genesis 28:10–22, Jacob had a dream in which he saw a stairway resting on the earth, with its top reaching heaven. The angels of God were ascending and descending on it.

There above it stood the LORD, and he said: "I am the LORD, the God of your father Abraham and the God of Isaac. I will give you and your descendants the land you are lying on. Your descendants will be like the dust of the earth, and you will spread out to the west and the east, to the north and the south. All people on earth will be blessed through you and your offspring. I am with you and will watch over you wherever you go, and I will bring you back to this land. I will not leave you until I have done what I have promised you (v. 13–15).

Jacob set up a pillar where he lay on the night that God gave him a vision. He named this place Bethel; although it used to be the town of Luz, he called it the "House of God, the gate of Heaven."

The memorial, Ebenezer, the Lord has helped us: In 1 Samuel 7:7–12, Samuel sacrificed the burnt offering as the Philistines drew near to battle. But that day, the Lord thundered with thunder against the Philistines and caused a panic, pushing them right into the Israelite's view. The Israelites rushed out and slaughtered the Philistines. God saved them from imminent danger. Samuel erected a large stone and called it "Ebenezer," the Lord has helped us, God's grace.

The memorial, The God who sees me: In Genesis 16:1-14: Another example is when Sarai, the wife of Abraham, who couldn't bear a child. She prayed and believed God would give her a child but grew weary in waiting and took the situation into her own hands. She had a servant named Hagar and thought maybe she could have a child in her place.

When Hagar became pregnant, Sarai was full of jealousy and mistreated her. Hagar ran away and hid by a well. An angel of the Lord came to talk to Hagar, relaying the message that the Lord had heard her misery. She named the well "Beer Lahai Roi," the God who sees me.

The memorial, God's grace in His presence and protection: I once did a Bible study by Blackaby called "Experiencing God." We had a young lady as our leader, named Laura Spencer. We came to the section on altars, and she gave us a gift bag with a glass jar with a lid and a bag of smooth rocks. She encouraged us to make our altars of memorials of all the times God was faithful in our lives. The stones would be a visual and physical example we could use to remind ourselves of His faithfulness, goodness, provision, and protection, the times He moved mountains and parted seas for us, and the moments He was tender with us and was our champion. These would be memorial stones of thankfulness for His forever grace in our lives.

As I look back over my stones in the jar, I gush with gratitude, and tears of thankfulness stain my face. Each altar stone was a whisper of His love, tender loving care, and a visual reminder of His faithfulness. He never left me; He knows me fully and provided the best solution while showering me with His grace

I recall a time I purchased a new van from a different state, and while I thought I paid the fees for the tags when I moved to another state, that was not the case. I drove for a long time with expired tags. I don't recommend this, and I am embarrassed to admit it. God kept me in a protective bubble. I prayed, gave thanks, and worshipped Him moment by moment; the van became my prayer closet. I would miss my exits because I was so consumed in prayer. He protected me as He equipped me. As I gave myself to Him, He gave Himself to me.

There were several incidences where it was a close call with the police; I would fervently pray and curl up in the palm of His hand, and His grace would pour over me. I did get the money together to get my tags, finally. The time spent in my prayer closet was immeasurable, full of grace, and made a sweet divot in my soul.

When that van broke down, I had to get a new car. I bawled as I cleaned out the van of my belongings; I saw the salesman give me a funny look. "You just don't know what this van meant to me," I said softly while I ached on the inside. The stone marked "van" represented the tangible presence of God; it was my meeting place, my prayer closet, and the place He covered me with His grace.

My altar stones are so precious to me, for it was in those moments God's heart was so connected to mine; He understood me, and while society might think I was being ridiculous to fret over such things, He took it seriously and moved on my behalf. How can a God so big care about the silly little thing bothering my heart? He is beyond our understanding and about loving us beyond eternity.

The memorial, Faith journey, deepening trust: Another significant stone in my life was the start of learning to walk by faith. Our church was helping with the Greg Laurie Crusades. We all took a spiritual gifts test and trained in proper etiquette and loving care for those who might come forward to receive Jesus.

We began prayer groups a few months in preparation, and we even marched around the venue location praying. While the results of the spiritual test were not a qualification needed to be involved with the crusade, it was instead a more profound look within ourselves and how we could be best used, and my results showed I didn't have as much faith as I thought I did. The stone marked "GL Crusade" represented the beginning of my faith journey experiences that catapulted me deeper into trusting the Lord with all that I am.

Just yesterday, I found a note I wrote in my budget book that I had been praying over and trusting God, and to no surprise, His grace covered me early! He is faithful!

If you think back over your life, you will be shocked at how many altar stones you have. The size doesn't represent the quality or quantity of the grace granted. It represents all the instances grace rushed in; they are monumental to me. May your past instances be numerous and precious evidence of His presence. The number of pebbles in the brook is infinite, and so is the Father's love.

Chapter 4

INTERRUPTING GRACE

∙∙

INTERRUPTIONS IN OUR life are seldom wanted. We like controlling circumstances; at least we *think* we have control. We like to keep things going when we are comfortable; if it isn't broken, why fix it, right?

One day, He might send an interruption in your life, and while it isn't a welcomed situation, He uses it to build you up, shake you up, refocus your views, and rearrange your steps to align with His will. He gets you back on the straight and narrow. While He can do a miracle anytime and anyplace, He involves others in the mix. He made us for connections and community. He doesn't waste any part of your experience; He allows it to be used for others while He builds us up.

God sent an interruption to Jonah by asking him to go to the great city of Nineveh and preach to them about their wicked ways (Book of Jonah). Jonah was scared, confused, and angry that he ran away from the Lord. He went to Tarshish and boarded a boat to Joppa, which would take him far away from Nineveh; it was actually in the complete opposite way from Nineveh.

There was a great storm, and the sailors started throwing heavy items overboard. Still, the storm raged. The Lord hurled a powerful wind over the sea, causing a violent storm that threatened to break the ship apart. They prayed to their gods and cast lots to see who was causing this calamity. The lots fell on Jonah. Once the truth came out that Jonah was running from the Lord and fearing for their lives, the sailors threw Jonah overboard.

The Lord sent protection for Jonah by sending a huge fish to swallow him. Jonah didn't feel the Ninevites deserved God's grace for all their wickedness. Spending three days in the belly of a huge fish brought Jonah to his senses. Jonah turned to obedience to God's instructions, and the nation was changed. (Highlights from the book of Jonah)

Things are not always as they seem. We don't have a perspective or view like our heavenly Father does. Little did Jonah know that God had been preparing the hearts of the Ninevite people to receive the message He sent through Jonah seven years prior!

We do not know what is going on in each other's hearts, but the Lord does. We aren't privy to information, secrets, aspirations, weaknesses, and the needs of others, but the Lord knows every detail of our lives. He decides who receives grace and the measure or dosage in which it will be given. God is always working on us and in our hearts. He allows things or circumstances to move us, mold us, pull off layers, fluff us, peel the veils from our eyes, build confidence, grow courage, and change our views and conceived thoughts to align with Him and His will. It might take years, but God never gives up on us! He never stops loving us! He only desires to be the keeper of our hearts.

Several times in my life, I have had grace lessons interrupt me and my thirty-six years of marriage. One of the big ones recently took place three-and-a-half years ago. Looking back, God began preparing us five years before our faith journey; He was gearing us up for what was to come. I prayed to the Lord to use us, and we would go wherever He wanted us to go. I probably should've told my husband what I had prayed. I am also learning that an interruption is on its way when life gets too comfortable.

My husband worked for the railroad, as did my mother, father, and grandfather. He worked hard and moved up the conductor, engineer, and management ladder. He was a meticulous, safe conscience, a walking rulebook encyclopedia, prompt, diligent, fair, and well-liked. He loved his job.

I felt the Lord telling me we were going to move. My husband's new job in management moved us an hour away from our family and church. We still made the trek to our church faithfully. We were comfortable; we all were connected in our church and so loved at our church and community, so why leave? I thought, well, maybe God meant this move; that wasn't so bad. So, we settled in, even though I still would feel his soft stirrings from time to time. I eventually would step out and try a new church and then split my time between churches.

I had several Bible studies in both churches; I am lost without my precious ladies and Bible studies. I still felt the soft stirrings. During our four years there, God grew our faith in and through circumstances so we could trust Him and be willing to step out when the time came.

That interruption started the day with a bizarre incident at my husband's work; without a valid reason, he lost his job! He was devastated. It made no sense to us, but I had this peace that came from out of nowhere. I just knew—I had confidence; I didn't have any fear; I didn't even worry (which is usually something I do). I had complete and utter peace! We lost our retirement if he couldn't find another railroad job, lost the pension he earned in management, and lost our house!

After eight months, moving to Missouri, and taking a lower-paying job, my husband finally humbly said, "Okay, God, if this is where you want me, I am okay with it." No exaggeration, within two days, the phone rang with a job offer for another railroad in Salt Lake City, Utah.

Things started happening very quickly, and God's grace was extravagant! My husband interviewed for one job, and they made him an offer on another job, a higher title, and higher pay than he had before, and it came with a moving package and stock option packages (these were out of our league). We had to leave our family and grandkids, but how do you tell God, "Oh, no, thank you, I am good here in this mess"? I knew God would be creative in seeing our family, and he has outdone himself doing it!

We were comfortable, and God had other plans. We stepped out and trusted that He knew best. He showered us with His grace every step of the way. We grew deeper in our faith; we grew in character, our passion was ignited in serving, and we found new perspectives and knowledge of "the hurting and the lost."

Our journey to Utah turned out to be for many reasons that we were not aware of. Amongst the Mormon culture, we were welcomed and cared for in our neighborhood during my open-heart surgery and foot surgery. We found unity and love and lifelong friendships. God placed several amazing and inspiring people in our lives! We found immeasurable support and training from our church, K2 The Church. It was such a fantastic experience, and we hold it so dear to our hearts. We continue to pray, support, and hold all of our precious Utah friends close in our hearts.

Not only did the Lord send protection for Jonah, but He also had an interruption of epic proportions planned. The Ninevites were wicked; why would the Lord send Jonah, the prophet, to preach to them? Why would the Lord choose grace for such wicked people?

With his whale experience vastly fresh, Jonah came to terms with the task the Lord had asked him to do and decided to trust Him even when it didn't make sense, even when it seemed like a waste of time, and even when his heart was not in it.

Jonah set out for a three-day walk into the city; along the way, he started proclaiming, "In 40 more days, Nineveh will be overthrown" (Jonah 3:4 NIV).

Now the word got back to the king of Nineveh, and he stepped down from his throne, took off his royal robes, clothed himself in sackcloth, and sat in the dust. What? This made Jonah mad, for he recognized that the Lord was at work and that the Ninevites would receive grace! They were wicked and had been wicked for decades; indeed, they couldn't have totally changed.

Jonah walked east of town and made a shelter to watch and see what happened. The Lord provided a leafy plant to grow over Jonah and give him shade. Now the Ninevites saw Jonah, the prophet, who was in the belly of the fish for three days and nights, as a sign from the Lord, for just like He was dead for three days and nights, He arose to save the world, our Lord and Savior Jesus Christ. They were open and willing to hear what the Lord had to say to them through the prophet Jonah.

Refocus your mind and heart to seek and trust God the next time an interruption comes into your life. It is for a reason that God allows it. He has only good plans for you, plans to prosper you and not to harm you, plans to give you hope and a future (Jer. 29:11). It might not look or feel like it, will not happen at the opportune time, and will not be just about you. Lean in, trust the Lord, and have your eyes wide open. He knows all the details, your concerns and shortcomings, and your heart and will carry you through it. You will see Him work, you will see His heart, and you will see His grace and love.

Chapter 5

GRACE TRADE

Come to me, all you who are weary and burdened,
and I will give you rest. Take my **yoke** upon you and
learn from me, for I am gentle and humble in heart,
and you will find rest for your souls. For my **yoke** is easy,
and my burden is light.
Matthew 11:28–30 (emphasis added)

TAKE THE LOAD off and give the burden to Jesus. Take His yoke. A yoke is a wooden harness attached to an animal's head or shoulder to help pull or carry a heavy load. Jesus's yoke is easy and light. He is offering for you to take His load, and He will take yours—a trade of grace.

A simple trade. Give up your heavy load, your burdens, and your worries. He will take it and give you His, which is light and easy, worry-free, and restful.

He will be the one to clean up any messes, reestablish your good name, remove all hindrances, begin working on broken relationships, and schedule a make-over of epic proportions. He will unplug any clogs that stop the flow of His love in your heart. You will be unrecognizable; the old you will be gone. You will be a new person with a new look, reputation, and perspective: a new temperament, one of peace and kindness, with no agenda or unrealistic expectations of performance. You will be more focused on loving others than conjuring up ways to get even. All your old ways and thoughts will be Jesus's problems. You will trade control of yourself and try to fix others over to Him. He has you; He has got this.

His ways are higher. He is the Rock; His works are perfect. He is faithful! His ways are always purposeful and good. He knows what is best for us.

The Heart of the Matter

You are precious to God, and all He wants is your heart. Where your heart is, so will you go. It is your heart that God looks at. He sees the real you, the genuine, honest you that is His creation. God wants to win your heart and affection. He wants to stir and capture your heart. He wants to empower your heart with compassion toward others. He wants to guard and protect your heart like the rare jewel it is. He longs to be in a relationship with you. He will never break your heart or forsake you.

No matter the situation or circumstance, our heart gives us away. We can't hide anything from God, who is omnipotent and omnipresent (all-knowing and everywhere), so I don't understand why we think we can. He knows already what our hearts are thinking. While that might sound creepy, it is extraordinary that He knows our heart and doesn't twist it to His advantage. He doesn't manipulate us into giving it to Him. He knows our next move yet lets us do what we want while He waits in the wings for us to whisper His name. He knows whether we are genuine or faking it, whether we are angry or selfish, coping an attitude or broken. Our hearts can be stubborn and driven in the wrong direction, but He doesn't judge; He faithfully loves and waits.

Where your heart is, where your treasure is, that thing you love to do and will do anything to do it, that is where your heart is. That craving or yearning that is so overwhelming you must satisfy where your heart is. That thing you put before everyone as a priority is where your heart is. That substance or event you use to try and fill a void in your life is where your heart is. The argument or grudge you are holding is where your heart is. The pit of pride you so protect, that is where your heart is. That person you look to for your happiness is where your heart is.

> "Above all else, **guard your heart**, for everything you do flows from it" (Prov. 4:23, emphasis added).

We must guard our heart, so it doesn't lead us astray. Keep watch of what situations and strongholds we could fall into. Sometimes we allow our heart to distract us, and it deceives us. You have heard the phrase, "The heart wants what the heart wants." Boy, is this the truth in many circumstances. It blinds us to the truth or reality of situations. It has no boundaries to keep from being taken advantage of. It rages with jealousy and deceitfulness. It twists our views and opinions to have more significant gains.

Keep a watchful eye on our heart. What you see with your eyes sends visual information to your brain. Be careful, for you can't "unsee" things. Your mind will recall these images at any given time. It could be a pleasant sensory reminder, a taunting temptation, or a horrible haunting. What you see your brain keeps locked away, and you may even continue to bring it back to contemplate on, to continue to process, to dream about, and make connections with it. It is the gateway to your heart, so be careful, selective, and intentional of what you allow your eyes to see. Don't allow your eyes to cause your heart to wander, for deceit is lying in wait to attack you.

Protect your heart. Don't allow yourself to get into a situation that isn't good for growth, that wouldn't be a place of kindness, that wouldn't cultivate good, and that wouldn't bring glory to God. You are not a child anymore; you have control of your heart, so be wise, be kind to yourself, and be loving toward others. Put a meter on your heart to gauge positive levels and negative levels. Stay in the positive and avoid things that would be negative for they allow doubt and fear in the mix; it brings you down, it is ruthless, and stomps on your heart.

Forgiveness

Harbored grudges suck the joy out of life. Revenge won't paint the blue back into the sky or restore the spring in your step. No. It will leave you bitter, bent, and angry. But to each one of us grace has been given as Christ apportioned it. (Ephesians 4:7)

Once I was asked how you let go of pain when you forgive. As in all things, it is a process, but ultimately, it is giving them to the Lord; take your hands off it and give it over to the Lord. What can you accomplish by hanging onto the pain, drudging up the past, voicing your hurt, or justifying your actions? Holding onto the hurt only causes bitterness and stops the flow of your blessings. We can't measure their hurtful actions on a scale that has our actions as the "best way" meter. It is God's way!

Who are we to decide if another person is right or wrong? The world's views are all about us and being true to ourselves. We all are selfish and think our way is the right way, and our thinking is more valuable than others. Our flesh gets in the way. Satan stirs the pot and uses those hurts to keep us from loving without borders and keeps us away from following the Lord. We need to put others' needs above our own as an act of love and align our lives with Christ.

> "Forgiveness is unlocking the door to set someone free and realizing you were the prisoner!'" —Max Lucado

Not forgiving a hurt done against you is giving the person who hurt you control to continue. They become the prison guard; they put up bars around you to prevent you from walking freely and drag you down. We even put up our walls to prevent it from happening again. Allowing your hurt feelings to keep you from a thriving relationship ruins your happiness. Avoidance and isolation from the situations drive a wedge deep in any relationship. Then darkness sets in, and you feel defeated and hopeless. You take on a negative outlook. Bitterness grows like a weed in your heart.

Don't allow it to keep you captive. Seeking revenge is not a sweet reward; it is an ego-boost that leaves you unfulfilled and even more bitter, with no relief. True forgiveness requires a heart change and the strength and power of our mighty God. Humbly forgive with a true heart and give them to the Lord (fully, physically, mentally, and ceremonially). He will take care of it and mend both hurts.

In all cases, when we react spiritually first, it places them and our hearts in the hands of the Father. We surrender to Him, and if we are out of line, He will let us know we are to make it right as best as we can. Our heavenly Father will give us the grace to walk through it and love them.

I have often even asked the Lord to give me His grace to love that person who has wronged me, and He does! When I rely on God to handle this situation and give it to Him, He moves in mysterious ways. He has revealed to me what the other person might be thinking or how their upbringing plays a part in how they relate to others. He has taken the veil off my eyes to see the error in my thinking and why I reacted the way I did. He even showed me why I am ultra-sensitive to what could have been an honest spoken-in-love comment and not an attack. He has opened my mind to give them a little room to process their reactions and see where they are coming from.

We all are hurting and, frankly, a mess, so our first reaction becomes an overreaction. We sometimes hurt back because we are hurt. We get blindsided and carry our emotions on our sleeves. Thinking of ourselves is our first reaction. While we might think we think of others above ourselves, it isn't true in our first instinct. We eventually get there most of the time, but those few times sting us.

We have to step back and assess the situation from every angle. Are they hurting? What is their motive or emotions at the time? Am I being sensitive? Am I not looking at the whole situation? What would the ramifications be? Am I being godly? WWJD (What Would Jesus Do)? Will my actions be a godly solution, or will I add salt to a wound or fuel the fire? Will I be an example of Christ, or will I taint His reputation? Is this about me, or is this an opportunity to love someone in Christ?

God's grace has no duration or expiration, and neither should ours.

When we have done all that we can and have given them grace, we have to move on in the knowledge that God will take it from here and through time, and if we stay unchanged, God will work it all out. We don't know how long it will take, but we must trust that He knows what He is doing, and if the relationship changes and may even grow distant, it is for a reason. He knows your path, and He knows theirs. He might be protecting you from something the other person is going through (tainted marriage, personal derailment, season of wrong choices). He loves you enough to move you out of a situation or not allow you to be involved in keeping you on the right track. He knows you! He knows you would try to carry their burdens, enable them, follow them, and that is not what He wants for you.

We give our whole hearts, and while that seems godly, there is a fine line (ego, ownership, idolatry). We also think our world is only what is in front of us, and if we only stay in one place, we end up with a tiny circle of relationships. Sometimes others are in our life for only a season. It could be a long one, or it could be a short one. Just as in all things that happen to us, it molds us as people and equips us to our calling, so are those relationships we have along the way. We keep a piece of every relationship in our heart, good or bad, horrible or sweet, and we will, one time or another, remember, and it will be part of who we are.

So, what kind of friends will we be? What kind of spouse will we be? What kind of parents will we be? What kind of employee will we be? What kind of servant will we be? What do we want others to remember about us? Our legacy is seen in our character and integrity.

We give what we get. When we get sarcasm, we give it back. We get attitude; we give it back. Hopefully, when we receive the grace, we will give it back!

Will your actions of unforgiveness be rewarding? Would your character be seen in a positive light in the bigger picture?

> "I, even I, am He who blots out your transgressions for My own sake, and I will not remember your sins" (Isa. 43:25 NIV).

Forgiving and Forgetting

We must follow God's example of forgiveness. We must learn to forgive AND forget. It is in the forgetting that the offense has no stronghold. Forgetting it gives freedom for love to take root and squeeze out unforgiveness. The forgetting allows love for one another to grow more deeply. God's love covers all things. May you give into His love and walk in freedom.

Not giving forgiveness is an entry on the tally sheet. It is still a record of wrong done against us. It is a reminder of the hurt. Unforgiveness over and over and over again turns into bitterness. It deceives us; it puts a wedge in our relationships and blocks us from being forgiven.

> "And as you stand praying, if you hold anything against anyone, forgive him, so that your Father in heaven may forgive you your sins" (Mark 11:25 NIV).

While it sounds easy, it is one of the hardest things to do. Handling the hurt right away is one way to help you forget quicker. Don't let it fester and build up to explode all at once. Don't push it to the side or under the carpet. Don't let your discomfort with confrontation keep you under a spell of anger. Deal with it head-on and right away.

I remember getting marital advice to not go to bed angry. We can still nicely voice our hurt or explain why we are bothered, and it helps to see where we are coming from emotionally, physically, or spiritually. We might have bad experiences and triggers going off. We all are in different places and mind frames. We might not have heard the other correctly. When we approach each other in love, the truth is brought to light. When we allow ourselves to be vulnerable, our true thoughts and fears surface, and we can tackle them together.

It is through repetition that we can change a habit or reaction. In repetition, it gathers new positive experiences that will overcome our old negative experiences.

We all have conflicts; the key is how we choose to allow them to affect us.

Another example is in my marriage. My husband and I hardly fight, but that is not to say we don't have fussy moments. For the most part, it is because of our first reactions. Do we snap, or do we process in love? Sometimes it is just letting the other voice their opinion, and then we discuss it from there. Giving value in being able to express ourselves is immeasurable. Sometimes we react from a place of fear from past hurts or failures, instead of learning to look at its face value.

When we choose to give grace first and work it out on all sides together, we grow deeper in love and confidence to trust each other with our hearts. The repetition of putting each other first and valuing each other has allowed positive experiences to build up confidence in each other, handling our hearts to the point that it isn't even a thought process anymore; it is freedom, free to be our true selves with wings of confidence. It is learning how we process things and use that to our advantage. My husband might think of a point I hadn't considered, or I might see it in a different light that would change the perception.

Faith

As we grow in faith, believing and trusting God with ALL things, the grace He gives us is replaced with a *fuller* grace. It doesn't stop there; it continues into eternity, grace upon grace upon grace, fuller and deeper, forever repeating. It reaches and consumes our innermost being. It removes any unholiness and replaces it with His love, truth, character, compassion, mercy, and wisdom, all for His glory. He pours all of Himself into our souls. He changes, mends, washes away, and buffs out the imperfections. He reveals and redeems, giving strength and confidence. He instills His character in us, and He seals our hearts to His. He equips us for our calling, empowers our minds, and anoints us to walk in His will. All of these actions come back to the depth of His love given through His grace.

> For it is by grace you have been saved, through faith—and this is not from yourselves, it is the gift of God—not by works so that no one can boast. For we are God's handiwork, created in Christ Jesus to do good works, which God prepared in advance for us to do.
>
> Ephesians 2:8–10 NIV

We can't achieve grace through our deeds, performing religious rules and traditions, or simply being good to others. Not to say these tasks aren't of value, but rather, grace results from your heart's motive in doing such good deeds.

Are you trying to perform the rules of religion to achieve holiness and respect? Are you striving to keep traditions perfectly to earn approval, and if so, from who? Are you trying to keep the status quo to carry on the family traditions, not to be the one to break them and be blamed? Performing good deeds out of obligation and duty to make yourself look good is dishonest. Are you striving for excellence in all categories to become worthy of God's affection? He wants your heart, not your service or sacrifice done with selfish gain or glory.

It is only by faith that grace is given to us as a gift from God. Through His son, a ransom was paid for all sin. We received a clean slate and walked into a new life free from our past to do good work that God had planned for us to do. We are His masterpiece; He is pleased with who He envisioned us to be.

Let your faith catapult you into His arms and give Him free rein in your life; you will never be the same and will live for eternity in heaven.

Through an ongoing relationship with Jesus Christ, grace upon grace is seen. Life is a constant battle against our flesh. When we learn to trust God entirely with every thought, every situation, and part of our lives, only then can we see and have an arsenal of experiences, graces upon graces, that build our faith.

> Now faith is confidence in the things we hope for and assurance in what we cannot see. Hebrews 11:1 NIV

Grace upon grace builds our faith and trust. It is hard for our brains to grasp this, and it seems too easy. Society teaches us that we must work hard, climb ladders, earn our way, be first, be the best at any cost, control, and create our destiny. This way of thinking only earns us exhaustion, bitterness, loneliness, and depression. Our ego is Satan's strategy to keep us in turmoil and away from God and eternal bliss.

Freedom

What bags are you carrying? I attended a Women of Faith conference, and the dramatist performed a skit on all the baggage we carry using purses. Which purse do you carry? Do you carry the purse of shame, the purse of failure, or the purse of mistakes? Do you carry the purse of jealousy, anger, pride, or fear? Do you carry the purse of abuse, addiction, or abandonment? We categorize each area of our life that is holding us hostage; we carry around these areas of our lives as a reminder, burden, or excuse that we are too messed up for God to want us. We give our purses (baggage) residency and validation in our lives. We provide them with power; they become our masks to hide behind our persona of wholeness. We allow them to become our identity, our lot in life; we are the victim, we deserve it, and this is just how life is. NOT TRUE!

It is time to purge your purses! Give them all to God. When we seek Him, we find Him; He is with us; call out to Him and give Him your heart and handbags. Allow Him access to all areas of your life. Trust Him with your secrets (He already knows them and still loves you!). He will forgive you, redeem the time lost, reveal His thoughts and affections, and begin restoration. He is **SO** ready for you to come to Him; He is eagerly waiting. He wants to wipe away your tears and blot out your hurts. He will remove them from your innermost being and show you who you were created to be.

He knew you before you were formed in your mother's womb (Ps. 139:13), and this baggage was not in the equation. He wants you to be free of all that pulls you away from Him. He wants you, mess and all. He is jumping up and down, anxiously waiting for you to choose Him. He is the WAY, He is the TRUTH, and the LIFE. He is your way to freedom and eternity. He will fight your enemies (Deut. 20:4), reward you (Heb. 11:6), has chosen you (Eph. 2:10, the depths of His love (Eph 3:18). See how head over heels in love with you He is! He has so much to show you and to grow you into what He envisioned for you. Don't allow your baggage to keep you from true freedom, distracted from what your life was meant to be, or from a love beyond what you can imagine.

True freedom is exhilarating! It gives empowerment and confidence, to know that you can freely be yourself and that you have a clean slate. His grace has validated your worth; it has turned the tables and broken the chains that held you. You have a renewed perspective and supernatural strength to keep walking. You can hold your head high now and profess high praises.

There is such freedom when we can now trust the Lord with any situation, concern, weakness, or loved one. His infinite grace and faithfulness build the bridge of complete trust, experience upon experience. We accumulate steppingstones of faith, trust, hope, and love through our walk with Him. Grace upon grace, we change, we grow, and we become a reflection of Him.

Knowing He is a God of grace and knows what is best for me gives me the freedom that I don't have to handle the situation, have all the answers, or be responsible for everyone. He gives us all free will and unlimited grace whenever we need it and when we choose to let Him be the God of our hearts.

I have only two things I can control: the words coming out of my mouth and my relationship with Christ. Everything else is out of our control, which is how it should be. God will take care of everyone else. And when there is a conflict, I remember He loves us all the same.

There might be more going on that I can't see, and we have our own free will. I choose to love even when it doesn't feel good. When I come close to God, He lets me see how he feels about that person and why He loves them. That melts my heart and allows me to give them grace. He is working, refining, or revealing a quality in them, and it is of most importance to stay in it and love them. It is very seldom about me; He works on all of us simultaneously. It is so precious, and it is freeing.

His grace is sufficient for you, for my power is made perfect in weakness... (2 Cor 12:9, so no more fear and no more shame. He covers every base and sets up things further down our path for the exact time we will walk in it. He is our champion, He fights our battles, and the victory is ours, so there is no need to worry and fret. We don't have to lose sleep and stress out; His grace is sufficient and perfect.

To know God is more significant than my problems is freeing. Circumstances will come; you can count on it, I have told you these things, so that in me you may have peace. In this world you will have trouble. But take heart! I have overcome the world (John 16:33 NIV).

Your best friend's sister is doing drugs, your marriage is a mess, you lost your job, or a friend betrays you. When you have your eyes on Jesus, you will see things differently. You will not be dragged down by all the drama or fall back into old habits. He is working things out on all sides, and you need to focus on Him and trust Him.

Sometimes we go through things because there is a lesson to be learned, and sometimes it is to build our faith. Sometimes it is to bring a situation to the surface to be dealt with. Sometimes it is just to feel you are being held while the storms rage around you. When we are deep in our messes, we can't see what He is doing and how He loves us.

He loves us enough to move us to another job that could bring us back on His path for our lives, restoke the embers of our heart's desire, or send protection in advance. He loves us enough to give us the grace to give to the friend who betrayed you, and now your relationship is even more vital. Put your marriage in His hands and stop hurting each other. Allow Him to give you both perspective, fine-tuned communication, and renewed love to weave you back together. Let His freeing grace have its way. We were made for so much more, and we will see it through His grace upon grace.

Chapter 6

GRACE STEPS IN

BY DEFINITION, GRACE is the free and unmerited favor of God, as manifested in the salvation of sinners and the bestowal of blessing; undeserving favor, do honor or credit to someone; a state of sanctification enjoyed through divine grace—a disposition to or an act or instance of kindness, courtesy, or compassion[1].

God's grace is so much more! His grace is forgiveness, a covering, and protection. His grace has resurrected, redeemed, and wholly transformed lives. His grace gives wisdom, freedom, and joy. His grace is humbling, illuminating, and set apart. It is full of power, truth, and fierce love. His grace is compassionate, provisional, and empowering. It bestows beauty, honor, and blessings. His grace is the action of His integrity and character. You can't earn His grace by your works; He gives it as a gift out of His love for you.

Because He is the creator of the universe, it stands to reason that we cannot fathom the depths of His power, creativity, thoughts, or unconditional love. He is more significant than any of our problems or failures.

To grasp the depth of the sacrifice bestowed upon us in one act of redeeming grace, how can we not let our appreciation be expressed in having an attitude of grace toward others? May we reflect the grace given to us as our anthem and catalyst to walk in His example.

> For the grace of God that brings salvation has appeared to ALL men. It teaches us to say no to ungodliness and worldly possessions and live self-controlled, upright, and godly lives in this present age. At the same time, we wait for the Blessed Hope—the glorious appearance of our great God and Savior, Jesus Christ, who gave himself for us to redeem us from all wickedness and purify for himself a people who are his very own, eager to do what is good (Titus 2:11–14 NIV).

This verse shows that God's grace teaches us how best to live. He uses each lesson, relationship, and failure. He sends others across our path to speak a word, send help in our time of need, or even send us someone to walk with us. Even if it is only for a season that He orchestrated others to grace our lives, it is intentional, inspirational, life-changing, and proof that He knows us intimately. His grace rushes in just at the precise moment we need it. Even if it is the tiniest gesture, it is pivotally huge in our life. He stirs the Holy Spirit inside us to prompt us when we might stray or need to pay attention. He speaks to us and teaches us through His Holy Spirit. He is ever aware of our needs and has our best interest at heart. He guides us to align with His will by teaching us His amazing grace.

In him, we have redemption through his
blood, the forgiveness of sins, by the riches
of God's grace (Eph. 1:7 NIV).

Grace stepped in. It is unfathomable to our minds
the whole concept and act of true grace bestowed on us
through Jesus Christ in laying down his life for us. I must
attempt to explain and hope I give the justice and reverence He so richly deserves.

I once had someone ask me why Jesus had to die for
me. My first thought was, "Well, you can't save yourself,"
then I was reminded of the blood significance. The Old
Testament spoke of the need to sacrifice animals as a sin
offering to be forgiven of our sins. It was a form of pay-
ment, action, or ransom that needed to be paid to satisfy
the debt of sin. A ransom was required after each sin. The
price was to be of great sacrifice to the sinner. It had to
be an animal that was the firstborn, flawless, and pure
specimen to honor God and represent the heart's pure
remorse for sin.

The Passover blood over the doors was a symbol of
God's grace bestowed on the Israelites when He brought
destruction to Egypt (Exod. 12). Grace stepped in, and the
doors marked with blood were to be "passed over" from
being destroyed.

Sacrificial blood was applied to the altar. In the ordi-
nation of Aaron and his sons for the priesthood, blood
was applied to the right ear lobe, the right thumb, and
the right toe (Lev. 8:24). While it can be viewed as ceremonial, it was without a doubt intentional. Aaron's sons
Nadab and Abihu haphazardly performed the ceremony

and didn't follow the ritual as instructed and without true honor in their hearts; they were killed immediately. That got my attention that the details were intentional and imperative.

A new blood covenant was coming! God sent His one and only Son to earth to live among us as an example, the teaching of the Father, and be the sacrificial Lamb of God, which would pay the ransom for all our sins. Our sins would be paid in full—no more need to continue with sacrificing and offerings. Jesus's sacrifice would be a seal of approval of authenticity and value because Jesus was the perfect, without a blemish, Lamb of God. His blood would pay the sin (death) price, wipe away the conscience guilt, and give us eternal life.

God loved us so much that He gave His only son that whosoever believes in Him will not perish but have everlasting life (John 3:16).

Well, that sounds ridiculous! What kind of dad was he to kill his son for all the world who were flawed, defective, ungrateful, and wicked? Jesus was a part of God; He was God in the flesh. He was a beacon, a portrait, and a portal to God. A pure sacrifice had to be made so that the world's sins could be completely forgiven for all time.

No more sacrificing is required, only that you give your heart to Jesus and follow His ways. Through Jesus, you will be made new, changed into His image. Jesus will intercede for you, and you can communicate to God directly. He wants to have a relationship with us. You will be given the indwelling of His Holy Spirit (helper, counselor, and guide). When you believed, you were marked in Him with a seal, the promised Holy Spirit (Eph 1:13).

God breathed the universe to life. He hung the stars in the sky, created man, and because of our sins, He sent His son, Jesus Christ, to pay our ransom by hanging on a cross. That is the biggest act of grace. He gave us the grace to overcome sin and walk with Him.

God is bigger than we can imagine. If we could figure Him out, then what kind of a God is he? Just like we saw with Moses, God's glory couldn't be contained (Exodus 33:18) nor could you see his face; His radiance would burn you up. Moses hid in a cleft of a rock with his back to the Lord, and when He passed by, a mere reflection of His radiance illuminated Moses's face beyond the forty days and forty nights he was in the Lord's presence.

In the life of Jesus, God split Himself into three persons: God the Father, God the Son, and God the Holy Spirit. He provided personal access to communicate with Him directly; He wants a relationship with us. We are wiped clean, made new in salvation, and given a seal of approval through the Son's sacrifice in paying for our sins. We may now have access to the presence of God the Father. Upon salvation, we are given the indwelling of the Holy Spirit as a helper and our guide to walking our life in godliness. This is the Trinity at work: God the Father, God the Son, and God the Holy Spirit. God will be with us all the time!

Cue music: the cocoon of stillness of the moment, and yet a rush of emotion is beginning to build, the moment you realize you are holding your breath. Your heart's whispered cry has been heard and...

Grace steps in.

Whether you are in the clutches of circumstance, hiding from view, or blatantly screaming, His grace is there for you to receive.

I know so many instances of God stepping down from heaven to intervene, speak, or quiet me. He uses everything and knows just what exact thing will speak to me to reveal His love for me.

Just this weekend, I had been feeling like I failed in finishing this book, I was quietly hiding and letting the voices tell me their lies to keep me away. I walked around aimlessly at a Brown's Orchard's and Farm Market" to fill the day and let all the crafts and lovely things comfort me.

A white-haired lady came down the aisle of the baked goods where I was choosing to linger, and she looked straight at me, held both of my arms softly, and began to pray and speak over me. She moved her arms to my forehead and, in a motion to draw a circle from my head to my heart, touched my heart lightly and said with authority, "Your amazing!"

I lost my breath; I had felt the Holy Spirit move in me and over me with a feeling of being lifted slightly and with a radiant warm glow surrounding me. I was moved and expressed back to her that she was amazing.

A woman who was her caregiver said, "Don't worry about her; she has dementia."

"Oh, well she just gave me a blessing," I replied.

"She probably did," replied the caregiving woman and called the little white-haired woman by her name, "Norma, bring your cart over here."

Grace stepped in, and God swooped down at that very moment and used Norma to deliver a message of His love and how He feels about me. He chose to give Norma clarity at that exact moment to be used to impact, and I am ever grateful! God knew I was struggling. He sent an angel to say, "Your Amazing", these two words of affirmation, two words to wipe away the lies, and only two words to reaffirm what He thinks of me and that I am the right one for my calling.

I tear up to think He stopped everything to send a message to one of his sheep. I am that important to him, and so are you! When you give him your heart, He takes every opportunity to love on you.

My girlfriend lost her dear mother-in-law, who was dear to me as well, last year and wait for it, wait, her name was... Norma! No, I haven't fallen off my rocker and thought she came back to life, but I do know that God uses everything and everybody dear to us or has a connection that would touch us.

That is how you know it is God. Only **He** knows all our thoughts, desires and dreams, secrets, pain, and every cell that He made us with. He knows our love language and our creative niches. He knows our Achilles heel and how to stir our hearts to sing. He uses His love and intimate knowledge of us to restore and decimate the lies that are scheming against us, to lift us, wipe us off, and restore us.

His Word says, "His mercies are new each day" (Lam. 3:22–23). His mercies never end, and you will never be cut off from His love.

I just thought of Dory from the Disney movie *Finding Nemo,* and she says, "Just keep swimming²." God is saying to us, "I still love you", - there is nothing we can do to stop or cut off His love for us. I am sure you might be saying, "Yeah, well, you don't know what I have done!" I know for a fact He does. 1) He can't go back on His promises, 2) He loves you to death and beyond, and 3) He doesn't see you as you and the world see you; He sees you as He created you—who you truly are deep down inside. He delights in who He made you before you were born because He had a plan with just you in mind.

God has a plan for each one of us and uses us for each other. He gives us each a unique quality, places us in the right place at the exact time and equips us with whatever is needed to fulfill His will and plan for our life. It is an honor and privilege to be chosen by God; we all are chosen and wonderfully made for His glory.

I was reading in Exodus 31:1-11 about the tabernacle, ark of the covenant, and how God specifically names Oholiab and Bezalel (I can't even pronounce their names) as the artistic directors. He gave them talents just for this specific job. He gave them creativity, workmanship skills, and knowledge of what would please Him. This is the first time you even read the mentioning of their names. They could have been beggars, the last of a long line of siblings overlooked in society or a gang of boozers at the watering hole, but God knew them and had a plan.

Grace stepped in. They were just in the background, and God was waiting to use them for the exact time the Israelites would turn from their other gods to choose to follow Him, the one true God. He was proud of His creation in Oholiab and Bezalel and for this exact moment to raise them for the utmost precedence of epic and holy proportions.

Esther was a beautiful orphaned Jewish girl who trusted God with her life and would change the heart of the king, and, in turn, it saved her people, a beautiful love story with a kingdom agenda. God raised her and placed her in the exact place she needed to be to derail evil plots to annihilate the Jewish community (Book of Esther).

It was her grace and poise that caught the eye and the heart of the king. It was her faith in God that her servants prayed and fasted for three days for favor and to be heard by the king. She was steadfast and willing to lay her life down in trusting God with the outcome of the situation. Grace stepped in and turned what was mean for evil to turn to good.

Rahab was the prostitute who hid Joshua's spies, who, in turn, spared the lives of her and her family (Joshua 2:1-24). Grace stepped in, and Rahab later became the mother of Boaz and was included in the lineage of Jesus Christ! Every life matters, even when you think you are too far gone or worthless. He has a plan for our lives no matter how much we mess our life up. His will be done.

When grace steps in to help Israel defeated the Amalekites:

> Moses commanded Joshua, "Choose some men to go out and fight the army of Amalek for us. Tomorrow, I will stand at the top of the hill, holding the staff of God in my hand." So, Joshua did what Moses had commanded and fought the army of Amalek. Meanwhile, Moses, Aaron, and Hur climbed to the top of a nearby hill. As long as Moses held up

the staff in his hand, the Israelites had the advantage. But whenever he dropped his hand, the Amalekites gained the advantage. Moses' arms soon became so tired he could no longer hold them up. So, Aaron and Hur found a stone for him to sit on. Then they stood on each side of Moses, holding up his hands. So his hands held steady until sunset. As a result, Joshua overwhelmed the army of Amalek in battle (Exod. 17:9–13).

That is such a visual example of God's power and how He uses us to accomplish His will. Grace steps in. Just as Aaron and Hur helped hold Moses's arms for victory, we might be called to hold each other up when we are in despair. May we be a shoulder to those in need and lift each other always.

Mary was a virgin engaged to Joseph, and God chose her to bring forth the awaited Messiah. She walked through a scandal to birth the Savior of the world, our holy champion and king, Jesus Christ. (Luke 1:26-38)

And what about Norma, the lady in the market? She was still used despite her dementia. Her caregiver wasn't surprised she blessed me; maybe she was a pastor's wife or came from a long line of godly women. I could see that even dementia wouldn't rob her or change her from who she was deep down, who God created her to be. She knew the voice of her God and was fearlessly obedient out of the reflection of His love. Oh, Father, I pray that I will be a Norma.

Sheltering Trees

An extension or manifestation of God's grace felt is through friends. God uses all things and circumstances to mold, grow, equip, and impact our lives. I truly believe that friends are one of the most precious avenues He uses; He allows his angels to entertain and commune with us.

The song "Sheltering Trees" by New Song[3] is delightfully accurate in naming friends sheltering trees, those friends who will get down on their knees for you.

Chorus:

> *We all need sheltering trees,*
> *Friends in our lives who will get down on their knees*
> *And lift us before the King of kings.*
> *We all need sheltering trees.*

May God reveal those who will be sheltering trees in your life. They are a physical expression of His love. He made us for the community, not to be alone. He sends us to help along the way of our life journey. It isn't an accident that others cross your paths; it is a divine arrangement. He is infinitely aware of our thoughts, doubts, concerns, weaknesses, fears, aspirations, and dreams. He continually pursues our hearts and sends blessings, favors, warnings, unseen protections, provisions, grace, and mercies. He uses everything and everyone around us. He gets you and He stirs you. He pairs us to help each other. We might be going through the same thing or be on the other side and can encourage another with our story.

Even in our pain, He can use us for others while He lifts us. Uniquely, our sheltering trees are spiritually compatible with an instant supernatural purpose and connection, sent from the heart of our tender and mighty God.

He speaks through others as He carries us through the storms. He sends helpers to walk shoulder to shoulder with us. He strikes the core of our hearts, meets us in the middle, and lifts our chin to His face. His mercies are new each day, and His love is forever. Look for Him, pursue Him, allow Him access, and be open. He will be there in your heart, mind, and spirit.

"For when two or three are gathered in My name, I am there among them."

Matthew 18:20 NIV

God brought sheltering trees alongside us on our new journey to Chicago. God guided us to our new church, Christian Life Church, and surrounded us with an amazing community of friends to live life together with; what a precious time! One day the Lord prompted our dear lifelong friends Andy and Karen Ill to come alongside us to minister to us as a helping hand pulling us up out of our pit of despair with finances. We hid in shame (which still chokes me up), and God sent us sheltering trees of grace.

There is strength in numbers. Satan is a tricky, deceitful adversary and wants nothing but to get you isolated. You will need those who are strong in their walk with Christ around you, those who will pray till the rooster crows, stand and hold your arms up, encourage you when you are down, and shout praises to the heavens when God's triumph is witnessed.

May you be a sheltering tree to those who cross your path. May you always be mindful that God will never leave you or forsake you!

> For I know the plans I have for you, declares the Lord, plans to prosper you and not to harm you, plans to give you hope and a future. Jeremiah 29:11 NIV

He Is with Us

When we face a tough situation, we know we need to give it to God, but it is so hard, and yet we know He sees all sides of the situation and works them out for us all. We have to trust Him and lean into Him, and soon we will be on the other side soaring with a full heart, clothed in His grace, validated special, and set apart, that **He** heard our hearts cry, and we are precious to Him.

While "give it to God" sounds easy, it is a struggle for control. We think we can fix it, carry the burden, and only rely on ourselves. Waiting on God takes too long; I want it taken care of now. I am a "getter done" person, and why put off what you can do now? It will save me pain and time. Just pull the band-aid off and move on.

Despite our best intentions and efforts, we can't see down the road, make others do what we think is best, and aren't considering the ramifications of doing things our way might be. Being rash or making a spontaneous decision is putting the horse before the wagon, counting the eggs before they are hatched, or putting your hope in the wrong basket.

Wisdom, timing, and heavenly perspective is the key, none of which we possess. We might have wisdom in the sense of living longer, seniority and all. We might have been around the bend a few times and learned many lessons, all the wrong way, and therefore have gained the title due to endurance. We might have obtained many degrees and have held high positions, but only God is omnipresent, all-knowing.

Timing is everything, and doing something right now without contemplation, knowledge, or prayer would be disastrous. God's timing is perfect. It never lines up with ours, for we have selfish reasoning and instant gratification as our guide. His timing lines up with His will, plan, preference, and delight. Putting a limit or time frame shortens the blessing and possibility to allow an epic turn of events to occur.

Having it our way, we cheat our experience, cheat others to learn or change, cheat ourselves of a blessing, and possibly miss an opportunity or pivotal moment in my life with my hurriedness.

Fruits need to ripen to a certain stage before picking. Crops must reach perfect growth before they are harvested. We need to trust the Maker; only He knows when the time is right.

He is the heavenly perspective that brings the answer, brings the long-awaited healing, and sends you strength in His joy, which will bring all things together for the good of all. It is His power that put the world into existence and His thoughts woven in all the intricacies and unique qualities we each have. Some answers might not be what we prayed for, or it might not look like we thought it would. I am extremely thankful I serve a big, creative, humorous, and gracious God! I have seen recently that He builds us up in layers. I think we limit what God has in mind. We need baby steps that lead to a big step to lead to a big change.

The same is true at the level of our trusting God. We need many good experiences to outweigh the bad ones so we can form a new database per se that when I trust God, I know He is faithful, and I know now that He does what is good for me in every situation no matter how I see things. I find great comfort in the verse:

> "The LORD himself **goes before** you and will be with you; he will never leave you nor forsake you. Do not be afraid; do not be discouraged" (Deut. 31:8).

He goes before me; he knows the road ahead, how I will react, and what will detour my heart to follow Him.

My Grace Is Sufficient

> My grace is sufficient for you, for my power is made perfect in weakness. Therefore, I will boast even more gladly about my weaknesses, so that Christ's power may rest on me" (2 Cor. 12:9 NIV).

The definition of sufficient is enough, as much or as many as required.[4]

God's grace is sufficient; His grace is complete. There is no need to add to it or tweak it. Bask in what measure He gives, for it is all you need. He gave it freely; it was at no cost to you. He bestowed it to you at the precise time. If He said He will do it, He will! No need for a backup plan. No need to publicize it to get more attention or steal a morsel of glory. There is nothing you can do to enrich the experience, for when He moves, it is of supernatural power; only He receives the glory.

I know I walk in faith and trust God completely; however, there are times when I walk more intentionally in faith—my crazy faith moments. I know God has me in the palm of His hand and is always mindful of me. There are some moments when you have more boldness and spiritual strength to dream bigger and want to take a huge step or leap for that matter.

We took a trip to visit my son and his wife to meet her parents in California. It was a lovely visit! God showed himself in every detail—I love when He does that! He leaves nuggets and surprises around every corner. He throws in animals and then stirs my heart in only a way He can do. He is so precious to me!

We stayed in an Airbnb, which was a remodeled airstream RV. It was so adorable and comfy with all the honeybee decorating details to make you feel loved. There was a tiny bookshelf beside the couch that caught my attention. A little yellow book jumped off the shelf to me, and it was by an author and speaker I had seen many times at the Women of Faith conferences many years ago. She was a spunky, charismatic, and contagious, classy lady named Thelma Wells. Her signature was a bee lapel pin. I squealed and started to cry... it could have only been God to move on the lady of the house who decorated the Airbnb to choose this book (maybe she was touched by Thelma as well), and it was no coincidence that we found this available Airbnb to stay in for our visit 2764 miles away in a town we have never been in on this particular weekend in December.

He arranged this time to touch and stir me. His grace was more than sufficient; it was a multifaceted and wonderous adventure! He repositioned my feet on the path. He rekindled fond memories and milestones I had tucked away in my heart. He re-stoked my heart's desire that I had humbly suppressed.

I was more open to whatever God had for me. I was getting the feeling that movement was going to happen or that I was beginning to be released from the job I was working unto the Lord at our local grocery store. My thoughts of growing into management, which was my experience, were not in God's long-term plan for me this time. God was simultaneously working on my husband's heart and used him in catapulting me backward to resurrect my heart's desire to be a flight attendant. This was a big step for him and a selfless one at that. I usually coax him along in faith walking, but now our lives are one faith journey to the next faith journey, and we are joyously following.

"There it is, done," my husband said.

"What is done?" I replied.

"Your application for a flight attendant," he calmly stated.

"My what? "I said, now on the floor crying.

Life started moving faster than expected. There was a recruiting event for SkyWest in Chicago, home to two of our children, six grandkids, an amazing aunt and her wonderful children, and many dear friends. Could this be happening? Every time I thought of it, I would get giddy and emotional. I knew I had to get it together and keep control of my emotions when I went to get my passport; I had to rewrite the paperwork three times! The officer handling me must have thought I was a hot mess; I was a giddy hot mess.

I was so humbled and excited it was hard for me to wrap my head around the idea that I was worthy and qualified for this job, but I still just wanted to lose a little weight, I thought I would feel better about myself, more confident, and fit the image more. I found a diet that was just a mixture additive to your drink, thinking it was not a big deal; it wasn't a starvation diet, and I would be drinking more water so that would be good, right? As I told myself, knowing deep down I felt I had to do more to make myself more attractive. I am so glad it was only eighteen dollars instead of the expensive plans or the contract ones you get caught in.

I didn't realize how much caffeine it had in it, and with my heart murmur and prior heart surgery, that would not be a good idea. Thank the Lord He protected my heart, but I got so sick for twenty-four hours; I had all kinds of symptoms. I had felt the Holy Spirit tell me before I drank it that this wasn't going to be a good idea and to stay trusting God and lean not on my understanding, but I chose to ignore it.

I learned a valuable lesson: God's grace is sufficient! Nothing else is needed or should be added to His grace. Nothing can better the feeling of God's approval and favor on us.

What was I thinking? It is amazing the grace He is giving me to fulfill my heart's desire, and I was trying to lose more weight when He already made a way. I felt the Holy Spirit whisper I shouldn't do it; I didn't think that my action was like saying that what God was doing for me wasn't good enough. I quickly came to my senses when I got so sick. I know now I am just walking in who God created me to be, and God will do the rest.

God's grace steps in at just the right moment. It is just the right amount needed. It is sufficient, the exact proportion that is needed to cover my weakness, failures, mistakes, messes, and shortcomings and then to lift me and dust me off so I can keep walking.

Remember when you were about to graduate high school and the pressures of knowing what you wanted to do with your life? I have always wanted to be a flight attendant but thought that it was not an option for me. I wasn't as strong spiritually then, and a cosmetologist can love on others, making them feel good about themselves, so that was the route I took. I came very close when I worked for a commuter airline, which was my favorite job, but I needed to lay it aside and raise our family. Thirty-four years later, God never forgot my dream, for I am sure He placed it there in the first place, and I had forgotten or counted myself out.

"Take delight in the Lord and He will give you the desires of your heart" (Ps. 37:4 NIV).

Tuck this one in your heart:

"The Lord makes firm the steps of the one who delights in Him, though he may stumble, he will not fall, for the Lord upholds him with His hand" (Ps. 37:23–24 NIV).

The time finally came for the recruiting event; my hair was rocking and my makeup looked good. I was wearing a skirt, blouse, and jacket, hopefully looking the part. It was one thing after another trying to break my confidence. I had a debacle at the gas station in deep snow and blowing rain. I arrived early to register, and while socializing and waiting for the event to start, I noticed I had mud on my shoes and pantyhose! I tried two times that evening to get it off. My shirt wouldn't stay tucked in.

There were many different walks of life, ages, and body types represented, which was comforting. I had to get up in front of the room and state why I would be a good flight attendant. I honestly don't remember much of what I said, for I had one minute to speak. I know I said I love people, which I do, and I know I said something about traveling around, but when I heard myself say something about Maryland crabs, I started to lose it. My brain was like, "The plane is on fire; it is going down." I panicked and ended it with details of having run restaurants. Ugh! I had to sit and listen to forty-six other speeches, and with each one, I was shrinking smaller and smaller.

When everyone was finished, we were to sit in the lobby for forty minutes and then come back, and if our name was on the list, we would advance to the interview. Well, I am sure my name wasn't going to be on the list; Maryland crab lady was leaving the building.

I sat down and started to eat my peanut granola bar, and of course, it broke off and landed peanut butter side down on my skirt! Holy cow! What else could happen? I let it roll off and decided to keep going for fear I would break down and cry. My prayers now were, "Okay, God, just give me the strength to handle the *no*. Help me keep it together until I get to the car, and then help me drive back home in my daughter's car without wrecking it, for my tears will be many. Thank you for this opportunity, Lord, Amen."

We reconvened to the outer room area anxiously awaiting our fate. I encouraged those around me and tried to keep positive. I was not going to go up and look at the list but would be their cheerleader while we waited. I approached one lady who had been a hospice nurse for twenty years! I thanked her for her service and told her that she was an angel for loving others. I hugged her and wished her good luck; I said a prayer for her on my way back to my huddle group.

The list was hung, and some of those around me came back with their names not on the list. I encouraged them to try again, and they said we could come back and try in ninety days. I was shocked one lady wasn't listed. She was so confident and charming.

There were only a few of us left, so I gathered up some courage and went to look for my name on the list. I refocused my eyes. I was on the list! I told myself, "Don't cry, don't cry... thank you, Lord!" Within minutes, I had my interview, and it went so well. The lady who interviewed me was lovely, and she was a small-town girl like me. What a rollercoaster ride with God that night! It wasn't about me; He did all the work. I just had to step out.

More time than expected had passed by since the interview, so I put in other applications for other airlines, knowing God had made a way; I just might have to search for the right door. I had foot surgery on my left foot, which required a long recovery period, and my right foot needed the same surgery. I had put it off for a very long time, but with a recent visit to the doctor, surgery was mentioned, and it was up to me.

I toiled and prayed all night. I woke up with a new perspective and focus. Maybe God wasn't saying no but maybe not right now. I was going to trust Him and started wrapping my head around possible surgery and how we would survive without my income.

I was on my lunch break when I got a call from a Utah-based phone number. I ignored it, but they left a message; it was from SkyWest! This was the airline I wanted to work for and had interviewed with when I went to visit my grandchildren in Chicago. It had been way past the time they said they would notify me, so I thought I didn't make it. It is when I was humbled that God's grace stepped in, and I landed the job! He stood in the gap when I didn't think I was worthy to have this position. He made a way! When I wasn't matched against all the other candidates, He moved on my behalf. Maryland crab lady was chosen because God shined for me! God's grace was sufficient! All I needed!

I was in a Bible Study of Hebrews and what a timely verse to savor:

> "So do not throw away this confident trust in the Lord. Remember the great reward it brings you! Patient endurance is what you need now so that you will continue to do God's will. Then you will receive ALL that He has promised."

> Hebrews 10:35–36

The words "this confident" struck me to my core; it means:

- How He saved you
- How He has always been faithful (remember all those times in your life)
- His reputation and integrity
- His promises are never broken
- He will never forsake you
- The peace He gives us that passes our understanding
- His Word is true and complete
- His gifts and call on our life are irrevocable (can never be withdrawn)

> For the gifts and the calling of God are irrevocable [for He does not withdraw what He has given, nor does He change His mind about those to whom He gives

His grace or to whom He sends His call].
Romans 11:29 AMP

Chapter 7

TRANSFORMING GRACE

Do not conform to the pattern of this world, but be
transformed by the renewing of your mind. Then you
will be able to test and approve what God's will is-His
good, pleasing and perfect will.
Romans 12:2 NIV

RENEWING YOUR MIND is allowing your heart and mind
to come in agreement with trusting and following our Lord
Jesus Christ. A transformation will be ignited, a new perspective and an insightful view through His eyes. You will
begin to take on His characteristics, to see His heart for
others as our hearts become one. He will wipe our sins
away and redeem what was lost.

The moment of transformation begins with the surrender of your heart and life to Jesus. While giving up
control is unfathomably hard, the first step is always the
hardest. But once you step out, the rest is a journey you
wouldn't want to miss.

In the Waiting

It is in the waiting that we humble ourselves to the knowledge that God can do anything and fix anything. We remember all the times we received grace. We truly let go of the issue when all we can do is wait. Sometimes we fret over it for days until we finally run out of backup plans and justification. We must pray about it and then let it go.

It is in the waiting that we realize our need for God's intervention. We undergo a perception adjustment. We find hope and see His love while He unfolds the tangled knots we are in or have made. We see He cares about each of us in the same way—that unconditional love. He considers each of our uniqueness that He has intricately created in us. He knows our hearts and how to take care of us. We might like to tell Him how best we would like it, but He knows the outcome and redirects us.

It is in the waiting that we learn more of His character and the depths of His love. He loves us, is patient with us, is kind, gives joy, gives us His peace, is gentle, is faithful, and has self-control. Thank goodness! I would have given up on myself a long time ago.

The songwriter wrote[1]:

> *He giveth more grace when the burdens grow greater,*
> *He giveth more strength when the labor increased.*
> *To added affliction, He added His mercy.*
> *To multiplied trials, His multiplied peace.*

It is in the waiting that He lavishes over me. He sends blessings, takes care of other concerns I have, and stirs my heart. He just doesn't take care of the situation; He takes care of me. I think of the Casting Crowns' "I Will Praise You in the Storm." A line in the chorus says: "Sometimes He calms the storm in me²." There are times He just calms me while the winds blow around me. He holds me in the palm of His hand.

I remember one time hateful words hurt my feelings, and it went down from there for the whole week. I prayed and asked Him to give me His grace so I could give to this person because I couldn't muster up any myself. He did, as well as reaffirmed my torment over having a lack of knowledge was just not true. He sent two boys to pull the weeds that were on my mind, and He arranged my radio music to minister to me! He knew what I needed and how the devil was trying to attack me, so He reminded me **whose** I am, how He feels about me, and that He had never left me. My lack of technology was not going to keep me from getting into Heaven, and He has my life marked with a plan.

I am sure those in cars around me probably thought I lost it as I praised my God while driving down the highway with the music cranked, wiping tears, and lifting my hands toward Him. He is just precious to me! I get choked up and even lose my breath just thinking of Him. He truly knows me and would move mountains to delight my heart.

A precious friend and woman of God, Jenn Smith, told me one time that it is like we all are on a timeline. We never know where each other might be on their timeline, just as we never know how we impact others. We might cross paths with them at the beginning of their timeline when they are just becoming spiritually curious. It might be in the middle where it is all messy and we are so distracted. It could be at the end of their searching, and they give in to His wooing of their hearts.

It is in the perfect timing that His transforming grace is revealed; all the occurrences of His gentle nudges, His whispers to our souls, His presence in the darkness, and His strength of peace in times we don't understand, those times He sends His angels into action or when His supernatural protection is felt. When He provides a need we haven't even spoken or thought about yet or when His Spirit is like a breeze blowing over us, He never stops wooing our hearts.

As I look back over my life, I see and remember those precious times He broke through and gave me a glimpse of Himself. It was in the waiting when I felt alone, and He came alongside me. I remember a time I flew on an angel's wings to work safely, as I was having an emotional breakdown while driving. I remember praying in desperation that He would send me an honorable man who loved me for me and not what I could give him. It was in the waiting that He fulfilled it two months later, and we are still married today. I remember all the precious ladies He brought into my life at just the right time. Funny, we needed each other at the same time. He orchestrates our paths to cross and then knits our hearts together.

I have learned through all the moving around we have done that He uses me for others and others for me. He is intentional and knows us intimately. He knows us better than we know ourselves. He delights in giving us the desires of our hearts; He never forgets our desires even when we do.

I tear up when I think of this. I had pushed some of my desires and things that made me happy aside, not intentionally; it just happened because life happened. However, He never forgot.

My husband traded the Army for the railroad, and we traveled with three children in tow. It was in that isolated time I spent with God until our next move that that my relationship with Him began to grow. He sent me messages through Chuck Swindoll's ministry on the radio, and He gave me creative ideas to spread out what very little money we had to live on. He sent me joy in the hard moments when we needed a battery and drove to the auto store on a flat tire in the snow.

In the house we were staying in, we didn't have a TV, and we certainly didn't have enough money for Christmas presents. A friend put our name on the list for those who need help. They called me to come get our gifts, and I stood there and bawled when they filled my trunk and back seat with presents. On Christmas morning, the kids opened the presents, and they were things they wanted, the colors they liked, and fun toys.

That also was the time I had to get food stamps. I dressed my daughter up in a frilly dress to cover up my shame. When I arrived I found I had to talk through this tiny hole in a huge glass wall that announced to the whole room of my need for food stamps, I was mortified. It still seems so crystal clear of all the details and moments of grace, even the songs on the radio then and the time sitting in the car waiting to pick up my boys from school events. As I began to give Him more time and include Him in my daily happenings, He lavished over us.

We had many adventures, and they are so very sweet to us. We were heading to Chicago, and this time I consulted God in every decision, and He chose our church for us, Christian Life Church in Mt. Prospect, Illinois. I started just as they were organizing a musical, yes, I said a musical! I forgot that I loved to sing and act. I was praying for Him to send me some ladies in my life; I was lonely. In one swoop, He answered my prayers and fulfilled a desire I had forgotten. This church was our cornerstone home for many years. My son even met his wife there and proposed in a musical we were putting on, just precious!

It was in the waiting that I felt Him move ever sweetly. He was right there by my side, and He lifted me when I was low and gave me joy and lavished grace over us. Oh, how precious all the "in the waiting" moments and memories are to me. I use the waiting moments as a sign or gauge that pending grace is on its way, for He is taking the time to spread it out for the perfect timing and fill it with many tiny blessings for a big outcome.

Fear

"For God did not give us a **spirit of** timidity *or* cowardice *or* **fear**, but [He has given us a **spirit**] **of** power and love and **of** sound judgment *and* personal discipline [abilities that result in a calm, well-balanced mind, and self-control]" (2 Tim. 1:7, emphasis added).

Fear is confusion in a capsule. It might be small at first and candy-coated, but it expands when digested. It wreaks havoc at every turn. It taints our views, and like a disease, it takes over our thoughts and ignites our irrational thoughts, resulting in unacceptable actions. We fear the judgment of others, we fear being left out, we fear our insecurities, we fear our failures will define us, we fear we won't be seen or heard, we fear being alone, we fear someone else's power is inferior to ours, we fear all that is bad will happen to us, and we fear, fear itself.

Fear is a state of turmoil, a stronghold, and sometimes it has been around so long we call it family. We become numb to its chaos and adapt without missing a beat. We contemplate and react in a fear mode. We allow it to weigh in on our decision-making and give control over it willingly. It is a taskmaster, and we fall in line obediently.

Fear has the power to make irrational thoughts look rational. It feels and looks mistakenly true. Your worst fears have occasionally happened, so you start believing it will happen again, so if you just accept it, it won't hurt as bad. NOT! It will trap you in bigger and deeper fear, and before you know it, you are paranoid and on the edge of insanity. Fear is not from God, so don't even give it a moment of your time. Speak out against it, challenge it, and stand firm on who you are in Christ Jesus. It doesn't have power over you; you are under God's authority!

Fear can be like an addiction. It starts as a hiding place, for we fear we are weak, exposed, vulnerable, and a failure, so much so that it becomes a misunderstood comfy chair. We receive a false sense of approval when we share with others. They validate us with their attention to try to help us, and it becomes an initiation into the worry group.

Everyone has fears, we tell ourselves. It seems harmless at first, and then it becomes an instant reaction, even an obligation to stay in the circle of fear. It is the popular status quo of most of our society today; vested interests in maintaining turmoil are a fire burning out of control. The presence of staying in fear becomes familiar, popular, and yet daunting, an evil taskmaster.

Blessings amid fear, we allow being misconstrued as a reward for fearing, so we continue to be afraid over and over again. It is now an expectation that we worry about all things. It becomes a weird adrenaline rush; we need more turmoil and chaos to fuel our feelings. Details, gossip, tabloids, lies, and self-doubt are needed nourishment. We can't get enough of the fear rush. We are hooked line and sinker into the mystical world of fear. We can't see any other way.

If fear is not of God, then who is its originator? Good versus evil, I can tell you, and God's Word tells you it is not of Him. Fear draws you further away from the heavenly Father.

God is not an evil king! He doesn't punish or leave you out to dry in a situation. He might allow a variance of a situation to happen but only to bring you closer to Him, to show you He is your champion, The solution: the Way, the Truth. He is your savior and your Grace giver. He has the best in mind for you! He is standing on the sideline anxiously awaiting to help you and lift you; won't you let Him? Choose good; choose God.

I remember watching a movie called *The Village*. It was weird and scary (which I usually don't watch), and in the end, the town-elected officials chose to use human instinctual fear to keep the town people in an isolated area and under their control. They were acting out of fear from past bad experiences and wanted to protect others from being hurt, so they played on their fear to keep them away from the possibility of getting hurt. They completely thought they were being kind and protecting them and taking care of them all by keeping them isolated.

Do you choose to be manipulated by others and by your fear? Do you let the past dictate your future? Do you think staying in fear will keep you safe? Is the faith step to trust God too risky?

Yes, we need to be aware of issues but not completely consumed that every waking moment we are in turmoil. Yes, we need to do research and from many sources; however, we need to put our concerns to prayer and seek God's answers. We need to trust God and not have our agenda to prove or try to make pieces fit where they don't. We tend to think we can figure God out and how things are going to work. We rely on information that may be false, past experiences, future prophecies we have heard for many years, and even science. Nobody knows what is going to happen.

Spoiler Alert: GOD WINS!

We need to remember to walk by faith and not by sight (2 Cor. 5:7), not by the popular choice, not by which way is prosperous, and not by whatever feels good. We walk by faith in our triumphant Savior Jesus Christ! We need to stay in the Word of God, trust Him at His Word, for He is faithful. Nothing is impossible for God (Luke 1:37 CSB). Stop worrying; He has got this! It might not look like you think it should. This time might not be comfortable or secure, but He will take care of you if you let Him.

Worthy

God doesn't analyze us, judge us, or pick us apart before granting us grace. He doesn't pull a reference check or see if our name was on the "naughty" or "nice" list. He doesn't keep a tally of how many days we came to church or if we gave money on the offering plate. He doesn't use a measuring tape to see how spiritual we are.

I couldn't wrap my head around that grace didn't depend on my worthiness. It was freely given to me by my Savior. I didn't have to prove myself or earn it. He gave it to me as a gift. No strings attached. I didn't have to be deserving of it for a good reason. He gave it despite my failures, behavior, and pride.

It doesn't matter what color we are, what shape we are, what financial class we are in, which church we go to, which car we drive, or what house we live in. It doesn't matter if we are an ax murderer, are into pornography, are a thief or money launderer, or are struggling with an addiction. He doesn't like sin, but He loves His creation.

His grace doesn't affect whether I have my act together. He loves and accepts me because of my mess. He is the mess cleaner-upper. When we think we have it all together and all our ducks in a row, pride sets in, and we think we don't need God.

I think we also alienate ourselves when we are so obsessive-compulsive in our efforts to be perfect; we push all those in our lives out because we can do it better. They don't do it right, and "I am better than you." Who wants to be around that person we will never measure up or be fully accepted and trusted?

Shame walks hand in hand with unworthiness. We might feel our shame is valid when, in reality, God sees us with the identity He created us with. His view of us is not tainted or changed because of our sins or shortcomings, the shame we feel, or the mistakes we have made.

For instance, Gideon was a mere weakling and common farmer tending to his wheat crop when an Angel of the Lord appeared and called to him. "…The Lord is with you, Mighty Warrior" (Judges 6:12). Now that had to have taken Gideon by surprise to be called a Mighty warrior. You see, God created Gideon for just this task. Gideon was to be the mighty warrior who, with 300 men, trumpets, and glass jars, would defeat the Midianites, who impoverished the Israelites by ravaging their land.

We were made with a specific identity unique to our purpose in His perfect will. He is pleased with how He made us. No one can take that away from us. God accepts us all no matter what kind of mess we are. We are all worthy of His affection and attention. There is nothing we have done that could stop the Lord from loving us, nothing! Sorry, you qualify for just being you, His perfect creation.

Perspectives

God has an uncanny way and timing to bring perspectives into play. Our human reactions to situations are always selfish. We think of ourselves first and always let past offenses come to the surface; things we thought we were over, and past forgiveness is given. It is the forgetting part that is hard. We must grab hold of those first reactions and throw them in the trash can! Allowing the past to creep back in is pointless, hurtful, and a timewaster. We fall back into prison and give evil a way into our hearts. Don't even go there! Lean into a godly perspective.

God's grace gives you the strength and love to forgive. It releases you and the offender. He gives us multiple second chances, and if you seek a godly perspective, He will enlighten, create a sweeter space than before, and soften your heart's pain as a new perspective arises.

Perspectives are a voice for the other side of a situation or person, where they are coming from or where the situation could be heading. It is in the details that I think God shines even brighter than I could have imagined. He knows all sides and, through His revealing grace, brings love and light to the situation. He knows both sides of struggles and knits a sweet connection in the end. He sees each side's motivation and weaves a scenic route through common ground. He has blessings in store for both sides and uses each other to facilitate them. He grows each side with love and encouragement by allowing His light to shine where darkness tries to invade. He knows each of us intimately and allows both sides to be valued.

Develop a slow reaction, taking into consideration that in due time all will be brought into perspective. Let it unfold, for a blessing is in the center of it. Big blessings sometimes come in small packages. Pause to consider the feelings of others, as well as what Christ has to say about it. Consider if the reaction is out of love, selfishness, hurt, or ego. Ponder if the motivation or outcome is eternal thinking or earthly thinking: "Will my reactions bring God glory or myself glory?"

Put on the glasses with a godly perspective. He knows all and sees all, for God is in control. He isn't in heaven wringing his hands with the worry of what to do now, when will that girl or boy learn, or what went wrong. This is a battle of a spiritual kind, a battle of your heart's allegiance. Keep your eyes on Him, for He has a plan and will make a way. Things never look like you think they will. Put on your God-perspective glasses and see what He has for you.

Perspectives give intentions a positive representation. Perspectives shed light and give your opinions a silent voice. Perspectives are unknown persuasions to view things differently. We need to know all sides before making a judgment or decision that could be irrevocable and damaging, words you can't take back or actions that are uncalled for. I am ever grateful for grace's perspectives on all things. It keeps my focus on what God thinks and how I can act in a way to give Him praise, glory, and honor. If it doesn't look like I thought it would, I still trust God because He sees what I can't and knows what I don't, and most of all, He has my best interests at heart. If He says so, it will return as a blessing back to me when His full light reveals. I will be so grateful I trusted Him.

May you "Be still and know" (Ps. 46:10) that God has His reasons and His perspectives. He will work all things out. He is the lover of my heart.

Drops of Grace

I now see where God rains down "drops of grace" when I need it. It might be along the road, when I step out in faith, when I am weary, or just because. I envision these drops as jellybeans, assorted candies, or my favorite chocolate. They are colorful and have all kinds of flavors and textures for all kinds of needs. His grace comes in all sizes, shapes, and for all occasions.

The tangy ones are bursts of joy. The sweet ones are a dose of heart pleasuring. The chocolate ones melt your heart with comfort, compassion, and gentleness. The hot and spicy ones burn with passion. The sour or tart ones are like a bitter pill and pack a punch when we need to pay attention. The whacky and fruity ones are God's sense of humor. The hidden treasure ones are nostalgic, unexpected blessings, and yet they are attitude changes. The chewy ones are for pondering and savoring. The ones you try to avoid in the box are undiscovered experiences with a chocolate grace covering for us to receive and heed.

It might seem silly to you, but it speaks to me. It is so awesome how intimately God knows us and all the ways that He draws, stirs our hearts, or touches us to hear Him.

He sends "drops" of encouragement through my husband when I feel I am not smart enough for a task or feel out of my league. My husband reminds me, "God doesn't call the qualified; He qualifies the called."

When I am plugging along, not wanting to complain or so involved in a project that I lose myself, He brings forth a "drop" of creativity in a task to distract and inspire me. He knows me so well; He renews my focus and stirs my heart.

When I am struggling and searching, He sends a "drop" of music to soothe my soul and wipe away the chaos. He embeds the right word in the chorus or verse that I can cling to. He stirs me with an emotion or passion that brings light to the situation and makes the darkness flee. My response to His call to worship Him heals and washes me in His Spirit.

A few times He has sent a "drop" of humility to keep me in the passenger seat as He takes the wheel, to remind me that His will and plan are the very best for me, more than I can imagine them to be. He will be in charge, and I just need to ride the wave with Him. It reassures me I can trust Him! He will bring things to fruition in His timing, and I will not fall or miss out; I will be lifted in His name.

In the time of utter need for forgiveness, He sends "drops" of mercy to cover you.

> The steadfast love of the LORD never ceases;
> his **mercies** never come to an end; they are
> **new every morning**; great is your faithfulness
> (Lam. 3:22–23 ESV).

His mercies for you are new every morning, for He is faithful! He shines a new love on you, for as sure as the sun will rise, so will God's mercy cover you.

There might be a time when God will "drop" a "beware" or "be mindful" in your path. He sends intuition through His Holy Spirit to warn, protect, and steer you away from folly. That still small voice guides you to stay clear, to help you stay on the right path, the one that leads to Him. He will allow a situation to happen while protecting you to give you the experience to draw upon for future reference.

He allowed this very thing to happen to me. One day at my job as a deli manager, a situation arose and a confrontation with a co-manager got heated. Thankfully, I didn't feel I was in danger. I only wanted to calm them down and handle it in the walk-in cooler instead of in front of the employees and customers. It wasn't a good move to trap or try to control the situation. I was oblivious to the potential dangers of the co-manager's reaction. We, of course, worked it out and are still friends.

I learned a few lessons that day. God used this experience to better equip me with handling this kind of situation if it should arise again, to give people space to process their way and in their timing. I tend to want to fix it right now so we can move on. We are all different and process things differently.

When I lose hope, He showers me with "drops" of hope. He won't allow me to stay in the space of hopelessness. He spares nothing to renew my hope. He sends others alongside me with encouragement, sends music, sends animals, and sends laughter and things that bring me joy, which is honey to my soul. He makes nature stand out to me to get my attention and stoke the fire of His love in me. He covers me in His fragrance, presence, and portion allotted just for me.

> For the LORD your God is living among you.
> He is a mighty savior. He will take delight in
> you with gladness. With his love, he will calm
> all your fears. He will rejoice over you with
> joyful songs" (Zeph. 3:17 NLT).

But they who wait for the Lord shall renew their strength; they shall mount up with wings like eagles; they shall run and not be weary; they shall walk and not faint.

Isaiah 40:31 NLT

For in this hope we were saved. Now hope that is seen is not hope. For who hopes for what he sees? But if we hope for what we do not see, we wait for it with patience.

Romans 8:24–25

He will rain down "drops" of grace on you. Open your heart and allow Him to move, stir your heart, and wipe away life's hopelessness.

Chapter 8

COVERINGS OF GRACE

I will greatly rejoice in the Lord, my soul shall be joyful
in my God; for He has clothed me with the garments of
salvation, He has covered me with the robe of righteousness,
as a bridegroom decks himself with ornaments, and as a
bride adorns herself with her jewels.
Isaiah 61:10 NKJV

Each of you should use whatever gift you
have received to serve others, as faithful
stewards of God's grace in its various forms.
1 Peter 4:10 NIV

THERE ARE VARIOUS forms of grace. In doing a search
of God's grace in the Bible, I found numerous verses that
speak of God's grace in various forms: the grace of salvation, kindness, favor, and blessings.

His greatest grace is salvation (saving grace), which
has wiped you clean, covered you, and applies the stamp
of belonging to Him. Kindness is gushed over you from
kind words to unexpected acts to gentle, genuine, loving
care. There is favor within relationships, receiving the

go-ahead or thumbs up, and being picked when odds were not on your side just because our God loves you. There are blessings from health to gifts to new beginnings to epic surprises.

Another form of grace is in wisdom. He provides wisdom in situations. Knowledge from out of nowhere; knowledge you had no past information to support. It is perfectly timed. It can even be wise to have restraint in not to speak foolishly or being quiet to allow processing. Wisdom in choosing your battles wisely and in choosing to allow respect to be given. Wisdom in seeking Him first

He gives grace in having compassion for the needy or oppressed. Grace in having a listening ear, or eyes to see those who feel they are not seen. He gives you grace to be vulnerable, to connect to others, and share the grace that God has lavished you with. He is the author of your heart and loves you endlessly.

God's grace gives freedom. Freedom from addictions, strongholds, shame, and guilt. Freedom from unforgiveness, from acts of violence, from whatever is keeping you from allowing God to have your whole heart. He doesn't want you tied up in knots and stuck in turmoil. He will give you grace to overcome! Grace to walk in freedom, leaving the past behind, blazing a new trail in a new life.

Grace as a covering favor, as a treasure of restoration, ornamentally as in glory and beauty.

His grace can be a supernatural covering, or a surrounding presence.

For one brief season of my life, I felt He had me in a protective bubble when I was in my van, and while I stayed in prayer, nothing could penetrate it, and I was invisible;

it was amazing (there isn't a word to describe how this feeling was). It reminded me of when Aaron and Hur held up Moses's arms to win the battle against the Amalekites (Exodus 17:11). It was when I was in prayer that I flew on angels' wings and the flood gates of His love covered me.

You are His priceless treasure! He will do anything, go anywhere, and chase you down till you are found and safe in His arms.

He gives the grace of restoration and redeeming the past.

He has given grace in exile and grace in rejection! His grace is heavenly intervention of protection as well as in fulfillment of His will. Apostle John was exiled to the island of Patmos, and that is where God used him to address the seven churches in Asia Minor and receive the vision from God of the future return of Jesus Christ and triumph over evil. There is a purpose in everything God does, and it is always for our good and the good of the body of Christ. While rejection is not a warm and fuzzy feeling, it serves a purpose. God knows what He has planned for you, and sometimes our path needs to be realigned. When these times come, look to Him with an assurance that He knows the way, and He is protecting you

The grace of protection, provision, and spiritual power: He covers us with His protection. It could be physical protection, roadblock protection, or even an interruption to maneuver us on a different path. He sends provision in our times of need and even when we don't know we need it. Provision could be monetary, wisdom, or insight in decision-making, or even in good health; the ways are limitless. We have the power of the Holy Spirit inside us, spiritual power to lead us, guide us, and inner intuition, to walk by faith, praise Him in the storms, stand on His promises, for healing power, and to be an overcomer in Christ Jesus.

The grace of joy, illumination, or enlightenment and the stirring of our instilled passions: He gives us overflowing joy in the morning, in the suffering, at work, and in Himself. We will make a joyful noise, have a joyful heart that is good medicine, and be graced with a joyful spirit. God will bring illumination or enlighten us through insight and extraordinary wisdom through the Holy Spirit (Heb. 6:4; Eph. 1:18). He will bring us to remembrance of His Word and truth (John 14:26). The stirring of our instilled passions is my favorite way He moves me. He knows us so intimately and gets us. He will stir my heart and soul most magnificently and tenderly that I know it can only be HIM! He is the keeper of my heart. He is my hiding place, my sure foundation, and my portion He is mine! My special personal allotment of Himself.

Obedience

The Lord calls us to obedience; the action of obeying what He has instructed us to do, the diligence to follow His command quickly, effectively, and to the best of our ability, the faithfulness to be consistent in putting His command before any other, and to execute His instructions to the letter. It may seem wild and silly, but it always has a purpose. He isn't trying to make you look like a fool. He is using it to equip you for the next step or the long haul. He has every detail planned for every angle of the task.

There is a reward for being obedient.

The Book of Genesis, chapters 37-50 tell of the life of Joseph and how he was a great example of obedience to the Lord. Joseph's brothers were jealous of him. They lied and came up with a deceitful plan to get rid of him, even tricking their father into believing Joseph was dead. Joseph trusted and believed in God beyond what he was experiencing. Joseph knew that the Lord would always take care of him. The Lord was with Joseph and made him prosper, enabling him to live with the Egyptian master Potiphar. Joseph found favor with Potiphar and became his attendant. From the time Potiphar put Joseph in charge of his household and all he owned, the Lord blessed Potiphar.

Joseph was a man of integrity in all situations, even when Potiphar's wife made advances on him. Even when Joseph was in prison, God gave him favor. When the tables turned and Joseph was back on top, he had an amazing opportunity to be the voice who would decide his brother's fate. He chose not to get revenge but give grace as our Father would give us, bringing all glory to the name of God. Joseph was obedient to the Lord in every situation, and the Lord blessed him. His relationship with his earthly father and brothers was restored, and the lonely void in his heart was mended.

Being obedient to God is showing Him honor. We respect Him enough to obey what he asks of us. We trust Him enough to know He is faithful, and He will take care of all our needs.

In the book of Daniel, Chapter 3 tells the story of Shadrack, Meshack, and Abednego who honored God by not bowing down to another king. King Nebuchadnezzar had an image made of gold resurrected and decreed, and

when the music sounded, all would bow down and worship the image. If you disobeyed, you would be thrown
into the fiery furnace.

When the sound was sent out, Shadrach, Meshach,
and Abednego would not bow down to the gold image;
they would only worship the true God of heaven. The king
was so furious he had his guards turn up the fire seven
times hotter and had the three men thrown into the fire.
The guards watching saw a fourth person in the fire. This
was alarming to King Nebuchadnezzar, and in fear, he had
them removed, for he realized the God Shadrack, Meshack,
and Abednego served was real and powerful enough to
protect them from the fire. They came out without burn
marks or singed smell. They were obedient in serving only
God, no matter the cost.

Stay steadfast and unmoving in your beliefs of the Lord
Almighty, for you know not an ounce of His mighty power;
you can't see all and know all. Your obedience gives God
the glory and honor that is due. To what lengths will God
go to rub His grace on you?

To be obedient is a representation of your faith, your
willingness to obey what is being asked of you, even when
it doesn't make sense and when you can't see the necessity
of the actions. Your actions show God that you trust Him.
We can't see what He sees, we don't know what He knows,
and we are selfish while He is wise. He has only the best
for us. If what He asks sounds silly or off base, confirm in
prayer and do it anyway, for He has wisdom beyond us
and already knows the outcome.

There have been many times the Lord has asked me
to do things, and I have been obedient. When He asked

me to step down from the worship team at church, it was dear to my heart and very hard to do, but I did. He showed me He had other plans for me and was going to use someone else for the team. He showed me I could worship Him in different ways, with different music styles, and help encourage others to join in. It also was a step in the process of what He had for me further down the road of which I had no idea.

Once I was watching TV, and the show I was watching seemed harmless; it ended up with a storyline of doubt and distrust between a married couple, and an affair began to happen. The Lord said to turn that off, and I did. He protected me, my mind, and our marriage. Sometimes we walk into things unknowingly, and thankfully, His Spirit in me diverted me.

Always have your ears and eyes open to heed His directions. You have no awareness of what He is saving you from or what He is equipping you for.

Being obedient is our testimony of God's grace in our life. With each opportunity to recant our story, it is not only a reminder but also a hope that all isn't ruined. It is an expression of the depth of His love and an affirmation of His infinite faithfulness.

Humility

In great reverence for our humility, God will give you the grace to give to another, to walk through your situation, and to overcome the impossible with grace and dignity.

Whenever a situation is wacky or kind of off, I know God is at work. He knows us intimately and uses all our experiences and sometimes even our hindrances to cata-pult us back onto the path of His will.

Having mentioned Jonah's story in Chapter 4, we see God extend grace upon grace even deeper still in Jonah's life. Jonah was a prophet who prided himself on being ahead of the game with his duties for the Lord, almost as if he knew what God would choose or do in a situation. Jonah followed the letter of the law, and those who didn't were to be punished. So, when God asked Jonah to go to Nineveh and tell the Ninevites to repent and turn from their wicked ways, he thought God was mistakenly soft and off his rocker. The Ninevites had been wicked their whole life, and he felt they didn't deserve another chance. No matter what, we all are worthy of God's grace and forgiveness.

Jonah couldn't be more wrong to think God would be predictable. Being thrown overboard and swallowed by a whale, how wacky is that? A God moment had to be just around the corner.

There may have been times in your life when you felt you were abandoned, exiled, or having a desert experience. This time, Jonah was orchestrated by God. Maybe we need to get away from a situation. Maybe we are not listening to God or need a time out.

At times, He shelters us from certain things or situa-tions that could derail our walk. Maybe He is making a way for us to take shelter in Him and be restored, refreshed, and redirected to the next journey He has for us. God won't ask you to do something that He won't give you the grace and strength to do. He will be your supply, and you will be His vessel.

Jonah received grace even in his defiance! God gave him safe passage in the belly of the whale to bring humbleness and perseverance to trek his way back to Nineveh and then supplied him with His grace to speak repentance and grace to the Ninevites.

Jonah knew God wanted to give grace to the Ninevites, and Jonah was angry because they didn't deserve that grace. Following the rules of religion, Jonah let his pride in get in the way of the holy path of relationship and righteousness.

Jonah ran from his obedience to do what God had asked, and calamity followed. I am sure as Jonah sat in the belly of the whale, he became humble and realized that God had his reasons to give Nineveh grace. Jonah soon found out that God would give him the grace to walk in obedience to fulfill His wishes.

Humility gives grace a blank canvas of opportunity to paint an impossible miracle in marvelous hues, colors, and perspectives. What God has planned is far more than we can imagine or try to make happen.

Humility keeps you mindful of where you have been and how much God loves you to scoop you up and brush you off.

Humility is willingly letting God have the reins to your life. Oh, what a ride it will be!

Humility is letting God have the glory that He deserves while you receive a blessing in being used by Him.

I leave you with this quote to visualize and savor, a nugget of revelation and a pause in time that takes our breath away. It is in our moments of humility we get a glimpse of Him.

"God never gives a thorn without this added grace, He takes the thorn to pin aside the veil which hides His face[1]." —Martha Snell Nicholson

Quiet Spirit

"Rather, it should be that of your inner self, the unfading beauty of a gentle and **quiet spirit**, which is of great worth in God's sight" (1 Pet. 3:4, emphasis added).

The word *gentle* we understand, but the word *quiet* unsettles me and yet resonates with me at the same time. Obviously, "quiet means no sound," but upon deeper thought, it means calm, wisdom, neutral, tender, patient, pure motives, peaceful, no judgment, and self-controlled actions and reactions[2]. It means thinking before you respond and loving no matter what. It means allowing others to be heard, with no retaliation, interruption, or confrontation. It sets the stage for honesty and vulnerability. A quiet spirit soothes anger like sweet honey on your lips.

A quiet spirit is an attitude of grace. It is an example of how Christ treats all of us. He doesn't yell and point out our mistakes. He doesn't respond with snide remarks and demeans us. He doesn't lose patience and gets fed up with us. We don't have to earn his love. He is a gentleman and lets us have free will. He waits patiently for us to call His name. He knows us intimately and handles our hearts with tender care. He gently corrects us when needed, and we still walk away feeling loved. He never leaves us, for He is faithful!

A quiet spirit is having the self-control to be silent, to allow others to reflect and vent while we remain calm, the restraint to not correct, criticize, or voice your own opinion. To give the grace of silence is the wisdom of kindness. We don't have to right all wrongs and put others in their place. It is in the quiet spirit that we allow the Christ in us to surface. We allow His wisdom and kindness to come through our every action.

When I picture Jesus, I see the Sunday school picture of Jesus with the little children. There is magnetism, a calmness, and yet an unconditional love that exuberates from His presence. When He is with us, it is as if all other things are not important, like a moment in time when chaos is frozen, and we hear only His heart.

I long and strive to be of a quiet spirit and great worth to God, to see others as God sees them, to love others as God loves them, to have wisdom, peace, and self-control, to put others before me, and to be Jesus with skin on.

I pray that all I say and do brings glory to God.

Extravagant Joy

Receiving grace creates extravagant joy. It is feeling God's presence break through Heaven and into our world on our behalf. It is the awe of His love for you, yet your worries are just as important to Him as it is to you. It is an uncontainable joy, for His grace was so freely spent on me!

When He breaks through, I cry and laugh at the same time; it is uncontrollable, and my emotions are all over the place. He so delights my heart. It gives me confidence and renewed strength to keep running the race. He reveals His heart's thoughts toward me. I am instantly whisked to cloud 9 with exhilaration. His joy elates and raises me higher. The higher altitude allows expression more robustly.

His joy gives me strength (Neh. 8:10) to keep going on, to believe in Him, and to believe in me, strength to do what He has called me to do, a strength I didn't know I had.

> Splendor and majesty are before him;
> strength and **joy** are in his dwelling place.
> 1 Chronicles 16:27 NIV

> But those who trust in the LORD will find
> new strength.
> They will soar high on wings like eagles.
> They will run and not grow weary.
> They will walk and not faint.
> Isaiah 40:31 NIV

May His strength and joy dwell in my heart forever.

His joy wipes out all fear, for fear is not of the Lord. He is the light and joy that will illuminate His presence and the depth of His love. A joyful heart has no room for fear or darkness, for the light of the Lord makes the darkness flee.

His joy is a refuge. I can remain in His joy. His joy will cover me and set me apart. His joy will be a testimony of His power and love. I can hide in Him, for His joy is a safe haven. His joy is freedom with no boundaries.

But let all who take refuge in you be glad;
let them ever sing for **joy**. Spread your
protection over them, that those who love
your name may rejoice in you. Psalm 5:11 NIV

His joy will cover my pain and renew my spirits. His
joy changes attitudes and our minds on things.

These things I have spoken to you, that my
joy may be in you, and that your joy may be
full. John 15:11 ESV

His joy cannot be contained; it is all-consuming and
contagious.

You make known to me the path of life;
you will FILL me with **joy** in your presence,
with eternal pleasures at your right hand.
Psalm 16:11 NIV

RESTORE to me the **joy** of your salvation
and grant me a willing spirit, to sustain me.
Psalm 51:12 NIV

May His joy flow over you like Niagara Falls. May you
stay in His presence and allow His joy to be a beacon and
unmovable force that shines for all to see. May you be consumed and covered by His joy. May His joy take up resi-
dence in your heart and push out all darkness and fears.
His joy is a priceless treasure. May you bask and savor
His joy, and may you store His joy in your heart and soul.

Chapter 9

REDEEMING GRACE

I have swept away your offenses like a cloud,
your sins like the morning mist. Return to me,
for I have redeemed you.
Isaiah 44:22 NIV

THERE ARE COUNTLESS stories of redeeming grace in the Bible—God is in the redeeming business. He is anxiously waiting for you. If you haven't given your life to Him, I would seriously and most definitely ensure that you do!

In the life of Abraham, he was a faith walker, obedient, and recognized by all for his relationship with God. Among all the miraculous ways God used him, the call to sacrifice his son Isaac was the ultimate example of God's redeeming grace.

Abraham trusted God completely, even with his long-awaited son's life. In a continuation of the story from Genesis 6:1-14, Abraham and his wife Sarah could not even have a baby, but we serve an amazing God. and so, He gave them a son. When the time came for Abraham to give his son Isaac as a sacrifice to the Lord, he did not hesitate. It was an epic moment of faith to not only lead his son up the mountain, gather the wood, and prepare the altar but to gently and willingly tie his son down and be ready to light the flame.

His obedience was imperative, and yet to have the peace that surpasses all understanding, he was willing to go through with it out of his deep love for God. It was in this act that God provided a substitute, a ram in the bushes, to take the place of Isaac. It was an exact foreshadowing of the substitution, the redeeming grace for each one of us because God loves us, so He gave His only Son, Jesus Christ, so that we may live and have a relationship with Him.

Not only did the Lord allow grace to be given to Ruth in the way of an interruption, but He also gave her redeeming grace. Here is a little more detail about her story from the Book of Ruth. Ruth, a Moabite, married a foreigner in her land. All the men of the family died in the war, leaving Ruth and her mother-in-law, Naomi, by themselves. Naomi released both of her daughters-in-law to go back to their homes. Orpah returned, and Ruth chose to stay with Naomi. Ruth was faithful to Naomi, for they had suffered significant loss together.

Ruth began to worship Naomi's God and witnessed Him take care of them. God saw Ruth's heart and had a plan for her with a distant relative (kinsman) of Naomi's family

Naomi and Ruth traveled to Bethlehem just as the harvest was beginning. Ruth offered to work in the fields for their food. Naomi had a relative on her husband's side living there named Boaz; he was a man of good standing. Boaz noticed Ruth working in the fields and asked about her.

Boaz heard of her loss and how she cared for and loved Naomi, her mother-in-law.

The tradition was that if the death of the male in the family occurred, a relative must take care of the other's wife, called a kinsman redeemer, redeeming the family line per se.

Boaz was immediately captivated by Ruth and asked the next family member's permission to redeem her if he could take Ruth as his wife. Boaz loved her and married her, taking on the responsibility of both Ruth and Naomi. This unexpected interrupting grace led to a sweet marriage and placed Ruth in King David's lineage and the Lord Jesus Christ!

God redeemed Ruth's sacrifice and faithfulness, not to mention a renewed heart to love again with the esteemed hunk of the land, Boaz. God is our kinsman redeemer! Upon our accepting Him in our hearts, He paid for our sins and saved us, redeemed us to His family, and willingly took on the role of caring for us.

Another example of God's redeeming grace is with the prodigal son (Luke 15:11-32). A father had two sons. The younger son asked for his inheritance in advance and when it was granted, he booked it out of town. It was not very long before the younger son squandered all his money. He became in dire need and remembered how good his father's hired men were taken care of. He knew he sinned against God and his father; he wouldn't blame his father if he allowed him to be like one of his hired men. His father instead prepared a grand celebration and adorned him with a robe, a ring on his finger, and sandals for his feet. The fattened calf was killed for an extravagant feast.

The Father said, "My son was lost and now he is found, He was dead and now he is alive" (Luke 15:24). What more would your heavenly father do for you? He waits as the father did, filled with compassion for you to come back home.

I read this quote once and wrote it down; it spoke to me, and I hope it speaks to you too.

> "I do not at all understand the mystery of
> grace—only that it meets us where we are
> but does not leave us where it found us[2]." —
> Anne Lamott

My favorite story is of Peter, the disciple who Jesus dearly loved. Peter swore he wouldn't deny knowing Jesus, and even though he made every effort to stand on his word, a moment of fear changed everything, signified by the crow of a rooster upon the third denial.

After Jesus's resurrection, he appeared to the disciples who were fishing without any luck. Jesus called out to them from the shore to throw their net on the right side of the boat, and when they did, they caught so many fish they were unable to haul them in.

Once Jesus spoke, Peter knew His voice and said, "It is the Lord," and jumped in the water to get to Him. They ate the fish together, and then Jesus asked Peter, "Do you truly love me?"

"Yes, Lord, you know that I love you," Peter replied.

"Then feed my lambs," Jesus responded.

"Do you truly love me?" Jesus asked again.

"Yes, Lord, you know that I love you," Peter replied.

"Take care of my sheep," Jesus responded.

"Do you love me?" Jesus asked the third time.

"Lord, you know all things; you know I love you," Peter said.

"Then feed my sheep, follow me," Jesus responded. John 21:15-17 NIV

I tear up to think this was intentional and significant of redeeming each denial Peter had made with each expression of love. What an incredible redeeming grace on display.

To be a recipient of God's redeeming grace, there aren't enough words to express the gratitude and humility that my God, who hung the stars in the sky, thought so much of me to send His redeeming grace to set me free and lift me to see His heart toward me.

Restoring

But those who hope in the LORD will renew their strength. They will soar on wings like eagles; they will run and not grow weary, they will walk and not be faint. Isaiah 40:31 NIV

God will heal you with restoring power. He will renew your strength and rebuild what once was lost. He will send healing and renewing of your heart.

"I shall restore to you the years that the **locust**, the swarming **locust**, the cankerworm, and the caterpillar **have eaten**—My great army that I sent among you" (Joel 2:25, emphasis added).

Mind-blowing! And it is true. He will restore things that have been lost to what it was or even better. He will wipe you off and lift you up, shiny and new. He will restore your reputation and give you grace to right the wrongs. He will renew your strength and confidence. He will give you a new song to sing and overflowing joy.

The Lord walked me through His redeeming grace in 2010 through 2011. I had a Chevy Cobalt, bright blue, so cute and sassy. I loved it and had it for a couple of years. When finances got rough, I struggled to make the payments; it was embarrassing, to say the least, and I had to let it be repossessed. Years passed, and in 2017, we found ourselves needing a new vehicle. We lived in a different state, and God had worked miracles with our finances. I was so nervous and hesitant to try to get a new car. I prayed and prayed. I was humble in whatever God had for us. I gave it to Him speaking out loud:

"Lord, you know what I need and how much driving I will be doing in the future. I trust you."

We saw an ad for a brand-new Ford Escape with a $5,000 rebate (you *never* see a rebate this high)! We went to the dealer to test drive it and try our luck with financing. It was the base model but was a nice ride, and the gas mileage was decent. The finance man deliberated for an hour, and to our surprise, we were approved. I could have fainted. We signed on the bottom line and drove it off the lot. I was overjoyed and sang praises to the Lord for His grace.

A couple of weeks later, we were sitting in church, and a sermon on redemption was being preached. When we walked out into the parking lot, it hit me when I walked up to my pretty, BRIGHT BLUE SUV. God not only redeemed our credit but gifted us with the same color vehicle that was taken away. He is a God of restoration! He knows my heart! He was restoring our loss, making us new, and blessing us in it.

Hosea, a well-known prophet of his day, was called by the Lord to go and marry a promiscuous woman and have children with her, for like an adulterous wife, this land was guilty of unfaithfulness to the Lord (Hosea 1:2). Hosea found Gomer and did as the Lord said. She had one child with Hosea but had two others from different men.

At first, you want to say "What!" Now take a moment and read it again. Gomer was an example of what Israel was being accused of. Israel was all caught up in adultery, idol worship, and blatantly walking away from God by doing their own thing (for the umpteen time). Ouch, isn't that just like us?

When you read a few more chapters, you are captivated and overwhelmingly mystified by the grace God extends to Gomer through Hosea. Hosea was called to love Gomer no matter if she showed him her affections, no matter how many times she ran back to her old sin and lovers, by accepting her children from other fathers as his own and by buying her back out of slavery.

Of course, the writer didn't emphasize any of the emotions that were raging. I am sure Hosea was angry and embarrassed by Gomer's actions and consequent reputation. I am sure Hosea struggled with loving a child who wasn't his blood. I am sure Hosea had dreamed of his future wife of purity, stature, and even nobility. I am sure what God asked Hosea was not in line with what he had planned for his life. I am sure he was repulsed and yet wounded that she ran to another man instead of wanting him; he was a great catch of the times. I am sure Hosea questioned why God was asking him to do this. It was his obedience that God counted on, and, thus, Hosea was used in healing the hurting heart of Gomer and sending the call of repentance to bring blessing to the Israelites.

I am sure Gomer was dumbfounded by Hosea's sudden interest in her. Who knows, maybe he previously snubbed her in the streets as he passed by her. I am sure Gomer carried a lot of baggage and wounds tied up with a little string of what self-esteem she had left.

We have all run back to our past sins; they are comforting in a weird sense, and yet we feel we know what to expect, even if it is unpleasant. We might have gotten our identity from our sins, and it is scary to think of changing. We have felt we deserve what we are in. The voices of lies are familiar, and yet the controlling aspect of them is your driving force.

In Chapter 3, Hosea was the valiant knight who rode in on a white horse, paying for her freedom, and rode away in the sunset. Pass the tissues, please! The knot in her throat of misbelief and gratitude was rock-hard. While scripture doesn't mention specific details of each character's reactions, for Gomer to see Hosea come back for her had to make a huge declaration of his devotion to her and to His God. To be loved so deeply even when you have chosen to run from it. To see forgiveness in a physical example and for all to see.

I am sure she didn't know her name would be printed in the most-read book in the world. I am sure she wanted to shrink into a hole and disappear, but God wouldn't have it. He raised her, wiped her clean, and gave her a new life. The restoring grace rushed in.

This story just moves my heart (I am still crying). Maybe it is because I am an emotional woman. It is knee-dropping amazing how intimately God knows us and the lengths he would go to win my heart. He knows me better than I know myself. He knows what makes my heart sing and how to get my attention. He delights in me in several avenues and is faithful to wait when I am being rebellious. He loves me and you like crazy! No mountain is too big. His restoring grace will cover me.

Another thought I wanted to express is with all the mess we have made of our lives, we can't just go back and fix them. But God can! He will walk us through those places of mistakes, failures, and blemishes of sin and intentionally wipe the black residue off and make our hearts white as snow. The past no longer has its hold on you! You are new; you belong to Jesus Christ!

Rescuing Grace

Through the Holy Spirit, He warns us if we are straying. He has an escape plan when we are tempted. Wait! Did you say God has an escape plan for us? Yes I did. Look at this verse:

"No temptation has overtaken you, but such
as is common to man; and God is faithful,
who will not allow you to be tempted
beyond what you are able, but with the
temptation will provide the way of escape
also, so that you will be able to endure it"
(1 Cor. 10:13 NIV).

You may have heard that God doesn't give you more
than you can handle. The **temptations** in your life are no
different from what others experience. And God is faithful.
He will not allow the temptation to be more than you can
stand. When you are tempted, he will show you a way out
so that you can endure

This verse has gotten lost in translation. It is the temptations that He will not allow you to handle more than
you can stand, NOT the situations in life. The great news
is He is with you on both plains. He will show you a way
out of temptations so you can overcome them.

Satan and his world will throw all situations at you,
but when you have God on your side, He will carry you.
He will walk with you and give you the strength to endure.
His grace rushes in, and within all the masterful mysteries
of His grace, you will have victory. In some instances, God
might allow some situations to happen in your life, not out
of spite or punishment but to reveal and grow you, like
refinement, purification, and an establishment of heavenly
accomplishments. It could be your defining moment, your
life changes to catapult you into a platform to reach the
masses of the world for His heavenly kingdom. It could be
your testimony that changes hearts and saves souls. It isn't

always about you! It **includes** you to pump up the magnitude! It is for the greater good, the good of God's greatness.

God's love rescues you by always showing you a way to Himself. He desires your heart no matter what and at whatever cost. He constantly searches for you, looks out for you, and is ready to grab you away from evil clutches. He makes a way when there is no other way. He makes the impossible possible. He would break down walls and come after you at a moment's notice.

Hallelujah! If He says it, He will do it! So, no worries when things are tempting you too much; lean on God. He will have an escape plan that will enable you to endure through it.

Have you ever needed to be rescued? Been so stuck and so desperate when, out of nowhere, a solution covers you? Have you had an instance that, looking back, could have been catastrophic, and you realize you were supernaturally spared? Was there a close call that took your breath away?

He sends rescuing angel armies to fight for us. He goes ahead of us and steers us away from danger. He puts up an invisible shield at the precise moment. He sends intuition in an instance that leads us away or causes us to hesitate.

Here is the chorus to Chris Tomlin's song "Whom Shall I Fear?" (God of Angel Armies).[3] It is a banner and promise you can claim and stand on!

> *I know who goes before me.*
> *I know who stands behind.*
> *The God of angel armies*
> *Is always by my side.*

He goes before you, and He has your back. He is omnipresent and omnipotent. He knows the beginning and the end. He only has the best in mind for you! His grace rushes in.

Lauren Daigle
"Rescue Song[4]"

> *I will send out an army to find you*
> *In the middle of the darkest night.*
> *It's true, I will rescue you.*
> *I will never stop marching to reach you.*
> *In the middle of the hardest fight,*
> *It's true, I will rescue you.*

How reassuring to know there is nothing that will stop God from finding you, saving you, and giving you another "do-over." He is waiting and watching. He knows the beat of your heart and longs to have you be only His.

His love conquers all—all fear, mistakes, weaknesses, doubts! He gave His life for you; His love is a bridge to bring you home to Him. This reminds me yet of another song. (He speaks to me through songs, nature, animals, and all things around me. If I am listening and looking for Him, He shows up, He delights my heart, May you experience all that He has for you.

The chorus from Casting Crowns' "The Bridge[5]"

Your love is the bridge
You built with a cross.
And Your truth is the light
That searches for the lost.
Your grace won't stop reaching.
Your mercy won't let go
Cause Your love is the bridge,
And Your truth leads us home, oh.
You lead us home, oh.

Genie

I always thought grace was like a genie in a bottle. I only had three wishes, three good reasons for a pardon, three chances to get it right, and three strikes, and I am out. I thought God only granted me grace when I really messed up with no way to fix it. He would only swoop in and rescue me when I was in insurmountable trouble. I used to think that you could only have your three doses of grace, if you were lucky, and find the bottle with the genie in it.

As if luck had anything to do with it... **not** What a relief to know all my preconceived ideas of when God would bestow His grace on me was not valid. I would have never been worthy of such a gift.

God isn't a genie who, when you ask nicely or do all the right stuff, lets you win the prize of His grace, His pardon, or seal of approval for a free passage—the prestigious "get out of jail free card." We can't wrinkle and twitch our noses and have all our dreams come true or escape tribulations. You can't put God in a glass jar or a tightly sealed box and expect to be saved. God isn't a fairy who waves a wand or a magician who says a catchy phrase to make your circumstances disappear.

God breathed the universe to life. He hung the stars in the sky, created man, and sent His Son, Jesus Christ, to pay our ransom by hanging on a cross because of our sins. That is the most significant act of grace. He gave us the grace to overcome sin and walk with Him.

God won't take away a bad situation, but He will give you the grace to walk through it. He provides us with a grace perspective change. Sometimes it is taking the veil from our eyes so we can see the broader spectrum of things. Sometimes it is pumping us up with the power to stand when we are overcome and persevere through a long season. Sometimes He changes those around us. Sometimes He just holds us while the storm rages.

I now realize that comparing God to a genie is small-minded and limiting. I couldn't visualize how BIG He is and that His capabilities are infinite! I thought I had to earn His favor or follow the religious rules to the letter when it was always about the RELATIONSHIP! He simply wants my whole heart. He wants to be number one in my life. There is no limit to His love, faithfulness, provision, protection, forgiveness, or grace. If it is His will to move the mountains and part the Red Sea, then He can take care of little 'ole me, for nothing is impossible for God! (Luke1:37 NLT)

Answer His call. Let Him be the champion and keeper of your heart. Let His grace rush into your heart, His love to the rescue. Let His love be a bridge, the access to the way home.

Grace of Possibilities

I love God's grace of possibilities and blossoming hope when things seem too far gone. Even when we are in the valley of darkness or wandering in the hopeless wilderness, a fresh wind of grace flows over me and lifts my eyes or a fresh fragrance that lifts my chin. His presence beckons me like a beacon or ray of light that pushes out the darkness, demanding attention. It points me upward, drawing me closer to Him.

It is an indescribable feeling when His grace rushes in at the exact moment while He is with you always, every second. It is the precise flicker of time that IF we are open and seeking Him, HE WILL make Himself known.

He will lift you out of the miry clay and wash you off. He will wipe away your tears and sit you up on His shoulders so you can see above your situation. He will give you a change of perspective. He will give you insight into who He made you to be and how He sees you. He sees you through His eyes, not the world's. He sees you in the way He created you to be. It is what He says that is the most important opinion you must cling to.

Lauren Daigle
"You Say" song:[6]

> *You say I am loved when I can't feel a thing.*
> *You say I am strong when I think I am weak.*
> *And you say I am held when I am*
> *falling short.*
> *And when I don't belong, oh You say*

I am Yours.
And I believe (I).
Oh, I believe (I).
What You say of me (I).
I believe.

Opinions—everyone has one—and I think most of them need a perspective element added to it. We make assumptions without any true perspectives or all the details before we quickly decide how we feel. Opinions are our idea or reaction to a subject. Not to be negative, but sadly, that is where the ego thrives, in the shallows of opinions that are hurtful and negative or a way to lash out in anger. It is when a glimmer of grace is applied that an opinion turns into encouragement. May we remain open to godly perspectives before we make judgments or assumptions and needlessly push our opinions on others.

Actually, the Lord has been working on me in this area, ouch! I have gotten my nose bent out of place about what I thought or assumed when, in fact, once valid points were revealed, I was proven wrong. I was upset for nothing, and in reality, I was being called to give grace, called to just listen or be there instead of letting it be all about me.

For example, as a flight attendant and as crew members, we should work together; however, one time I had a fellow crew member who was controlling and running around doing everyone's job (especially taking over my duties, which was very hard to be quiet and allow). I was secretly fuming, and, well, maybe it wasn't as secret as I would have hoped. They were like a bee running hither and fro doing everyone's job and butting in on mine, and they seemed nervous and out of control, trying to enforce control. I prayed for patience, I prayed for strength to endure, and by the third flight together, I was fed up. Then it slowly came out that this person was having horrible back and leg pain, and keeping busy walking around seemed to be the only thing they could do to get relief. Out of pain on the inside, they were trying to keep it together, but it was spewing out on the outside as a crazy person.

Maybe I was the only one who felt they were making me feel like I couldn't do my job, but in trusting the Lord, He gave me His grace and changed my frustration into a calm safe place where they could confide in what they were dealing with. I wished I would have trusted the Lord sooner; I wouldn't have suffered, but most importantly, maybe I could have offered a suggestion or some way to ease her pain.

I have since gathered additional godly perspectives personally in this same area. He revealed I was trying to gain validation of my skills by being super-efficient in my position, which alienated my partner, unintentionally, of course. He allowed others to show me how they physically set up their area in a different way, inviting their partner to not only help but to have a sense of support and confidence to present a top-notch service team.

As a result, we both shined. This was an intricate process, but I needed to learn it in the way He showed me. He is in the details. He cares enough about us and how we have relationships with others that He takes the time and repositions us to cross paths to help each other. We are sharpening and buffing each other to shine for His glory, for we are His prized possessions.

We all have our things going on, and when you are captive in a plane at 35,000 feet, God still works things out, He still sees you and never stops thinking about you; He is faithful! I am humbled He can use me for someone else and humbled He uses others to help me. His grace is relentless, limitless, and infinite!

Godly perspectives and revelations are His specialty. He is tender in delivery and powerful in solutions. God is fantastically creative! He has crazy math and crazy hope-filled solutions.

When we had to move away from our grandchildren for a time, He sent me babies and children to babysit for. He creatively made a way to see each other in special monumental moments, like in hotels (a provision from a job perk) where my grandchildren could swim. We played games, ate, laughed, talked for hours, and squeezed in lots of loving in a quick visit that would become memories to look back on.

Another godly creativity is through technology. Through FaceTime, my grandchildren could see us as we talked. I remember one time, my granddaughter Olivia was just over two, and we were talking without FaceTime. She said, "Grandma, turn on the light. I can't see you." It was everything to her to see us when we talked. It was a connection being made even though we were miles apart. It was so dear to my heart. I couldn't hug and kiss them, but I could see their faces and have interactions. We had special times and special conversations with all our grandkids.

Along came Portal, and we had more interactions via a bigger span of space so they could show us a new trick, a dance move, or show us their boo-boo (we sent air kisses).

You could play karaoke and apply silly facial changes and even read a book together; it was awesome!

God has crazy math if you believe and trust Him.

We haven't been the best with our budgeting money. God has sent us a precious couple to help us in times of need with perspectives, generosity, and sound advice. He has sent us through Dave Ramsey's financial training. There have been times when He gave us specific dollar amounts to give or we have received the exact amount we needed. When we are humble, His grace rushes in, and in His magnificent intentional way, He lets us know that it is Him who takes care of us. He uses life circumstances to build our faith through several lessons, all to draw us to trust Him and follow Him. What an awesome God!

Grace Knows Your Name

As Shakespeare would say in a line from Romeo and Juliet[7]: "What's in a name? That which we call a rose by any other name would smell just as sweet."

Many avenues go into naming your child. Usually, you are named after someone dear to your parents. Your middle name might be after a father, grandfather, or even a family name passed down. Heritage, tradition, and nobility might influence the name you have been given. We all roll our eyes at some of Hollywood's names given to their children, but uniqueness was the goal. Your name might have come from your mother's favorite soap opera or hero in a novel they just read.

When I had my first child, we had a few options we liked, and my husband said, "Let's just wait and see what the baby will look like." Our baby boy went a few hours without a name, and then when the nurse said we could give him as many names as we wanted, we gave him three.

Popularity plays a huge role nowadays when naming your child. We scour many books or lists on baby names. With technology, you can do it with a touch of a finger and sort it to a specific quality. You could choose one that means strength or beauty, one that is old-fashioned, nationality-specific, virtuous, warrior, biblical, or of stature. Your name might come from an expression of a season or trial, a marker of time or event, or a heartfelt emotion at the precise timing of your coming into the world.

No matter the reason you were named, and while that makes you who you are, it is the unique name God has chosen for you that validates your being. I knew you before I formed you in your mother's womb. Before you were born I set you apart... (Jeremiah 1:5 NLT) and He has a will and purpose for your life.

He knows you only by that name, so when you mess up and are not living out your life as intended, He still sees you by your given name. When you are rebelling and running as fast as you can away from Him, He still sees you with the eyes of His creation. He doesn't see you as a failure or lost cause. He is patiently and tenderly waiting. He calls you by your name each time as He pours out a drop of his grace on you. For He knows the real true you, and He wipes away each fragment that tries to mar His handy work in you.

You might not recognize that He is calling your name. You might not be listening or even think He would be aware of your every move. You might have lost hope and are drowning in your mess to even expect Him to consider looking your way. You might not know His voice, hear it in the chaos of life, or question why He would care about you. Yet, He is patiently and tenderly waiting. He redirects your path to intersect with His grace. He goes before you and prepares for you in advance. For He knows you intimately, and He sees you with His eyes of creation.

Remember Gomer, Hosea's wife, whom we previously touched on. Grace knew her name, and while He had continually poured out His grace on her, He never gave up, never lost sight of who she was made to be. No matter all the things she did, it didn't change WHO she was to Him. Grace knew her name, and it will always stay the same.

Is Grace—God—calling you? Is He whispering your name? Are you feeling a pull in His direction? Is His peace, presence, and love attracting you away from life's chaotic pull?

If you are feeling His pull and His whispers, don't hesitate or discount what you are experiencing. Be brave and allow Him access to your heart. Please pray this prayer:

Lord Jesus, I invite You into my life. I believe You died for me and that Your blood pays for my sins and provides me with the gift of eternal life. By faith, I receive that gift, and I acknowledge You as my Lord and Savior. Amen.

Jesus knows your past, your secrets, and everything about you, but best of all, He knows your future! He has plans for your life. He is your number-one fan and best friend. He is a true friend! You are part of the family now. You are not alone, and you have a new beginning.

You might be very emotional; I was when I asked Jesus into my heart. I urge you to get connected to a church so you are surrounded by fellow Christians who can help and encourage you.

We all need fellowship; we weren't created to be alone. Join a Bible study or group to suit your needs. We all need a safe space to grow and gather knowledge, someone to walk side by side with, and those to help us flourish. All of heaven is giving you a standing ovation! Welcome, precious child of God!

Chapter 10

ECHOING GRACE

....

> But my life is worth nothing to me unless I use it for
> finishing the work assigned to me by the Lord Jesus
> Christ—The work of telling others the Good News
> about the wonderful Grace of God
> Acts 20:24 NLT

THIS VERSE IS my life's mission.

Let the roar of grace echo in your life. God's grace is
like a roaring lion. His grace breaks through and devours.
His grace is a reckoning force and a redeeming kiss. His
grace is authoritative, final, and infinite.

We need to have an attitude of grace because of the
grace given to us. We need to allow our experiences of God
intervening on our behalf to be echoed by others.

When we collect all the God experiences in our hearts,
it grows our trust in Him. Through this trust, we are
fearless and step out more. We grow in confidence and
strength. Our lives become beacons to the glory of God.

Pay It Forward

In Acts 2:42-47, it talks about the first church. It was a utopia of love and taking care of each other. If someone had a need, they would band together to take care of the need. There were no hesitations to share or sell one's land to provide for one another. All the believers were of one heart and mind. All their property or possessions were for everyone to benefit. There were no homeless or starving people. They truly took care of each other and had a community together. They had *Koinonia love*[1] (Greek for taking care of each other) for each other. The Bible said they testified to the resurrection of Jesus Christ, and much grace was upon them all (Acts 4:33). Wow, if only it was like that today, right?

If you had the pleasure to see the movie *Pay It Forward*, I know you were richly blessed. What an impact it made on many hearts to step out and pay kindness to someone in need. I still see or hear about people paying for someone's meal in the drive-thru or the checkout line of the grocery store. I have been a part of it on both sides. It blessed me in both instances.

In listening to the Holy Spirit, He moves upon me when I am amid someone who could use some help. It is exhilarating and humbling at the same time. I have been there, and to know He sees me wherever I am and moves others on my behalf is so very, very precious to me!

I challenge you to listen to the Holy Spirit's prompting; you never know who is in need just by looking, and you never know if you might have to walk in different shoes.

We were created for relationships—relationships with God, with our family, and with our friends, as well as, with strangers, our neighbors, the needy, and those from foreign lands. We have opportunities placed before us. Seize them! We can have a little piece of the first-church attitude and *Koinonia love* by paying it forward and putting others before ourselves.

Be an Ambassador

When you hear the word *ambassador*, you think of dignitaries from a foreign country, those who represent or symbolize a stand-in for someone of authority who couldn't be present. You are the front man or spokesman for a higher authority figure.

> "We are therefore Christ's **ambassador**s, as though God were making his appeal through us. We implore you on Christ's behalf: Be reconciled to God" (2 Cor. 5:20).

We are God's ambassadors, and we should let our light and testimony of Christ be seen by all. We need to stand in honor and humble gratitude for what has been done for us.

There is no other God like Him. He asks only a little of us and gives us unmeasurable grace and love. We must stand on truth and speak the truth in love.

Upon the receiving of Christ in our hearts, the transformation process begins. Through His grace and love, we are re-molded and shaped to reveal His intentions and visions of who we were made to be.

As a potter lovingly crafts his creations, every attention to detail is taken. If the clay has an imperfection, it is reworked and readjusted to enhance its uniqueness. Through kneading, an intimate relationship is formed. Just as with the potter and the clay, so is your relationship with Christ. He knows you intimately and admires His work in your uniqueness.

We became an ambassador the moment we received Christ. He marked us with a seal. The heavens cheered, and the angels bowed. We are His. We chose Him as our God.

And you also were included in Christ when you heard the message of truth, the gospel of your salvation. When you believed, you were marked in him with a **seal**, the promised Holy Spirit (Eph. 1:13NIV).

The Reflection of Christ

When we are filled to the point of overflowing with God's grace and love, His reflection is seen in us. From our heart of gratitude to our expressions of worship, His presence emanates from us.

When we allow him control of our life, tuck his Word into our hearts, and obey, the fruit of His Spirit blossoms in our relationship with Him and is seen by all. We are changed. We no longer have the characteristics of our old selves; we have new ones.

We take on God's attributes: love, joy, peace, patience, kindness, goodness, faithfulness, gentleness, and self-control. This could be a change of epic proportions that render us unrecognizable. Anger is replaced with kindness. Negativity is replaced with contagious joy. Deceitfulness and selfishness are replaced with pure goodness. Critical and mean-spiritedness is replaced with tender gentleness. Maniac drill sergeant on fire is replaced with humbled self-control. To have God's character enveloped in you is to reflect who He is mirrored in all of us.

Giving grace to others reflects the grace given to us. It is a living testimony of the grace given to you that causes you to reflect it on someone else by not judging first but loving always and by putting them first before ourselves. Let your first motive be to give grace to another when you know they are making a mistake and choose to still love them. The grace you give reflects the highest glory back to God.

Opportunities

"Though I am the least deserving of all God's people, He graciously gave me the privilege of telling the Gentiles about the endless treasures available to them in Christ" (Eph. 3:8 NLT).

His grace gives you countless opportunities to spread the good news of Jesus Christ. His ultimate act of grace is to pay the continual price for all mankind's sins. His grace continues to cover us and redeem our past mistakes, cruelties, or shortcomings. His grace gives us a do-over, makes us new, lifts us, and sets our feet back on the right path. He wipes away the yuck and reveals the real radiant you, the one He had in mind; the apple of His eye.

His grace opens opportunities to walk in freedom, to hold your head high and shine for all to see. He gives you the strength to do things you had no idea you could do. He sends encouragement right when you need it. He sends others to hold you up when you are shaky. He might even set up a roadblock or detour to keep you on the right path and out of harm's way. He walks with you each step of the way.

There will be opportunities and privileges to be used for another person or persons. He will use you if you allow Him to. It is such a double blessing! He will give you opportunities to build up your spiritual muscles and equip you with all you need for whatever is coming your way.

Will you have hard situations come your way? Yes. We aren't exempt from hard situations or circumstances. He gives us what we need to overcome. He will walk with you through it and sometimes carry you. He uses everything for our good, and while that doesn't seem fair or appealing, He weaves it in a way to grow and elevate. If He knew you couldn't handle it, He wouldn't allow it.

You will be allowed to witness or observe His grace in action, seeing Him in action and His heart for someone else. It is mind-blowing and humbling.

Walking in His grace will afford you an experience you would never have had you chosen to not heed His call. He has abundantly more for you than you can imagine. You might be used in a BIG way, used intricately, or mentor someone who will play a strategic role. We all have unique skills, strengths, and personalities that play an important part in the body of Christ.

Don't hesitate or put off His call; you could miss out on so much. You have so much potential in His eyes. He has a plan for you, and He can't wait to call you His child.

Getting to share your experiences about the Lord is amazing. You look back over your life and see all the times He rescued you, applied grace to your situation, covered you with His grace as protection, and broke through the walls you put up. He knocked down walls to find you and heard your heart whisper a concern and took care of it.

It has always been so precious to me when God sprinkles grace on the little thing that is big to me. It is in the sharing that God receives the glory, the grace He gives echoes through me and touches those who need to hear. It reignites hope, reflects His love, and reveals His faithfulness.

The opportunities are unlimited! With God, **ALL** things are possible! (Matt 19:26)

Rub Some Grace on It

Grace is giving a pardon when it isn't deserved. It is holding your tongue and allowing another person to be right. It is putting others first. It is loving others no matter what they have done to you. It is being the bigger person and stepping aside. It is being tender, patient, and kind. It is giving another person a chance no matter who they are. It is standing by someone even when it seems hopeless. It is giving forgiveness while you are being wronged.

It is a huge opportunity to rub grace on those who are different from us. It could be a difference in religion, and we are called to unity, so we need to find what we agree on and let that be a starting point of giving and walking in grace with them. It might be lifestyles. We must love one another as God loves us, no matter what. We should be Jesus with skin on. Jesus hung out with thieves, murderers, prostitutes, and tax collectors, all the unlikely people to hang out with. He didn't judge or criticize them. He was accepting and loving. Continue His legacy and let your life reflect Jesus to them.

We need to give grace even to repeat offenders. We need to have grace and forgiveness ready and waiting. There is a learning curve we all struggle with. We might not even realize we have been offensive again. Some of us need second, fifth, and twelfth chances. Peter came to Jesus and asked, 'Lord how many times shall I forgive my brother or sister who sins against me? Up to Seven Times?' Jesus answered,' I tell you, not seven times, but seventy-seven times.'(Matthew 18:21-22 NIV). It is in our reactions of grace and forgiveness that Christ is seen by others. It is being faithful, doing it over and over. It is giving the situation to God and trusting He will fix them, and He will give you what you need to do so. Don't limit your love; let it increase. God's love is unconditional and infinite.

If we would just rub the attitude of grace onto every situation, the outcome would be revolutionary for both parties, just like when you bless someone, it blesses you most. If we choose to forgive just as God has forgiven us, there would be no bitterness, and instead an overflowing of unstoppable joy.

When things are trying, and you have been offended, rub some grace on it! When you have been wronged and misjudged, rub some grace on it! When trusting is not your thing and you can't forgive, ask God for some of His grace so you can rub some grace on it!

★★★★★★★★★★★★★★★★

We can echo God's grace in many ways. We can love others in Christ's love. He loves them, and so should we. Sometimes just remaining quiet or in prayer for another as they are going through something that the Lord is addressing is a huge help. We might need to just be there, hold their hands, or listen. Sometimes it is best to remain quiet, trusting that the Lord is aware and working. They might need to get the words out with you first before they approach God in prayer. We would be echoing His non-judgment, His silence, even when being accused, and an example of His unconditional love.

This verse contains good advice:

> "Understand this, my dear brothers and sisters:
> You must all be quick to listen, slow to speak,
> and slow to get angry" (James 1:19 NLT).

We can echo God's grace through our actions; by showing integrity even when nobody is looking, by doing the right thing no matter what, without hesitation, and being humble and vulnerable.

Nobody is king, only Jesus Christ. We are not here to right all the wrongs; we are here to love one another and lift each other. We must be approachable, honest, and positive. Our words can be weapons, and they can be honey to a hurting heart. BE KIND In your reactions and interactions, with all kinds of people, family members, coworkers, strangers, and from all kinds of backgrounds. Be respectful! Let's be the hands and feet of Jesus to all.

We must be a blessing to everyone and on purpose. There is no room for selfishness, prejudice, grudges, personal gain, intimidation, or fears. Be the last and allow others to be first. Give without expectations and sometimes anonymously. Allow others to have the last word. Don't step on others to make yourself look bigger. Let others cut the line in front of you, take the smallest piece of cake, acknowledge others for their accomplishments, strive to inspire others, and be a great friend. Be compassionate, trustworthy, and genuine. Keep your promises and make time for others.

Treat others as you want to be treated. Care for others as you would want someone to take care of you. Take care of the widow and the needy. Give your best to others, for you know not who you might be caring for. You might be entertaining angels or the Lord all mighty Himself.

May you reflect on your life and see all the instances God has showered you with grace, favor, and blessing. I am blown away by His continual grace and love throughout my life; it is unlimited and infinite. The smallest things seem like even bigger blessings, for He knows my heart, my concerns, and He gets me!

His grace might not always feel like a favor or blessing, but it is in His grace that He protects me, uses it to redirect me, or sometimes carries me through things with His ever-tender ways. He still brings out the good, even in a bad situation. His grace might be character-building, or a "time out," so I can regroup or have a perspective change. It could be developing or equipping me for a new thing down the road that I can't see yet. It might be a blessing given before I need it or one to bless others.

He might want me to walk with someone so they can see Him in a different light. No matter the reason, He has a purpose and has the best for me always in mind. I need to trust Him. He receives all the glory, honor, and praise, all the "atta boys," kudos, and high-fives. He works in me and through me. He is the master.

"For out of His fullness" (John 1:16 MSG).

He gives us His best, His abundance, and His truth. We receive grace upon grace. The more we trust and believe, the more we give Him access to our hearts. As our relationship grows deeper and deeper with Him, we see and feel His love and grace revealed. Through our faith walking, we see and feel His protection, provision, His presence, and His peace, grace, and favor. He gives me "my portion" of Himself, my piece, my special part of the God of the universe. He thinks of each one of us and sings songs over each one of us. He is relentlessly devoted to each one of us.

Verses to savor and encourage, His Word of truth:

> The LORD bless you and keep you [protect you, sustain you, and guard you]. The LORD make His face shine upon you [with favor] And be gracious to you [surrounding you with lovingkindness]. The LORD lift His countenance (face) upon you [with divine approval] And give you peace [a tranquil heart and life].

> Numbers 6:24–26 AMP

But those who trust in the LORD will find new strength. They will soar high on wings like eagles. They will run and not grow weary. They will walk and not faint.

Isaiah 40:31 NIV

For I know the plans I have for you," says the LORD. "They are plans for good and not for disaster, to give you a future and a hope. In those days when you pray, I will listen. If you look for me wholeheartedly, you will find me.

Jeremiah 29:11–13 NLT

May you have the courage to pursue a relationship with our Savior Jesus Christ.

May you open your eyes, ears, and heart to our God.

May you believe with childlike faith.

May you supernaturally encounter the Lord.

May you seek and chase after God.

May you soar on His wings as He reveals His wonders.

May you feel Him holding you when times are dark.

May you "be still" and know He is God... (Psalm 46:10 NLT)

May you worship Him with abandon.

May you know that God loves you with an everlasting, never-ending love.

May you be blessed beyond your comprehension with God's infinite and extravagant grace upon grace.

Grace and peace to you from God our Father and the Lord Jesus Christ. Philippians 1:2

NOTES

Chapter 1: Grace Loves

Jordan Feliz. *Never Too Far Gone*. CD. *The River*. Nashville, Tennessee: Colby Wedgeworth, 2016.

Lucado, Max, and Chris Shea. *God thinks you're wonderful!* Nashville, TN: J. Countryman, 2003.

Jesus Culture. *Fierce*. CD. *Your Reckless Love*. Sacramento, California: Jeremy Edwardson, 2015.

Boom, Corrie A.J. ten, Elizbeth Sherrill, and John Sherrill. *Hiding place*. Ada, MI: Baker Publishing Group, 2006.

Chapter 5: Grace Protects

Lucado, Max. *You'll get through this: Hope and help for your turbulent times*. Nashville, TN: Thomas Nelson, 2015.

Chapter 6: Grace Steps In

"America's Most Trusted Dictionary." Merriam-Webster, 2023. https://www.merriam-webster.com/.

Finding Nemo. United States: Buena Vista Pictures, 2003.

New Song. CD. *Sheltering Tree*. Nashville , TN: Benson Music Group, n.d.

"America's Most Trusted Dictionary." Merriam-Webster, 2023. https://www.merriam-webster.com/.

Chapter 7: Transforming Grace

Flint, Annie Johnson. "He Giveth More Grace." Hymnary.org, 2024. https://hymnary.org/text/he_giveth_more_grace_as_our_burdens.

Casting Crowns. CD. *Lifesong*. Nashville, TN: Beach Street Records, n.d.

Chapter 8: Coverings of Grace

"The Thorn - by Martha Snell Nicholson." The Cotton Apron, September 18, 2016. https://thecottonapron.blogspot.com/2016/09/the-thorn-by-martha-snell-nicholson.html.

"America's Most Trusted Dictionary." Merriam-Webster, 2023. https://www.merriam-webster.com/.

Chapter 9: Redeeming Grace

Lamott, Anne. *Traveling mercies: Some thoughts on faith*. New York, NY: Anchor Books, 2000.

Chris Tomlin. *Burning lights*. CD. Brentwood, TN: Sparrow, 2012

Lauren Daigle. *Rescue*. CD. *Look up Child*. Franklin, TN: Sentricity, 2018

Casting Crowns. *The Bridge*. CD. Nashville, TN: Casting Crowns, 2018

Lauren Daigle. *You Say*. CD. *Look up Child*. Franklin, TN: Sentricity, 2018

Shakespeare, William, and Horace Howard Furness. *Romeo and Juliet*. Philadelphia, PA: Lippincott, 1913.

Chapter 10: Echoing Grace

"America's Most Trusted Dictionary." Merriam-Webster, 2023. https://www.merriam-webster.com/.

Printed in the USA
CPSIA information can be obtained
at www.ICGtesting.com
CBHW021924081024
15576CB00006B/38

9 798868 502163